Full Range Leadership Develop

D0153653

It has been more than 30 years since Bernard M. Bass presented an integrated overview of Full Range Leadership Development (FRLD), which has since become the standard for providing leadership training around the world in business, military, religious, and educational contexts. This book teaches how to use FRLD to grow transformational leaders in organizations. Organizations that support and develop transformational leadership at all levels are more productive and profitable, attract and retain top-notch talent, promote creativity and innovation, garner trust and commitment from employees, leverage sustainability and workplace safety efforts, and are strategically positioned to respond well to uncertainties and changes in the market.

Retaining the conversational style of the first edition, this second edition contains several new features, such as: updated leader profiles and leadership examples, including more international cases; expanded discussion of gender diversity and leadership in teams; and new Summary Questions and Reflective Exercises.

The book's practical action steps make it of use to both practitioners and students and well-suited as a core leadership textbook or supplement in leadership development courses.

John J. Sosik is Professor of Management and Organization at Great Valley School of Graduate Professional Studies, The Pennsylvania State University, USA.

Dongil (Don) Jung is Professor and Department Chair of Management at the School of Business, Yonsei University, Republic of Korea.

"The character-based leadership concepts in this edition are presented in a conversational manner and are an essential guide for leaders at all levels, whether leading a team of five people or thousands. This book is a moral compass for those who strive to be transformational leaders."

—Maj Gen John Gronski, U.S. Army Europe, Deputy Commanding General, Army National Guard

"Backed by an enormous body of research on the theory, *Full Range Leadership Development* uses that knowledge to establish state-of-the-art standards for developing leadership potential and competencies. Do you want to become a better leader? Here is your roadmap."

—Ronald E. Riggio, Henry R. Kravis Professor of Leadership and Organizational Psychology, Claremont McKenna College, USA

"One of the most extensively researched and strongly validated models of leadership, Transformational Leadership (TL), has led to one of the most widely used and well-developed education and training programs, Full Range Leadership Development (FRLD). Fortunately, John J. Sosik and Dongil Jung, two of the best-known researchers on TL, who are also two of the best-known educators/consultants/trainers using FRLD, have chosen to share their knowledge, experience, and practical applications in this book, *Full Range Leadership Development: Pathways for People, Profit, and Planet*. They have taken what they researched and learned, and how they applied that information in their work with various organizations, to produce a volume that is a must-have for any manager or student who wants to know more about leadership and/or develop and grow his/her own leadership skills and talents. Enjoy and use this book!"

—Francis J. Yammarino, SUNY Distinguished Professor of Management; Director, Center for Leadership Studies, State University of New York at Binghamton, USA

Full Range Leadership Development

Pathways for People, Profit, and Planet

Second Edition

JOHN J. SOSIK
DONGIL JUNG

Routledge
Taylor & Francis Group

NEW YORK AND LONDON

Second edition published 2018
by Routledge
711 Third Avenue, New York, NY 10017

and by Routledge
2 Park Square, Milton Park, Abingdon, Oxon, OX14 4RN

Routledge is an imprint of the Taylor & Francis Group, an informa business

© 2018 Taylor & Francis

First edition published by Psychology Press 2010

Library of Congress Cataloging-in-Publication Data
Names: Sosik, John J., author. | Jung, Don I., author.
Title: Full range leadership development : pathways for people, profit, and planet / John J. Sosik and Dongil Jung.
Description: Second edition. | New York : Routledge, 2018. | Revised edition of the authors' Full range leadership development, c2010. | Includes bibliographical references and index.
Identifiers: LCCN 2017058022| ISBN 9781138053649 (hardback : alk. paper) | ISBN 9781138053670 (pbk. : alk. paper) | ISBN 9781315167206 (ebook)
Subjects: LCSH: Leadership.
Classification: LCC HD57.7 .S6928 2018 | DDC 658.4/092—dc23
LC record available at https://lccn.loc.gov/2017058022

ISBN: 978-1-138-05364-9 (hbk)
ISBN: 978-1-138-05367-0 (pbk)
ISBN: 978-1-315-16720-6 (ebk)

Typeset in Univers LT Std
by Keystroke, Neville Lodge, Tettenhall, Wolverhampton

Contents

About the Authors

John J. Sosik (Ph.D., State University of New York at Binghamton) is professor of management and organization, and chief architect of the Master of Leadership Development program at the Pennsylvania State University, Great Valley School of Graduate Professional Studies, where he has received awards for excellence in research, faculty innovation, teaching, and service. Dr. Sosik teaches leadership, organizational behavior, and research methods courses. He is an expert on transformational leadership, having published over 100 articles, books, book chapters and proceedings, delivered over 90 academic conference presentations since 1995, and has conducted training and organizational development programs for a wide variety of profit, non-profit, and military organizations such as Altria/Phillip Morris, Boeing, Sanofi Aventis, Siemens, the Institute of Management Accountants, the U.S. Air Force, and Wyeth. His Google Scholar *h*-index was 52 as of January 2018. He is the recipient of the Center for Creative Leadership/Leadership Quarterly Award for his research on personality, charismatic leadership, and vision, and Sage Publication's Best Macro Contribution Award for his work on the application of the Partial Least Squares data analytic technique to group and organization research. Dr. Sosik serves on the editorial boards of *The Leadership Quarterly, Group & Organization Management*, and *Journal of Behavioral and Applied Management*. He is the lead author of the book, *The Dream Weavers: Strategy-focused Leadership in Technology-Driven Organizations* (2004, Information Age Publishing). His second book, *Leading with Character: Stories of Valor and Virtue and the Principles They Teach*, was named one of the 30 best business books of 2007 by Soundview Executive Book Summaries, and is now in its second edition (2015, Information Age Publishing). Dr. Sosik was awarded a grant from the National Science Foundation to study e-leadership of virtual teams at Unisys Corporation.

Dongil (Don) Jung (Ph.D., State University of New York at Binghamton) is professor of management at Yonsei University, School of Business, in Seoul, Korea. He formerly taught at San Diego State University. He teaches leadership in organizations, organizational behavior, and negotiation courses at the undergraduate and graduate levels. His areas of expertise include leadership, innovation, strategic thinking, organizational culture, and talent management. He has been very active as a leadership consultant and trainer for a number of global companies such as Qualcomm, HP, Samsung, LG, SK, and Hyundai Motors. He also provided leadership training for several military organizations such as the U.S. Army, Navy Seals, and Korean Army. Dr. Jung's publications have appeared in many top-tier scholarly journals such as the *Academy of Management Journal, Journal of Applied Psychology*, and *The Leadership Quarterly*. His awards include a Best Paper Award from the Center for Creative Leadership/Leadership Quarterly, the Ascendant Scholar Award from the Western Academy of Management, a Faculty Contribution Award from the College of Business Administration at San Diego State University, and several Best Teaching Awards from Yonsei School of Business. He was selected as one of the Top 30 Prominent Business Thinkers in Korea by *Mae Kyung Business Daily*, the largest business newspaper. He published a best-selling leadership book in Korea called *Develop Your People as A Leader* and it received the prestigious Jung Jinki Press and Culture Award from *Mae Kyung Business Daily*.

Foreword

In the last edition of this book, I provided some historical background to the origins of a full range model of leadership and its development. In this revised version, I retained a large part of the earlier edition below because retaining how this model came into being remains critically important to understanding the arc of its growth and impact over the years on both leadership research and practice.

Although much of the foundational work on transformational and transactional leadership can be attributed to James McGregor Burns, many of the extensions to this work via a full range model of leadership came from practice. This model and the thousands of articles written about it, in my view, is a perfect example of where practice and science can be completely integrated versus being artificially divided. Indeed, I would personally like to think that the bridges built across the science and practice domains as represented by this full range leadership model, and its development, may be one of its greatest contributions to the field of leadership.

Looking back in history, Bernie Bass and I were working with the Fiat organization to design a leadership training intervention for its top 250 managers around the globe. As we built out the program on one of the most validated models of leadership, we had many discussions on how we could best frame the type of leadership we intended to develop in individuals, teams and indeed entire organizations. In fact, from the very outset in planning these interventions, we took a multi-level view of leadership, examining transformational leaders, shared transformational leadership, and transformational cultures.

After a number of brainstorming sessions, we settled on the idea of calling the model "a full range model of leadership." Our choice of this term was based on three criteria. First, we wanted to challenge participants to continually expand the breadth and depth of "their range" as they learned about leadership throughout their careers. Second, we knew that by choosing the term "full range" some of our academic and practice colleagues would immediately challenge whether "full" actually was completely "full." Our choice was our way of intellectually stimulating the field of leadership to ask, "what's missing and why?" Finally, we were well aware of the theories and models of leadership that preceded ours, and we wanted to honor and include them in "the full range."

You will see in this book that much of what Bernie and I had hoped for, regarding this slice of our work together, has come to fruition. For example, I can tell you of numerous conversations and citations where someone has tried to add to "the" (we really meant "a") full range model with this or that leadership style or concept we had left out, including now the full range of mechanisms it impacts before it effects performance.

Over the last three decades, we have also seen a substantial amount of evidence not only supporting the full range model in individual and meta-analytic studies published in the literature, but also training interventions that have provided support for challenging participants to expand their implicit notions of what constituted their leadership. Regarding our third criterion, the model has now been incorporated into the leadership literature and in many ways, has become even more integrated with prior models of leadership, while serving as an important organizing mechanism for pulling together the leadership literature.

With that as background to this book, you will see in the following pages an evidenced-based model of leadership unfold in unique and creative ways. This book still covers a very broad range of leadership styles, with many applications of the model that will help any reader come to understand what it means to lead across the full range of leadership behaviors, actions and potential. John and Don attempt to convey, in many ways, the breadth and depth of these constructs of leadership. Now with additional years of experience under their belt, what I still find interesting is how far this work has come, particularly in terms of application and relevance. This book is a testament to those achievements.

In closing, if you engage this book from front to back, you will no doubt positively expand your understanding of a full range of leadership potential and impact. I say no doubt, because after over 30 years of accumulated evidence, there is *no doubt*. Now go enjoy all of your travels along a full range of leadership challenges and successes.

Bruce J. Avolio
University of Washington
Michael G. Foster School of Business

Preface to Second Edition

We begin by pondering an apropos parable told by investment oracle Warren Buffett. The moral of this tale is that it is a fortunate person who sits under comforting shade today only because a wise person had the foresight to sow the seeds of a mighty oak tree many years ago. With this life lesson in mind, it is hard to believe that almost 25 years have passed since we parted ways as doctoral students graduating from the Center for Leadership Studies (CLS) at the State University of New York at Binghamton. It is there that our passion for research on transformational leadership was first ignited by our former professors Bernie Bass, Bruce Avolio, Fran Yammarino and others at the CLS. We agree that there is nothing in this world that we would trade for the rigorous training, lasting friendships, and wonderful experiences we were blessed with in Binghamton. The knowledge, skills, and abilities that we gained there have served us well throughout our academic career and in life. And for that, we are most thankful.

Our appreciation has grown exponentially since the first edition of *Full Range Leadership Development: Pathways for People, Profit, and Planet* was published in 2010. We intended our book to be the "go-to source" for transformational leadership training that originated at the CLS. Since then, it has been used by a wide range of corporate, not-for-profit, educational, and military organizations. For example, tenets of Full Range Leadership Development (FRLD) are included in the U.S. Air Force's Squadron Officer School at Maxwell Air Force Base, U.S. Air Force Academy, Officer Training School, Senior Non-commissioned Officer Academy, First Sergeant Academy, International Officer School, and in graduate-level electives at Air Command and Staff College and Air War College. We have used FRLD in our leadership training and consulting for a number of global companies such as Boeing, Hewlett Packard, Qualcomm, Samsung Electronics, LG, Hyundai Motors, Sanofi, and Wyeth. Numerous universities around the world also have adopted our book as part of their leadership development and MBA graduate degree programs.

We wrote this book for intelligent managers and business students who are serious about developing their full leadership potential with knowledge backed up by a solid foundation of academic research. In this updated and redesigned second edition of *Full Range Leadership Development: Pathways for People, Profit, and Planet*, you will read how our students, clients, and colleagues have used FRLD to enhance their leadership skills, advance their career, and make the world a better place. The second edition is written in the same conversational style as the first edition, but contains several new features that our readers will appreciate:

- Restructured and focused chapter content explaining what each FRLD component is, why it is important, what its effects and outcomes are, and how to use it
- Updated Leader Profiles and leadership examples with more international cases
- Expanded discussion of gender diversity and team member-exchange topics
- Revised connections of FRLD to specific leadership theories such as ethical leadership and servant leadership, and leadership organizing theories such as the Total Leadership System
- Updated figures and illustrative photos since many of our students and clients are visual learners, and
- Simplified, amended, and new Summary Questions and Reflective Exercises, limited to those most popular with our students and clients.

These features should assist you in the leadership learning process that we introduce in Chapter 3 and advocate throughout the book. If you carefully read our book, think about its ideas, and practice them every day, you should not only gain a thorough understanding of the tenets of FRLD, but also be able to produce positive changes in people, teams, organizations, and our world.

We are grateful for the assistance of numerous individuals in our effort to bring this second edition to fruition. Decades of scholarship on FRLD by our academic mentors, colleagues, and other researchers have contributed to our insights on leadership development described in this book. We owe a debt of gratitude to our current and past academic colleagues and students at Penn State University, Yonsei University, San Diego State University, and SUNY-Binghamton for their research, teaching, and assistance over the years. Equally deserving of appreciation are the many executives and managers from organizations where we provided training and consulting services throughout our careers. Special thanks to Christina Chronister, Julie Toich, Emily Boyd, John C. Cameron, Jae Uk Chun, Erica Vinski, Kaushik Krishnaswamy Kumar, Ziya Ete, John F. McKenna, Fil J. Arenas, Michael Palanski, Ron Riggio, Joey Tsai, Minyoung Cheong, Kendra Ingram, and the Immaculata University Gabriel Library staff for their encouragement and expertise in support of the second edition. We dedicate this book to our parents and mentors who long ago planted the seeds of education, transformational leadership, and social responsibility in our hearts and minds. May these pursuits offer you a place in the shade, where you can smile at the sun shining from your very own transformational leadership.

John J. Sosik
The Pennsylvania State University
School of Graduate and Professional Studies at Great Valley

Dongil (Don) Jung
Yonsei University
School of Business
January 2018

Preface to First Edition

Transformational and transactional leadership and its elegant expression in Bernard Bass and Bruce Avolio's Full Range Leadership Development (FRLD) model has become the premier leadership research paradigm. More importantly, countless educators, trainers, and practitioners in a wide range of industries and countries around the world have embraced the FRLD model. We wrote this book with the objective of demonstrating how ordinary people in all walks of life have used FRLD to achieve extraordinary results of developing people to their full potential, boosting company profits, and creating sustainable business practices. In essence, our purpose is to tell the story of how research on FRLD is being taught at our universities, trained in our clients' organizations, and applied by aspiring leaders to sustain performance excellence.

We feel well qualified to tell this story. We earned our doctoral degrees under the tutelage of Bernie Bass and Bruce Avolio at the Center for Leadership Studies at the State University of New York at Binghamton. As their students, we worked with our colleagues on many research projects on transformational leadership conducted at SUNY-Binghamton and elsewhere. During this time, we became close friends, honed our research skills, and vowed to carry on the work of researching and training transformational leadership over our careers. Looking back, our Binghamton experience was nothing short of wonderful. It led us to one of the most exciting and important research topics in our field. We're glad it happened to us.

After graduating, we became accomplished leadership scholars, trainers, and educators in our own right at Penn State University and San Diego State University. Our training, teaching, and life experiences inspired us to develop courses on FRLD at our schools, and an AACSB-accredited Master of Leadership Development (MLD) graduate degree program at Penn State. By sharing our knowledge of FRLD with our students and clients, we have personally witnessed FRLD's effectiveness in promoting positive change in individuals, teams, organizations, communities, and nations. FRLD is part of what has kept us united both as friends and advocates of transformational leadership over the years.

Our story began in the early 1990s when we were attracted to SUNY-Binghamton's doctoral program in management for one primary reason: Bernie Bass and his colleagues. Bernie entered academia in 1946 and had published over 400 books and articles on leadership by the time we joined him. His association with the classic Ohio State leadership studies, excellent pedigree provided by Ralph Stogdill and others, tireless work on the *Handbook of Leadership* (an encyclopedic anthology of leadership research findings and applications), and *Leadership and Performance Beyond Expectations* (the seminal work on transformational leadership) were huge draws for us.

During our days at Binghamton, we learned an important lesson: not only was Bernie a giant in the field of leadership, he was an extremely kind and nurturing man with an overflowing well-spring of knowledge as well. Both of us remember spending time with Bernie in countless mornings, asking him many silly questions. At that time, we were deadly serious about our questions. We even dared to challenge him. However, he never showed any sign of getting tired of naïve doctoral students. He always smiled like a Zen master! His willingness to spend time nurturing us clearly demonstrated that he was a transformational leader himself. Bernie also helped launch many vehicles that advanced the field of leadership such as *The Leadership Quarterly* and the Center for Leadership Studies. We were privileged to be able to study and work with someone who had such a profound impact on our field, and a heart of gold that personified idealized leadership. For these reasons, we dedicate this book to the memory of Bernie Bass.

Intended Audience

In the spirit of Bass' notion of transformational leadership, we wrote this book as an in-depth overview of the FRLD model and how it has been applied in a wide range of real-life situations by people just like you. We wanted to show our readers that the FRLD model was not designed exclusively for world-class CEOs and high-rank executives. It was designed for leadership development for everyone. Therefore, the intended audience is undergraduate and graduate classes in management, leadership, educational leadership, faith community leadership, industrial and organizational psychology, social services, health care and biotechnology management, social entrepreneurship, public administration, criminal justice, and training and development.

This book is a suitable compliment to a growing number of university programs, such as the MBA and MLD programs at Penn State University, that are using the Multifactor Leadership Questionnaire (MLQ; www.MindGarden.com) to assess students' leadership development. Thus, this book may be used as a central text in leadership courses or as a supplement in an organizational behavior or human resource management course. Managers of organizations at all levels in all industries, trainers, business professionals, entrepreneurs, community leaders, or any readers interested in becoming better leaders should also find this book motivating and useful.

Features

Our book has several important and distinctive features. It is written in a clear, conversational and thought-provoking style. It challenges you to think about what you are learning and how you can apply this knowledge to your personal leadership situation. It contains many profiles of famous leaders and colorful examples that bring FRLD concepts to life. In addition, several other features make this book useful and unique:

- Much of the application of FRLD has been tested and applied in Penn State's MLD program. Our book gathers this evidence together to provide a rich description of how transformational and transactional leadership can be successfully applied in real-life situations. We buttress this evidence with results of scientific research that makes this book both rigorous and relevant. We believe that there are many leadership books available, but many of them lack a fine balance of practical discussion and rigorous scientific validation.
- Each chapter describes in actionable ways what leaders need to do to be more successful in demonstrating transactional and transformational leadership and reaping the benefits of developing associates into leaders themselves. Thus, the book can serve as a "how-to" training guide that explains *how*, *when*, and *why* FRLD leadership behaviors work.
- Each chapter provides vivid examples and anecdotes about the nurturing of FRLD in organizations. We share many personal examples of how ordinary managers became extraordinary leaders through the FRLD model and training.
- Each chapter contains summary and reflective questions that reinforce the learning process and provide ideas for applying what is learned through experiential exercises. These exercises are designed to develop your full leadership potential and facilitate your learning. These include exercises linked to the measurement of FRLD behaviors summarized on Mind Garden, Inc.'s MLQ feedback report.
- Chapter 1 links FRLD to other leadership theories. A brief history of the development of leadership thought provides you with an understanding of how FRLD fits into and extends the leadership literature.
- Chapters include testimonials of key FRLD scholars and practicing managers who have used the FRLD model in their personal and professional lives. Their words can help you to understand the history and nuances of FRLD and how you too can benefit from the lessons in this book.

The book contains ten chapters and an appendix. Chapters 1 and 2 provide foundation material. Chapters 3 through 6 cover transformational leadership behaviors. Chapter 7 describes transactional leadership behaviors. Chapter 8 examines passive forms of leadership behavior. Chapter 9 explains how FRLD can be shared within teams. Chapter 10 presents how FRLD can be used as a strategic intervention in organizations and communities through evidence from research and testimonials from managers and other practitioners. The appendix describes the philosophy and content of Penn State's MLD program, which is structured around the FRLD model.

Acknowledgments

Working on this book has been a labor of love, a nostalgic return to our roots, and a hopeful vision of a bright future for our students, clients, colleagues, and you the reader. It is a privilege to acknowledge the great debt of gratitude to those individuals whose cooperation, assistance, and advice have made this book possible.

The first word of thanks goes to Bernie Bass and Bruce Avolio for their tireless mentoring and collegiality over the years. In August 2004 at the National Meetings of the Academy of Management in New Orleans, Bernie asked if we would be willing to integrate material from the transformational leadership training workshops into book form. Shortly before Bernie's passing in October 2007, we spoke with Bruce to get his opinion on our interest to write such a book. He expressed a need for such a book and supported our idea to write the book in a style that is both relevant and rigorous in terms of research support and integration. Bruce kindly provided generous and excellent feedback on our book proposal and we greatly appreciate his support and encouragement for this project, and his outstanding mentoring over the years.

We thank our colleagues at the Center for Leadership Studies at the State University of New York at Binghamton. We owe a considerable debt of gratitude and friendship to Fran Yammarino, Don Spangler, Ruth Bass, Surinder Kahai, Shelley Dionne, Howard Powell, Al Pellicotti, Lisa Wolf, Diane Thomas, and Wendy Kramer for their counsel, mentoring, and assistance during our days in Binghamton and throughout our careers.

Our thanks go as well to our friends and colleagues at Penn State Great Valley and San Diego State University: the late Effy Oz, Jae Uk Chun, Denise Potosky, Simon Pak, Daniel Indro, Janice Dreachslin, Pastor Robert Scott, Alex DeNoble, Lynn Shore, and Moon Song for their help and support during this project. We thank and continue to be inspired by the numerous Penn State and SDSU students who have contributed testimonials on the effectiveness of FRLD in developing people, building profits, and saving our planet's natural resources and environment. Our students are transformational leaders in every sense of the word and we are very proud of them.

Our editor, Anne C. Duffy at Taylor & Francis, has been a valuable resource throughout the project. We also thank Robert Most at Mind Garden Inc., Darryl Walker, and Louise Whitelaw for their super job of editing and critiquing the manuscript. We must also thank Andrea Laine, JoAnn Kelly, Susan Haldeman, Sue Kershner, June Gorman, Pat Misselwitz, Michael Lomax, Silviu Rechieru, Lisa Baker, Karen Norheim, Nisha Desai, Neal Generose, Brian and Cristina Powell, and Sean Travers for various forms of assistance and support.

Finally, our profound thanks to John G. and Josephine A. Sosik, the late Ann Drost, Sinyoung Choi, Austin and Celeste Jung for their love, patience, perseverance, and support during this project and over the years. Their lives give meaning to transformational leadership to which we owe a special debt of gratitude.

John J. Sosik
The Pennsylvania State University
School of Graduate and Professional Studies at Great Valley

Dongil (Don) Jung
School of Business
Yonsei University

February 2009

Chapter 1

Introducing Full Range Leadership Development

In her role as a project manager for Element Environmental Solutions (EES), Shannon Crooker enjoyed being creative, collaborating with her teams, and leading the charge in her company's sustainability mission. As a child, she loved to explore and learn about the world through books and writing. She studied communications in college in hopes of eventually becoming an editor of *George*, the political magazine founded by John F. Kennedy, Jr. But the high cost of college tuition curtailed her plans and she joined the United States Air Force (USAF) for six years to help pay for school. While serving in the USAF, she enrolled in a management degree and took marketing classes which she really enjoyed. After watching the documentary *An Inconvenient Truth* by Al Gore, she became committed to saving the earth and dedicated her post-military career to combatting climate change. She was searching for an opportunity to take part in something that is bigger than herself.

Shannon's life changed in profound and positive ways when she and her husband launched EES in 2013 to combat climate change, remediate contaminated land, and promote corporate social responsibility. These social and environmental initiatives are closely tied to marketing and communications, but they don't work without collaboration and effective leadership. They are fields that are always changing and expanding with plenty of opportunities to learn. In her leadership role, Shannon ignited people's passions by leading by example and communicating how and why EES is cleaning up sites. She encouraged her associates to become part of the solution by developing themselves, their associates and community to higher levels by working to achieve EES' triple bottom line's environmental, social, and financial targets. In working toward these noble goals, all aspects of Full Range Leadership Development should come into play and help Shannon earn the respect and trust of her associates in her new role as a director at Sustainable Energy Fund. Shannon's example of outstanding leadership illustrates that we can do good for people and the planet while making a profit.[1]

What do outstanding leaders like Shannon Crooker have in common? Our work and research show that they are committed to growing and developing their followers and making positive impacts for their organization and world. If we aspire to be an outstanding leader, we need to consider several key issues as we start reading this book. Take a few minutes now to reflect upon your responses to each of the following questions:

- Do you have a workable plan to cultivate the greatness of the people in your organization?
- How can you help them realize their potential to succeed?
- Are you able to carefully scrutinize and evaluate their actions for growth?
- Are you able to set goals for them and use rewards and punishments to move them closer to these goals?
- Can you role model in your own behavior what you expect from them?
- Is it possible for you to inspire them to cooperate with your organization's internal and external stakeholders?
- Are you capable of challenging them to rethink their basic assumptions and rework their ways of doing things?
- Are you patient enough to coach them in a way that develops their strengths to their full potential, while recognizing and addressing their weaknesses?

If you are willing to work to achieve these ends, you are in good company. Recognizing and developing the full leadership potential of people has become a strategic initiative in today's most successful global organizations. For example, General Electric (GE) has expanded its famous executive-level leadership development program to middle-managers, with a focus on growing its talent pool, broadening employee skillsets, and shortening the time it takes to be promoted. GE customizes leadership development plans with specific content tailored to each participant, who is provided with feedback on assignments, 360-degree leadership surveys, and sponsorship by executives. Coca-Cola sends its promising leaders on six-week excursions to plants and customer sites located around the world. During these learning experiences, they learn Coca-Cola's core values, customer preferences, and innovation practices. The United Way offers its annual Loaned Executive Program to teach key personnel in local companies fund-raising and community leadership skills, and sponsors its Executive Fellows Program to train directors of member agencies on effective leadership. While these organizations differ in size, age, industry, and mission, they have one thing in common—they realize that leadership development gives them a competitive edge in adapting to the rapid changes and challenges of our global and technology-driven world.[2]

These organizations have realized that leadership is not just about moving people, teams, and organizations to get from point A to point B, and simply achieving goals. It's also about displaying behaviors and creating an organizational culture that encourages leaders to develop future generations of leaders. It involves moving leaders and followers from passive to more active styles of leadership, elevating followers' motivation and performance to levels of excellence, creating a positive and results-oriented organizational culture, and being committed to environmental stewardship as well.

The big question is: how do we develop more proactive leaders in our organization who motivate employees to perform beyond their expectations? We believe that the Full Range Leadership Development (FRLD) model,[3] a research-based and practically oriented leadership paradigm, can help accomplish that goal. That's why we wrote this book, to share our more than 25 years of experience in researching, teaching, and consulting the FRLD model with you. The FRLD model is a leadership training system that proposes that leaders vary in the extent to which they display a repertoire of leadership behaviors, ranging from active and more effective leadership to passive and less effective leadership. To fully develop the potential of leaders and followers who can achieve extraordinary levels of success requires an understanding of a full range of leadership behaviors suitable for today's complex world. The focus of this book is to help leaders recognize what leader behaviors they exhibit now and how they can transform their leadership from a reactive or passive approach to a proactive approach.

Why Full Range Leadership Development Is Essential for Exceptional Performance Today

The time is right for leaders at all levels in today's organizations to use FRLD. That's due to the many dramatic changes that we face in our life. Shifting demographics, refugee crises, workforce diversity, geopolitical alterations, technology innovation, threats to the environment, shifts in the economic prowess of nations, and collaborative business practices are just some of the trends today's leaders must face. These changes are occurring at an accelerated pace due to cultural changes, advances in technology, globalization, and the information age in which we live. We believe that the following changes have created a new need to develop and practice a relevant leadership paradigm such as FRLD.

Leadership for Our Dynamic World and Lives

We live in a world that is constantly changing—and changing at a rapid rate. These changes require leadership that is more adaptive and dynamic. Let's take a look at several sources of these big changes that are affecting us today.

Demographic Changes

Each new generation of workers brings different values, mindsets, and ways of living. Do you know how to motivate different generational cohorts (e.g., Baby Boomers, Generation X, Generation Y/Millennials, Generation Z/Boomlets) in your organization? Increased diversity and shifts in demographics in today's workplaces add complexity in terms of how we can leverage individual differences among people. For example, the Hispanic, Asian, and Muslim populations in the United States have grown significantly over the last ten years. These trends pose interesting leadership challenges. How has the collective face of your workforce changed in recent years, and what are you doing to leverage the power of such diversity? By the year 2050, today's majority groups will become minorities, and vice versa. We believe that one of the most important roles you have to face as a leader in the future is to figure out how to leverage diversity for innovation and performance in our ever-changing environment.

Technology Trends

Advances in technology bring new opportunities and methods to socialize, share ideas and experiences, and conduct business. Our world has become fully connected via social networks, virtual reality, artificial intelligence, and data mining. These new technologies are creating new markets and industries at a rate that only a handful of companies can handle. Leadership based on strategic thinking is needed to identify ways to take advantage of these emerging technology systems to build social and collaborative networks and accelerate the development of associates and the success of organizations.[4] Are you leveraging leadership in a way that coordinates both the social and technology systems in your organization?

Geopolitical Alterations

The geopolitical alliances and boundaries that we grew up with have morphed into new configurations that require novel approaches for conducting business. Who would have predicted the United Kingdom's "Brexit" from the European Union, the emergence of the Islamic State of Iraq and Levant (ISIL/ISIS) as a potent source of terrorism and genocide, the re-emergence of populist and nationalist movements along with a renewed Cold War between the United States and Russia, or that the "global war on terror" would continue to fester? An increasing amount of political, economic, and social attention is shifting to the Asian and African continents, along with a renewed focus on the Middle East. Forces of internationalization and globalization bring both opportunities for market growth and the responsibility to address some of the world's most menacing problems, such as terrorism, poverty, and disease. Is your leadership operating in such a socially and politically responsible fashion? Leadership can play a vital role in finding ways to deal with these challenges based on strong and meaningful visions and purposes. The FRLD model presented in this book is a leadership system that can help answer these questions.

New Generations of Workers Bring New Ideas

The associates in your organization also bring with them leadership challenges. Because today's employees are better educated and more experienced than ever before, they demand more of an active role in the leadership of their organization. For example, the Generation Y "millennials" (those born between 1976 and 2001) find serving their organizations and communities to add meaning to their lives. They enjoy connecting with their friends and colleagues almost 24/7. While they can be brash, narcissistic, and entitled, they also tend to be more inclusive and tolerant of different social groups than previous generations. In contrast, the Generation Z "Boomlets" (the generational cohort born after the millennials) tend to possess traits of being cautious, mature and in control, private in their online and real lives, and more pragmatic in their careers than millennials.[5]

Leadership is needed to bring such associates' knowledge, skills, and abilities into the leadership equation to offer optimal solutions to the problems we face. The FRLD model helps build a leadership system that develops and utilizes potential talent among both younger and older generations. Based on a large volume of research evidence accumulated to date, we know that people who display such leadership are more capable of producing and sustaining the high levels of performance required for succeeding in today's global market and society.

Organizational Modifications

Does your company have the adaptive capacities and structure to deal with emerging changes effectively? Indeed, adaptation has become a fact of life for most organizations. Increasingly, organizations are turning to their leadership at all levels to promote more active participation among their employees and create flatter organizational structures. In today's business environment, we need more responsive and horizontal leadership. Organizations that support and develop this form of leadership across organizational levels are more productive and profitable, attract and retain high-quality associates, promote creativity and innovation, garner trust and commitment from employees, and are strategically positioned to respond well to changes in the market. Leadership can help by fostering strategies and systems that promote adaptation instead of rigidity. FRLD strives to grow change-oriented leadership in organizations at all levels (including followers), thereby generating these positive outcomes at all levels as well.[6]

Environmental Issues

Worldwide environmental problems pose additional challenges for contemporary leaders. Many of the world's metals and fossil fuels, such as oil, coal, and natural gas, are nonrenewable. In 2017, we heard that most world regions will experience energy demand growth and increased fossil fuel consumption. With the world's demand for fuel increasing beyond what we can presently supply, leaders must help identify alternative sources of energy to meet demand.

In addition, a variety of pollutants are wreaking havoc on the environment. Forests are being destroyed at an alarming rate as the world is being concreted over with new developments. Land that was once functional is being rendered useless through desertification. An unholy host of pollutants are making their way into our water, soil, and air. These include chemical pollutants (e.g., fertilizers, detergents, pesticides, plastics), solid waste pollutants thrown out by individuals and industry, and water pollution coming from a plethora of nasty sources. Industry, farmers, and cities are producing toxic waste. Hospitals, universities, and industrial plants are generating radioactive emissions. Air pollution and acid rain represent additional environmental threats. Sadly, little has changed since the first edition of this book was published in 2010. Such social, economic, political, and environmental challenges require a new form of leadership based on FRLD. Our book offers a more systematic approach to leadership that integrates a vast amount of research results in order to help you to develop more effective leadership. We need leaders like *you* to solve these problems.

And the Research Says . . .

To begin solving these problems with the right leadership paradigm, you need to seriously consider your options, just as you would if you were facing a major health concern. Would you subject yourself or family members to a medical treatment or procedure that has not been validated in systematic evaluation? Probably not. Then why would you subject yourself and your associates to any leadership paradigm that has not been rigorously validated? Rest assured, the FRLD model is supported by an extensive research base and applications in corporate, military, religious, educational, and nonprofit training settings worldwide. It is based on Bernard Bass' *Leadership and Performance Beyond Expectations*, the seminal work on the transformational-transactional leadership paradigm published in 1985. Building upon Bass' work in 1999, Bruce Avolio published *Full Leadership Development: Building the Vital Forces in Organizations* and updated it in 2011. The book you are reading builds upon and extends their work.

The work of Bass, Avolio, and their associates at the Center for Leadership Studies at the State University of New York in Binghamton and at other universities has provided the foundation for leadership training around the world in many areas, including stand-alone specialized graduate degree programs in leadership development being taught at a number of universities. For example, Penn State University's Master of Leadership Development program, which John created and led, uses the transactional-transformational leadership paradigm as the foundation for its courses. We will present evidence of the development of leaders from this program throughout this book to support its key lessons.

The advent of Bass and Avolio's FRLD model has led to a surge in research attention on the transformational-transactional leadership paradigm since its inception in the mid-1980s. According to a 2014 review of leadership theory and research published in *The Leadership Quarterly*, the transformational-transactional leadership paradigm dominates the leadership field and ranks #1 among all leadership theories reviewed. It is *the* premier leadership paradigm, currently garnering more research attention than any other leadership theory or model. Several meta-analyses (i.e., a quantitative academic study summarizing the results of many studies) by and large have validated the FRLD model.[7]

In summary, we are confident that the FRLD model presented in this book will give you a competitive edge in dealing with today's internal and external issues that your organization is now up against. We are faced with challenging problems every day at work, and within and between the nations on earth. Solving these problems requires us to be creative and innovative. We need to constantly challenge and develop our colleagues so that we can select and retain the best and brightest. When we utilize FRLD, we are able to attract new high-quality personnel, and grow their skillsets and talents more fully. We can respond more quickly and effectively to changes in the market. We are able to generate more creative solutions to our problems. We are able to project an image of confidence, commitment, and mission focus to our employees, customers, and other organizational stakeholders. All of these processes result in higher satisfaction, productivity, and profits.[8] And they have the wonderful potential to enhance the welfare of our planet as well.

The Components of Full Range Leadership Development Theory

Now it's time to briefly introduce the components of the FRLD model. Together, we will expand our understanding of these leadership styles in subsequent chapters. At this point, consider the FRLD model shown in Figure 1.1. According to this model, leadership across the range is represented by five specific behaviors

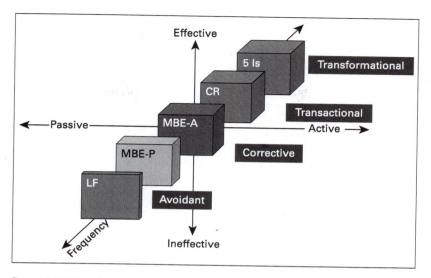

Figure 1.1 **Full Range Leadership Development model. (Reproduced by special permission of the publisher, Mind Garden, Inc., Menlo Park, CA, www.mindgarden.com from the *Multifactor Leadership Questionnaire Feedback Report* by Bernard M. Bass and Bruce J. Avolio. Copyright © 1996, 2003 by Bernard M. Bass and Bruce J. Avolio. All rights reserved. Further reproduction is prohibited without the publisher's written consent.)**

and one attribute. A *behavior* is something a person does or says that can be observed, described, and recorded. In contrast, an *attribute* is a characteristic that is ascribed to a person by others based on what the person is perceived to be. Behaviors are actions whereas attributes are personal characteristics or traits.[9] These five behaviors and one attribute describe different forms of leadership. According to the FRLD model, leaders display a repertoire of both passive and active forms of leadership. The more active forms of leadership are associated with higher levels of effectiveness and satisfaction than the more passive forms of leadership.

The passive forms of leadership in the FRLD model include laissez-faire and passive management-by-exception leadership. More active forms of transactional leadership include active management-by-exception and contingent reward leadership. At the uppermost end of the range is transformational leadership, which research has linked to the highest levels of individual, group, and organizational performance. Let's establish transformational leadership as our goal and work up starting at the bottom of the model.

Laissez-Faire

Have you ever worked for a leader who sees the development and performance of followers as someone else's responsibility and avoids taking a stand on issues at all costs? How did you and your associates respond to this individual's behavior? What was the end result of such a lazy attitude toward leadership?

Figure 1.2
**Not interested.
Laissez-faire
behavior is
associated
with the
lowest levels
of individual,
team, and
organizational
outcomes.**

When leaders abdicate responsibility, delay in responding to urgent requests, or do not follow up on issues, they display laissez-faire leadership. When they avoid involvement in tasks, are indifferent about important issues, or avoid making decisions or dealing with chronic problems, they display laissez-faire leadership as well. Laissez-faire leadership might be called "absence of leadership" or "non-leadership" because there is no exchange relationship between the leader and the follower. A leader who displays this form of nonleadership is perceived as not caring at all about others' issues. The laissez-faire leader shown in Figure 1.2 is lost in his own thoughts and is certainly absent from his team and their professional responsibilities. Laissez-faire leadership is associated with the lowest levels of performance and satisfaction.

Passive Management-by-Exception

A slightly more effective style of leadership in the FRLD model is called *passive management-by-exception*. When a leader waits for mistakes to happen before stepping in to attempt to fix the problem, the leader displays passive management-by-exception. The leader's attitude is "if it's not broken, don't fix it." A leader who displays this form of leadership "fights fires" and intervenes only when standards are not met. Because the leader springs into action only when something went wrong, the leader is not perceived by followers as active or effective.

Passive management-by-exception leadership also can be illustrated with the "cop in the donut shop" stereotype often seen on television shows and illustrated in Figure 1.3. Imagine a policeman placing an order before leisurely sitting in a Dunkin' Donuts® shop drinking coffee. Then his police radio goes off, beckoning him to a disturbance at the local shopping mall. He takes no action unless a problem arises. After the problem is fixed, it's back to normal functioning—a warm and comfortable booth at the coffee shop.

Figure 1.3
**Waiting
for trouble.
Passive
management-
by-exception
leadership
behavior
points out
what's gone
wrong after
the fact.** Image
by David
Shankborne.

Active Management-by-Exception

If passive management-by-exception behavior is like the cop in the donut shop,
you can imagine *active management-by-exception* behavior as "Robocop,"
"Rambo-in-Pinstripes," or a spy looking for a problem. Instead of waiting for
things to go wrong before taking action, a leader who displays active management-by-exception micromanages processes and takes corrective action, often
before or soon after the problem arises. Such behavior involves closely monitoring work performance for errors and arranging to know if and when things go
wrong. As shown in Figure 1.4, the leader scanning his cellphone and computer
is monitoring performance very closely. He is clearly focusing much attention on
operations of the day instead of considering the entire year. Here the leader's
attention is on mistakes, complaints, failures, deviations from standards, and
infractions of rules and regulations.

While active management-by-exception may be effective in high-stakes
or life-or-death situations (e.g., nuclear power plants, military operations) or in
problem-solving contexts (e.g., auditing, information systems development
and maintenance), leaders in other contexts who display this behavior are
likely to promote fear and stifle innovation among associates. It is difficult for
followers to identify with and place trust in a leader who constantly focuses
on the negative and constantly keeps systems in check. Consequently, followers' commitment and motivation levels are not typically optimized with active
management-by-exception.

**Figure 1.4
Tech-savvy
micromanager.
Active
management-
by-exception
leadership
behavior
seeks to avoid
mistakes
before they
happen. But
its focus on
the negative
can be
de-motivating.**

Contingent Reward

Moving up the FRLD model, we now come to *transactional contingent reward*, an active and generally effective leader behavior, often displayed by politicians and other dealmakers such as U.S. President Donald Trump. Contingent reward leadership is a constructive transaction—a type of implied contract. It represents an exchange relationship between the leader and the follower. The leader sets goals, clarifies roles, and explains expectations for the follower regarding performance targets. In return, the follower promises to meet the performance expectations

**Figure 1.5
Keep up the
good work.
Transactional
contingent
reward
leadership
behavior
sets goals for
followers, and
rewards them
for a job well
done. Pormezz
/ Shutterstock.**

set by the leader. If the follower meets expectations by following through with his side of the deal, the leader rewards the follower in accordance with their implied contract. If the follower fails to meet the goal, he does not receive the reward.

In essence, contingent reward is an approach to leadership that relies on extrinsic motivation to drive followers toward the goal and then reward achievement. In Figure 1.5, we see a leader praising his follower for a job well done. The follower was able to accomplish his task properly because the leader was clear in setting and communicating his goals for the report. Research has shown that contingent reward leadership is generally effective in building base levels of trust and commitment in followers, and for meeting targeted performance levels.

The 5Is of Transformational Leadership

While contingent reward may be an effective way to motivate followers to reach targeted goals, such an approach might have limited success in today's innovation-based economy, where people need to have both extrinsic and intrinsic motivation to succeed. We need someone who leads us with a clear vision and confidence. A transformational leader inspires followers to exceed these goals—to perform beyond expectations. Transformational leaders promote positive and meaningful changes in people, teams, organizations, nations, and even societies, as illustrated in the leader profile of Muhammad Yunus in Box 1.1. There are five components of transformational leadership, which are called the 5Is of transformational leadership: idealized influence (behavior), idealized influence (attributes), inspirational motivation, intellectual stimulation, and individualized consideration. Let's briefly examine each of these components of transformational leadership.

Idealized Influence—Behaviors and Attributes

You might have felt that Muhammad Yunus seems like a current-day version of Mohandas Gandhi, who advised his followers to always aim for complete harmony of thought, word, and deed. Transformational leaders, such as Yunus and Gandhi, often seek this authenticity by displaying high levels of moral behavior, virtues, and character strengths, as well as a strong work ethic.[10] Transformational leaders talk about the importance of values, beliefs, purposes, a collective mission, and the benefits of trusting each other. They set aside their self-interest for the good of the group. Their words and deeds represent *idealized influence behaviors*. When followers witness a leader's idealized influence behaviors, they attribute *idealized influence* to the leader, as shown in Figure 1.7. Here you can see that the leader is well respected and admired by his team members. This leader instills a sense of pride and respect in his team members because of his achievement of the collective mission and bringing values and beliefs to life.

Box 1.1 Leader Profile: Muhammad Yunus

Bringing vision into action is a hallmark of transformational leaders. One man's vision is the total eradication of poverty and hunger from the world—a vision based on core values of altruism and generosity, instead of self-interest and political empire-building. That man is Muhammad Yunus, recipient of the 2006 Nobel Peace Prize for his work in fighting world poverty. Yunus (shown in Figure 1.6) is the Bangladeshi economist, professor, politician, and founder of the Grameen Bank (Village Bank). This organization transformed the financial services industry by introducing the concept of providing small loans to poor people at reasonable interest rates. These microcredit loans have helped reduce poverty in Bangladesh and in hundreds of countries around the world. Grameen has diversified beyond banking into the agriculture, irrigation, software, telecommunications, and clothing industries—all with a focus on fighting poverty and helping to promote social entrepreneurship.

Yunus is using part of his Nobel Prize award money to create another company that will make low-cost, high-nutrition food for the poor. He also works with G 20 leaders to promote youth entrepreneurship initiatives, and eradicate youth unemployment with the help of governments, businesses, and social organizations. He is a former member of the Global Elders, a multinational group of political leaders, including Desmond Tutu, Nelson Mandela, and Jimmy Carter. This group shares its leadership wisdom in an effort to solve the world's most pressing problems of poverty, disease, and social and economic injustice.

Yunus displayed intellectual stimulation by venturing where traditional banks would not dare to go. He did this by extending high-risk microcredit loans to the poor. He displayed individualized consideration by

Figure 1.6 **Muhammad Yunus at the University of Salford in 2013. Image by University of Salford Press.**

expanding his business model beyond finance so that more poor people could benefit from the products and services of his Grameen enterprises. Yunus is the epitome of transformational leadership in the realm of social entrepreneurship.[11]

Figure 1.7 Hooray for our team! Idealized leaders talk about the importance of teamwork and the collective success that energizes followers to emulate the leader. KeyStock / Shutterstock.

The idealized leader's role modeling of high levels of performance and ethics is admired and respected by followers as well, thereby adding to the idealized influence followers attribute to a transformational leader. As a result, followers identify strongly with a leader, show high levels of trust in and commitment to the leader, and exert high levels of drive and motivation. Indeed, idealized influence (behavior and attributes) represents the very pinnacle of leadership within the FRLD model, as shown in Gandhi's call for authenticity, which increases followers' willingness to trust and emulate the leader.

Inspirational Motivation

Closely related to idealized influence is *inspirational motivation*, a leader behavior that involves developing and articulating a vision. Examples of positive visions include Steve Jobs' "How to Live Before You Die" speech to Stanford University graduates, Dr. Martin Luther King's "I Have a Dream Speech," Oprah Winfrey encouraging young women with her Leadership Academy, and Professor Randy Pausch's "Last Lecture" on life lessons given at Carnegie Mellon University. If you have not witnessed these visionary speeches, we encourage you to view them on www.YouTube.com. Such visions paint an optimistic and enthusiastic picture of the future that "raises the bar" for followers. The status quo is unacceptable to the transformational leader; the alternate future presented in the vision is considered a must-achieve scenario. Often this vision elevates performance

expectations and reframes the organization's purpose as meaningful. Raising the bar and highlighting significance is a way to inspire followers to put forth extra effort in their work.

By using inspiration, transformational leaders express confidence in followers and their shared vision. Inspirational leaders energize followers and create synergistic energy for collective action based on an exciting vision. Like the entrepreneur shown in Figure 1.8, inspiring leaders frame and articulate a clear vision of the future, and with confidence in their message of team synergy and collective success.

Both inspirational motivation and idealized influence elicit very strong emotional bonds, deep trust, and commitment between leaders and followers. As a result, inspirational motivation increases followers' willingness to excel.

Intellectual Stimulation

While inspirational motivation triggers the emotions of followers, intellectual stimulation increases followers' rationality and intellect. The great thinkers of history, such as Thomas Aquinas, Albert Einstein, and Maria Skłodowska Curie, were strong advocates of rational thinking, considering opposing points of view, and systematic analysis as means of creative problem solving and innovation. So too are contemporary leaders such as Jeff Bezos of Amazon, Ginni Rometty of IBM, and Larry Page and Sergey Bren, the founders of Google, Inc. When leaders encourage followers to challenge old ways of doing things, they are displaying *intellectual stimulation*. Seeking different perspectives, reexamining assumptions that are no longer valid, getting others to look at problems in new ways, and encouraging nontraditional thinking as well as rethinking are all forms of intellectual stimulation. These behaviors get followers to become more creative and innovative, and more willing to change people, processes, products, and services

Figure 1.9
Let's try it this way. Intellectual stimulation gets followers to look at old problems in new ways. Syda Productions / Shutterstock.

for the better. In essence, intellectual stimulation increases followers' willingness to think out of the box.

As shown in Figure 1.9, the leader is challenging his team to reexamine assumptions and seek perspectives that are not the norm. He is encouraging his team to think in a different way and be creative. As a result, his intellectual stimulation creates an environment of rational thinking that supports the development and use of followers' natural talents and strengths.

Individualized Consideration

Transformational leaders' ultimate aim is to develop followers into leaders themselves.[12] Who in your life has been such a transformational leader to you? Who has helped you recognize the greatness that grows in you? Pause for a moment and think of some of those people who wanted the best for you in your life. Who helped to transform you into your best possible self?

The developmental nature of transformational leadership is best illustrated through *individualized consideration*. When leaders spend time listening, coaching, and teaching for followers' development they are displaying individualized consideration. When leaders treat others as individuals with different needs, abilities, and aspirations (and not just part of a group of subordinates), they are displaying individualized consideration as well. As shown in Figure 1.10, the leader reaches out to address his follower's concern. He understood the problem facing the follower and supported him in facing a challenge. Individualized consideration involves showing empathy, valuing individual needs, and encouraging continuous improvement. As a result of such attention, individually considerate leaders increase followers' willingness to develop.

To summarize, the FRLD model proposes the notion that leaders who achieve extraordinary levels of performance are those who build people up through transformational leadership. These leaders are exemplary role models, have an exciting vision, challenge the status quo and continually innovate (even at the peak of

Figure 1.10
A helping hand. Individually considerate leaders coach and mentor followers by appreciating their uniqueness and helping them build their talents into strengths. PannrayS / Shutterstock.

success), and coach and mentor their associates toward their full potential. Effective transformational leadership is built upon a foundation of transactional contingent reward leadership, an exchange relationship between the leader and follower that sets well-defined roles and expectations and uses extrinsic rewards to achieve desired performance. Less effective leadership styles search for what's done wrong, not what's done right (active management-by-exception), patch problems and focus on mistakes only after they have occurred (passive management-by-exception), and avoid leadership and relinquish responsibility (laissez-faire).[13]

Full Range Leadership Development and the History of Leadership Thought

Theory and research on FRLD is connected to and built upon a long and interesting history. For centuries, man has considered the concept of leadership. But it was not until the 20th century that the disciplines of political science, psychology, sociology, history, anthropology, and management converged to make major contributions toward our understanding of leadership.[14] Guided by Table 1.1, let's briefly examine the history of leadership thought and how FRLD relates to a variety of other leadership theories. As we often tell our students, please consider a theory to be a useful tool that explains how and why things happen, rather than an abstract and useless idea. As psychologist Kurt Lewin once said, "There is nothing more practical than a good theory."[15]

Table 1.1 How Full Range Leadership Development Relates to Other Leadership Theories

Theory	Source(s)[18]	Key Concept(s)	Relationship to FRLD Theory
Trait theory	Bass (2008); DeRue et al. (2011); Judge et al. (2002); Rubin et al. (2005)	Innate qualities and personality characteristics are found in "great" leaders (e.g., intelligence, self-confidence, determination, integrity, sociability).	Traits and personality not considered in FRLD model. But research indicates that positive, adaptive, active, interpersonal, and developmental leader traits support social influence process for most effective leaders.
Psychodynamic theory	Freud (1938); Kets de Vries (1994); Shamir (1991); Zaleznik (1977)	Self-concept, ego states, and personality issues underlie a parent–child relationship for leaders and followers. Leaders and followers develop through self-awareness.	Ego, self-concept, and personality not considered in FRLD model. But research links positive life experiences, prior leadership experience, and relational, other-oriented and positive self-concepts to most effective leadership.
Skills theory	Goleman (1995)	Emotional awareness and control are essential to leadership effectiveness.	Emotional connection and social comfort between leader and follower key to leadership effectiveness.
	Mumford (2006)	Problem solving, social skills, and knowledge impact leadership effectiveness.	Rationality and intellectual curiosity required on part of leaders and followers.
Style theory	Judge et al. (2004); Stodgill (1963)	Task and relationship leader behaviors influence followers' performance and satisfaction.	Most effective leaders pay attention to both task and relationship issues with followers.
Situational leadership-oriented theory	Blanchard et al. (1993); Thompson & Vecchio (2009)	Followers' competence and confidence determines appropriate leader behavior (i.e., direct, coach, support, delegate).	Most effective FRLD behaviors universal across many situations and cultures. Most effective leaders can be either directive or participative.
Contingency theory	Fiedler (1967)	Match leaders to the appropriate situation depending upon task/relationship orientation, relations with followers, task structure, and position power.	Most effective FRLD behaviors universal across many situations and cultures. Some situations may require more task-focused and less developmental behaviors.
Path–goal theory	House & Mitchell (1974); House (1996)	Leader considers task and follower characteristics and selects appropriate behavior (i.e., directive, supportive, participative, achievement).	Most effective leaders clarify expectations to clear a path for followers. Raising self- and collective efficacy is vital. Most effective leaders can be either directive or participative.

Table 1.1 continued

Theory	Source(s)[18]	Key Concept(s)	Relationship to FRLD Theory
LMX theory	Graen & Uhl-Bien (1995)	Quality of leader–follower dyad determines in-group, out-group, and effectiveness.	Most effective leaders give individualized attention to followers through coaching, mentoring, and diversity.
Servant leadership theory	Greenleaf (1977); Liden et al. (2014); Kool & van Dierendonck (2012)	Leader acts as a prosocial community steward empowering, healing, and developing others, humbly and ethically.	Empowerment, ethics, community, and relational focus are consistent with transformational leadership.
Ethical leadership theory	Brown et al. (2005); Brown & Treviño (2006)	Leader promotes ethical conduct by being a moral person and moral manager.	Leader role model ethics with idealized influence and hold followers accountable for ethical conduct through transactional leadership.
Authentic leadership theory	Avolio & Gardner (2005); Banks et al. (2016); Zhu et al. (2011)	Positive psychological states, organizational contexts, and self-development promote positive outcomes.	Most effective leaders are true to themselves and others, self-aware, positive, and development oriented.

Trait Theory

Scholars first studied leadership in terms of the traits, or fixed personal characteristics and innate qualities, found in great leaders. These "Great Man" theories linked qualities such as intelligence, self-confidence, determination, integrity, and sociability to leadership effectiveness.[16] For example, think about the types of strong characters that movie actors John Wayne, Denzel Washington, or Russell Crowe played across their careers and you will get a sense of what the Great Man theories espouse. These theories also describe similar "great women," such as Margaret Thatcher, the strong-willed former prime minister of Great Britain, who was dubbed the "Iron Lady" by the Soviets. Other examples include Hillary Clinton, former U.S. first lady and secretary of state, and Angela Merkel, the chancellor of Germany.

There are several problems with trait-based leadership theories. For example, leaders can share many of the same traits, yet behave in different ways and produce starkly different outcomes. Consider Mohandas Gandhi, Winston Churchill, Franklin Delano Roosevelt, Charles de Gaulle, Adolph Hitler, Joseph Stalin, Benito Mussolini, and Francisco Franco. Each of these charismatic leaders of the mid-20th century possessed self-confidence and determination, but some led followers in destructive ways, while others were constructive. This is also true for more contemporary leaders, such as Vladimir Putin, Donald Trump, Angela Merkel, and Xi Jinping. Trait theories ignore what these leaders do, namely, how they behave. Trait theories also ignore the characteristics of followers and the situation, which also determine leadership effectiveness. For these reasons, by the 1950s, leadership scholars shifted their attention to leader behaviors and characteristics of followers and the situation.

FRLD primarily focuses on leader behaviors and does not consider leader traits and personality. However, a recent resurgence of interest in trait-based explanations of leadership has linked leader traits to aspects of the Big 5 personality model (i.e., emotional stability, openness, conscientiousness, extraversion, and agreeableness) and several other traits.[17] In general, this line of research indicates that leaders who are positive, adaptive, interpersonally engaging and aware, and developmental in nature are the most effective leaders.

Psychodynamic Theory

Some psychologists and sociologists have used psychodynamic theory to explain leadership processes as the making of meaning, protection of followers by the leader, and emphasis on development of the self and others. While psychodynamic approaches to leadership are varied, one common theme is that leaders play a key role in influencing how followers think, feel, and act. This theory assumes that the world can be a hostile, turbulent, and unpredictable environment. Followers look for a leader who can make sense of such crises for them. This way of describing leadership may explain why in the midst of major global economic, social, and political turmoil, Donald Trump was able to win the 2017 U.S. presidential election. Trump was able to make sense out of the turmoil for people, communicate with a sense of confidence, and make many campaign promises that only he could lead efforts to meet these challenges.[19]

Many leaders successfully overcome personal challenges or organizational crises in their own lives and share their life lessons with followers. Through introspection and learning, these leaders gain greater self-awareness of who they are, what their strengths and weaknesses are, and how they can best contribute in their leadership role. Some trainers schooled in the psychodynamic approach use the Myers–Briggs Type Indicator® (MBTI) to help leaders better understand their psychological type and preference for leadership or follower-ship. While most MBTI consultants may not see themselves as psychodynamic counselors, they are coaching leadership as a personality style measured by the MBTI, as opposed to training leadership as a set of behaviors that can be learned independent of personality, as proposed by FRLD consultants. After experiencing personal growth through the psychodynamic approach, some leaders are able to present themselves as role models worthy of protecting and guiding followers, similar to parents with their children.[20]

For example, one of our colleagues uses psychodynamic theory with her executive clients to identify sources of their aloof leadership behavior. One such client is "Richard," a 60-year-old entrepreneur who identified several critical events in his early childhood that hindered his ability to interact effectively with his associates. Richard's father was very harsh, strict, and cold in his relations with his wife and children. To compensate for this liability, Richard's mother and sisters smothered him with love and affection because he was the baby and only boy in the family. Richard's upbringing has fed a strong need for attention, standoffishness, and huge ego. In addition, Richard has few male friends due to his hypercompetitive and manipulative manner. He also feels more comfortable around women at work, but only if he is in charge and gets his way. Doesn't he sound somewhat child-like? After counseling, Richard has identified these roadblocks to his leadership effectiveness, understands where they came from, and is working on a plan to address his issues.

Psychodynamic theory provides leaders such as Richard with a better understanding of who they truly are so that they may grow in their self-awareness and improve their leadership. Concepts of self, ego states, and personality are not considered in FRLD theory. However, some evidence exists that transformational leaders have a preference for intuition, empathy, and extraversion, while transactional leaders have a preference for logical thinking and practicality. In addition, research indicates that positive life experiences (e.g., having challenging but supportive parents), prior leadership experiences, and relational, other-oriented and positive self-construals are associated with the most effective leaders in the FRLD model.

Skills Theory

Some scholars take a more practical view by describing leadership as a way to solve problems. Here the emphasis is on solving social problems that arise in relationships, teams, organizations, communities, and nations. These perspectives are grounded in theory and research on emotional intelligence and problem solving.

Emotional Intelligence

Emotions and the information they contain can help leaders do their job. Emotions, such as happiness, amusement, sadness, and concern, influence our thinking and decisions on how to act. The emotional intelligence perspective proposes that emotional awareness and control is essential to leadership effectiveness. For example, the level of emotional intelligence that Donald Trump and George W. Bush used in their leadership pales by far when compared to that of Barack Obama or John F. Kennedy.

While there is some debate on whether emotional intelligence is a constellation of traits or a collection of skills, most leadership trainers assume the latter to be true. Emotions contain valuable information such as hints at psychological states and underlying intentions. Many people think with emotion and also think about emotions. Therefore, there is skill and knowledge involved in dealing with emotion. As such, emotional intelligence skills allow individuals to recognize their emotions and the emotions of others, and use this information to adapt their behavior and influence others' behavior to produce a more satisfactory and effective outcome.[21]

For example, Tanya received incorrect feedback from her manager, Clyde, who pointed out her "mistakes" in the presence of coworkers. By doing so, the boss sent an implied message to others that Tanya is incompetent and could not control situations. Such messages usually trigger emotions (e.g., fear and resentment) and physical reactions (e.g., tense body and wide-open eyes). These reactions typically produce a defensive mindset and a fight-or-flight behavioral reaction. Instead of allowing these effects to dismay her, Tanya recognized what she was feeling and was able to calm herself down by rationally challenging the underlying assumptions that triggered her fear. She calmly confronted Clyde and pointed out the error in his thinking. In this case, Tanya's emotional intelligence helped her exert upward influence on Clyde, her misinformed micromanaging boss.

According to FRLD theory, the level of emotional connection and social comfort between leader and followers is oftentimes associated with transformational leadership effectiveness. Emotionally intelligent leaders and followers are better able to create the positive and developmental relationships found at the pinnacle of the FRLD model.

Pragmatic or Problem-Solving Leadership Theory

Another skills-based leadership perspective proposes that leaders play a very practical role in helping followers solve organizational and career-related problems. According to this view, leadership is nothing more than a series of opportunities for problem solving. In these situations, leaders' cognitive and social skills, coupled with their life experiences and knowledge base, influence their leadership effectiveness. Problem-solving leadership theory also proposes that innate and learned intelligence and the abilities stemming from them, along with personality and motivation level, influence these problem-solving skills.[22]

For example, when Walt arrived at his new managerial post, he saw himself as the "organizational savior," who was appointed to fix all that was wrong in an organization that had run amok prior to his arrival. Based on his 20 years of experience in the Defense Ministry, Walt felt that he possessed the systems thinking skills, ability to judge under uncertain conditions, and judgment to determine whether or not a solution was a good fit for any organizational or personnel problem that came his way. He thought that these skills, along with his accumulated wisdom, allowed him to fix any problem, whether it was mentoring a colleague or designing a new metric to assess organizational performance. Walt's leadership strength could not be explained by personal charm, charisma, or inspiring words. Instead, his leadership prowess was based on his ability to use organizational resources to solve organizational problems.

The problem-solving perspective to leadership can also be illustrated by many politicians who claim that they have solutions for social, economic, or political problems. By framing themselves as a problem solver, they hope to appeal to the rationality and practicality of voters who are looking for someone who could address these problems. According to FRLD theory, such rationality and curiosity are required for the intellectual stimulation of both transformational leaders and their followers.

Style Theory

By the 1950s, scholars realized that the trait approach for explaining leadership was inadequate. It was not enough to know only what personal characteristics great leaders possessed; there also was a need to know what these leaders do (i.e., how they behave). So scholars from Ohio State University and the University of Michigan analyzed a wide variety of leader behaviors and distilled them into two main types of leadership: (1) *task- or production-oriented leadership*, which focuses on providing structures and pathways for followers to effectively perform tasks, and (2) *people- or relationship-oriented leadership*, which focuses on building and maintaining good relationships with followers by being considerate. According to style theory, leaders who lack either of these leader behaviors can be problematic and less effective than those who display high levels of both styles of leadership.[23]

Consider the leadership style of a charming middle-aged professor named Norton. When Norton was appointed academic head of a department at a local college, faculty and staff were thrilled. Norton was famous for his brief interactions with colleagues that were laced with compliments, flattery, and humorous quips uttered in the style of a pompous, yet gregarious thespian. Norton would frequently utter witty comments such as "Erica couldn't get elected dog catcher," "Now there's a dangerous duo . . . how are you, my young ladies?," or "I think I can work for the new boss—I can dance with her." Norton ingratiated everyone that he came into contact with, and as a result was well liked by a highly satisfied but unproductive staff. He was very considerate and supportive with all colleagues and thus displayed very high levels of people-oriented leadership. Unfortunately, the faculty tired of Norton's excessive and almost exclusive display of people-oriented leadership, and he left the campus to work in a consulting practice for federal agencies.

As Norton's example shows, you need to find the right balance between *getting things done* and *being a nice guy* if you want to perform well <u>and</u> gain trust and respect from your followers. One thing in common between style theory and FRLD theory is that they both use leader behaviors to explain leadership processes and outcomes. Transformational leadership is associated with many of the same outcomes (e.g., followers' job satisfaction and leadership effectiveness) as people- or relationship-oriented leadership.[24] These behavior-based theories make leadership development more promising because behaviors are more changeable and thus trainable than personal attributes proposed in the trait theory discussed earlier.

Situational Leadership Theory

Situational leadership theory (SLT) seeks to match an appropriate leader behavior to various situations defined primarily by the follower's readiness to perform a task independently. These leader behaviors shift from task-oriented to relationship-oriented or supportive leadership, and from leader-dominated action to follower-dominated action. Followers' readiness is defined by their competence and commitment levels as perceived by the leader.

When the leader perceives the follower to possess low levels of competence and commitment, SLT prescribes the leader to be *directive* with the follower by clearly stating what needs to be done. When the leader perceives the follower to possess a low level of competence but some commitment, the leader is advised to *coach* the follower to develop his/her skills. When the leader perceives the follower to possess a high level of competence and some commitment, the leader is advised to *support* the follower by soliciting suggestions from the follower and making the decision based on that input. When the leader perceives the follower to possess high levels of competence and commitment, SLT prescribes the leader to use *delegation* with the follower by permitting the follower to make the decision within limits set by the leader. As followers' levels of competence and commitment increase, the use of authority by the leader diminishes and amount of empowerment of followers increases.[25]

To illustrate, Rhonda supervises a group of internal auditors at a large public accounting firm. Due to the high turnover rates in entry-level positions in public accounting, Rhonda's firm hires several college graduates every June. When the new hires join her group, Rhonda spends much time directing them regarding the firm's standard operating procedures and adherence to new statements published by the Financial Accounting Standards Board and the International Accounting Standards Board. Rhonda and her senior colleagues coach those that remain with the firm past the first year and whom they perceive to be increasing in their competence and commitment levels. As the junior staff gain more experience and knowledge, Rhonda spends less time with them and empowers them with the necessary resources and decision-making authority. Therefore, the leadership behaviors Rhonda displays with her staff members depend upon her perception of their competence and commitment to her group and the firm.

Many organizations use SLT in their training and development programs because SLT is intuitive and easy to understand. However, SLT also has been criticized by leadership experts on several fronts. For example, SLT has received little empirical support from rigorous scientific research, and newer "refinements" of the theory have been shown to perform worse than the original conceptualization. It also suffers from conceptual and measurement ambiguity, lacks a solid theoretical framework to explain the effects proposed by the theory, and fails to account for demographic differences in leaders and followers that may influence its predictions across situations.[26] In contrast, research on the FRLD model indicates that the most effective leader behaviors (i.e., transformational and transactional contingent reward leadership) are generally universal across many situations and cultures. Depending on the situation, leaders can blend directive or participative approaches with transformational and contingent reward leadership to maximize leadership effectiveness.[27]

Contingency Theory

Another popular situational approach to understanding leadership is contingency theory, developed by leadership researcher Fred Fiedler. Contingency theory seeks to match leaders to appropriate situations. Leaders are assumed to possess a preference for task- or relationship-oriented leadership. This preference is assumed to be measured with an instrument called the Least Preferred Coworker survey. Respondents are asked to describe a coworker with whom they have the biggest problem getting work done together. Those who describe their least preferred coworker more critically are said to possess a task-oriented leadership style. Those who describe their least preferred coworker more leniently are said to possess a relationship-oriented leadership style. Since contingency theory assumes that leaders are fixed in either of these leadership styles, they must be fit into a situation that best suits their leadership effectiveness. This approach is much like a bullpen pitcher in baseball who is brought into the game based on whether he is right- or left-handed and whether the hitter bats from the right- or left-hand side of home plate.

The appropriate fit for task- or relationship-oriented leadership depends on the nature of the situation as assessed by three critical situational factors:

- The quality of the leader–follower relations
- The leader's position power (i.e., authority to reward or punish followers based on position in the organization)
- The task structure (i.e., whether the task is clearly defined and easily understood or ambiguous and complex)

Contingency theory predicts that task-oriented leaders are best suited for very favorable (e.g., good leader–follower relations, strong position power, structured tasks) or unfavorable (e.g., poor leader–follower relations, weak position power, unstructured tasks) conditions. In contrast, relationship-oriented leaders are said to be a good fit for moderate conditions (e.g., good leader–follower relations, weak position power, unstructured tasks). According to contingency theory, the relationship-oriented leadership style is a good fit for followers performing tasks that cannot be performed by simply adhering to standard operating procedures, but must rely on their collective experience and skillsets to make sense out of the difficult task. Based on these assumptions, top management should be familiar with their leaders' preferences for leadership and carefully assess the aforementioned situational characteristics so they can match the right leader to situations that arise.[28]

FRLD theory differs from contingency theory in at least two ways. First, FRLD theory does not assume that leaders are fixed in terms of their predisposition for a certain style of leadership. Rather, FRLD theory assumes that leaders possess the ability to display the repertoire of leadership behaviors shown in the model. Second, the most effective FRLD behaviors are universal across many situations and cultures. Some of these situations may require more task-focused (e.g., active management-by-exception and contingent reward) and less developmental (i.e., transformational) behaviors, and vice versa. Therefore, FRLD argues that the leader must assess the situation to determine whether he or she is using the right mix of active or passive leadership behaviors.

Path–Goal Theory

Perhaps a more useful situational approach to understanding leadership is path–goal theory. According to path–goal theory, one of a leader's main functions is to pave the way for followers by clearing a path for them to achieve organizational goals. To do this, the leader must first assess (1) personal characteristics of the follower, such as perceived ability and locus of control (i.e., the degree to which you believe you control your own destiny), and (2) environmental characteristics, such as task structure, authority system, or work group characteristics. Once this assessment is made, the leader chooses one of four behaviors to display: *directive* (leader tells followers what to do), *supportive* (leader attends to needs of followers), *participative* (leader invites followers to share in the decision-making process), or *achievement-oriented* (leader sets high performance expectations and challenges followers to meet them). Path–goal theory proposes that selecting the right leader behavior for the personal and environmental characteristics results in followers' motivation to perform and reach high levels of productivity.[29]

While taking one of our MBA courses on leadership, a group of students once produced a training film for path–goal leadership that we used in our teaching. This humorous video illustrates how Steven Peppers, an ex-Army sergeant, attempted to motivate a follower to perform a data analysis task. The video scenes depict Steven's successful and unsuccessful attempts at leadership. For example, Steven failed when he used participative leadership with an inexperienced follower working on an ambiguous task. Here Steven should have used directive leadership, which provides guidance and structure for followers working on complex tasks with unclear rules. Supportive leadership provides consideration to followers who desire affiliation with others working on mundane or repetitive tasks. Participative leadership works best when followers are experienced and professional, but need the leader to add some understanding to the complex tasks they perform. Achievement-oriented leadership is appropriate for leaders like Steven whose followers have high needs for achievement but are faced with challenging tasks. When Steven finally got it right, his followers called out for a group hug and exclaimed, "You're transformational beyond transformational!"

Path–goal theory teaches leaders how to structure the transaction they enter into with followers. This is what the most effective leaders using FRLD theory do when they display transactional contingent reward leadership and clarify expectations to clear paths for followers. Path–goal theory also describes how leaders can raise followers' self-efficacy and collective efficacy, as described in motivation-based theories of charismatic and transformational leadership. Transformational leaders in the FRLD model can use either directive or participative approaches to leadership, and these behaviors are listed among the choices for leaders in the path–goal theory.

Leader–Member Exchange (LMX) Theory

Ever wonder why some people get so worked up over leadership changes in their departments? One reason is provided by leader–member exchange (LMX) theory. According to LMX theory, leaders form a unique relationship with each of their followers due to constraints (e.g., time, resources, differences in preferences and personalities, etc.) and then create in-groups or out-groups. In-group members receive preferential treatment from the leader, such as receiving privileged information, highly sought-after resources, and mentoring. Out-group members receive support from the leader, but they are not treated as well as in-group members. Thus, in-group followers enjoy higher-quality relationships with the leader than do out-group followers. As followers demonstrate their competence and loyalty to the leader, their roles may change from being treated like a stranger, to being treated like an acquaintance, and finally like a partner in the high-quality exchange seen in in-groups.[30]

Consider the case of Eleanor, who was suddenly removed from a leadership post by senior management and replaced with Peter. All at once, it seemed that those who were close to Eleanor had lost their power derived from the perks of her position and their closeness with Eleanor. Because Eleanor was not friendly with Peter, those formerly in the in-group now found themselves part of the new out-group. Their influence on management was now second fiddle to that of Peter and his in-group. It would take time before the members of the new out-group could scheme to gain more influence over the senior managers. Indeed, LMX theory sheds light on the nature of the leadership dynamics for Eleanor, Peter, and their associates. Such variation in the quality of relationships can also be found among members of a team, and are explained by a related theory called team-member exchange (TMX), which we will discuss in Chapter 9.[31]

LMX theory is similar to FRLD theory in at least two ways. First, LMX theory describes the nature of the social exchange between the leader and the follower. FRLD's transactional contingent reward behavior is also based on an exchange relationship. Here, the leader clarifies goals and expectations, and in exchange for a follower's promise to meet the performance target, the leader rewards the follower for meeting the expectations. Second, transformational leaders give individualized attention to followers through coaching, mentoring, and appreciating the unique knowledge, skills, and abilities followers possess. This individualized approach to leadership is also described by LMX theory.

Servant Leadership Theory

Much like today, the turbulent 1960s and early 1970s were marked by racial tensions, civil rights rallies, social unrest, protests against government policies on war, economic inequities among social groups, and contentious national leaders. Servant leadership theory emerged out of this era based on the ideas of Robert Greenleaf, a former top executive at AT&T. Greenleaf's ideas radically challenged the prevailing tough-looking and authoritative behaviors exhibited by many traditional leaders of the time. This enlightened view of leadership requires a heightened sense of spirituality, humbleness, and ethical understanding. Its goal is to elicit trust among followers and solve problems by listening first to the concerns of others within the community and then envisioning a better future for all.

The servant leader engages in several behaviors that set him or her apart from a traditional leader. He promotes the emotional healing of followers and is sensitive to their needs. As a steward of community wellbeing, he creates value for the community by providing direction, soliciting volunteerism, and humbly engaging in the work required to address the community's needs. The servant leader also empowers and develops followers, and is an advocate for their success. For these behaviors to be displayed, the servant leader requires the motivation to lead as well as the personal characteristics of self-determination, moral reasoning acuity, and cognitive complexity (i.e., the ability to distinguish nuances among concepts and find similarities among seemingly distinct ideas). Those who lead in cultures with a humane orientation, decentralized decision-making, and less emphasis on deference to those in power are more likely to be successful servant leaders. Outcomes of servant leadership include high-quality leader–follower relationships, self-actualization, positive attitudes and performance outcomes for followers, and sustainability and corporate social responsibility for organizations.[32]

A colleague named Clifford personifies the characteristics of a servant leader. Clifford joined the university after spending many years as a legal counsel for a regional hospital. While in the health care field, Clifford witnessed many social injustices that oriented him toward servant leadership. In his current role as an educator, Clifford shows a deep concern for the welfare of others. Guided by his deep faith, he often goes out of his way to help associates overcome challenges, understand dilemmas, and develop as business professionals and human beings. His service to others often comes at his own expense, which he makes up by putting in long hours on the job. Nevertheless, Clifford's servant leadership has gained him the respect and admiration of students, staff, and faculty, who have awarded him for his teaching and service to the university and community.

In regard to the FRLD model, servant leadership shares several character-istics with transformational leadership. Servant leadership's goal of empowering and developing others is almost identical to the notion of individualized considera-tion that we described earlier. Its focus on community welfare and stewardship is similar to idealized influence behaviors that challenge followers to put their self-interests aside for the good of the group. Transformational leaders can ben-efit from servant leadership principles which serve as guideposts for promoting the development and wellbeing of followers in a more spiritual, self-aware, and enlightened manner.

Ethical Leadership Theory

The inner battle between self-serving and other-oriented motives that charac-terizes human nature sometimes leads to human failings and ethical scandals in organizations. Examples of recent ethical scandals in business include Wells Fargo's fake customer accounts, former Fox News top executive Roger Ailes' and movie mogul Harvey Weinstein's sexual harassment of women, the Mylan's EpiPen price gauging of those suffering anaphylactic shock due to allergic reac-tions, and the Samsung Galaxy Note 7 battery fires and subsequent recall.[33] The world has become more transparent and leaders need to establish higher levels of ethical standards because with today's technologies and interconnectedness, everyone is watching. Therefore, leaders should aim to be both a *moral person* and a *moral manager*. As a moral person, they personify and role model the high-est levels of honesty and trustworthiness in their decision-making and behavior. When it comes to personal integrity, they are beyond reproach. As a moral man-ager, they emphasize and enforce moral policies among their followers so an ethical climate can exist in their organization.[34]

The Penn State/Sandusky sexual abuse scandal illustrates breakdowns in ethical leadership. As a Penn State football defensive coordinator, Jerry Sandusky used his position, connections, and power within the local community to sexually abuse at least ten boys. These horrendous crimes were covered up for over a decade. But in 2012 Sandusky was convicted of 45 counts of child abuse. The scandal cost Penn State over $237 million dollars in fines and legal fees, and caused significant damage to its reputation as one of the world's finest educational institutions. How did Penn State's top leadership and its iconic football coach Joe Paterno allow for such a tragedy? Paterno's moral persona as a developer of character and strong supporter of educational values was well-established for many years. But he failed as a moral manager in his response to Sandusky's actions when informed by graduate assistant Mike McQueary and while reporting the incidents to administrators who some critics claim propped up a culture that valued the football legacy (and all the money it generates) over ethics and the human dignity of the victims.[35]

This tragic case shows that ethical leadership parallels aspects of the FRLD model in two ways. First, the moral person aspect of ethical leadership is similar to the idealized influence attributes and behaviors components of transformational leadership. Second, the moral manager aspect of ethical leadership is similar to the transactional leadership behaviors of contingent reward (e.g., setting ethical standards) and active management-by-exception (e.g., addressing ethical violations with appropriate sanctions). Both similarities are important because followers learn what is and what is not acceptable from transformational leaders, who are supposed to provide ethical guidance for their followers. Consistent with these similarities, meta-analytic research shows that both ethical leadership and transformational leadership produce similar positive effects on followers.[36]

Authentic Leadership Theory

The abovementioned affliction of lies, corruption, and other unethical behavior that plagued top management of organizations including Enron, WorldCom, Volkswagen, faith communities, and governments has spawned a call for more ethical approaches to leadership. But this new way of explaining leadership goes back to some very old ideas pondered by the Greek philosopher Socrates and English poet and playwright William Shakespeare. Socrates called for men to know themselves. His philosophy influenced Shakespeare in *Hamlet* to write: "This above all: To thine own self be true, and it must follow, as the night the day, thou canst not then be false to any man." More recently, leadership practitioners and researchers have proposed that leaders and followers must also be true to themselves and others in order to produce exemplary, ethical, and sustainable results.

Such calls for authentic leadership have been made by Bill George, former CEO of Medtronic, Warren Buffet, CEO of Berkshire Hathaway, and Pope Francis. Instead of riding in an enclosed "Pope Mobile," Pope Francis prefers an open-air small and unpretentious automobile. Instead of living in the Apostolic Palace, he resides in a humble guest house for Church officials near St. Peter's Basilica. Instead of appearing stuffy and standoffish, the Pope displays an easygoing manner. He uses Twitter to send out his messages, some of which include humble off-the-cuff remarks such as "Who am I to judge?" These authentic behaviors make him down-to-earth instead of distant and unapproachable. As a result, his followers feel close to him and hopeful.[37]

Authentic leaders are known to be transparent; they openly share appropriate information with their associates. They are moral and ethical in their personal and professional lives. They use their personal values as a guideline to behave consistently across different situations. They believe in associate building and developing the full leadership potential of their followers. They make decisions in fair and balanced ways. And they aim to produce positive and sustainable impacts on individuals, team, organizations, and the environment. This set of qualities makes them authentic.[38]

To illustrate, consider Jim, a Canadian-born engineering executive. When Jim assumed a new leadership post, he promised himself that he would lead based on the same set of principles that he uses in his personal life. He wrote out and posted these principles in his office so that he could read them any time he was challenged by a difficult boss or situation. Jim quickly became well-liked by his staff because he stood up for them while he advanced the best interests of the organization. He is known as a man of his word as well. People know what Jim stands for and will not stand for. He openly communicates with his staff and doesn't hide things from them. He shares his positive vision of the future with them in a way that includes their opinions in the decision-making process. In many ways, Jim is considered to be an authentic leader by most of his associates.

Authentic leadership theory is proposed to subsume many forms of leadership, including transformational leadership within FRLD theory. The most effective leaders in the FRLD model are true to themselves and others because they demonstrate consistent behaviors that reflect their values. The notions of authentic leadership and transformational leadership overlap to a great extent and are somewhat redundant.[39] Research indicates that transformational leaders, like authentic leaders, are self-aware, positive, and future-oriented in their vision and attitudes, ethical in their thinking and actions, and development-oriented in their quest to build followers into future leaders. These elements of authentic leadership share a common foundation with transformational leadership: promoting positive change in people, teams, organizations, communities, and the world.

Our overview of the FRLD model and its relationship to other leadership theories provides us with theoretical bases to improve as leaders. Our experience in teaching and researching leadership has taught us that the best way to become skilled in FRLD, or any leadership topic for that matter, is *learning by deeply understanding and then doing*. To help achieve this goal, we provide several summary questions and reflective exercises at the end of each chapter. Please carefully review them before moving on to subsequent chapters. In the next chapter, we turn our attention to examining the dynamics of leadership situations, paying particular attention to how the leader, follower, and situation interact to produce important outcomes.

Summary Questions and Reflective Exercises

1. What is the greatest leadership challenge facing your organization today? What is your greatest personal leadership challenge? How can the FRLD model help you to successfully face these challenges?

2. Think of an individual in your life who has had a profound effect on your personal growth. For example, this person may be a parent, a boss, a pastor, a teacher, a coach, etc. With this person in mind, list three traits and three behaviors associated with him or her. (A trait is a stable personality characteristic, whereas a behavior is a specific action displayed by this person.) How do these traits and behaviors map onto the FRLD model introduced in this chapter? What situation gave rise to the effectiveness of this person's leadership effect on you?

3. You can measure your FRLD behaviors as perceived by yourself, your subordinates, peers, superior, and other associates with the Multifactor Leadership Questionnaire (MLQ). The MLQ is a reliable and valid online survey tool that provides feedback reports on how you and others perceive the frequency of different FRLD leadership behaviors that you exhibit, as illustrated in Figure 1.11. The most recent version of the MLQ report uses the following labeling for the FRLD behaviors and attributes: *Builds Trust* = idealized influence attributes, *Acts with Integrity* = idealized influence behaviors, *Encourages Others* = inspirational motivation, *Encourages Innovative Thinking* = intellectual stimulation, *Coaches & Develops People* = individualized consideration, *Rewards Achievement* = contingent reward, *Monitors Deviations & Mistakes* = active management-by-exception, *Fights Fires* = passive management-by-exception, and *Avoids Involvement* = laissez-faire. These customized reports can help you to develop plans for enhancing the full range of leadership potential for individuals, teams, and organizations. Visit www.mindgarden.com to learn more about the MLQ and to order this valuable tool prior to developing a plan for achieving your full leadership potential.

4. Instructors in our FRLD university classes and corporate training workshops are often asked if leaders are born or made. The answer is both. We are yet to see a leader who was not born, although some are so bad that we wonder whether they need to be born again, or what leadership scholar Abraham Zaleznik called "twice born."[40] But seriously, leaders are shaped by both their genetics and life experiences.[41] Which of your personality traits are beneficial to your leadership development? Which are liabilities? What experiences in your life have shaped your behaviors as a leader?

5. Think of situations where you have used FRLD behaviors. How did your followers and associates react to your use of these behaviors? Which behaviors resulted in positive outcomes? Negative outcomes? Why?

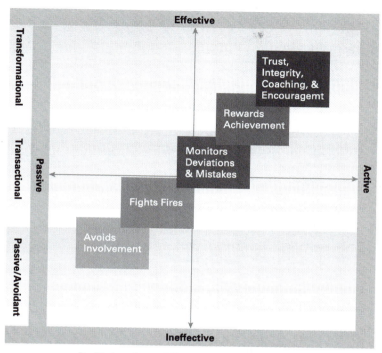

Effective

Transformational

Transactional

Passive/Avoidant

Passive ←→ Active

Trust, Integrity, Coaching, & Encouragemt

Rewards Achievement

Monitors Deviations & Mistakes

Fights Fires

Avoids Involvement

Ineffective

Profiled against a full range of leadership styles

Frequency
0 = Not at all
1 = Once in awhile
2 = Sometimes
3 = Fairly often
4 = Frequently, if not always

Your Raters' Average Scores

	0 0.5 1 1.5 2 2.5 3 3.5 4	Score
Transformational Leadership (5)		2.1
Rewards Acheivement (5)		1.9
Monitors Deviations & Mistakes (5)		2.1
Fights Fires (5)		2.1
Avoids Involvement (5)		2.2

Figure 1.11 **Selected pages from the *Multifactor Leadership Questionnaire™ 360 Leader's Report*. (Reproduced by special permission of the publisher, Mind Garden, Inc., Menlo Park, CA, www.mindgarden.com from the *Multifactor Leadership Questionnaire™ 360 Leader's Report* by Bernard M. Bass and Bruce J. Avolio. Copyright © 1996, 2003, 2015 by Bernard M. Bass and Bruce J. Avolio. All rights reserved. Further reproduction is prohibited without the publisher's written consent.)**

5. Full-Range Leadership Profile – Aggregate Scores

Section 5 presents your aggregate ratings and your self-rating. Use the key below for interpretation:

Frequency
0 = Not at all
1 = Once in awhile
2 = Sometimes
3 = Fairly often
4 = Frequently, if not always

The number of raters is shown below in parentheses.

Transformational Leadership

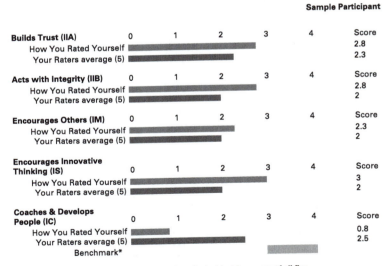

Transformational Leadership (Total Average)

	Score
How You Rated Yourself	2.3
Your Raters average (5)	2.1
Benchmark*	

*According to the Research Validated Benchmark, the ideal frequency of all five Transformational behaviors should be a "Fairly Often" rating of 3 or greater.

Builds Trust (IIA)

	Score
How You Rated Yourself	2.8
Your Raters average (5)	2.3

Acts with Integrity (IIB)

	Score
How You Rated Yourself	2.8
Your Raters average (5)	2

Encourages Others (IM)

	Score
How You Rated Yourself	2.3
Your Raters average (5)	2

Encourages Innovative Thinking (IS)

	Score
How You Rated Yourself	3
Your Raters average (5)	2

Coaches & Develops People (IC)

	Score
How You Rated Yourself	0.8
Your Raters average (5)	2.5
Benchmark*	

*According to the Research Validated Benchmark, the ideal frequency of all five Transformational behaviors should be a "Fairly Often" rating of 3 or greater.

Figure 1.11
Continued

6. Self and Rater Feedback (By Level)

Section 6 presents a breakout of Leadership style group frequency ratings
for each rater level. The graphs can be interpreted using the key below:

Frequency
0 = Not at all
1 = Once in awhile
2 = Sometimes
3 = Fairly often
4 = Frequently, if not always

The total number of raters at each level is shown below in parentheses.

Transformational Leadership

Transformational Leadership (Total Average)

	Score
How You Rated Yourself	2.3
Above (1)	2.3
Same (2)	2.2
Lower (2)	2

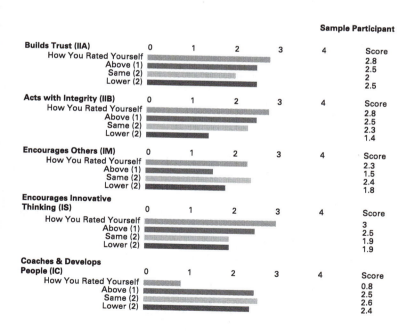

Builds Trust (IIA)

	Score
How You Rated Yourself	2.8
Above (1)	2.5
Same (2)	2
Lower (2)	2.5

Acts with Integrity (IIB)

	Score
How You Rated Yourself	2.8
Above (1)	2.5
Same (2)	2.3
Lower (2)	1.4

Encourages Others (IM)

	Score
How You Rated Yourself	2.3
Above (1)	1.5
Same (2)	2.4
Lower (2)	1.8

Encourages Innovative Thinking (IS)

	Score
How You Rated Yourself	3
Above (1)	2.5
Same (2)	1.9
Lower (2)	1.9

Coaches & Develops People (IC)

	Score
How You Rated Yourself	0.8
Above (1)	2.5
Same (2)	2.6
Lower (2)	2.4

Figure 1.11
Continued

Notes

1   Crooker, S. (2017). *Character strengths when I was performing at my best*. MGMT 507. Malvern, PA: Penn State Great Valley; and http://e2s.us/about/; and Crooker, S. (2017, May 29). Personnel communication.

2   Krishnamoorthy, R. (2014, May 16). How GE trains more experienced employees. *Harvard Business Review*. Retrieved from https://hbr.org/2014/05/how-ge-trains-more-experienced-employees; and Wartzman, R. (2015, May 4). Coke's leadership formula: Sending its rising star execs away for six weeks. *Fortune*. Retrieved from http://fortune.com/2015/05/14/coke-leadership-program/?iid=sr-link2.

3   Bass, B. M., & Avolio, B. J. (1994). *Improving organizational effectiveness through transformational leadership*. Thousand Oaks, CA: Sage.

4   Avolio, B. J., Sosik, J. J., Kahai, S. S., & Baker, B. (2014). E-leadership: Re-examining transformations in leadership source and transmission. *The Leadership Quarterly, 25*(1), 105–131.

5   Williams. A. (2015, September 18). Move over, millennials, here comes Generation Z. *The New York Times*. Retrieved from www.nytimes.com/2015/09/20/fashion/move-over-millennials-here-comes-generation-z.html?_r=0.

6   Bass, B. M., & Avolio, B. J. (1999). *Training full range leadership: A resource guide for training with the MLQ*. Palo Alto, CA: Mind Garden.

7   A comprehensive qualitative review of leadership theory and research is provided by Dinh, J. E., Lord, R. G., Gardner, W. L., Meuser, J. D., Liden, R. C., & Hu, J. (2014). Leadership theory and research in the new millennium: Current theoretical trends and changing perspectives. *The Leadership Quarterly, 25*(1), 36–62. Several meta-analyses validate the FRLD model and its ability to predict individual, group, and organizational performance, including Judge, T. A., & Piccolo, R. F. (2004). Transformational and transactional leadership: A meta-analytic test of their relative validity. *Journal of Applied Psychology, 89*(5), 755–768; Lowe, K. B., Kroeck, K. G., & Sivasubramaniam, N. (1996). Effectiveness correlates of transformational and transactional leadership: A meta-analytic review. *The Leadership Quarterly, 7*(3), 385–425; and Wang, G., Oh, I., Courtright, S. H., & Colbert, A. H. (2011). Transformational leadership and performance across criteria and levels: A meta-analytic review of 25 years of research. *Group & Organization Management, 36*(2), 223–270.

8   Bass & Avolio (1999). As cited in Note 6.

9   Cooper, C. D., Hellriegel, D., & Slocum Jr., J. W. (2017). *Mastering organizational behavior*. Boston, MA: Flat World/Boston Academic Publishing.

10 Comprehensive overviews of authentic leadership are provided in Banks, G. C., MacCualey, K. D., Gardner, W. L., & Guler, C. E. (2016). A meta-analytic review of authentic and transformational leadership: A test for redundancy. *The Leadership Quarterly, 27*(4), 634–652; George, B., & Sims, P. (2007). *True north: Discover your authentic leadership*. San Francisco, CA: Jossey-Bass; Shamir, B., & Eilam, G. (2005). "What's your story?" A life-stories approach to authentic leadership development. *The Leadership Quarterly, 16*(3), 395–417; and Sosik, J. J. (2015). *Leading with character: Stories of valor and virtue and the principles they teach* (2nd ed.). Charlotte, NC: Information Age Publishing.

11 Yunus, M. (2017). *A world of three zeros: The new economics of zero poverty, zero unemployment, and zero net carbon emissions*. New York: Public Affairs; and www.muhammadyunus.org.

12 Burns, J. M. (1978). *Leadership*. New York: Harper & Row.

13 Bass & Avolio (1999). As cited in Note 6.

14 Bass, B. M. (2008). *The Bass handbook of leadership: Theory, research and managerial applications* (4th ed.). New York: Free Press.

15 Lewin, K. (1952, p. 169). *Field theory in social science: Selected theoretical papers by Kurt Lewin*. London: Tavistock.

16 Bass (2008). As cited in Note 14.

17 DeRue, D. S., Nahrgang, J. D., Wellman, N., & Humphrey, S. E. (2011). Trait and behavioral theories of leadership: An integration and meta-analytic test of their relative validity. *Personnel Psychology*, *64*(1), 7–52; Judge, T. A., Bono, J. E., Ilies, R., & Gerhardt, M. W. (2002). Personality and leadership: A qualitative and quantitative review. *Journal of Applied Psychology*, *87*(4), 765–780; and Rubin, R. S., Munz, D. C., & Bommer, W. H. (2005). Leading from within: The effects of emotion recognition and personality on transformational leadership behavior. *Academy of Management Journal*, *48*(5), 845–858.

18 References for Table 1.1 citations are Avolio, B. J., & Gardner, W. J. (2005). Authentic leadership development: Getting to the root of positive forms of leadership. *The Leadership Quarterly*, *16*(3), 315–338; Banks, G. C., McCauley, K. D., Gardner, W. L., & Guler, C. E. (2016). A meta-analytic review of authentic and transformational leadership: A test for redundancy. *The Leadership Quarterly*, *27*(4), 634–652; Bass, B. M. (2008). *The Bass handbook of leadership: Theory, research and managerial applications* (4th ed.). New York: Free Press; Blanchard, K. H., Zigarmi, D., & Nelson, R. B. (1993). Situational leadership after 25 years: A retrospective. *Journal of Leadership Studies*, *1*(1), 21–36; Brown, M. E., & Treviño, L. K. (2006). Ethical leadership: A review and future directions. *The Leadership Quarterly*, *17*(6), 595–616; Brown, M. E., Treviño, L. K., & Harrison, D. A. (2005). Ethical leadership: A social learning perspective for construct development and testing. *Organizational Behavior and Human Decision Processes*, *97*(2), 117–134; DeRue, D. S., Nahrgang, J. D., Wellman, N., & Humphrey, S. E. (2011). Trait and behavioral theories of leadership: An integration and meta-analytic test of their relative validity. *Personnel Psychology*, *64*(1), 7–52; Fiedler, F. E. (1967). *A theory of leadership effectiveness*. New York: McGraw-Hill; Freud, S. (1938). *The basic writings of Sigmund Freud* (A. A. Brill, Ed.). New York: Modern Library; Goleman, D. (1995). *Emotional intelligence: Why it can matter more than IQ*. New York: Bantam; Graen, G., & Uhl-Bien, M. (1993). Relationship-based approach to leadership: Development of leader-member-exchange (LMX) theory over 25 years: Applying a multi-level multi-domain perspective. *The Leadership Quarterly*, *6*(2), 219–247; Greenleaf, R. K. (1977). *Servant leadership: A journey into the nature of legitimate power and greatness*. New York: Paulist Press; House, R. J. (1996). Path-goal theory of leadership: Lessons, legacy, and a reformulated theory. *The Leadership Quarterly*, *7*(3), 323–352; House, R. J., & Mitchell, T. R. (1974). Path-goal theory of leadership. *Journal of Contemporary Business*, *3*, 81–97; Judge, T. A., Bono, J. E., Ilies, R., & Gerhardt, M. W. (2002). Personality and leadership: A qualitative and quantitative review. *Journal of Applied Psychology*, *87*(4), 765–780; Judge, T. A., Piccolo, R. F., & Ilies, R. (2004). The forgotten ones? The validity of consideration and initiating structure in leadership research. *Journal of Applied Psychology*, *89*(1), 36–51; Kets de Vries, M. F. R. (1994). The leadership mystique. *Academy of Management Executive*, *8*(3), 73–92; Kool, M., & van Dierendonck, D. (2012). Servant leadership and commitment to change, the mediating role of justice and optimism. *Journal of Organizational Change Management*, *25*(3), 422–433; Liden, R. C., Wayne, S. J., Liao, C., & Meuser, J. D. (2014). Servant leadership and servant culture: Influence on individual and unit performance. *Academy of Management Journal*, *57*(5), 1434–1452; Mumford, M. D. (2006). *Pathways to outstanding leadership: A comparative analysis of charismatic, ideological and pragmatic leaders*. New York: Psychology Press; Rubin, R. S., Munz, D. C., & Bommer, W. H. (2005). Leading from within: The effects of emotion recognition and personality on transformational leadership behavior. *Academy*

of *Management Journal, 48*(5), 845–858; Shamir, B. (1991). The charismatic relationship: Alternative explanations and predictions. *The Leadership Quarterly, 2*(2), 81–104; Stogdill, R. M. (1963). *Manual for the Leader Behavior Description Questionnaire Form XII.* Columbus, OH: Ohio State University, Bureau of Business Research; Thompson, G., & Vecchio, R. P. (2009). Situational leadership theory: A test of three versions. *The Leadership Quarterly, 20*(5), 837–848; Zaleznik, A. (1977). Managers and leaders: Are they different? *Harvard Business Review, 55,* 67–80; and Zhu, W., Avolio, B. J., Riggio, R. E., & Sosik, J. J. (2011). The effect of authentic transformational leadership on follower and group ethics. *The Leadership Quarterly, 22*(5), 801–817.

19 Politifact (2017, May 16). Trump-o-meter: Tracking Trump's campaign promises. Retrieved from www.politifact.com/truth-o-meter/promises/trumpometer/.

20 Freud (1938). As cited in Note 18; Kets de Vries (1994). As cited in Note 18; Shamir (1991). As cited in Note 18; Sosik, J. J., Chun, J. U., Blair, A. L., & Fitzgerald, N. A. (2013). Possible selves in the lives of transformational faith community leaders. *Psychology of Religion and Spirituality, 5*(4), 283–293; and Zaleznik (1977). As cited in Note 18.

21 Goleman, D. (1995). *Emotional intelligence: Why it matters more than IQ.* New York: Bantam.

22 Mumford (2006). As cited in Note 18; and Zaccaro, S. J., Harding, F. D., Jacobs, T. O., & Fleishman, E. A. (2000). Leadership skills for a changing world: Solving complex social problems. *The Leadership Quarterly, 11*(1), 11–35.

23 Judge et al. (2004). As cited in Note 18; Piccolo, R. F., Bono, J. E., Heinitz, K., Rowold, J., Duehr, E., & Judge, T. A. (2012). The relative impact of complementary leader behaviors: Which matters most? *The Leadership Quarterly, 23*(3), 567–581; and Stogdill (1963). As cited in Note 18.

24 Piccolo et al. (2012). As cited in Note 23.

25 Blanchard, K. (2007). *Leading at a higher lever: Blanchard on leadership and creating high performance organizations.* Upper Saddle River, NJ: Pearson-Prentice Hall; and Blanchard, K., Zigarmi, P., & Zigarmi, D. (1992). *Leadership and the one minute manager.* Escondido, CA: Blanchard Training and Development.

26 Northouse, P. G. (2016). *Leadership: Theory and practice* (7th ed.). Thousand Oaks, CA: Sage; Thompson & Vecchio (2009). As cited in Note 18; and Yukl, G. (2012). *Leadership in organizations* (8th ed.). Upper Saddle River, NJ: Pearson-Prentice Hall.

27 Bass, B. M., & Riggio, R. E. (2006). *Transformational leadership* (2nd ed.). Mahwah, NJ: Lawrence Erlbaum Associates.

28 Fiedler (1967). As cited in Note 18.

29 House (1996). As cited in Note 18; and House & Mitchell (1974). As cited in Note 18

30 Graen & Uhl-Bien (1995). As cited in Note 18.

31 Chun, J. U., Cho, K., & Sosik, J. J. (2016). A multilevel study of group-focused and individual-focused transformational leadership, social exchange relationships, and performance in teams. *Journal of Organizational Behavior, 37*(3), 374–396; and Seers, A., Petty, M. M., & Cashman, J. F. (1995). Team–member exchange under team and traditional management: A naturally occurring quasi-experiment. *Group & Organization Management, 20*(1), 18–38.

32 Greenleaf (1977). As cited in Note 18; Liden et al. (2014). As cited in Note 18; and van Deirendonck, D. (2011). Servant leadership: A review and synthesis. *Journal of Management, 37*(4), 1228–1261.

33 Matthews, C., & Helmer, M. (2016, December 28). The five biggest corporate scandals of 2016. *Fortune.* Retrieved from http://fortune.com/2016/12/28/biggest-corporate-scandals-2016/.

34 Bedi, A., Alpaslan, C. N., & Green. S. (2016). A meta-analytic review of ethical leadership outcomes and moderators. *Journal of Business Ethics*, *139*(3), 517–536; Brown et al. (2005). As cited in Note 18; and Brown & Treviño (2006). As cited in Note 18.

35 Alderfer, C. P. (2013). Not just football: An intergroup perspective on the Sandusky scandal at Penn State. *Industrial and Organizational Psychology*, *6*(2), 117–133; and Bidgood, J., & Pérez-Peña, R. (2017, March 24). Former Penn State president found guilty in Sandusky abuse case. *The New York Times*. Retrieved from www.nytimes. com/2017/03/24/us/graham-panier-jerry-sandusky-penn-state.html?_r=0.

36 Bedi et al. (2016). As cited in Note 34.

37 Bruenig, E. (2015, September). Pope Francis' radical authenticity is revolutionizing the Catholic Church. *New Republic*. Retrieved from https://newrepublic.com/article/122868/pope-francis-radical-authenticity-revolutionizing-catholic-church.

38 Avolio & Gardner (2005). As cited in Note 18; Banks et al. (2016). As cited in Note 18; and Zhu et al. (2011). As cited in Note 18.

39 Banks et al. (2016). As cited in Note 18.

40 Zaleznik (1977). As cited in Note 18.

41 Arvey, R. D., Zhang, Z., Avolio, B. J., & Krueger, R. F. (2007). Developmental and genetic determinants of leadership role occupancy among women. *Journal of Applied Psychology*, *92*(3), 693–706; Avolio, B. J., & Hannah, S. T. (2008). Developmental readiness: Accelerating leader development. *Consulting Psychology Journal: Practice and Research*, *60*(4), 331–347; and Sosik, J. J. (2006). Full range leadership: Model, research, extensions and training. In C. Cooper & R. Burke (Eds.), *Inspiring leaders* (pp. 33–36). New York: Routledge.

Chapter 2

The Full Range Leadership Development System

Today's most progressive organizations are revamping their leadership processes based on Full Range Leadership Development (FRLD) to make it more systematic and consistent for different individuals and situations. For example, consider MBA student Justine Clark and the story of her colleague CEO Jay Sidhu and his longtime friend and business partner COO Dick Ehst. After many years, these executives created Customers Bancorp and Customers Bank of Wyomissing, PA. This organization provides financial solutions to customers with low to no fees. It offers truly outstanding customer service, has a socially responsible focus, and operates with high levels of ethics and technological integration. As an associate in Customers Bank, Justine began her leadership development journey focused on how she could advance her own career. However, Sidhu and Ehst's vision and ethical standards have helped Justine to focus on a more other-oriented leadership style. They helped Justine to understand how each bank department interacts with other executives and departments. They showed her how each executive works to fulfill the mission of the company by keeping the customer-focused corporate culture alive and well. Sidhu's strong vision and strategies for adapting to a tumultuous marketplace keep associates focused and reaching for higher standards. Justine plans to introduce FRLD training to these executives so that they can put a name to their leadership behaviors with the hope of them passing the knowledge along to other associates. She also thinks that FRLD training can make it easier for executives in her company to reflect and evolve as leaders. Justine also intends to further her own leadership development by thinking about it through the FRLD systems lens so she can continue her leadership evolution.

The way we study and practice leadership has come a long way as well. We have broadened our perspective on leadership to focus not only on characteristics of leaders that make them great, but also on characteristics of followers and the situations that add to their greatness over time. Before taking action, smart leaders reflect upon the relationships between leader and follower, leader and situation, follower and situation, and the confluence of leader, follower, and situation. They also think about how these relationships change over time. The events that shape leader–follower interactions and the situation that embeds them depend upon broader societal, cultural, historical, and technological trends and circumstances. Therefore, like Justine Clark, you also need to think of leadership as a system of which you are an integral part.

One way to gain this systems point of view about leadership is to develop your *perspective-taking capacity*. Higher levels of perspective allow you to look at a situation from multiple viewpoints and to integrate these viewpoints in a way that is easily understood by others.[1] To better understand this, consider the motion picture-making process and the responsibilities that actors, actresses, and directors have for specific tasks in preparing for and creating a movie. Actors and actresses are responsible for reciting their own lines and knowing when to come in on the script. Directors are responsible for much more. They must understand set design, lighting, special effects, and how all the actors and actresses interact according to the script. Directors have to view the production from a systems perspective in the sense that they understand who, what, when, where, and how all the elements come together in the performance. Therefore, a director's perspective needs to be broader than an actor's perspective, but both must work together to satisfy the audience with a great production.

Now, think of the leadership process as a type of movie production where the leader is the actor/director, and the followers are actors who play roles in the leadership performance for audience.[2] An outstanding leader must also possess a director's mindset, in addition to acting along with the followers. If, as a leader, you are always thinking about what's best for you, then you have limited your perspective and range of potential, and you're likely to be a lousy actor (or a leader who displays laissez-faire behavior). Why? Because people put forth their best efforts for role models who make personal sacrifices for the good of everyone. If you want to limit your followers' potential, take care of your own needs with a laissez-faire approach to leadership. However, if you want to reach your full leadership potential and theirs, then act like a transformational leader by looking at things from their perspective, considering their needs, and making some sacrifices. Your short-term sacrifices will pay off in the long run with much more significant achievements and perhaps an "Academy Award" for your leadership performance.

This chapter shows you how to view FRLD as a system by broadening your perspective so that you can take away the skills required for effective leadership and performance. We present three tools that will assist you to better understand the systems nature of leadership. Let's begin by considering a case we have used in class for many years to teach graduate students how to view leadership as a system.

Sidney Poitier and *To Sir, With Love*

Films are a great way to illustrate various leadership behaviors and the dynamics of the leadership system as well. People often comment that once they watch the numerous film clips throughout their FRLD training, they can never view movies the same way. Thereafter, they view movies through a leadership systems lens.

One of our students' favorite films to illustrate leadership systems is *To Sir, With Love*,[3] starring Sir Sidney Poitier, the Academy Award-winning Bahamian American actor, film director, and social activist. In this classic movie, Poitier portrays Mark Thackeray, an unemployed communications engineer who takes a teaching job in a rough English high school in the late 1960s. The film shows how he is able to overcome many challenges to ultimately inspire his students to reach their full potential. The film deals with the timeless issues of social and racial prejudice, motivation, teenage angst, and inspirational leadership, among others.

Our students often comment that the film is as relevant today as it was when it was first released. They cite today's calls for social and economic change, political tensions and divisions, workforce diversity issues, empowerment of youth, and troubled times as examples of its relevance. Many subsequent films, such as *Stand and Deliver*, *Dangerous Minds*, and *Freedom Writers*, follow somewhat similar storylines. If you have never seen *To Sir, With Love*, we strongly recommend that you view it. You are sure to thoroughly enjoy the film and Sidney Poitier's role. Poitier's fine performance illustrates a teacher's evolution from a traditional transactional taskmaster. At first, he falls victim to the students' tormenting and unruly behavior. But over time he transforms into an inspiring and intellectually stimulating pragmatist who wins over his students and gains their respect and admiration.

The movie's plot illustrates how characteristics of the leader, the follower, the situation, and their interaction over time produce either positive or negative outcomes. According to the story plot, Thackeray, the movie's aspiring leader, was born and raised in British Guyana. He goes on to earn his university degree in the United States. After graduating, he is frustrated by many unsuccessful job applications to numerous engineering firms in England. The movie implies that he is turned down because he is a person of color. To make ends meet during his extended job search, he takes on a teaching post in a predominantly white high school in a lower-class East End London neighborhood.

Thackeray stands in stark contrast to his jaded, bitter, and unmotivated fellow teachers who have been worn down over the years by their students. Instead, Thackeray presents himself as a sharply dressed, refined, calm and collected, intelligent, and idealistic teacher. As a victim of racial discrimination throughout life, he feels compelled to overachieve to fit in with his colleagues and gain the respect of his underachieving students. At first, he tries traditional teaching methods, strict discipline, and formality in his teaching. These methods do not work. Thackeray is baited, jeered, and easily manipulated by students who view the classroom as their turf.

Although Thackeray's humble background is similar to his students', everything else was different between them. His students are mainly Caucasian, unmotivated, rude, and selfish. They show little concern for their appearance and less respect for their elders. They view their coursework as an impractical waste of time. They believe most of the boys will end up working in factories like their fathers, and most of the girls will end up as stay-at-home moms. These were typical career paths for students in economically disadvantaged areas in England during the 1960s.

The situation that surrounds Thackeray and his students makes matters even worse. The political and social climate of the 1960s promoted questioning of authority and nonconformity. These were ideas that students brought into the classroom and acted out on their teachers. The students' home lives were filled with parental disputes, alcoholism, and drug abuse, also depicted in contemporary films such as *Thirteen* and *Girl on the Edge*. To make matters worse, they suffered from a lack of support and encouragement from their parents. Many were forced to take on part-time jobs to help make ends meet. At school, they were constrained by the rigid factory-like English educational system of the time that sought the mind control of students rather than developing their creativity and expressiveness. This approach to education viewed students as merely products who are churned out regardless of the amount of knowledge, skills, and abilities they possessed at graduation. The negative and cynical attitude of their prior teachers created an "us versus them" culture, so adeptly described by Roger Waters of Pink Floyd in his classic song entitled "Another Brick in the Wall (Part II)."[4] (Please view the video for this song on YouTube.com to see what we mean.) It seems impossible for any teacher (or leader) to make a difference in the lives of unmotivated and unruly students (or followers) in these circumstances.

However, Thackeray never gave up. At the point Thackeray's "kids" are just about to drive him crazy, he realizes that treating them as kids is the problem that made the situation even worse. He realized that he should stop treating them as kids by constantly focusing on correcting their mistakes. Instead, he must start treating them as adults by engaging them as partners rather than products of the learning process. Fellow leadership scholar Bruce Avolio pointed out that treating followers as children who are at a lower stage of development is the way active management-by-exception leadership achieves its goals.[5]

Thackeray understood this concept and applied a new transformational approach to teach the class. He demonstrated intellectual stimulation by throwing out all of the textbooks and allowing his students to choose what topics they'll study. He showed inspirational motivation by taking his students on a field trip to a museum. He demonstrated individualized consideration by encouraging them to attend the funeral of a student's mother. Most importantly, he displayed idealized influence by insisting that they use proper forms of address toward him and among themselves, taking pride in their appearance, and fine-tuning their personal demeanor. By the end of the film, Thackeray is recognized as a gifted teacher by his colleagues. He also wins his students over as they present him with a pewter mug and serenade him with the movie theme song at the graduation dance.

Sidney Poitier's portrayal of Mark Thackeray in *To Sir, With Love* teaches us an important lesson: coordinating all the roles your followers play and developing them along the way is essential to creating and sustaining a successful leadership system. What role will you play in optimizing your organization's leadership system?

Leadership Is a System

English poet John Donne once wrote, "No man is an island entire of itself; every man is a piece of the continent, a part of the main."[6] Likewise, *To Sir, With Love* illustrates that it takes a system to produce positive leadership effects. That is, it takes the right leader, followers, and situation, working in concert as a system, to produce outstanding results. Therefore, you must examine and understand the

Figure 2.1
**Components
of the
leadership
system.**

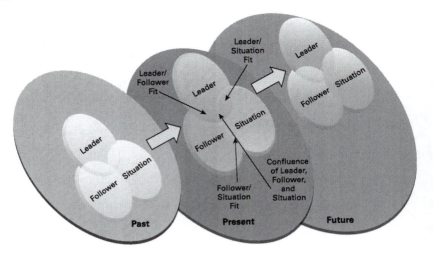

linkages and interactions between the leader, follower, and situation over time to optimize your leadership.[7]

To Sir, With Love illustrates several obvious components of the leadership system. Mark Thackeray represents the leader. His students represent the followers. The historical period and place (i.e., East End London high school circa 1967) represent the situation. As shown in Figure 2.1, the leader, follower, and situation represent the three core components of the basic leadership system, which we will elaborate upon later.

There is another important system component that is not quite as obvious. That component is the element of time, ranging from the past to the present to the future. Each of these time periods are depicted as circular platters in Figure 2.1. The *past* represents previous time periods that provide cultural traditions, experiences, and events from which leaders and followers can learn and make appropriate changes. The past also teaches us what has worked in specific situations and what does not work, so that we do not repeat our mistakes. For Thackeray, both the criteria he eventually used to assess his students' performance in class and his teaching style evolved based on his initial failures. How do leaders in your organization build upon the past to make things better for their followers?

The *present* time period represents the "now moment" that provides current opportunities, challenges, events, and experiences that shape an entirely different configuration for the leader, followers, and situation from that of the past. Many leaders consider the present to be most relevant because it allows them to make decisions based on what they currently see around them, rather than expectations of what they hope to see. Leaders cannot change the past, or create a future with absolute certainty. In *To Sir, With Love*, Thackeray did not waste his present now moments. He was quick to recognize how his leadership behaviors were being received by his students, how his students were being influenced by their surroundings, and what opportunities and challenges the present situation offered for creating a better future.

Transformational leaders, like Thackeray, relish in imagining *future* time periods comprised of new and exciting interactions among the leader, followers, and situational elements of their leadership system. You can think of the imagined future as a canvas upon which transformational leaders paint their compelling vision for the better future. Thackeray presents a much better and meaningful life for his students as a way to overcome the "present" situation and obstacles. Oftentimes, the better future suggested by the leader creates exciting "now moments" and unites followers with a common objective and purpose. Smart leaders assess the present situation, try to find a way to improve it, and bring about changes for the better future. Therefore, the future time period becomes an integral part of the leadership system.

To summarize, FRLD requires you to view leadership as a system. Like ecosystems, leadership is a dynamic and complex whole based on our relationships with others. It involves willing collaboration between leaders, followers, and other constituents. Energy (i.e., motivation and effort), materials and resources, and information flow between these elements of the system. These flows can be observed and described with effects traced back to specific activities or behaviors. Because of these actions, the leadership system is a community situated within a broader environment that can provide or take away the energy, resources, and information to and from the system. All components of the leadership system are interdependent. They can only exist as a whole; they cannot exist independently, especially the core systems components of the leader, follower, and situation. It is through the evolution and changing interactions of these components that the leadership system operates—by being firmly grounded in the past, seizing opportunities and addressing challenges in the present, and constantly imagining better futures.

Leader

A *leader* is someone who influences others to achieve a goal. Leaders are real people. They are not perfect. While they strive to display virtues and character strengths in their behavior, they also are challenged by their own personal vices and idiosyncrasies.[8] Their genetic makeup predisposes them to certain personality traits, such as confidence, extraversion, or narcissism. Such traits are generally stable over the life span. They have their own set of personal values, beliefs, and ideas about how things are and how they should be. Based on their life experiences, they think of themselves in a particular way. This self-perception shapes their self-concept, the image some project to followers, and that some attempt to conceal.

U.S. president Donald Trump presents an image of strength, confidence, and knowledge. Trump's projected self-image stems from a personality characterized by narcissism, disagreeableness, attention-seeking, and grandiosity. As a child of a privileged family, Trump was provided with all that money can buy. He also learned the ways of the world from his father. One lesson that he learned is that life is extremely competitive and tough, so the way to win in life is to hit your competition much harder than they hit you. As an adult, Trump has actively pursued the accumulation of wealth through real estate dealings, with a focus on looks, wealth, women, and power. In his 2016 victory over Hillary Clinton in the race for the presidency, he reached the ultimate destination in the pursuit of power.[9]

As with President Trump, the family background of leaders shapes their attitude about themselves and about life in general. Both genetics and upbringing by parents and relationships with siblings and other family members shape their willingness to influence others. Their motivation to lead often comes from other environmental influences, such as educational, religious, and leadership experiences, support from peers, role models or mentors, unexpected opportunities, and overcoming personal and professional challenges.[10] These genetic and environmental influences shape the leader's character and style, which he or she brings into the leadership system. For example, former U.S. president Bill Clinton's father was absent during his childhood. This forced Clinton to assume a parental role of overseeing and nurturing his siblings. This role taught him the importance of building and maintaining personal relationships. Relationship building and maintenance is an essential principle of transformational leadership. These lessons were essential to Clinton's successful political career, but were ignored in the mistakes he made in his personal life.[11]

One mistake that aspiring leaders (even successful ones) often make is to assume that it is the job of leaders to get things done all by themselves. However, we do not believe that this process can be called leadership because it does not involve the whole leadership system. It is better called self-leadership.[12] That's because followers are not involved in the process. Leadership is about getting things done *with and through* followers. This principle becomes even more important as the unit/organization you lead gets larger and the goal you are trying to accomplish gets bigger and more complicated. FRLD considers leadership to be a development process that views followers not only as a means to accomplish tasks, but also as an end in themselves. In the end, followers should be developed to their full leadership potential and transformed into leaders themselves.

Self-centered leaders who ignore this developmental viewpoint are like Spanish playwright Miguel de Cervantes' character Don Quixote, the "Man of La Mancha." This elderly gentleman was so obsessed with notions of chivalry and righting injustice that he lost his mind and set forth as a knight on an ill-fated mission.[13] His only follower was his "squire," Sancho Panza. To "dream the impossible dream" with one or no followers is a nice notion for a novel or film. But it holds no value for leadership systems in the real world. Leaders need able followers to make organizational dreams come true.[14]

Follower

A *follower* is someone who chooses to follow a leader because of the leader's character, ability, knowledge, position, or vision. Because of their respect and admiration for the leader, followers often imitate a leader in thoughts, words, and deeds. They become motivated to work in the service of the leader. Wouldn't it be nice if we could pick the best followers we could get, like schoolchildren who pick their own teams during recess? Nice thought, but highly unlikely.

Like it or not, most of us either inherit our followers or choose them through inadequate selection systems. Because followers are only human, they are imperfect, just like leaders. Followers bring into the leadership system the same baggage that leaders bring with them—all of the personal characteristics derived from one's genetic makeup and life experiences. If we have unable and/or unwilling followers in our leadership system (just as Mark Thackeray inherited), all we have is struggling leadership. For example, Thackeray's leadership didn't function effectively until he took into account his students' characteristics and situations. Therefore, a good leadership system can't be developed without integrating followers and what they bring into the system.

Great followers sometimes follow and sometimes lead. They often possess detailed knowledge and personal connections that allow them to step up into leadership roles that the leader cannot assume. At other times, followers can struggle in areas of communication, teamwork, creativity, and ethics, and therefore require the guidance of a leader. Transformational leaders understand when followers must follow and when they are capable of leading. They provide followers with the resources, support, and confidence required to overcome these struggles.

When Howard Schultz, former CEO of Starbuck's Corporation, passed the leadership torch of the global coffee chain to current CEO Kevin Johnson, expectations were high. Founded under the principle of treating all people with respect and dignity at all times, Starbucks is consistently mentioned as one of the most caring and socially responsible places to work. The company has hired thousands of U.S. military veterans and plans to hire 10,000 refugees worldwide over the next several years. Under Johnson's leadership, Starbucks has increased employee wages and paid employees for six weeks of parental leave. They also initiated several HR programs built upon the core value of compassion, first espoused by Schultz. As the company has grown over the years, Starbucks has remained true to its heritage by providing a connection and a sense of community for its employees and customers. Personal interactions between top leaders and employees allow them to share their ideas and concerns and show that the CEO cares.[15] If you keep this in mind and start viewing your followers as associates to develop rather than coworkers to tolerate, you are already moving up the FRLD model by imagining a better place for all of you.

Situation

A *situation* describes the relative circumstances, position, or context in which the leader and followers interact and achieve outcomes. There are many ways to describe a situation. The historical context shapes the social culture, world events, and ways of thinking for a particular period of time. For example, the 1960s, with its anti-establishment and change-oriented values, were a perfect stage for Mark Thackeray's intellectually stimulating behaviors in *To Sir, With Love*, just as they are for today's business and national leaders. The economic, social, and political conditions that pervade a particular time period and geographic region place boundaries on what is possible for leaders and followers to achieve. For example, the civil unrest and bigotry in America in the 1960s severely limited

Martin Luther King Jr.'s ability to enact many of the ideals outlined in his "I Have a Dream" speech. These limitations and his competition (i.e., enemies and racists) ultimately led to his death. Fortunately, Dr. King's followers and the majority of Americans have embraced many of his ideas, and we are making progress toward achieving his vision. In 2008, Americans elected Barack Obama as the first African American U.S. president. But given recent tensions between minority and law enforcement agencies, we still have a way to go.

Situations have other elements as well. Competition can be nonexistent (as with monopolies) or it can be fierce. Business and political environments can be turbulent or relatively stable. Faster global growth, changes to U.S. tax and spending policies, U.S. withdrawal from the Paris Climate Agreement, China's shift from relying on exports to domestic consumption, and the British exit from the European Union place many limitations on social and economic development. Such historical, political, and economic conditions are important aspects to consider when assessing the situation in the leadership system. These are issues facing today's world and business leaders.

Beyond timeframe and markets, the geographic context is important to consider. Geography specifies a particular national or regional culture with its own particular values, traditions, and practices. For example, collectivistic (group-oriented) national cultures that we find in China, Korea, or Japan and their emphasis on team, organization, and country rather than self can create a better context for transformational leadership. These contexts focus on cooperation and self-sacrifice advocated by transformational leaders. In addition, the industrial context dictates specific laws, regulations, and technologies unique to a particular industry. Leadership styles that work in one industry (e.g., active management by exception in accounting and auditing) may be a big turn-off in others (e.g., marketing and higher education).

Organizational contexts define the situation as well. Whether an organization chooses an adaptive or rigid strategy to deal with the aforementioned external conditions also affects the situation. How the organization is structured also matters as well. Some organizations are highly bureaucratic with tightly controlled top-down hierarchical communication and reporting structures, formalized policies and procedures, and specialized functions performed by particular personnel. Governmental agencies are notorious when it comes to such bureaucracy. So are companies like Sears Holding Corp, with its history of red tape and mechanistic operations. Sears, once America's largest retailer, is failing because it refused to make its structure flatter and more efficient. It filtered bad operational news from top management. And its culture valued protecting the status quo instead of re-inventing itself, adopting trends of online shopping, and responding to its competitors with innovative strategies.[16] No wonder Sears, Kmart, and other major brick-and-mortar retailers were on the verge of bankruptcy in 2018. We do not believe that transformational leadership with its change-oriented nature will flourish under these environments.

Others are structured as organic organizations with flat communication and reporting structures, less hierarchy of authority and rules, and functions shared by crossed-trained employees and teams. Organic organizations, in contrast, facilitate transformational leadership. Some organizations deploy cutting-edge technologies as an integral part of their strategy, while others depend less on such technologies. All of these contextual characteristics determine whether or not a particular FRLD behavior is appropriate, or whether leadership development is possible. For reasons given in Box 2.1, we believe that General Electric (GE) is one of the best companies in which leadership development is not only encouraged but also required proactively through a systems view of leadership.

The structure and demands of the task also dictate what FRLD leadership styles will work in a given situation and which ones will not. For tasks that are highly structured and easily understood, active management-by-exception leadership is likely to be perceived by followers as unnecessary and redundant. For tasks that are unstructured and complex, contingent reward and individualized consideration displayed by leaders are likely to be valued by followers. That's because such behaviors clarify how to perform tasks. To master FRLD, you need to consider all of these aspects of the situation to know the appropriate time and place to display each of the leadership behaviors in the FRLD model. In other words, the overall effectiveness of FRLD is determined not only by the transformational leadership qualities that a leader possesses, but also by the combination of other factors in the leadership system.

Box 2.1 General Electric and its Passion for Leadership Development

GE is the only original Dow Jones Industrial Average company remaining on the list. In 2016, GE was ranked number one among publically traded companies for leadership development by *Chief Executive* magazine. Rankings were based on five criteria: (1) quality of formal leadership development process in place, (2) CEO commitment to top leadership development measurement, (3) depth of leadership succession pool, (4) number of executives recruited by other companies, and (5) shareholder value growth over ten years.

GE is a huge global organization formed in 1892 whose beginning can be traced back to Thomas Edison and the invention of the lightbulb. At that time, GE's leadership recognized the huge opportunity that tapping into electricity could provide for businesses and households alike. This imaginative quest parallels GE's current focus on facilitating the global exchange of innovation technology, talent, expertise within and between the world's continents and industries, and environmental initiatives for a more sustainable and greener world. GE's vast array of products and services include power generation technologies, wind turbines, hydropower solutions, turbomachinery, drilling equipment, commercial and military engines and aviation systems, health care diagnostic imaging systems, locomotives, diesel engines, power grid management systems, and financial services. With customers in more than 170 countries, GE has more than 330,000 employees worldwide. Such a scope of operations presents both great opportunities and daunting challenges for its leadership, which requires a strong system of leadership in order to meet these challenges.

GE's large investment in leadership training is part of a culture of leadership development first embraced and supported by former CEOs Jack Welch and Jeffrey Immelt, and continued by current CEO John Flannery. All of these top leaders realized that GE's priority is not only providing its wide variety of products and services globally, but also developing GE's associates into leaders through an emphasis on ethics, collaboration, diversity, simplification, innovation, mutual accountability, and high performance. In his letter to the shareholders in GE's 2016 annual report, Immelt stated, "We win by being a valuable, global company and by engaging members of every community we operate in all over the world . . . We are building a culture that is simpler, faster, and more accountable." Motivating individuals to adopt this systems-perspective of leadership through a strong culture of positive change and performance excellence contributes to the collective success of GE. This is what FRLD aims to achieve.[17]

Confluence of Leader, Follower, and Situation

Meteorologists tell us that combinations of geography, ocean temperatures, jet stream flow, and time of the year often interact to create conditions for developing storms. Just as the right mix of ingredients is needed to fuel a storm, the right combination of leader, follower, and situational elements is needed to produce a potent leadership effect over time. To desire leadership, followers must feel challenged by their current situation or perceive themselves as victims of a crisis situation that is destroying their future career or hampering their performance. When followers feel ready to embrace change, we have *follower–situation fit*, depicted by the overlap of the follower and situation circles in Figure 2.1. In this case, the leader must help followers make sense out of the crisis situation that threatens them. By rejecting the status quo and providing an evocative and compelling vision, leaders give new meaning to followers about the situation they face and build their hope for a better tomorrow. When the leader's vision is seen as a viable and inspiring alternate to the status quo, then the leader is the right person for the times and we have *leader–situation fit*, depicted by the overlap of the leader and situation circles in Figure 2.1. A leader must also provide the right message that followers are waiting to hear. Followers must view the leader as someone who is capable of giving them what they need to overcome their struggle and succeed. When these two conditions occur, the leader and followers are able to bond and we have *leader–follower fit*, depicted by the overlap of the leader and follower circles in Figure 2.1. A careful review of Figure 2.1 indicates that when you possess good leader–follower, leader–situation, and follower–situation fits, your leadership system is primed to be the most powerful human force in the universe.

Over the course of history, we've witnessed many examples of this powerful force. Major General John L. Gronski's leadership of U.S. Army forces in Europe is one example (see Box 2.2 and Figure 2.2). Another is Tesla CEO Elon Musk, who has helped define what the future of the automobile and commercial space travel will look like. At Southwest Airlines, we've seen how Herb Kelleher was able to create a fun-filled and positive organizational culture that selects and develops employees who are passionate about their jobs and company. The result is a company with an amazing 45-year track record of financial success that is the envy of the airline industry. This reputation is one that current Southwest Airlines CEO Gary Kelly has sustained.

Box 2.2 Leader Profile: Major General John L. Gronski

I was first introduced to the concept of transformational leadership by Dr. Sosik when I was working on my MBA at Penn State in the late 1990s. The elements of transformational leadership resonated with me primarily due to the foundational principles of character (displayed with idealized influence) and providing a vision (displayed with inspirational motivation) and the concept of servant leadership (displayed with idealized influence and individualized consideration). As my career advanced and I moved from tactical leadership positions to more strategic level leadership positions, I found the elements of transformational leadership to serve as an excellent guide for leading effectively. In order to get the most out of the concept of transformational leadership, I had to personalize it to my own style in order to be authentic. My leadership philosophy has evolved to what I call CVRC2: Character, Vision, Resiliency, Competence, and Care. The highlights of my leadership philosophy and their relationship to transformational leadership are:

Character

Character is the root of leadership. A leader cannot possibly lead effectively if he does not establish credibility among his followers and others with whom he works. By displaying idealized influence, a leader with strong character will exhibit integrity and act in other ways that grow trust. An organization whose members exude trust will flourish and accomplish its goals. Although there are other important components of leadership and other key leadership traits, character is the foundational bedrock of outstanding leadership.

Vision

A leader must be able to develop and communicate a shared vision of the future. This requirement is satisfied by displaying inspirational motivation.

Followers need to know what target they are moving toward. It is impossible for an organization to reach an objective it cannot see or is ambiguous. Without a vision, there may be a great deal of organizational activity, but there will be no tangible results. A lack of a vision leads to frustration and confusion. Once a leader creates a picture of the future, he must communicate this vision over and over again so everyone on the team understands. The leader must be able to articulate a simple, unique, and ideal image of the future. He must also provide a sense of purpose with the picture of the future he paints in the minds of those being led. He must explain the "why" behind the vision and tell followers what he believes. When a leader provides a purpose and a vision, he instills confidence in followers and provides inspiration that fuels energy in an organization that will lead to success.

Resiliency

Armchair psychologist and hall of fame pro football coach, Vince Lombardi, famously said, *"The greatest success is not in never falling, but it is in rising every time you fall."* Anyone who has ever led anything will say that at some point in time the organization will face adversity. For that matter, every living person faces adversity at some point in life. It all comes down to how prepared one is to face these challenges and how one responds. Through a combination of idealized influence and intellectual stimulation, a leader must prepare self and others to overcome challenges. The preparation takes the form of habits that promote psychological, physical, mental, and spiritual wellness. Resiliency is much more than fighting through tough times. It is also about developing into the best person one can be. A resilient person will become an overachiever along with being the type of person who meets challenges head on and wins. Optimism and enthusiasm are two key traits of a resilient person, and can be seen in the display of inspirational motivation. Like any other trait, they must be exercised in order to become a strong part of one's make-up.

Competence

There are four elements of competence. Competence has to do with (1) knowing the technical aspects of the job, (2) knowing yourself and others (i.e., having emotional intelligence), (3) knowing how to solve problems and make decisions, and (4) knowing how to coach and develop others. The first and third elements come with the display of intellectual stimulation. The second element is realized through enhanced self-awareness and the display of idealized influence. The fourth element comes with the display of individualized consideration.

Care

It is important to strive to be an individually considerate servant leader. A servant leader is one who does not seek preference as he is promoted within an organization, but rather takes on more responsibility for one's followers. A servant leader cares more about those being led than about himself. By being individually considerate, we look out for the person on our left and the person on our right. We sacrifice ourselves so others may gain. This aspect of caring for those we lead is what makes being a transformational leader a noble calling.

In conclusion, my current position serving on active duty as the U.S. Army Europe Deputy Commanding General for Army National Guard has reaffirmed that the concept of transformational leadership and that the way I have personalized it for my own leadership philosophy is effective. This philosophy has served me well in a myriad of situations in my career, from leading soldiers of all ranks through engaging senior U.S. military and civilian leaders, as well as leaders and heads of state of foreign governments.[18]

— Major General John L. Gronski

Figure 2.2 **Major General John L. Gronski, U.S. Army Europe's Deputy Commanding General, visits 30th Medical Brigade headquarters in Warsaw, Poland in 2016. Image by 30th MED.**

Other events, such as the Genghis Khan's Mongol conquests, Joseph Stalin's ruthless murder of millions of people to advance changes to the Soviet economic and social landscape, and the Holocaust, provide somber reminders of the potential for disastrous effects of leadership. Such effects come from the confluence of an evil charismatic leader, visions of ethnic cleansing, followers thirsting for self-esteem, and untenable economic and social conditions that prompt followers to view the leader as a savior capable of extracting them from their undesirable situation. We will elaborate on this important cautionary tale in Chapter 4.

The Total Leadership System

Leadership is indeed a system. But research now suggests that this system is much more complex than we had earlier believed. Leadership systems must not only consider characteristics of the leader, follower, and situations, but also explain the transmission modes/mechanisms and sources/loci of leadership given the advent of advanced information technologies (AIT) that can aid leaders and followers. Over the last century, leadership theories focused on the traits, behaviors, cognitions, or emotions leaders and followers display, and/or the situations that embed them.[19] These theories only provided piecemeal explanations of leadership processes and outcomes without yielding a grand theory of leadership that integrates the elements of leadership in a comprehensive theoretical framework.

In an attempt to fill this gap in the literature, scholars have developed a comprehensive framework for understanding leadership by identifying the mechanisms and loci of leadership processes and outcomes.[20] *Mechanisms* represent the means by which leadership is transmitted by leaders and received by followers. Leadership is transmitted through traits, behaviors, cognitions, or affect. *Loci* represent the source of the leadership. Leadership can emerge from individual leaders or followers, leader–follower dyads, groups/teams, organizations, or organizational contexts. These loci parallel organizational levels of analysis (i.e., entities of study) described in the leadership literature, namely, individuals, dyads, groups, and collectives.[21] Cycles of events surrounding these entities form opportunities for leadership emergence, development, or disruption.[22]

Building upon this stream of research, leadership scholars have introduced the idea of the *total leadership system* by defining it as:

> representing vertical, horizontal, and diagonal forms of leadership, as well as leadership exhibited by individuals and through groups/entities. This entails examining leadership within and across all organizational levels based on the new connections made possible with AIT—including leading peer-to-peer and leading up management levels.[23]

These forms of leadership represent a second tool to understand leadership's complex systems nature and can be best understood by carefully examining the various panels of Figure 2.3.

As shown in Panel A of Figure 2.3, leaders and followers can transmit leadership through four modes:

- Traits—who we are (e.g., extroverted vs. introverted, humble vs. narcissistic).
- Cognition—how we think (e.g., linear vs. parallel processing, degree of integrative complexity).

- Affect—how we feel (e.g., determined vs. dejected, calm vs. jittery).
- Behavior—what we do (e.g., ignore, micro-manage, reward, or inspire others).

Leaders and followers can use these modes to transmit leadership from several sources or levels of analysis represented by the five planes that emerge across the panels of Figure 2.3. These include the individual, dyad, group, organization, and context. The individual level of analysis is the source we're most familiar with because it pertains to leadership emerging from the traits, cognitions, affect, and behavior of a *single leader*. For example, while attempting to influence a depressed follower over a period of time, a leader might display a funny personality, think of things in novel or witty ways, frequently be in a good mood, and/or use humor to diffuse tense situations. These modes of transmission can be achieved in person or via technologies such as Facebook, Twitter, Instagram, or text messages.

As shown in Panel B of Figure 2.3, individuals are nested within dyads. At the dyad (two-person group) source, we see unique relationships take shape between a leader and each of her followers as described by LMX theory that was discussed in Chapter 1. Each party in the relationship might share traits, cognitions, affect, and behavior that affect the quality of the relationship. For example, a leader and follower in the leader's in-group might form a dyad through day-to-day interactions. Their dyadic interaction might influence the dynamics and outcomes of other individuals, groups, or even the organization.

Shifting our attention to Panel C of Figure 2.3, we see that dyads and individuals are nested within groups. At the group or team source we observe members, including the leader and followers, display traits, cognitions, affect, and behavior that influence the group process and dynamics. Here leadership can come from a single leader (leadership OF the team) or be shared by all members (leadership BY the team), both of which we elaborate on in Chapter 9. As the leader and followers continue to interact with one another, the group develops its unique characteristics and culture called group norms. These norms further influence the leader's and followers' behaviors.

In Panel D of Figure 2.3, we see that groups, dyads, and individuals are nested within organizations. At the organizational level, members are expected to follow particular guidelines and values. These shared expectations and behaviors create a certain climate and culture that can exert strong influence within and outside of the organization. For example, Apple holds its annual Worldwide Developer Conference (WWDC) that brings employees and outside experts together to hear the latest regarding Apple's new product offerings and industry trends, and provide responses to users' needs through the design of new apps that can run on Apple's products. You might think of this organizational event as a massive meet up designed to "create new ideas and experiences that push society forward."[24] The collective action might influence other individuals, groups, and organizations.

Moving our focus to Panel E of Figure 2.3, we see that individuals, dyads, groups, and organizations are all nested within the context. This context might be different industries, businesses, and social/political environments that can encapsulate each of the previous levels, and have a profound influence on them. For

Figure 2.3
The Total
Leadership
System.

A

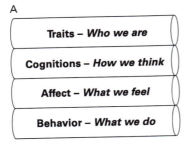

Transmission Mechanisms

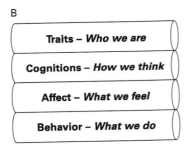

Individual

Transmission Sources

B

Traits – *Who we are*

Cognitions – *How we think*

Affect – *What we feel*

Behavior – *What we do*

Transmission Mechanisms

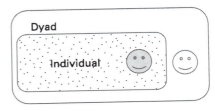

Dyad

Individual

Transmission Sources

C

Traits – *Who we are*

Cognitions – *How we think*

Affect – *What we feel*

Behavior – *What we do*

Transmission Mechanisms

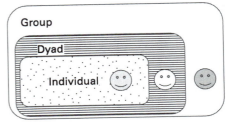

Group

Dyad

Individual

Transmission Sources

D

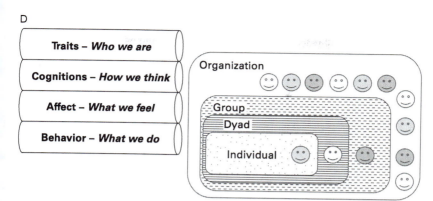

Traits – *Who we are*

Cognitions – *How we think*

Affect – *What we feel*

Behavior – *What we do*

Organization

Group

Dyad

Individual

Transmission Mechanisms　　　　　　**Transmission Sources**

E

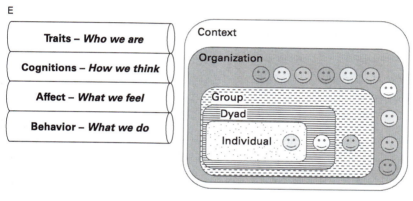

Traits – *Who we are*

Cognitions – *How we think*

Affect – *What we feel*

Behavior – *What we do*

Context

Organization

Group

Dyad

Individual

Transmission Mechanisms　　　　　　**Transmission Sources**

F

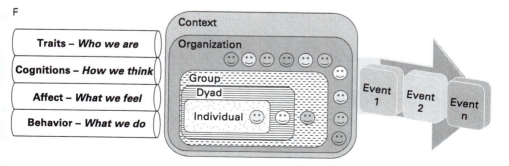

Traits – *Who we are*

Cognitions – *How we think*

Affect – *What we feel*

Behavior – *What we do*

Context

Organization

Group

Dyad

Individual

Event 1　Event 2　Event n

Transmission Mechanisms　　　　**Transmission Sources**　　　　**Events**

example, the Brexit (the United Kingdom's exit from the European Union) in 2016 pointed to trends of nationalist and populist movements that may have profound effects on international trade, leadership of multinational firms, and the redefinition of what globalization should look like. This political change event that took shape within the context may have influenced many individuals, dyads, groups, and organizations.

In summary, leadership can emerge and be displayed via traits, cognition, affect, and behaviors, at any and all of the levels across events that happen over time, as presented in Panel F of Figure 2.3. The Total Leadership System perspective can help you to understand how your leadership mechanisms (including the FRLD behaviors that you use) directly and indirectly influence followers. These different levels of leadership environments and processes can make your leadership efforts more effective in certain conditions while they add more complexities and challenges in other conditions. Therefore, if you want to make the most out of your leadership, assessing your environment carefully is crucial. (Please return to Chapter 1 where we summarize what these situations are and how they affect your leadership effectiveness in the *Contingency Theory* section.) By recognizing these leadership environments systematically, you may maximize your leadership potential.

Full Range Leadership Systems Thinking

Many aspiring leaders have focused on their own behavior, personality traits, self-awareness, and other types of personal attributes as their only means of leadership development. However, we have learned through 30 years of research that leaders can increase their insight on leadership by better understanding the process through which leadership occurs. Let's examine one such process model that will guide your FRLD learning throughout this book.

Process Model for Understanding Full Range Leadership Development

To assist you in understanding and applying FRLD theory, we present a process model that allows you to predict what leadership styles will work with specific followers in particular situations to produce a variety of positive outcomes for individuals, teams, and organizations. This research-based model is shown in Figure 2.4.

Since we're using a systems-based approach, this model has a number of systems components. The inputs to the system appear on the left-hand side of Figure 2.4 and are labeled "Antecedents," because they come before behavioral actions and motivational processes in the model. These elements reflect the personal attributes of the leader and followers. Examples of these attributes include age, gender, race, religion, self-concept, self-esteem, life experiences, values, beliefs, attitudes, and personality traits/skills such as emotional intelligence and the ability to feel positive emotions.[25] Take a few moments to reflect upon how each of these attributes shapes how you practice leadership and how

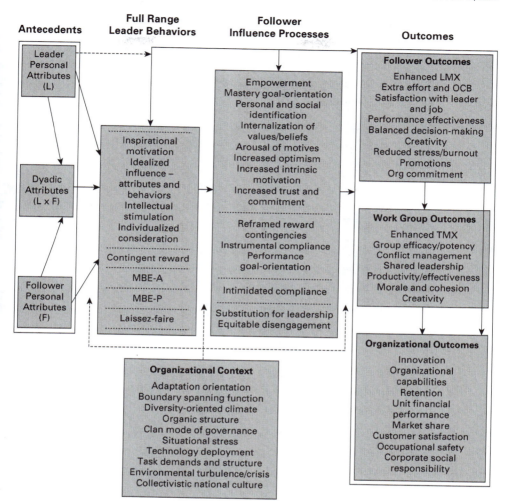

Figure 2.4 **A process model for understanding Full Range Leadership Development. (Adapted with permission from Sosik, J. J. [2006]. Full range leadership: Model, research, extensions and training. In C. Cooper & R. Burke (Eds.),** *Inspiring leaders* **[pp. 33–66]. New York: Routledge.)**

your followers react to your leadership. What new insights have you gained from your reflection?

Also included in the system are attributes that describe each unique leader–follower relationship or dyad. Have you ever wondered why you get along with some of your followers while have conflicts and misunderstandings with others? The answer might be in the quality of dyadic relationship you create with each follower. Several factors known to influence the dyadic relationship include attributes of the dyad such as length of relationship, gender composition, attitudes toward learning, and mutual trust, loyalty, and commitment to each other. Dyadic attributes are important indicators of the amount of bonding between the leader and follower. They differ across each relationship a leader has with followers. These attributes determine the quality of each dyadic relationship; higher-quality relationships are closer and more productive than lower-quality relationships.[26]

Based on the quality of the relationship and the attributes of the leader, follower, and situation, leaders can choose which behaviors in the FRLD model to display. Each of the FRLD behaviors motivates followers in a unique way. We see from the two interior rectangles in Figure 2.4 that the 5Is of transformational leadership influence followers by making them identify with the leader and the organization's mission. Research has also shown that followers internalize and share values and beliefs of the transformational leader and become more motivated to fulfill their needs for achievement, power, and affiliation. Followers also become optimistic and work harder to achieve the mission that they perceive as important or a job they perceive as meaningful. Followers feel more empowered and engaged in their work and exert extra effort when they experience transformational leadership. They develop a passion for their work and a "growth mindset" or a love of learning that assumes that abilities can be developed through achieving learning goals through hard work and dedication.[27] These are powerful forms of intrinsic motivation. Followers of transformational leaders are motivated by increased levels of trust and commitment as well.

These processes are illustrated by the way CEO Satya Nadella has transformed Microsoft's cautious bureaucratic culture into one that encourages learning, risk-taking, and empowerment. Employees connect with Nadella because he takes the time to listen and learn from employees. He allows employees to work on projects they have a keen interest in, and joins them in company-wide "hack-a-thons" that have greatly expanded their cloud services and artificial intelligence markets. This example illustrates the power of transformational motivational mechanisms and their dramatic results.[28]

The motivational mechanisms for transactional contingent reward leadership differ from those for transformational leadership. Unlike transformational leadership, which relies on intrinsic motivation, extrinsic motivation is the primary driver that prompts followers of contingent reward leaders to work toward their goal. When leaders present clear goals to followers and offer them rewards upon successful attainment of the goal, followers set performance goals and become willing and able to meet performance expectations to prove their competence to others. These *reframed reward contingencies* help followers to see the path they must travel to reach their goal. They comply with the leader because it will result in receiving a reward that they value. Leadership researchers call this *instrumental compliance* because the follower complies since she perceives the leader's contingent reward behavior as being instrumental to her goal attainment and success. This is the kind of motivation we often see from politicians like former U.S. presidents Abraham Lincoln and Lyndon Baines Johnson, who cut deals with other players and constituents and mastered the political system to achieve specific goals.[29]

Whereas contingent reward leadership uses reframed reward contingencies and instrumental compliance processes to motivate followers, management-by-exception (active and passive forms) relies upon *intimidation* to motivate followers and get them to comply with requests. When leaders wait for problems to arise or seek out problems before they occur, followers focus on avoiding mistakes or deviating from policies and standard operating procedures. They often fear the consequences of their failure to comply with standards, policies, regulations, and requests. For example, one school administrator used the guise of a social hour with students as a means for intelligence gathering of negative information to be used for reprimands. The days after these events were filled with phone calls to program administrators regarding "problems that needed to be solved." Research has shown that such a negative focus instills fear in followers because they become afraid of "being caught" and reprimanded by the leader for their miscues.[30] Interacting in such police state conditions inhibits the innate creativity and proactive participation that are becoming more and more important in today's knowledge-based economy. So, a primary reason that followers comply with leaders who display management-by-exception leadership is because they are afraid of the consequences of crossing the leader.

Fear of a different sort is involved in the motivational process associated with laissez-faire leadership. This type is a fear of failure. When asked how to deal with a superior who displays laissez-faire behavior, the majority of aspiring leaders we have taught over the years responded that they "do it themselves." In other words, they substitute for the superior's lack of leadership. They are able to do so because they possess the professionalism, knowledge, or character to make up for what their leader fails to add to the leadership system. However, those followers who lack these qualities engage in *equitable disengagement*. Since most people operate on principles of fairness or equity, these followers are likely to exert an amount of effort equal to the effort the leader exerts. If the leader is laissez-faire and thus exerts little or no interest or effort, such followers are likely to reciprocate and become disengaged from their work, thus displaying equitable disengagement. That's because they don't want to be perceived as suckers who are taken advantage of by others.[31]

As a result of the interaction of the leader, follower, and situation, numerous outcomes shown in Figure 2.4 emerge from the leadership system. The individual and group-level outcomes can cascade up to produce several organizational-level outcomes, especially with the more active and effective leadership styles in the FRLD model. These include innovation, employee retention, organizational commitment, organizational capability, increased unit financial performance, improved market share, customer satisfaction, corporate social responsibility, and occupational safety.[32] Examples of organizations that have experienced these outcomes as a result of a transformational culture include Amazon, Netflix, Apple, Microsoft, and Priceline, among many more.[33] Using the 5Is is more effective for producing the follower, work group, and organizational outcomes of leadership when the organizational context includes one or more of the situational elements shown in Figure 2.4 that are conducive to transformational leadership.[34]

Putting Full Range Leadership Development Systems Thinking into Practice

Books are great ways to learn the concepts of FRLD. If you think carefully and critically while reading, books can be a learning laboratory for your mind. But the real learning laboratory is your personal and professional life. That's where you can put these ideas into action. Your world provides you with many opportunities to put the leadership concepts discussed in this book into practice. And that's the only real way to fully develop your leadership potential. Developing leadership potential is a long and arduous journey that takes a lot of focus, dedication, and hard work. Practice makes perfect.

You need to start by making a commitment to putting into practice what you've learned so far and will learn in subsequent chapters. Once you have made the commitment to start applying what you've learned from this book to your world, you're ready to move toward reaching your FRLD goal. Here are some steps to get started on your FRLD journey.

Be Honest with Yourself

No one is perfect. But as iconic NFL coach Vince Lombardi once said, challenging oneself and striving for perfection allows us to catch excellence.[35] A lot of highly successful leaders we know had less than perfect experiences before they began improving their leadership skills systematically. This was the case for Kurt Linneman, founder and president of Crocodile Catering, a quirky and successful food catering company and restaurant that is beloved by its fiercely loyal customers. Before he embraced FRLD, Kurt jokes that he was known by his employees as "Kurt-ler" (a sarcastic twist on Hitler). This nickname was the result of his single-minded focus on details and the bottom line, to the exclusion of his employees' needs, desires, strengths, and potential for development. With his newfound passion for FRLD principles, Kurt has evolved into a transformational leader who has created a strong culture that encourages leadership development, fun, employee engagement, and creativity at work. (Visit www.croccater.com for an in-depth look at this unique transformational culture.) As Kurt learned, once you begin to identify with the 5Is of transformational leadership, you can commit to developing an action plan to achieve your full leadership potential. Try to find a way to impose some reinforcement and accountability while practicing FRLD. Remember that if there are no serious consequences or rewards, people are not likely to change their behaviors and thoughts. Be patient, and start slow and easy. The journey to leadership development is a marathon and not a sprint.

Personal Reflections are Essential for FRLD

Practicing FRLD requires a lot of reflection. It involves a lot of questioning, strategizing, and planning. Rethinking assumptions about leadership didn't come easy for Matthew Dever when he first attended Penn State's FRLD graduate-level course. As an introverted computer engineer working at Cerner Corporation,

Matthew assumed that leadership was only about solving problems within his team to help the organization achieve its goals. But then he learned that his new job role as a Wellness Knowledge Architect required a systems' view of leadership influence. Matthew now sees his role in terms of influencing a wide network of peers and direct reports by developing close personal relationships (dyadic leadership), setting an example through his work ethic and values-based decision-making (idealized influence), and by listening closely to their perspective (individualized consideration). He also realizes that he can influence his superiors by delivering on company commitments consistently (idealized influence), keeping them informed of issues and potential options to resolve, and appealing to their interests using logical analysis (intellectual stimulation). After much hard work involving reflection and refining of his leadership development plan completed as part of the course, Matthew became a FRLD systems thinker.[36]

Fortunately, you have three tools that can help guide your systems thinking about FRLD—the Leader/Follower/Situation model (Figure 2.1), the Total Leadership System (Figure 2.3), and the FRLD process model shown in Figure 2.4. Consider the elements in the latter model. Think about what positive and negative personal attributes you bring to the table in interactions with your followers. Make a list of all of your key followers along with their strengths and weaknesses. Consider each of your followers one at a time. What is good about your relationship with each follower? What is bad? What is the level of developmental readiness that each possesses? What behaviors and motivational processes are likely to be useful to produce desired leadership outcomes for your associates, teams, and organization? Which of the organizational context elements in Figure 2.4 describe your leadership situation? Remember, if you don't think of leadership as a system that extends beyond your behavior, you won't be able to maximize the benefits of FRLD training and development.

Take the Multifactor Leadership Questionnaire Now

Since all leadership systems evolve over time, you will need to establish a baseline measure of your FRLD profile in order to track your progress over time. Your leadership behavior can be measured validly (what is supposed to be assessed is in fact assessed) and reliably (consistently over time) with the Multifactor Leadership Questionnaire (MLQ). It is easier to understand the concepts in this book when you see how they relate to you personally. Results from the MLQ make these concepts less abstract and easier to practice when they are quantified and measured within your personal situation. At this point, be sure to visit Mind Garden's website to order the MLQ before you read the next chapter, especially if you have been inactive in your leadership or are just beginning FRLD training.

This is very important because the way you view your leadership behavior may be very different from the way your boss, peers, subordinates, and other raters perceive your style. This so-called "360-degree feedback" can provide you with a reality check on your leadership style and pinpoint any discrepancies that can limit your potential to become a transformational leader. We often find that people are shocked by these multisource views. Well, most of us tend to think of ourselves as an above-average leader. Right? After receiving this feedback, we should become humbler and more willing to change our leadership style.

Establish a Personal Leadership Mission Statement

Every exemplary leader has an overarching purpose that drives him to carry on in good times and bad. This notion has been explored by several psychologists, including Viktor Frankl, who calls this *purpose in life*, as well as Daniel Levinson, who discussed the importance of each person having a *dream* that directs one's life.[37] Sometimes these dreams also direct the lives of many others, as Dr. Martin Luther King showed us. Your purpose may be to create a new business, hire and develop the best staff possible, or make the world a better place to live. Your purpose may change over time, but the values that provide the foundation for your purpose are relatively stable. Examples of values include love of learning, truth, optimism, financial independence, and self-control, among many others. Values are abstract representations of what are deemed to be most important in life. They can be strong motivators of leadership behaviors that put these values into action.[38] For example, a leader who values love of learning may use intellectually stimulating behaviors to reflect this preference.

It is important for you to create a short personal leadership mission statement (PLMS) that links your purpose, values, and FRLD behaviors. This mission statement represents a constitution that can guide your leadership development and provide you with direction in the leadership roles you assume. It can also serve as a standard against which you can compare your MLQ results. When

---

Box 2.3 A Personal Leadership Mission Statement

My mission is to lead people towards becoming their best self through improving habits, health, and happiness. I teach people about physical and mental fitness, inspire, coach, and guide them towards achieving their personal and professional goals and leads teams who build systems that encourage healthy behaviors.

I value health and potential. I believe health is the foundation for reaching one's full potential and that is the best form of self-expression. One might choose to apply one's potential to family, work, community, or other areas. Some people feel selfish putting their health first, but I believe that it's a prerequisite to delivering the maximum value for other priorities in the long-term.

I put my values into practice, primarily using Idealized Influence and Inspirational Motivation. I live every day as a healthy role model for my team, my students, and my clients. I communicate a vision for how our products can help people live healthier and give speeches and one-on-one coaching on how to improve health. I aim to infuse people with energy, optimism, and confidence in themselves in all my interactions.[39]

MLQ results are less desirable than what you espouse in your PLMS, you can create action steps in your leadership development plan to improve in these areas. Matthew Dever's PLMS is shown in Box 2.3. Matthew is responsible for enthusiastically communicating Cerner Corporation's vision and his Wellness team's vision to Cerner's associates. A reflective exercise for creating your own PLMS is presented in the following summary questions and reflective exercises.

Find a Learning Partner

Starting your FRLD training with a learning partner can increase your chances of benefiting from it and help you to stick with it as well. If you have a learning partner who is also interested in studying transformational leadership, you can encourage, motivate, and challenge each other. Learning partners can share their thoughts and comment on them. They can talk about the similarities and differences in their personal leadership situations and evaluate them from a different point of view. Besides, learning can be pretty lonely, so if you have a learning partner, it will make your journey to master FRLD far more enjoyable.

The benefits of learning with a partner are illustrated by Dion Robinson and Richard Lancaster, two colleagues from Lincoln University and Arcadia University, respectively. As friends from their college days, Dion and Richard decided to complete Penn State's MLD degree program together. They took almost all of their courses together. They worked in the same teams. They challenged each other in all of their classes. They worked together to apply their FRLD knowledge in their university settings. Dion is now shaping the lives of young men and women as Undergraduate Admissions Counselor and Head Cheerleading Coach at his school. Rich is leading his school's recruiting efforts as Associate Director of Alumni Relations.

Make FRLD Reflection a Part of Your Schedule

Include a five to ten-minute slot in your daily planner just as you would with any other appointment. At the end of each day, find a comfortable chair in which to sit and reflect upon what FRLD leadership behaviors you used during the day. What worked well? What didn't work so well? What lessons did you learn about leadership today? Use the Total Leadership System model in Figure 2.3 to locate targets for your leadership within and outside of your organization. Use the FRLD process model in Figure 2.4 to explain how and why things went the way they did. This technique trains you to view leadership as a systematic process and to fine-tune your leadership skills over time as well. You can also plan ahead for the week so that you have an idea regarding what FRLD behaviors you can use with followers and associates. Even if you are pressed for time one day, a little self-reflection is better than none at all. Do what you can to fit it in, even if you have less time than you expected.

Gail Cooperman is no stranger to very hectic schedules. As a strategic marketing and growth consultant, adjunct professor, and busy working mom, Gail knows the challenges of time management. Despite her challenges, Gail stays focused on her daily FRLD reflection. This helps her to plan for unexpected leadership emergencies. As Gail says, "If you take the time to reflect and plan every day, you'd be amazed how that cuts out a lot of potential problems that spring up."

Use Self-Rewards and Positive Affirmations

When you receive MLQ feedback from your associates and get in the habit of thinking about your leadership on a daily basis, take some time to celebrate small successes. Giving yourself little rewards such as your favorite food or drink, socializing with friends and family, and taking some much-needed rest and relaxation are great ways to help you stay on track. Affirmations can also help train your mind to accept new beliefs about leadership as a developmental process. You might say to yourself a few times a day: "I am evolving into a transformational leader by practicing what I am reading about." And, of course, be sure to be true to yourself and do what you're telling yourself. This can build your motivation and confidence levels as you develop your full leadership potential over time. It's the kind of confidence we see in leaders like Rajesh Bandekar, Ph.D., associate director of biostatistics at Johnson & Johnson, who is constantly evolving his leadership by applying many of the FRLD concepts described in this book to his department.

Set Goals with a Personal Leadership Development Plan

Setting goals can be helpful in keeping you motivated and helping you to improve your leadership potential, but remember to keep them realistic. As part of the personal leadership development plans we create in our FRLD training and graduate courses, we specify action steps along with timetables and measurement requirements to help our participants stay on track. Short-term and long-term goals can make accomplishing these action steps easier. For example, what will you do to improve your idealized influence score? How much time will you give yourself to improve your score? How will you assess whether you have made any progress? Readministering the MLQ and reflecting upon its results is certainly a good means to answer these questions. Plan these actions with specific timeframes such as once a week for 30 minutes, or 5 minutes daily.

Congratulations! You are now ready to learn about each of the FRLD behaviors in detail. In Chapter 3, we'll start at the pinnacle of the model with idealized leadership. This form of influence exemplifies the essence of transformational leadership.

Summary Questions and Reflective Exercises

1. This exercise helps you to gain perspective on the role of leadership in your life. Develop your personal leadership mission statement (PLMS) by following these steps. Devote at least 30 minutes to this exercise. Go to a quiet room in your house or somewhere else that you can be alone. Set the tone by listening to some relaxing background music (perhaps classical or soft music—whatever soothes you) with earphones connected to your stereo or iPod. Then meditate on how you would answer the following questions:

   - Who is someone you deeply admire? Why?
   - Who are you without your job or your money? Describe in detail.
   - What activities could you add to your life that could be a source of joy for others?
   - What gives you the greatest joy, satisfaction, and renewal in your life? Can you do more of it?
   - If you were on your deathbed and you wanted to tell people close to you the three most important things that you learned in your life, what would they be?

   Once you have meditated on the questions above, your mind should be in tune to complete the actual PLMS. Be sure *not* to answer these questions in your PLMS. Instead, your PLMS should be written clearly and concisely and contain three paragraphs. In the first paragraph, describe your overall *purpose in life* at this point in your life. Be sure that your purpose is directed toward serving others. In the second paragraph, define your *personal values* that are reflected in your purpose in life. In the third paragraph, explain how you will put each of these values into action through *specific FRLD behaviors*.

2. This exercise helps you to view leadership as a system. Draft an outline for your personal leadership development plan by following these steps. Your complete leadership behavior profile will come from the MLQ report you will receive from www.mindgarden.com. The profile will contain a summary of leadership ratings generated by those who report to you directly, your superior, your peers, your self-ratings, and normative data for comparison purposes. Your MLQ report also will contain qualitative comments from your raters. You should use this array of data to examine your personal strengths and weaknesses with respect to the specific FRLD behaviors. Participants in our courses produce a 15-page doubled-spaced written report with the following sections:

- Personal leadership mission statement.
- Tabular or graphical summary of MLQ feedback. This section should describe how you saw yourself as a leader, how your followers saw you as a leader, the discrepancy between your self-ratings and your followers' ratings of you, how your results compare to those of others in your training program, and how your results compare to normative results.
- Strengths.
- Areas for development (weaknesses).
- Organizational opportunities for leadership development.
- Organizational stumbling blocks impeding leadership development.
- Action steps to address weaknesses and accomplish personal leadership mission.

Once you have received and analyzed your MLQ results, you can embellish your outline.

3. This exercise involves using systems thinking to analyze a real-world scenario. The names have been changed to protect the innocent. Imagine that you have been hired by Whitless Corporation, a privately owned 50-year-old medium-sized manufacturing firm, to develop an organizational change program to address its quality, employee, and customer satisfaction problems. Whitless's CEO, Bob Bossanova, utilizes top-down, authoritarian, and directive leadership to control the firm's specialized divisions. Whitless's organization structure is characterized by task specialization and rigidity, strict hierarchy of authority, centralized decision-making (i.e., Bob calls the shots), and vertical/one-way communication.

In recent years, Whitless's sales, profits, and employee morale have fallen off to uncomfortable levels. Puzzled as to why his management strategies are not as effective as they once were, Bob hollers, "I wonder if we have a *quality* problem! Who's @%*$ing up this time?" He has responded by tightening financial controls on each department, especially manufacturing, by requiring all department managers to prepare monthly budgets. Department managers receive monthly performance reports from Leona Ledger, CPA, Whitless's controller. These reports compare budgeted to actual costs and highlight variances between these costs. Managers are required to provide written explanations to Bob for unfavorable variances exceeding 5% of budgeted cost.

a. Indicate reasons why Bob's management strategies may not be as successful as they once were. Be sure to consider factors both internal and external to the organization.

b. How would you describe Bob's style of leadership in terms of the FRLD model? Why?

c. Which styles of leadership do you feel would have positive effects on Whitless's total quality management (TQM) efforts? Negative effects?

d. In developing a TQM strategy for Whitless, what specific behaviors would you prescribe for training managers and employees? How would you describe these behaviors in terms of the FRLD model? *Hint:* TQM is based on three concepts: customer satisfaction, continuous process improvement, and employee learning and empowerment.

4. In addition to the PLMS you thought about in Exercise 1, it is important to develop a set of principles to practice when you work with your followers. What principles will you use consistently when influencing others, making a leadership decision, or working on a project? Each principle should be somewhere between two to five sentences. Write them down here and share them with your followers at work. We provide the first one as an illustration.

a. *I will respect my followers' opinions. I will use them when I make decisions and interact with my followers.*

b. _____
    _____
    _____
    _____

c. _____
    _____
    _____
    _____

d. _____
    _____
    _____
    _____

e. _____
    _____
    _____
    _____

5. Interview a top executive in your organization regarding how he or she evaluates the leadership potential of people in the organization. How much of a systems view does this leader possess? How can you help this leader to improve in this area?

Notes

1 Sosik, J. J. (2015). *Leading with character: Stories of valor and virtue and the principles they teach* (2nd ed., p. 55). Charlotte, NC: Information Age.

2 Gardner, W. L., & Avolio, B. J. (1998). The charismatic relationship: A dramaturgical perspective. *Academy of Management Review, 23*, 32–58; and Wilson, N. (2013). Interaction without walls: Analyzing leadership discourse through dramaturgy and participation. *Journal of Sociolinguistics, 17*(2), 180–199.

3 Clavell, J. (Producer/Director), & Braithwaite, E. R. (Writer). (1967). *To sir, with love* [Motion picture]. Culver City, CA: Columbia (British) Productions.

4 Waters, R. (1979). Another brick in the wall (part II) [Recorded by Pink Floyd]. On *The wall* [CD]. Hollywood, CA: Capitol Records.

5 Avolio, B. J. (2011). *Full range leadership development* (2nd ed.). Thousand Oaks, CA: Sage.

6 Donne, J. (1959, originally published 1624). *Devotions upon emergent occasions*, no. 17, pp. 108–109. Retrieved from www.bartleby.com/73/134.html.

7 Ackoff, R. L., & Addison, H. J. (2012). *Ackoff's f/laws: The cake*. Devon, UK: Triarchy Press; Avolio (2011). As cited in Note 5; and Shamir, B. (2011). Leadership takes time: Some implications of (not) taking time seriously in leadership research. *The Leadership Quarterly, 22*(2), 307–315.

8 Sosik (2015). As cited in Note 1.

9 McAdams, D. P. (2016, June). The mind of Donald Trump. *The Atlantic, 317*(5), 76–90.

10 Arvey, R. D., Zhang, Z., Avolio, B. J., & Krueger, R. F. (2007). Developmental and genetic determinants of leadership role occupancy among women. *Journal of Applied Psychology, 92*, 693–706; and De Neve, J. E., Mikhaylov, S., Dawes, C. T., Christakis, N. A., & Fowler, J. H. (2013). Born to lead? A twin design genetic association study of leadership role occupancy. *The Leadership Quarterly, 24*(1), 45–60.

11 Clinton, W. J. (2004). *My life*. New York: Knopf.

12 Neck, C. P., & Manz, C. C. (2017). *Mastering self-leadership: Empowering yourself for personal excellence* (6th ed.). Upper Saddle River, NJ: Prentice-Hall.

13 Hiller, A. (Producer/Director). (1972). *Man of la mancha* [Motion picture]. Santa Monica, CA: Distributed by Metro Goldwyn Mayer.

14 Kellerman, B. (2008). *Followership: How followers are creating change and changing leaders*. Boston, MA: Harvard Business Press; and Sosik, J. J., Jung, D. I., Berson, Y., Dionne, S. D., & Jaussi, K. S. (2004). *The dream weavers: Strategy-focused leadership in technology-driven organizations*. Greenwich, CT: Information Age.

15 Tu, J. I. (2017, March 22). Longtime Starbucks chief Schultz hands the key to new CEO. *The Seattle Times*. Retrieved from www.seattletimes.com/business/retail/starbucks-annualmeeting/.

16 Colvin, G. (2016, December 9). Why Sears failed. *Fortune*. Retrieved from http://fortune.com/2016/12/09/why-sears-failed/.

17 GE Annual Report. Retrieved from www.ge.com/ar2016/; and Whylly, L. R. (2016, January 27). Chief Executive Magazine announces its 2016 best companies for leaders. *Chief Executive*. Retrieved from http://chiefexecutive.net/chief-executive-magazine-announces-its-2016-best-companies-for-leaders/.

18 Gronski, J. L. (2017, June 5). Personal communication.

19 Bass, B. M. (2008). *The Bass handbook of leadership: Theory, research and managerial applications* (4th ed.). New York: Free Press; and Yukl, G. (2010). *Leadership in organizations* (7th ed.). Upper Saddle River, NJ: Prentice Hall.

20 Hernandez, M., Eberly, M. B., Avolio, B. J., & Johnson, M. D. (2011). The loci and mechanisms of leadership: Exploring a more comprehensive view of leadership theory. *The Leadership Quarterly, 22*(6), 1165–1185.

21 Dionne, S. D., Gupta, A., Sotak, K. L., Shirreffs, K. A., Serban, A., Hao, C., Kim, D. H., & Yammarino, F. J. (2014). A 25-year perspective on levels of analysis in leadership research. *The Leadership Quarterly, 25*(1), 6–35.

22 Eberly, M. B., Johnson, M., Hernandez, M., & Avolio, B. J. (2013). An integrative process model of leadership: Examining loci, mechanisms, and event cycles. *American Psychologist, 68*(6), 427–443.

23 Avolio, B. J., Sosik, J. J., Kahai, S. S., & Baker, B. (2014, p. 126). E-leadership: Re-examining transformations in leadership source and transmission. *The Leadership Quarterly, 25*(1), 105–131.

24 Retrieved from https://developer.apple.com/wwdc/.

25 Harmes, P. D., & Credé, M. (2010). Emotional intelligence and transformational and transactional leadership: A meta-analysis. *Journal of Leadership and Organizational Studies, 17*(1), 5–17; and Joseph, D. L., Dhanani, L. Y., Shen, W., McHugh, B. C., & McCord, M. A. (2015). Is a happy leader a good leader? A meta-analytic investigation of leader trait affect and leadership. *The Leadership Quarterly, 26*, 558–577.

26 Dulebohn, J. H., Bommer, W. H., Liden, R. C., Brouer, R. L., & Ferris, G. R. (2012). A meta-analysis of antecedents and consequences of leader-member exchange: Integrating the past with an eye toward the future. *Journal of Management, 38*, 1715–1759; Graen, G. B., & Uhl-Bien, M. (1995). Relationship-based approach to leadership: Development of leader-member exchange (LMX) theory of leadership over 25 years: Applying a multi-level multi-domain perspective. *The Leadership Quarterly, 6*, 219–247; and Sosik, J. J., Godshalk, V. M., & Yammarino, F. J. (2004). Transformational leadership, learning goal orientation, and expectations for career success in mentor-protégé relationships: A multiple levels of analysis perspective. *The Leadership Quarterly, 15*, 241–261.

27 Dweck, C. S. (2006). *Mindset: The new psychology of success*. New York: Random House; and Hamstra, M. R. W., Van Yperen, N. W., Wisse, B., & Sassenberg, K. (2014). Transformational and transactional leadership and followers' achievement goals. *Journal of Business and Psychology, 29*, 413–425.

28 Anthony, S., & Schwartz, E. I. (2017, May 8). What the best transformational leaders do. *Harvard Business Review*. Retrieved from https://hbr.org/2017/05/what-the-best-transformational-leaders-do.

29 Woods, R. B. (2006). *LBJ: Architect of American ambition*. New York: Free Press.

30 Carver, C. S., & Scheier, M. F. (1990). Origins and functions of positive and negative affect: A control-process view. *Psychological Review, 97*(1), 19–35.

31 Adams, J. S. (1965). Inequity in social exchange. *Advances in Experimental Social Psychology, 62*, 335–343.

32 For a multilevel overview of outcomes of the FRLD system, see Sosik, J. J. (2006). Full range leadership: Model, research, extensions and training. In C. Cooper & R. Burke (Eds.), *Inspiring leaders* (pp. 33–66). New York: Routledge. Also, see Clarke, S. (2013). Safety leadership: A meta-analytic review of transformational and transactional leadership styles as antecedents of safety behaviors. *Journal of Occupational and Organizational Psychology, 86*, 22–49; and Schweitzer, J. (2014). Leadership and innovation capability development in strategic alliances. *Leadership & Organizational Development Journal, 35*(5), 442–469.

33 Anthony & Schwartz (2017, May 8). As cited in Note 28.

34 Oreg, S., & Berson, Y. (2015). Personality and charismatic leadership in context: The moderating role of situational stress. *Personnel Psychology, 68*, 49–77; and Sosik (2006). As cited in Note 32.

35 Maraniss, D. (1999). *When pride still mattered: A life of Vince Lombardi*. New York: Simon & Schuster.

36 Dever, M. J. (2017). *Leadership development plan [for LEAD 555]*. Malvern, PA: Penn State Great Valley School of Graduate Professional Studies.

37 Frankl, V. (2004). *Man's search for meaning: An introduction to logotherapy*. Boston, MA: Beacon; and Levinson, D. J. (with Darrow, C. M., Klein, E. G., Levinson, M. H., & McKee, B.). (1978). *The seasons of a man's life*. New York: Knopf.

38 Sosik, J. J. (2005). The role of personal values in the charismatic leadership of corporate managers: A model and preliminary field study. *The Leadership Quarterly, 16*(2), 221–244.

39 Dever (2017). As cited in Note 36.

Chapter 3

Idealized Influence Behaviors and Attributes

The Humane Side of Transformational Leadership

Some people seem to have it all. When it comes to charm, personality, intelligence, and friends, Bill Jordan can win a prize. As vice president and deputy head of U.S. clinical research at pharmaceutical leader Sanofi, Bill is well respected by many colleagues and is making his mark as a transformational leader. Bill's jet-set corporate lifestyle involves frequent travel to Europe, grueling 12-hour days, plus role modeling leadership excellence for his associates. His far-flung personal and professional network stems from his innate ability to connect with people at all organizational levels and in almost any walk of life.

Despite his corporate star power, Bill carries himself with an unusual air of modesty and quiet confidence. For an experiential exercise in our Master of Leadership Development (MLD) program at Penn State, Bill took his protégé Michael Agard back to Camden, New Jersey, where Bill grew up. Bill showed Michael his humble beginnings. Bill's parents operated an inner-city grocery store where he learned the importance of personal relationships and how to interact with all kinds of people. Bill worked three jobs to pay for college and help his parents and family. These experiences shaped the positive way Bill treats his associates today and helped him understand leadership from different perspectives. Through hard work, insightfulness, and persistence, Bill now commands the loyalty, respect, and trust of his associates at Sanofi and in his community.

Being recognized as a leader in your organization or community can bring many benefits. Like Bill Jordan, you may be viewed by others as an important authority on key issues, a spokesperson for your group, a provider of desirable resources, and a person of power and influence. You are likely to receive preferential treatment by others. You may command the attention and respect of your peers and subordinates as well. You may even become an idol to them. For example, consider the amount of idolization famous sports figures like Wayne Gretzky, Lebron James, or Serena and Venus Williams receive from their fans. But no one, including each of these stars, is perfect. Creating and sustaining positive influence over other people is a difficult, but effective, way to expand your leadership reach. That's why the idealized influence attributed by followers to leaders is important.

Having a greater level of influence comes with the responsibility of being a role model for your associates. This can be a heavy cross to bear. As the leader, all eyes are fixed on what you do, all ears are tuned to what you say, and all minds are focused on evaluating how you think. People want to know if you exemplify your organization's values. They watch to see if you conduct yourself in a socially and morally acceptable manner. And they judge whether you can add social, economic, and market value for your organization through your leadership. In essence, everything you say, do, and think is scrutinized and becomes an important message to your followers. People constantly test you to see what you stand for and what you will not stand for.

Yes, it's a tall order to embody societal virtues and character strengths, epitomize organizational values, and produce sustainable performance results through your leadership. And, that's precisely why we challenge our students to see if they are *ready* to lead. When people think about leadership, they oftentimes think about the many perks, not the added responsibilities that come with leadership. When this happens, people working under such leadership may begin suffering, just like the many people who worked for Enron under Kenneth Lay's leadership did. If you don't consider these obligations, we don't believe that you are ready to meet your leadership challenges.

Many leadership challenges are easier to meet when you realize that the success of your leadership is achieved through the support from others. Your personality and behaviors have an effect on their motivation and influence the processes they use to achieve the outcomes of leadership. These outcomes of leadership are rarely directly related to a leader's personality or behaviors. A number of factors, such as economic conditions, strategy content and execution, and available resources, also determine organizational performance in today's complex environments. In fact, leadership research has repeatedly found that a single leader's personality and behaviors explain very little variation in organizational performance.[1] Nevertheless, how well your organizational unit performs can produce attributions of leadership effectiveness that can bolster your leadership prowess, as illustrated by the example of Jack Welch in Box 3.1.

Jack Welch's success story teaches us that the relationship that leaders have with their followers is created and maintained through social exchanges that go both ways. Leaders behave in certain ways that influence followers' motivation, values and beliefs, and organizational performance. Followers perceive these leader behaviors and performance outcomes and attribute either positive or negative characteristics to the leader. Because of this mutual influence, you should view leadership as a combination of actual leadership behavior displayed by the leader <u>and</u> socially constructed images of the leader created by followers.

This chapter shows you how to display idealized influence so that you can gain positive attributions and personify the very best of transformational leadership. Let's begin by considering the case of one of the greatest idealized leaders of the 20th century.

The Idealized Leadership of Mohandas Gandhi

Ever since we began teaching Full Range Leadership Development (FRLD) over 20 years ago, we've used the case of Mohandas Gandhi to illustrate a process

Box 3.1 Leader Profile: Jack Welch

Jack Welch is the iconic former CEO of General Electric (GE). If you browse Amazon.com or the business section of your favorite book store, you will likely find numerous books on leadership written either by or about Jack Welch.[2] With all this attention, it's as if he is the "patron saint of CEOs." Why? It's mainly because under Jack Welch's leadership tenure as CEO, GE was able to create a whopping $320 billion of stock market value for its shareholders. This represents phenomenal performance, especially compared to his two predecessor CEOs, who were only able to add about $1 billion in stock market value.[3] No wonder why *Fortune* named him "Manager of the Century."[4] Although he was criticized for his strong focus on performance at all costs, Welch's leadership and performance at GE is still highly admired.

How did Jack Welch do it? He used drastic cost cutting, including employee layoffs, in his early tenure. As a result, he was dubbed "Neutron Jack." He told his business units that their goal was to become number one or two in their markets, or they would exit that business sector. He championed continuous process improvement, total quality management, and Six Sigma initiatives aimed at promoting quality and efficiencies within and between GE's operating units. Later on at GE, Welch championed leadership development initiatives to enhance the knowledge, skills, and abilities of its employees. He valued being generous in caring for employees' developmental needs, providing clear direction and feedback, and advocating for them. As a result, GE's achievements under Welch became the envy of corporations around the world. Today, many seek to follow his lead and replicate what Welch had done for GE in their own organizations. This is what it means to exert idealized influence in corporate settings.[5]

through which leaders influence their followers based on ideals such as values, visions, and pride. His strong character and exemplary leadership led India to the successful quest for independence from Great Britain. He's been the subject of many books and movies. Indeed, Gandhi is perhaps the closest human example of idealized influence in history. His legacy is a collection of wise thoughts, ideas, words, and deeds that have changed the world. The changes he helped produce in India became the foundation for future social justice causes, such as the civil rights movement in the United States, the fight against Apartheid in South Africa, and the quest for increased human rights in China. His actions inspired leaders in other times and places to stand up for important principles such as human dignity, independence, and freedom of thought and expression. Gandhi's amazing story is relevant today because justice and human dignity are pro-social values that people will always be willing to live and die for.

The idealized leader reflects the most important pro-social values, beliefs, and aspirations of followers. Through consistency in thoughts, words, and deeds, the idealized leader becomes a symbol for the followers' cause. Recognizing his symbolic leadership role, Gandhi was very careful to portray himself as an imperfect "work in progress" instead of an infallible icon. He presented himself as being similar to his followers instead of being superior to them. He did this by shifting the focus of attention away from himself and toward important ideals and values he espoused. He did not want to create a "cult of personality" and receive the entire spotlight. Instead, he preached the importance of living a life of practical nonviolent moral action grounded in several spiritual and religious traditions. The only violence he condoned was "violence against the self" aimed at breaking down excessive ego. According to Gandhi, this helps one to be selfless by focusing on the needs of others and inspiring them to reach their full potential. These aspects of Gandhi's philosophy supported his ultimate quest and passion for truth in all situations.[6] Interestingly, Gandhi's words and deeds demonstrated the notion of "authentic leadership" long before former Medtronic CEO Bill George highlighted the term.[7] Gandhi practiced what he preached. His authenticity is why his followers and admirers even to this day respect him so, as shown in Box 3.2.

One of Gandhi's quotes defines the essence of authentic leadership: "Always aim at complete harmony of thought and word and deed."[9] The assumption in this statement and in theory on authentic leadership is that thought is indeed grounded in good or positive other-oriented values. However, it is also possible that a leader's thoughts are grounded in bad, self-centered, or egoistic values. What happens when a leader like Kim Jung-un (the infamous leader of North Korea), Abu Bakr al-Bagddadi (ISIS), or Travis Kalanick (Uber) is authentically self-centered or evil because he or she acts consistently with his or her egoistic beliefs at the expense of others? Being authentic does not always equate with good or moral leadership. Therefore, a high level of ethical standards and positive personal values are also important requirements of being authentic leaders.

Gandhi's ideas about service and stewardship (i.e., advocating the best interest of another person or entity) have influenced numerous leadership writers such as Robert Greenleaf, who identified Gandhi as an example of servant leadership (discussed in Chapter 1). Greenleaf's research identifies two requirements for servant leadership: the servant leader must elicit trust and have a sustaining spirit. Gandhi elicited trust through his consistency between his thoughts, words, and authentically altruistic actions. Gandhi sustained his spirit through a deep Hindu faith and informed knowledge of other world religions, such as Christianity.

Similarly, Greenleaf's conceptualization of servant leadership is not limited to one religious tradition or cultural context. In his writings, Greenleaf integrates ideas from Christian, Jewish, Hindu, and Buddhist traditions, and Western and Eastern cultural customs to explain his notion of servant leadership. And he illustrates this by pointing to Gandhi as the embodiment of servant leadership and idealized influence. To fully appreciate the example of Gandhi as an idealized leader, you should view Richard Attenborough's award-winning film *Gandhi*.[10] To gain a rich understanding of how Gandhi's ideas are being applied in leadership situations, visit www.greenleaf.org/ and watch clips from the film *Gandhi* on YouTube.com or Netflix.

Box 3.2 Gandhi's Impact Today

Gandhi scholar and historian J. V. Naik was delighted to hear of Gandhi's example being used in our FRLD courses. Naik taught history at Elphinstone College, then at the Government of Maharashtra I.Y. College. Before his retirement, he was professor and head of the Department of History at the University of Mumbai in India. He shared the following thoughts with us, which shed more light on the nature of Gandhi's idealized influence, and authentic and servant leadership qualities:

What is great and admirable about Gandhi is that he never claimed infallibility. Instead, he admitted that he committed some "Himalayan blunders" in his life. His greatness lay in the fact that in pursuit of The Truth that was God for him, he told us some simple truths such as "There cannot be oppression unless the oppressor and the oppressed cooperate with each other." He conquered the two greatest enemies of mankind: fear and malice. Once he removed fear from the minds and hearts of the Indian people, the British Empire collapsed because it existed basically with the support of military strength. He also taught us that "you can't fight evil with evil because if you do it multiples. Instead, you need to fight evil with good." He was the friend of the poorest, loneliest and the lost. He also advised us that if we want to have a just and equitable social order, then we should not commit the following seven social sins:

1. Politics without principles
2. Commerce without morality
3. Wealth without work
4. Education without character
5. Science without humanity
6. Pleasure without conscience
7. Worship without sacrifice.

All in all, Gandhi lifted us from dust to dignity. He gave us our self-respect. His mission and message was: HUMANISE, EQUALISE and SPIRITUALISE.

Idealized influence involves a set of leadership principles, a high level of morality, hard work, and strong character. It also involves focusing on others instead of the self, being guided by an inner voice that knows right from wrong, and making personal sacrifices for the good of the group. We believe that idealized influence is helpful in responding to Gandhi's call to avoid the seven social sins both today and in the future.[8]

Idealized Influence Behaviors: Definition and Examples

We believe that idealized influence is an important concept that differentiates transformational leadership from other types of leadership. However, you don't need to be at Gandhi's level to practice idealized influence and become a transformational leader. The current CEO of Pepsi, Indra Nooyi, demonstrates several ways to practice idealized influence today, especially in a corporate setting (see Box 3.3). In this section, we will explain what idealized influence is and how you can practice it every day based on six key transformational leadership behaviors.

Box 3.3 Leader Profile: Indra Nooyi

Consistently ranked among the world's most powerful women, Indra Nooyi, CEO of PepsiCo, uses her power in a positive way to empower her associates and women all over the world. Prior to coming to PepsiCo, Nooyi grew up in Madras (Chennai), India. She earned undergraduate degrees in mathematics, physics, and chemistry and an MBA from schools in India before earning a graduate degree in public and private management from Yale University. She gained corporate experience working at Johnson & Johnson, Boston Consulting Group, Motorola, and Asea Brown Boveri before joining PepsiCo in 2001 as CFO. In 2006, she became President and CEO of PepsiCo and redirected company strategy to produce and sell healthier foods. With her strategic leadership, she has helped her company achieve extraordinary performance in a turbulent global economic environment.

Nooyi often provides advice to aspiring executives regarding skills associated with her success that she calls the "5 Cs of leadership." The first skill involves developing a set of *competencies* or talents for which you are known. *Courage and confidence* are the next skills she advocates because they are needed to demonstrate your competence and speak up when necessary. To be able to speak up, *communication skills* are required to effectively motivate associates and influence others. Her fourth requirement is *consistency* in words and deeds based on a set of principles that guide decision-making and behavior. The fifth requirement is what she calls *compass* or possessing the integrity that serves as the foundation for the previous elements of her leadership philosophy. Nooyi's 5 Cs of leadership are helpful because courage, confidence, consistency, and compass (integrity) represent core aspects of idealized influence and authentic leadership.[11]

Talk About Your Most Important Values and Beliefs

Scott Mullner is a client service specialist at Energage, a company that fosters the employee engagement of its clients. With this focus on building employee engagement, Scott's team spends a lot of time talking about their company values and "living the mission." However, they rarely talked about how the company values of helpfulness, open-mindedness, and teamwork mesh with their own personal values. After recognizing this concern, Scott decided to bring up how important values are to their everyday lives in a team meeting. He started a discussion about his personal values. He asked his team members to join in with their own thoughts. He described his value of integrity. He then explained how he tries to connect his own integrity to being helpful and open-minded with coworkers and clients.

At the beginning of the conversation, many of Scott's colleagues rolled their eyes and shifted uncomfortably in their seats. After a few awkward moments, one colleague volunteered that she values helpfulness in her own life. This makes it easy for her to live that value at work. Once she answered, more of Scott's colleagues started to answer as well. His manager said that he tries to stress honesty and tolerance at home with his family and in his own life, and believes that open-mindedness closely aligns with that value. Another coworker agreed that being willing to help others has always been a part of her life. She then told a story of a *Habitat for Humanity* club and the impact it had on those they helped. By the end of the meeting, each member of Scott's team had talked about their values and made connections between their personal lives and their work lives.

The impact of discussing important values and beliefs on Scott's team has been powerful and tangible. Scott followed up by further working with his teammates on the values that they said were closest to their own. He has seen his teammates acting in a similar way. Those who said they value helpfulness have been taking extra time to explain something to a client, or work with one of their coworkers on a problem. Discussing personal values and their connection to the company values has reenergized the motivation in Scott's team. The team members now feel trust and respect growing between them. They now see each other as valuable individuals who go beyond their self-interests for the good of others and their team.[12]

Scott gained trust from his colleagues by bringing up his important values. This process illustrates what idealized influence is all about. When you talk about your important values and share them with your followers, you can establish a strong foundation that motivates them to achieve collective confidence and success, not just personal confidence and success. And when followers see consistency among their leader's ideas, words, and actions, they are likely to attribute idealized influence to the leader. What important personal or company values can you highlight for your staff?

Talking about important values and beliefs is important in all areas of life. As shown in Figure 3.1, for people of faith, religious ceremonies often highlight what's most important to strive for and how to live one's life. Organizational leaders also must guide their followers and point them in the right direction. For example, Tony Dungy, the first African American NFL coach to win the Super Bowl, has used his faith to direct players and others in the game of life.[13]

However, our experience with many students and executives while teaching leadership has taught us about one common problem. People rarely spend time thinking about what values are important to them. To test this, we ask our

Figure 3.1
**Values to live
and lead by.
The priest
performing
the baptism
ceremony
talks about the
importance
of Church
values and
beliefs and the
responsibilities
of the parents
and the
godparents in
leading and
developing
the child to
be a person of
faith.**

students to write down the five most important values that they use to guide their behaviors and decision-making processes every day. Surprisingly, more than half of them have a hard time writing down even two or three values. They are all managers, but they do not have a set of well-defined personal values. One common excuse for not having a set of personal values is that they are just too busy at work. Or, some people say that they will develop them when they become senior executives and when they really need them. We believe that it is very important to establish a clearly defined set of values early on and practice them every day. This will make you more of an authentic transformational leader. What are your top five important values? Can you pass this test by writing all five and living by them?

Talk About the Importance of Trusting Each Other

Elizabeth D'Eramo is a Procurement Specialist at a large utility company. Her team hired another person at her same level and job description. Although they report to different managers, they are on the same team and sit in the same office. Competitive by nature, Elizabeth felt threatened by Lucy, the new team member, and apprehensive to start a friendship or share any tips. Elizabeth avoided going to lunch with her on her first day or stopping by her cubicle. Then they were given an assignment to attend training for SAP software and were delegated as the key contacts of their group for any SAP purchase related questions. After the training, they were responsible for transferring over one hundred purchase orders from Oracle to SAP. Having prior experience in SAP and purchase orders, Elizabeth found this exercise to be easy. Lucy, on the other hand, had no prior supply chain purchasing experience, and Elizabeth sensed her confusion. They were both given a firm deadline for completing purchase order transitions. Elizabeth finished a few days ahead of time, but she overheard that Lucy was struggling with the task. So, she decided to offer a helping hand to Lucy.

Elizabeth realized that her overly competitive, covert nature was the wrong way to develop her leadership. Ironically, by hesitating to be helpful to others in pursuit of her self-interests, Elizabeth was only hurting herself. With this in mind, and to Lucy's surprise, Elizabeth started rapport on how her transition was going, and she asked how Lucy was fairing with the project. After hearing her frustration, Elizabeth considered this the opportune moment to extend herself as a leader. She offered to set up time on her calendar before working hours to finish this initiative. During their meeting, she shared her notes on purchase orders, computer screenshots, and her training binder with extra materials. Elizabeth also offered to process a quarter of the purchase orders on her own time so that Lucy could meet the deadline. In addition to the training, Elizabeth provided positive encouragement and assured Lucy that learning SAP is difficult at first.

With Elizabeth's instruction and help with a portion of the purchase orders, Lucy was able to meet the deadline and gain a better understanding of SAP. When Lucy received positive feedback from their Director, she copied Elizabeth's manager on an email and thanked her for the assistance. Elizabeth was delighted by Lucy's accomplishment and gratitude. In helping Lucy, Elizabeth also built her reputation with her manager and others on the team. The two team members felt the positive effects of collaboration, and more importantly, Elizabeth felt that she had earned Lucy's respect and trust. After this meeting, Lucy felt comfortable reaching out to Elizabeth with other questions. Elizabeth is now excited about developing their friendship, and now often assists others on her team.[14]

As illustrated by Elizabeth's story, giving out appropriate help to associates before it is asked for is absolutely, positively essential in leader–follower relationships, as it is in any interpersonal relationship. While trust levels vary, most people believe that trust either exists or does not exist. Pretending that trust exists (when in fact it doesn't) runs counter to Gandhi's concepts of truthfulness and authenticity. If issues with trust exist in a group, they cannot be swept under the rug. Instead, they must be dealt with by discussing the sources of mistrust and working to eliminate them. Even when trust levels are sufficient, trust needs to be reinforced periodically so that the leader can continue to establish her image reflecting integrity, competence, openness, and consistency. When followers feel that they can count on their leader, they are more likely to not want to let their leader or team down, as shown in Figure 3.2.

Figure 3.2
I believe in you! The pitcher is gaining confidence in his ability to throw strikes because he trusts his idealized leader, who has coached and watched over him.

So, what is your source of trust that creates positive influence for followers? If you do not have a clearly defined source of positive influence, then you are not likely to establish a trustworthy relationship with your followers. It could be authenticity (just like Gandhi), expertise, keen insights for work, extensive experience, or willingness to help (just like Elizabeth). Either of these sources is appropriate to practice idealized influence. Simply figure out what you have and how you will go about practicing it consistently.

Specify the Importance of Having a Strong Sense of Purpose

Have you ever felt like giving up when faced with a seemingly impossible task? Perhaps it was when you were working for a very difficult boss. Perhaps it was when you were completing your degree while you worked full-time. Perhaps it was when you were forced to take a statistics course you thought you'd never pass. Whatever the case, chances are you stuck it out because you had an important reason or motive for reaching your goal. Your reason might have been to make someone in your family proud of you. It might have been to establish or reestablish an important personal relationship. Or it simply might have been to complete an important work that no one else would be capable of doing.

This is the kind of motivation that sustained Lori in her leadership role as a middle manager in an international banking firm. Lori assumed her leadership post just as Willie joined her bank as the new director of operations and her superior. Willie had a notorious reputation for being an overbearing, number-crunching, command-and-control freak with an ego as tall as the Empire State Building. Willie had spent many years in the military's finance offices before he transitioned into industry a few years prior to a planned retirement at age 65. Imagine a cigar-smoking, crass, overweight, and opinionated middle-aged executive, and you'll get the picture. According to Lori, Willie is not a micromanager; he is a *nano-manager!* Sounds like active management-by-exception on steroids, doesn't it?

On account of Willie, Lori's days at work were replete with endless frustrations, nit-picky questions, illogical responses, and denials of resource requests. In short, Willie made Lori's and every other manager's life miserable. Escape from this situation was impossible because Willie's superior was his best buddy, and Willie had no intention of leaving. Like prisoners crossing off the days on a calendar as they passed, Lori and her colleagues counted down the days until Willie's planned retirement. What helped Lori and her colleagues keep their wits and willpower to carry on for the greater good of their firm?

It was their strong sense of purpose coming from a will to help their firm be successful despite Willie's mean-spirited motives and actions. This was their mission: to help each other and their associates get through the tough times, and to learn something from it. As mentioned in Chapter 2, their approach is what Viktor Frankl referred to as purpose in life and what Daniel Levinson referred to as the dream. When leaders talk about the importance of having a strong sense of purpose, followers are more likely to endure their current challenges and develop confidence in their ability to overcome them. Their confidence oftentimes

becomes contagious to other people in the organization. Furthermore, leaders' strong sense of purpose gives followers a reason to persist, a cause to champion, and a reason to fight the good fight when times get tough. As shown in Figure 3.3, the passion that leaders and followers possess can provide purpose for persevering and transcending the challenges that life throws at us. What sense of purpose can you share with your followers? How can you use purpose to help your organization overcome difficult challenges that competitors inside and outside of your organization throw at you? Before you think about motivating your followers, be sure to create an important purpose that you can share with your followers and organization.

Consider the Moral/Ethical Consequences of Your Decisions

The United States Air Force (USAF) promotes the ethical decision-making of its men and women by fostering three core values that reflect idealized influence. The first value is "Integrity First" which means that airmen do the right thing and are honest, self-controlled, and courageous. The second value is "Service Before Self" which means that an airman's professional duties must supersede personal desires. The third value is "Excellence in All We Do" which means that airmen continually work to improve processes and personal skills to achieve the highest levels of performance. Each of these values pertains to the consideration of moral/ethical consequences. Idealized leaders make decisions and act with integrity that is beyond reproach. They strive to serve others, often at their own personal expense. And they exemplify performance excellence and let their performance speak for them.[15] It is this set of core values displayed through idealized influence behaviors that Dr. Fil Arenas and his Air University staff at Maxwell Air Force Base instill in their students as part of FRLD training (see Box 3.4).

Box 3.4 FRLD Education at Air University, Maxwell Air Force Base

In the USAF, basic leadership development begins at various entry-level programs. For the enlisted force that begins with basic military training and for officers several accession programs exist; the U.S. Air Force Academy, Officer Training School, and the Reserve Officer Training Corps to name a few. As airmen progress throughout their careers they are provided professional development opportunities based on their career levels referred to as professional military education (PME). The PME for the enlisted force includes: the NCO Academy, SNCO Academy, and the Chief's Leadership Course. The officers begin with Squadron Officer School (SOS), Air Command and Staff College (ACSC), and finish with Air War College (AWC); the latter two programs offer master degrees.

Air University located at Maxwell AFB, Alabama directs professional military education. Since 2010, SOS has offered full range leadership development (FRLD) to their captains, international officers, and civilian equivalents. In their short six-week program, they must leverage a leadership model that is not only intuitive, but easily adopted in the dynamic military environment. Throughout their experiential exercises and leadership problem scenarios, they can quickly discern differences between transactional and transformational behaviors while discussing the importance of adapting their styles as needed. The SNCO Academy provides this model as well to not only help develop followers into leaders, but improve organizational relationships. Further, ACSC has delivered several FRLD graduate-level elective courses since 2013. The courses "Developing Your Full Range of Leadership" and "North Star Leadership" focus on principles of transactional and transformational behaviors across all Air Force organizations in an effort to create a common leadership language throughout levels of PME. These courses have also been delivered to senior officers at AWC over the last few years with the goal to take a familiar leadership model from the junior ranks to the most senior officers to create a common leadership foundation.

Utilizing a common leadership lexicon across the Air Force for thousands of PME students annually would have a significant impact on the ability to inculcate empirically proven leadership behaviors. Moreover, enhancing leader behaviors with virtuous character strengths will produce more personable leaders. The tenets of FRLD are ideal for this vibrant military setting, whereby developing followers into leaders is a revolving necessity.[16]

– Dr. Fil J. Arenas

Transformational leaders, such as Dr. Fil Arenas, are responsible for a broad range of followers with diverse interests and agendas. As role models for followers, transformational leaders must make decisions using a perspective that transcends their own narrow self-interests. This perspective-taking capacity, introduced in Chapter 2, is critical to the display of idealized influence behavior. That's because idealized leaders talk about important moral and ethical values and therefore must use these values in their own decision-making processes in order to gain credibility from followers. For example, before the Enron scandal, Kenneth Lay, its deceased former CEO, was frequently depicted as one of the most capable and charismatic CEOs of America. But, we know what happened when such a capable and charismatic CEO doesn't have strong moral and ethical standards.[17] This cautionary tale becomes even more important today than during the Enron scandal era because everything is connected and shared through social media now. We can't hide our behaviors behind a black curtain anymore.

Therefore, if your goal is to display idealized influence, it is not enough for you to talk about such values. You must use moral and ethical values to guide your decision-making processes and use them to justify your decisions if and when you come under fire from others. Like Gandhi and Arenas, you must strongly believe in a core set of moral and ethical values, use them in your decision-making, talk about them to your followers and others, and bring them to life with behavior that is consistent with what you espouse. As shown in Figure 3.4, remember that your values and personal beliefs shape your leadership behavior. As you continually display this behavior over time, your character is shaped.

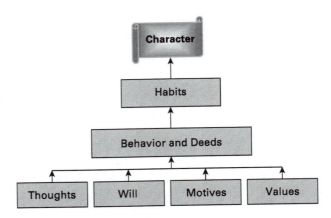

Figure 3.4 **Building character. Idealized leaders build their character upon a solid foundation of ideals, behaviors, and practices.** (Reprinted with permission from Sosik, J. J., Jung, D. I., Berson, Y., Dionne, S. D., & Jaussi, K. S. (2004). *The dream weavers: Strategy-focused leadership in technology-driven organizations* [p. 158]. Charlotte, NC: Information Age Publishing.)

Emphasize the Importance of Teamwork

If you have ever watched the Penn State Nittany Lions football team, you've probably noticed that the players do not have their last names printed on the back of their jerseys. While this is unusual, that's the way Coach James Franklin likes it. Upholding a tradition established by Coach Joe Paterno, Franklin feels that the absence of player names on jerseys places the focus of effort on the team instead of the individual player and therefore promotes team spirit and cooperation. What a great way to erase the big egos from these husky football players! This concept is what social psychologists call *de-individuation*, or the temporary loss of personal identity from being part of a group.[18] De-individuation shifts the attention of players from their individual needs and wants to those of their team because they are not easily identified at the individual level. They are, however, easily connected to their team because they share a common uniform and a common identity.

This shift of focus from individual to collective interests is a very important element of transformational leadership. A transformational leader's focus on collective interests raises followers' level of moral development because individuals whose perspective is on others rather than the self tend to possess higher levels of moral reasoning and perspective-taking capacities. Leaders like Gandhi or Franklin who focus the attention of followers on the cause rather than the leader are *idealized* rather than *idolized*. If the focus is mainly on the leader, a cult of personality is a real and dangerous possibility. But if the focus is on the team, vision, or mission, leaders are seen as servant leaders who display idealized influence. It's essential for you to highlight the importance of teamwork to your followers so that they will identify with you as a worthy role model (see Figure 3.5). What can you talk about to foster teamwork in your organization? How can you design work processes so your followers can focus on teamwork naturally?

Figure 3.5
All for one and one for all. Idealized leaders promote solidarity and teamwork among their followers, who look to them as role models.

Champion Exciting New Possibilities That Can Be Achieved Through Teamwork

Once you've established the importance of teamwork in conversations with followers, you need to get them excited about synergies that can emerge from teamwork. *Synergy* is defined as a process in which two or more entities acting together create an effect greater than any outcome resulting from the separate effects of the individual entities. For example, John can recall his first year of doctoral studies at the State University of New York at Binghamton. He came into the program with strong corporate experience gained at RJR Nabisco and a desire to learn leadership theory and research methods. Also new in the program at the time was Don, fresh from studying under Dr. Orlando Behling at Bowling Green State University. Don brought with him a background in history and military experience. As they discussed their research interests, they found that Don's knowledge of history was a perfect complement to John's knowledge of business. Their personalities complemented each other and a shared passion for leadership research and academic success made them click almost instantly. Their unique knowledge bases and skills synergized into a productive relationship that has generated a solid stream of research. An equally important by-product of their synergy is a friendship that has lasted a quarter of a century.[19] Neither of them could have achieved alone what they achieved together.

Pointing out the potential for your followers to collaborate and attain such synergies builds your image as an idealized leader. Oftentimes, we have found that one of the most important reasons that a work group fails is that members don't recognize potential benefits of working together. Similarly, when your followers don't recognize you as someone who is instrumental in achieving success, you are not likely to win their support and willingness to collaborate. By explaining the needs and benefits of interdependence among followers, you will be perceived by your followers as a leader with high perspective-taking capacity associated with high levels of moral development. And that's the essence of idealized influence.

Idealized Influence Attributes: Definition and Examples

When your followers see you displaying these idealized influence behaviors, they are likely to attribute certain positive characteristics to you. Because of your idealized behaviors, your followers will reflect charisma back at you. That's because when you display idealized behaviors, you are a shining star in the eyes of your followers. They perceive you as a glowing role model, akin to a gem. The more they see your idealized leadership brilliance, the more they will polish your shine and admire your glimmer. Because followers naturally recognize and appreciate beauty and excellence, and leadership is a process of mutual influence, they ascribe attributes of idealized influence to you. *Idealized influence attributes* are positive personal characteristics of the leader that are socially constructed in leader–follower relationships. The range of these attributes is wide and varied. They occur across many leadership contexts described later. How can you benefit from the attributes of idealized leadership that your followers attribute to you? Let's find out by now examining five essential attributes of idealized leaders.

Instill Pride in Others for Being Associated with You

Do your followers have a sense of pride in working with you? Is it a source of their satisfaction and happiness? These questions are very important in gaining attributions of idealized influence because people like being associated with winners. That's why so many sports fans are extremely proud of their teams during winning seasons? It makes them feel good about themselves because they are seen by others in a positive light. Their team's success becomes their own success. Ask any fan of the Green Bay Packers during the Lombardi years or those of the Philadelphia Eagles and New England Patriots in more recent years, and they're sure to agree.

If you are a top performer, chances are your associates will want to learn about your winning ways. They'll respect you for what you've accomplished and envy your success. They also may admire you for what you stand for as a person, as well as the tough stands you've taken during difficult times. They might like you for the values you demonstrate by your behavior. For example, we admire our mentors Bruce Avolio, currently of the University of Washington, and Fran Yammarino of the State University of New York at Binghamton. Bruce demonstrated his love of learning through his strong work ethic and intellectually stimulating behaviors that challenged his Ph.D. students' ways of thinking about leadership. Fran demonstrated his keen intellect through no-nonsense directives that clarified what needed to be done. His tough love fostered a sense of family that made students feel good because technical *and* social support were there for them. Being associated with Bruce, Fran, and all the other fine colleagues at the Center of Leadership Studies at the State University of New York at Binghamton has given us an immense amount of pride because of their positive values and achievements in cutting-edge research and training. As shown in Figure 3.6, pride is a powerful motivator for followers because it propels them to the same levels of excellence as their high-performing role models. If you want your followers to feel

Figure 3.6 **Pride in the name of love. These team members are proud of the achievements they attained together and their team's excellence.**

that same way about you, start thinking about what you can or should do to make your followers develop a sense of pride in being associated with you as a leader. That sense of pride can go a long way to help them endure many challenges and produce synergies that lead to success.

Go Beyond Self-Interests for the Good of Others

Peter accepted a challenging role as head of an academic department in a private university during a very difficult time. He put aside his research agenda for over two years to serve the faculty. He used a transparent and principle-centered approach to leading while dealing with the many challenges of a demanding faculty and administration and fierce competition from other schools. He led by following a set of virtues and principles outlined in Box 3.5. Peter often was the first to enter the office in the morning and the last to leave. Because of the grueling hours and nature of his leadership position, he was forced to forgo attending daily Mass, an experience he loved sharing with his wife for many years. These and other personal sacrifices did not go unnoticed by others as they attributed idealized influence to Peter. As a result, the vast majority of faculty and staff considered Peter to be the greatest department head in its history.

Idealized leaders such as Peter are seen as selfless servants to followers. Their followers perceive them as putting others' interests ahead of their own interests. Because of these idealized influence behaviors and perceptions, they are seen by others as possessing altruistic (i.e., other-oriented) goals as opposed to egoistic (i.e., self-centered) goals. Social psychologist C. D. Batson defined altruism and egoism in terms of goals. According to Batson, if the ultimate goal is to increase another's welfare, then the motivation is *altruistic* (even if the helper benefits in the process). If the ultimate goal is to increase one's own welfare (even if the one being helped benefits), the motivation is *egoistic*.[21] When followers see you as helping them achieve their goals, your behavior reflects the notion of altruism, as shown in Figure 3.7. When your behaviors are seen as altruistic, your followers are more likely to perceive you as an authentic leader as well.

Altruism is a core behavior discussed in research on organizational citizenship behavior (OCB). This discretionary behavior is not part of one's formal job requirements, but promotes the effective functioning of organizations.[22] Research indicates a positive relationship between OCB and performance for leaders and their organizational units.[23] Whether you spend time being altruistic with your followers, promote interpersonal harmony between followers, or are conscientious about your role as leader, your followers will see you as a more positive role model. As a result, followers wish to develop an intimate association with you and will attribute idealized influence to you. Therefore, one important question you need to answer is: what sacrifices can you make for the betterment of your followers and organization? Remember, you don't need to make a big sacrifice. It is more important to give sincere assurance to your followers that you are willing to make a sacrifice for the good of the team and organization.

Box 3.5 Leadership Principles of Bishop Filipe J. Estevez

Bishop Filipe J. Estevez is truly a global transformational leader. Prior to assuming his current role as Bishop of the Diocese of St. Augustine, Estevez came to the United States from Cuba, and is fluent in four languages. His impressive education includes a doctorate in sacred theology from Pontifical Gregorian University in Rome, Italy. He has served the Catholic Church in both Honduras and the United States in roles ranging from pastor to campus minister at Florida International University, from seminary faculty member to the dean of spiritual formation at St. Vincent de Paul Regional Seminary, Boynton Beach, Florida, and from Auxiliary Bishop to General Vicar of the Archdiocese of Miami.

Based on his extensive leadership experience, in 1984 he developed a set of ten practical leadership principles that illustrate idealized influence and other aspects of transformational leadership:

1. People are more effective when they do what they can do best—discover *talents*, affirm talents, challenge talents.
2. Each one is part of a *team*, a body—a team is more effective than the individual—that seeks to promote a collaborative stand from each one of the team.
3. *Responsibility.* Be alert to respond well, as soon as possible, and as far as possible to meet the need in its own terms.
4. *Clarity of direction.* Be sure to always have a vision and a plan of action—to know where the group is going. A sensitive plan is in touch with the history of the group and, above all, with the unique circumstances of the group.
5. Talk the language of *deeds*. Words fade away, but people esteem and respect you because of your deeds.
6. *Modesty.* The poor of the world are too many for seeking expensive, luxurious ways—modesty, sobriety, and simplicity at all times.
7. Seek the *involvement* of others. Delegate and share responsibilities as much as possible; then trust the persons involved. Praise their accomplishments publicly.
8. Seek *information*. It is indispensable for good decision-making. Encourage people to make decisions, but hold them accountable to share information about what they are doing.
9. Value the *permanent education* of each person—the improvement of skills and acquisition of new methods and ways. Allow time for this!
10. Offer all your accomplishments to *the Lord*. Ask Him to purify your intentions so that His will may be done in all things at all times, and to make up for what our abilities may lack.[20]

Figure 3.7
I can help.
Idealized
leaders take
time out of
their busy
schedules to
assist their
followers.

Act in Ways That Build Others' Respect

Transformational leaders gain attributions of idealized influence from their followers the old-fashioned way: they earn it. They earn it by behaving in ways that reflect virtues and character strengths that are perceived as such by their followers.[24] Andee realized this when she accepted the role of development officer at a small nonprofit organization. Her first days on the job were quite challenging given a small group of needy and contentious direct reports. This demanding group introduced conflict into Andee's department and sought to undermine her authority in the eyes of the other staff members. Andee was initially upset by their escapades and quickly became disheartened by their motives. Andee knew she had to confront their dysfunctional behavior and "nip it in the bud." How could she send a strong message without alienating all of her new staff?

Andee considered her conflict with this group as an opportunity to strengthen interpersonal relationships with them. She spent time in private meetings with each malcontent, listening to their opinions and ideas, and learning about how they best could serve her department. She framed the conflict as one of ideas or approaches, not of people. By keeping the conflict impersonal, Andee was able to present rational arguments that made sense to the large majority of her staff. She was not condescending and did not show contempt for those who threatened her by using sarcastic or abusive language. She did not shout or use emotional displays. Instead, she outwitted her challengers on a rational basis with calm and lucid reasoning supported by timeless virtues of wisdom, integrity, and justice. As a result, Andee was able to manage this initial challenge constructively and build her direct reports' respect for her.[25] A key challenge for many newly appointed leaders is how to go about building trust and gaining respect from their followers, as Andee did.

Display a Sense of Power and Confidence

One of the things that people most appreciated about Peter's leadership was his strong advocacy for the faculty. Rather than acting as a "leader on a leash" held by top administrators, Peter was a champion and spokesperson for his group. He championed the best interests of his faculty, while also seeking to cooperate to achieve broader university goals and policies. He was willing to stand up for them when they needed his support on important issues, such as faculty hiring, market equity in salaries, and funding for research. He didn't back down in the face of intimidating threats from individuals who possessed greater position power than he held. Peter made himself visible on important issues in a way that was consistent with leadership advice once given by civil rights activist and politician Jesse Jackson: "Leadership cannot just go along to get along. . . . Leadership must meet the moral challenge of the day."[26] Peter's ability to meet his challenges was based on strong convictions in the moral justification of his actions and his strong faith. And that's a source of power and confidence that can move mountains.

Do not confuse a sense of power and confidence with abuse of power, cockiness, or arrogant overconfidence. We are not recommending any form of abusive leadership which almost always leads to negative outcomes.[27] Instead, we recommend that you must be careful to hold back on temptations to use your power in ways that are self-serving and dismissive of viewpoints of your followers and associates. Therefore, your ultimate leadership challenge is to be able to exercise influence over people around you even if you don't have any leverage, such as your title and authority. Here's a reality check for you: do you believe that you can influence your subordinates when they no longer work for you?

As shown in Figure 3.8, displaying a quiet confidence can go a long way to avoid the pitfalls of an air of superiority. Remember that it takes many years to gain the trust and respect of followers and associates. But it only takes a few

Figure 3.8 **You can always count on me. As an idealized leader, this soldier offers hope and security to his followers in a confident and friendly manner.**

minutes to destroy the idealized influence that you have built through your history of interactions with your followers. Next time you see a leader in your organization who displays a sense of power and confidence that benefits others, thank her for being a fine example of idealized influence, and ask her how she does this. Then reflect on how you too can gain such attributions of idealized influence.

Reassure Others That Obstacles Will Be Overcome

Many successful leaders are natural optimists and they emphasize the importance of having positive perspectives quite frequently. For example, the French military and political leader Napoleon Bonaparte once said, "Leaders are dealers in hope." In 1988, Democratic U.S. presidential candidate Jesse Jackson challenged his followers with the mantra "Keep hope alive!" And to many people, former U.S. president Barack Obama represented the great hope of a brighter future for the world. Followers look to their leader to make sense out of crises or challenges that they are struggling to overcome. It's the leader's job to explain why things are so, why the status quo is unacceptable, and what followers must do to overcome their struggle and prosper in the future. Transformational leaders are able to present an exciting and compelling vision of change that boosts followers' collective confidence that they can bring about positive change. Their positive words and "can do" attitude make them admired role models in their followers' eyes.

This form of reassurance worked well when Brian Naviglia first joined his educational institution as a HR consultant. The most frustrating matter he dealt with involved unreasonable expectations. There was a shared idea within the culture that a new employee should know where to find information needed to perform the job (even though no training was offered or formal introductions to people or resources provided). Brian also didn't know the roles of key individuals and who to contact as resources for various matters that he faced. Additionally, when others would attend meetings, they would not share information. As a result, Brian felt disconnected from the organization and wondered if it valued the strengths, work history, and contributions that he possessed. However, he eventually found people in the organization that were encouraging and helpful. He relied on them for insights and guidance. As a result, his attitude changed from discouraged to encouraged. Brian is now very hopeful because he has experienced how his organization provides opportunities to network and learn from others.[28]

Do you look at situations as if the cup is half-empty or half-full? Do you focus on things that are positive or negative? Do you complain about a challenge or talk about a solution? If you want to gain attributions of idealized leadership from your followers, focus on something positive and develop a sense of optimism.

Rationale for and Effects of Idealized Influence Behaviors and Attributes

Now that you've been introduced to the concept of idealized influence, we'd like you to understand why it is important and what effects it can have on your followers. Idealized influence is important because followers learn through their own experience by observing others such as leaders who they respect. One of the best ways for people to learn is to observe and emulate another person's behavior. For this reason, it is important for you as a leader to act in a way that your followers can be proud of and respect you. When followers pay attention to and emulate the behaviors of leaders who display idealized influence, strong cultures of learning and development are created which can promote organizational effectiveness.[29]

Idealized influence can produce several positive effects on followers. The role modeling of moral and ethical considerations and the demonstration of high level of performance by an idealized leader makes followers more willing to trust the leader. That's because trust is based on perceived character and competence. Idealized influence also makes followers want to be like the leader who is perceived to possess a high level of integrity and success. Because leader–follower relationships are based on a social exchange involving norms of reciprocity and obligations to return favors, followers also desire to achieve to show support for the idealized leader. Idealized influence also causes followers to have a strong emotional attraction to the leader in which they identify with the leader as someone to whom they can relate.[30]

Associated with this last positive effect, however, is the fact that idealized influence can also produce a surprising negative effect. With a follower's strong emotional attraction to the leader forged through idealized influence comes the danger that followers can become too dependent on the leader. This dependence on the leader may stem from a lack of a personal identity or self-concept that is independent from the leader. Such followers may succumb to manipulation by the leader. (We will discuss this possibility in more detail in Chapter 6.) However, authentic transformational leaders do not develop such followers. They empower and develop followers who are their own persons capable of thinking for themselves and expressing their unique self.[31]

Putting Idealized Influence into Practice

So far, you have learned what it means to display idealized influence, why it is important, and how it affects followers. You are now ready to identify action steps for putting idealized influence to work in your leadership system. This section presents a few suggestions that you may find useful in exemplifying idealized influence and building your full leadership potential. Everyone is different. So, our recommendation is to develop your unique action plan based on your personal style and circumstances.

Display the Behaviors Described in This Chapter

The easiest way to begin practicing the idealized influence behaviors is to consider the behaviors we presented in this chapter and select the top three behaviors that you want to try out first. Alternatively, identify the top three behaviors that you feel most confident in practicing at your job and in your home. Then, develop

Figure 3.9
**Leadership
learning
process.**

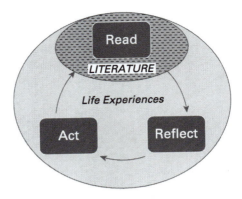

a specific time table such as "I will do #1 for 30 minutes every week or every other week." Every time you practice it, write something down in a leadership journal that you can re-read and think about using the process shown in Figure 3.9. You should continue this process of reading-practice-reflection until such behavior become part of your personal habits. Remember, life experience is the best teacher of leadership, and you need to practice leadership not as a one-time event but as part of your daily routine.

Identify and Leverage Your Strengths and Those of Others

To be an idealized leader requires an understanding of your professional and character strengths. It requires that you appreciate your followers' strengths as well. You can achieve both of these goals by administering two reliable and valid surveys. Gallup's Clifton StrengthsFinder survey identifies individuals' top talents that make them stand out from others. For more information, you are encouraged to visit their website (www.gallupstrengthscenter.com). Another valuable survey is based upon 24 character strengths that reflect the absolute best in humanity and transformational leadership. You can assess your character strengths using this framework at www.viacharacter.org/www/. Many of John's MLD students and their associates have taken these surveys. As a result of administering these surveys, they claim to possess a greater self-awareness of their strengths. They now have a clearer understanding of what they stand for, where they are strong, and where they need further development. This knowledge has helped them present themselves as idealized leaders in a more authentic manner. Remember, your leadership development journey should start from finding out what you don't know and what you need to know.

Improve Your Perspective-Taking Capacity

When you shift your perspective from a self-centered to other-oriented focus, you make decisions that are in the best interest of your group. This selfless approach to leadership builds attributions of idealized influence. You can enhance your perspective-taking capacity by solving ethical dilemmas presented in corporate ethics training classes, courses on ethics in universities, or those embedded in tests of moral reasoning ability. One such test is James Rest's "Test of Defining Issues,"[32] which can be ordered at http://ethicaldevelopment.ua.edu/. By taking this test, you can get a baseline measure on your perspective-taking capacity or level of moral reasoning. Do you reason at the preconventional level based on avoiding punishments or seeking rewards? Do you reason at the conventional level based on laws and conforming to group norms? Or do you reason at the postconventional level based on universal principles that sustain fairness, justice, and care in social systems? Research indicates that transformational leaders typically reason at the postconventional level, while self-centered charismatic leaders reason at the preconventional level.[33] Once you gain an awareness of how you reason, you can work to broaden your perspective by immersing yourself in situations that take you out of your comfort zone. These experiences can make you question your basic assumptions about life and broaden your perspective.

Work on Your Self-Awareness

Understanding the image you desire to project to your followers requires a heightened degree of self-awareness. There are private and public aspects of self-awareness. Private self-awareness involves an understanding of your personal values, beliefs, and attitudes. Public self-awareness involves an understanding of how other people see you in your leadership role and requires a degree of self-regulation. You can enhance your private self-awareness by clarifying your purpose in life by writing a personal mission statement (see Chapter 2), ranking your most important values, and ascertaining your character strengths. You can enhance your public self-awareness by participating in a 360-degree feedback assessment. (We assume that you have already or soon will administer the Multifactor Leadership Questionnaire [MLQ]. Hint. Hint.)

This two-pronged approach to improving self-awareness is something that Patricia Bonner, a high school administrator, found to be very effective. Prior to undergoing this process, Patricia complained about never really understanding the real substance of her leadership. And her associates never understood what she stood for. After examining her private and public self-awareness levels, Patricia became better aware of her self-identity. As a result, she was better able to present the leadership image she desired to share with others—an image of care, concern, and quiet confidence.

Gauging Your Leadership Self-Awareness

An effective way of assessing your level of self-awareness as a leader involves determining your level of self-other rating agreement. When you administer the MLQ, you provide self-ratings of your FRLD behaviors. Your supervisors, peers, subordinates, and others (e.g., customers, clients) also rate you on these leadership behaviors. These multiple sources of data allow you to determine the level of agreement between your self-ratings and your superior's, peers', subordinates', and others' ratings. In other words, this determines how you see yourself as a leader versus how others see you. A comparison of self-ratings and the specific other rating source of interest (e.g., subordinates) is made to classify you into one of four categories:

- *Overestimators*, those who produce self-ratings that are significantly higher than others' ratings of leadership behavior
- *Underestimators*, those who produce self-ratings that are significantly lower than others' ratings of leadership behavior
- *In agreement/good*, those who produce self-ratings that are similar to others' ratings of leadership behavior, when others' ratings are above the average of MLQ norms
- *In agreement/poor*, those who produce self-ratings that are similar to others' ratings of leadership behavior, when others' ratings are below the average of MLQ norms.[34]

Leaders categorized as overestimators and underestimators lack self-awareness. Those who are in agreement/good or in agreement/poor are self-aware, but the former is aware of her good performance while the latter knows that she lacks the ability to display a specific leadership style. These leaders differ in terms of personal characteristics, behaviors, and performance outcomes.

Overestimators are not emotionally intelligent. They can be arrogant, narcissistic, belligerent, and easily angered by others. They are publically self-conscious and possess a self-centered purpose in life. Think of people who you know who fit the description of an overestimator and you'll soon realize that they don't create positive self-images. Their negative attitude fuels an untrusting/suspicious nature and low levels of organizational commitment. They are not trusted by their colleagues. These personal characteristics prompt several negative behaviors. For example, overestimators ignore feedback from others because they think they know it all and are superior to others. They use intimidation tactics on their followers. They are poor at rational persuasion, inspirational motivation, mentoring, and exchange relationships. As a result, they make less effective job decisions, perform poorly, and often derail their careers. But with focused effort and determination, they can improve. Unfortunately, we have seen a fair number of overestimators in our teaching and corporate consulting experience.

Underestimators lack self-confidence and are too hard on themselves. Their high personal standards make them believe in continuous personal improvement. They are the least publically self-conscious and lack a strong purpose in life. But they are pleasant to be around and are somewhat trusting of other people. They are the most trusted of among the leader categories. These personal characteristics trigger several positive behaviors. Underestimators improve their self-evaluations based on the feedback they receive. They are most effective at rational persuasion, inspirational motivation, and mentoring. They are adequate at exchange relationships. As a result, they typically make inadequate job-related decisions and produce mixed, but generally positive performance outcomes. They are seen by superiors as more promotable than overestimators. In our experience, underestimators tend to be authentic idealized leaders who focus more on others than themselves.

In agreement/good leaders are emotionally intelligent and possess a healthy self-concept and adequate level of public self-consciousness. They hold a strong prosocial purpose in life. They have a positive attitude and are trusted by their followers. They are most trusting of others and committed to their organization. These personal characteristics prompt several positive behaviors. In agreement/ good leaders respond well to feedback and adapt their behavior appropriately. They are effective at rational persuasion, very inspiring, and good mentors. They are skilled at exchange relationships. As a result, they make good job-related decisions and produce very good and innovative job performance outcomes. Superiors and peers consider them more promotable than the other types of leaders.

In agreement/poor leaders are self-aware but may lack emotional intelligence. They have an unhealthy self-concept and inadequate knowledge, skills, and abilities. They have a negative attitude and poor self-esteem. They may lack the motivation to improve if they think their abilities are fixed. These personal characteristics prompt several negative behaviors. In agreement/poor leaders are frequently absent from their job because of their low level of organizational commitment. They often quit their job. They accurately assess their weaknesses, but are lax in working to address them. As a result, they make ineffective job-related decisions and are unsuccessful poor performers (but not as bad as overestimators). The good news for these leaders is that with the proper training and a positive attitude, they can improve their leadership and performance, as we have seen in our consulting work.[35] ·

Think about the personal characteristics, behaviors, and performance outcomes associated with these profiles and their potential implications for you. Then be sure to work on Exercise 2 at the end of this chapter.

Learn About Becoming an Authentic Transformational Leader

Greater self-awareness and self-regulation are required to be true to yourself and others. These concepts are at the core of authentic leadership, which builds upon ideas in the FRLD model. While it is beyond the scope of this book, the concept of authentic transformational leadership is a subject worthy of additional study. Numerous books, articles, websites, and workshops on authentic leadership are available to assist you in developing your ability to display idealized influence.[36] The idealized influence that comes from being true to yourself and others is a powerful force that can help you inspire others to work together to achieve extraordinary outcomes. Let's turn our attention to such inspirational behaviors that motivate followers to perform beyond expectations in the next chapter.

Summary Questions and Reflective Exercises

1. This exercise uses results of your Multifactor Leadership Questionnaire (MLQ) report to assess your level of idealized influence behavior and attributes. Compare your idealized influence behavior and attributes ratings with the research-validated benchmarks. How did your self-ratings, ratings from subordinates, ratings from peers, ratings from superiors, and ratings from others compare against the benchmarks? On which specific MLQ items (i.e., questions) did you score highest? Lowest? Consider the item with the highest score to be your most positive strength. Keep working on it so that it can become your defining image. Consider items with the lowest scores to be your weaknesses. What can you do to improve your weaknesses?

2. This exercise also uses results of your MLQ report to assess your level of idealized influence behavior and attributes. Compare your self-ratings on *idealized influence behavior* with ratings provided by subordinates, peers, superiors, and others. Compute the difference score (d) as the difference between your self-rating score and the specific other rating source score of interest (e.g., scores based on follower ratings). If d is less than .5 and the other rating source score is less than 2.8 (use 2.9 for idealized attributes), then you are considered to be *in agreement/poor*. If d is less than .5 and the other rating source score is greater than 2.8 (use 2.9 for idealized attributes), then you are considered to be *in agreement/good*. If d is equal to or greater than .5 and the self-rating score is greater than the other rating score, then you are an *overestimator* on this dimension. If d is equal to or greater than .5 and the self-rating score is less than the other rating score, then you are an *underestimator* on this dimension. Consider the category under which you fall in terms of idealized influence behavior. What are the implications of this categorization for you? Are there any things you can do to improve in this area? Repeat this exercise for idealized influence attributes.

3. Visit www.viacharacter.org/www/ and take the Character Strengths survey. What are your top five character strengths as described by the survey? How can you put these character strengths into practice through idealized influence behaviors? What specific idealized behaviors can reflect your character strengths in a way that allows you to be true to yourself and others?

4. Identify an individual in your organization or family whom you would consider a follower who needs attention. This may be a person who lacks self-confidence, self-efficacy, purpose in life, trust, or commitment. This person might be going through a personal or professional crisis. Alternatively, it might be someone who has great leadership potential but needs some direction and encouragement. Once you have identified this person, think about one or more of the behaviors

of idealized influence to address the issue you identify. Then have a 30-minute conversation with this person about the issue. During the conversation, focus on being a good listener, instead of being a good talker. At the end of your conversation, summarize what you have just heard and help your follower to develop a specific action plan to address the issue.

5. At your next department meeting, set some time aside to talk about your organization's core values. Highlight your personal values that are consistent with your organization's values. Ask your followers and associates what they can do to reflect those values in their behavior at work or in the organizational initiatives you are leading.

Notes

1   Meindl, J. R., Ehrlich, S. B., & Dukerich, J. M. (1985). The romance of leadership. *Administrative Science Quarterly, 30*, 78–102.

2   A variety of books have been written about or by Jack Welch. Some of our favorites include Baum, S. H., & Conti, D. (2007). *What made Jack Welch Jack Welch: How ordinary people become extraordinary leaders*. New York: Crown Business; Lowe, J. C. (2008). *Jack Welch speaks: Wisdom from the world's greatest business leader*. New York: Wiley; Welch, J. (2006). *Winning—the answers: Confronting 74 of the toughest questions in business today*. New York: Collins; and Welch, J., & Welch, S. (2015). *The real-life MBA: Your no-BS guide to winning the game, building a team, and growing your career*. New York: Harper Collins.

3   Bartlett, C. A., & Wozny, M. (2000). *GE's two-decade transformation: Jack Welch's leadership (multimedia case)*. Boston, MA: Harvard Business School Press.

4   Colvin, J. (1999, November 22). The ultimate manager in a time of hidebound formulaic thinking, Jack Welch gave power to the worker and the shareholder. He built one hell of a company in the process. *Fortune*. Retrieved from http://archive.fortune.com/magazines/fortune/fortune_archive/1999/11/22/269126/index.htm.

5   Hayden, J. (2017, May). Jack Welch reveals the number 1 quality every great leader possesses. *Inc*. Retrieved from www.inc.com/jeff-haden/jack-welch-reveals-the-one-quality-every-great-leader-possesses.html; and Welch, J. (2001). *Jack: Straight from the gut*. New York: Warner Business Books.

6   Gandhi, M. (1957). *An autobiography: The story of my experiments with truth*. Boston, MA: Beacon; Morselli, D., & Passini, S. (2010). Avoiding crimes of obedience: A comparative study of the autobiographies of M. K. Gandhi, Nelson Mandela, and Martin Luther King, Jr. *Peace and Conflict: Journal of Peace Psychology, 16*(3), 295–391; and Weber, T. (1999). Gandhi, deep ecology, peace research and Buddhist economics. *Journal of Peace Research, 36*, 349–361.

7   George, B. (2003). *Authentic leadership: Rediscovering the secrets to creating lasting value*. San Francisco, CA: Jossey-Bass; George, B. (2016, July 6). *HBS: The truth about authentic leaders*. Retrieved from www.billgeorge.org/articles/hbs-the-truth-about-authentic-leaders/; and George, B., & Sims, P. (2007). *True north: Discover your authentic leadership*. San Francisco, CA: Jossey-Bass.

8   Naik, J. V. (2017, March 20). Personal communication; and www.indussource.com/Author/J-V-Naik/12.aspx.

9   Gandhi, M. (1959). *An autobiography: The story of my experiments with truth.* (M. Desai, Trans.) Boston, MA: Beacon.

10 Attenborough, R. (Producer/Director), & Briley, J. (Writer). (1982). *Gandhi* [Motion picture]. Hollywood, CA: Columbia Pictures.

11 Annaporna (2013). *Indra Nooyi: A biography.* New Deli: Rajpal & Sons; and Wattles, J. (2017, March 18). Pepsi CEO Indra Nooyi gets big pay bump. *CNN Money.* Retrieved from http://money.cnn.com/2017/03/18/news/companies/pepsi-indra-nooyi/index.html.

12 Mullner, S. (2016, March 30). *Leadership experiential exercise post [LEAD 555].* Malvern, PA: Penn State Great Valley.

13 Dungy, T., & Whitaker, N. (2008). *Quiet strength: The principles, practices & priorities of a winning life.* Carol Stream, IL: Tyndale House; and Dungy, T., & Whitaker, N. (2011). *The one year uncommon life daily challenge.* Carol Stream, IL: Tyndale House.

14 D'Eramo, E. (2016, November 8). *Leadership experiential exercise post [LEAD 555].* Malvern, PA: Penn State Great Valley.

15 United States Air Force (2017). *Core values.* Retrieved from www.airforce.com/mission/vision.

16 Arenas, F. J. (2017, June 19). Personal communication.

17 An interesting account of the Enron corporate scandal can be found in McLean, B., & Elkind, P. (2013). *The smartest guys in the room: The amazing rise and scandalous fall of Enron.* New York: Penguin.

18 Diener, E. (1977). Deindividuation: Causes and consequences. *Social Behavior and Personality, 5,* 143–155.

19 The earliest of our collaborations goes back to work published while we were still doctoral students, namely, Jung, D. I., Bass, B. M., & Sosik, J. J. (1995). Bridging leadership and culture: A theoretical consideration of transformational leadership and collectivistic cultures. *Journal of Leadership Studies, 2*(4), 3–18; and Sosik, J. J., & Jung, D. I. (1994). A theoretical consideration of leadership and the global heterarchy. *Journal of Leadership Studies, 1*(4), 10–27.

20 Estevez, F. J. (2008). A vision of management and leadership (personal communication); and www.dosafl.com/bishop-felipe-j-estevez/.

21 Batson, C. D. (1991). *The altruism question: Toward a social-psychological answer.* Hillsdale, NJ: Lawrence Erlbaum Associates; and Sosik, J. J., Jung, D. I., & Dinger, S. L. (2009). Values in authentic action: Examining the roots and rewards of altruistic leadership. *Group & Organization Management, 34*(41), 395–431.

22 Podsakoff, P. M., & MacKenzie, S. B. (1997). The impact of organizational citizenship behavior on organizational performance: A review and suggestions for future research. *Human Performance, 10,* 133–151.

23 Cameron, K. S., Bright, D., & Caza, A. (2004). Exploring the relationships between organizational virtuousness and performance. *The American Behavioral Scientist, 47,* 766–790; Podsakoff et al. (1997). As cited in Note 22; and Sosik et al. (2009). As cited in Note 21.

24 Sosik, J. J. (2015). *Leading with character: Stories of valor and virtue and the principles they teach* (2nd ed.). Charlotte, NC: Information Age Publishing.

25 Bass, B. M., & Avolio, B. J. (2011). *Multifactor leadership questionnaire: MLQ leader's workbook.* Palo Alto, CA: Mind Garden.

26 Frady, M. (2006). *Jesse: The life and pilgrimage of Jesse Jackson.* New York: Simon & Schuster.

27 Mackey, J. D., Friedlier, R. E., Brees, J. R., & Martinko, M. J. (2015). Abusive supervision: A meta-analysis and empirical review. *Journal of Management, 43*(6), 1940–1965; and Tepper, B. J. (2007). Abusive supervision in work organizations: Review, synthesis, and research agenda. *Journal of Management, 33*(3), 261–289.

28 Naviglia, B. (2016, August 25). *Frustrating challenges at work post [MGMT 507]*. Malvern, PA: Penn State Great Valley.

29 Bandura, A. (1977). *Social learning theory*. Englewood Cliffs, NJ: Prentice Hall; Bass, B. M., & Avolio, B. J. (1994). *Improving organizational effectiveness through transformational leadership*. Thousand Oaks, CA: Sage; and Bedi, A., Alpaslan, C. N., & Green. S. (2016). A meta-analytic review of ethical leadership outcomes and moderators. *Journal of Business Ethics, 139*(3), 517–536.

30 Bass, B. M., & Avolio, B. J. (1990). *Full range leadership development: Basic workshop.* Binghamton, NY: Center for Leadership Studies/SUNY-Binghamton; Blau, P. (1964). *Exchange and power in social life.* New York: Wiley; and Kramer, R. M., & Tyler, T. R. (1996). *Trust in organizations: Frontiers of theory and research.* Thousand Oaks, CA: Sage.

31 Kark, R., Shamir, B., & Chen, G. (2003). The two faces of transformational leadership: Empowerment and dependency. *Journal of Applied Psychology, 88*(2), 246–255.

32 Rest, J., Narvaez, D., Bebeau, M., & Thoma, S. J. (1999). DIT-2: Devising and testing a new instrument of moral judgment. *Journal of Educational Psychology, 91*, 644–659; and Thoma, S. J. (2014). Measuring moral thinking from a neo-Kohlbergian perspective. *Theory and Research in Education, 12*(3), 347–365.

33 Kuhnert, K. W., & Lewis, P. (1987). Transactional and transformational leadership: A constructive/developmental analysis. *The Academy of Management Review, 12*(4), 648–657; Sosik, J. J., Juzbasich, J., & Chun, J. U. (2011). Effects of moral reasoning and management level on ratings of charismatic leadership, in-role and extra-role performance of managers: A multisource examination. *The Leadership Quarterly, 22*(2), 434–450; and Turner, N., Barling, J., Epitropaki, O., Butcher, V., & Milner, C. (2002). Transformational leadership and moral reasoning. *Journal of Applied Psychology, 87*(2), 304–311.

34 Yammarino, E. J., & Atwater, L. E. (1997). Do managers see themselves as others see them? Implications for self-other agreement for human resource management. *Organizational Dynamics, 25*, 35–44.

35 Fleenor, J. W., Smither, J. W., Atwater, L. E., Braddy, P. W., & Sturm, R. E. (2010). Self-other rating agreement in leadership: A review. *The Leadership Quarterly, 21*(6), 1005–1034; Gentry, W. A., & Sosik, J. J. (2010). Developmental relationships and managerial promotability in organizations: A multisource study. *Journal of Vocational Behavior, 77*(2), 266–278; Sosik, J. J., Jung, D. I., Berson, Y., Dionne, S. D., & Jaussi, K. S. (2004). *The dream weavers: Strategy-focused leadership in technology-driven organizations* (p. 230). Charlotte, NC: Information Age Publishing; and Yammarino & Atwater (1997). As cited in Note 34.

36 Banks, G. C., MacCualey, K. D., Gardner, W. L., & Guler, C. E. (2016). A meta-analytic review of authentic and transformational leadership: A test for redundancy. *The Leadership Quarterly, 27*(4), 634–652; George, B. (2003). *Authentic leadership: Rediscovering the secrets to creating lasting value.* San Francisco, CA: Jossey-Bass; www.authleadership.com/about-the-institute; www.authenticleadershipinc.com/; and www.billgeorge.org/authentic-leadership.

Chapter 4

Inspirational Motivation

The Emotional Side of Transformational Leadership

Several years ago, during the first day of the Full Range Leadership Development (FRLD) course, a confident executive MBA student stood up and made a bold statement. He said, "John, I'm expecting nothing less from this class than a Saul of Tarsus transformation!" And John wouldn't have expected anything less challenging from Philip O'Reilly, who, at the time, was a swashbuckling CEO of an entrepreneurial firm specializing in mergers and acquisitions. Phil's positive attitude, intelligence, and enthusiasm inspired many business associates and friends. His gregarious and charming personality added to his love for adventure in all aspects of his life. Phil would often take colleagues and friends scuba diving or on rides in his small-craft airplanes. His zest for life and risk-taking behavior were apparent whether he was talking to his employees about his Multifactor Leadership Questionnaire (MLQ) results or charting the course for his next business venture or airplane glider trip.

Today, Philip O'Reilly is world-wide vice president of Switching, Routing, and Analytics at Extreme Networks, a San Jose, California, developer of Ethernet computer network technology. Prior to his current role, Phil spent several years as vice president of sales at Brocade Communications Systems and Juniper Networks, both California-based tech companies. In his present role, Phil has excelled at inspiring sales growth and partnering with other organizations to provide more "green solutions" for customers.[1] These organizations are going through a digital transformation of their legacy IT systems to more energy- and cost-efficient technologies. For example, Brocade provides products that improve processing efficiencies by a factor of 6, strengthen cybersecurity, and reduce total costs of operation between 20–40%.[2] This efficient solution provides outstanding platforms for innovation and energy conservation/management, and demonstrates sustainability practices and corporate social responsibility. Like O'Reilly's passion for airplanes, his visionary leadership for providing efficient eco-friendly data infrastructures is boosting sales and profits to ever higher levels.

Airplane pilots, like O'Reilly, are responsible for leading their craft from point A to point B. But airplanes do not fly in a vacuum. Rather, they fly in turbulent environments that include unpredictable weather conditions, strong airstreams, and wind shears. So if a pilot simply aimed his plane for point B (see Figure 4.1) without accounting for drift from down winds, his plane would veer off course

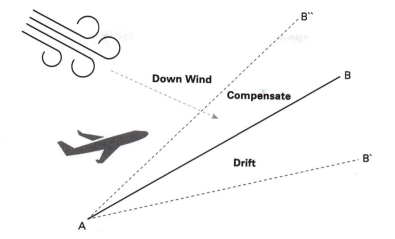

Figure 4.1
Charting the
right course.
Like airplane
pilots, leaders
must set their
sights on the
right path for
their followers
to take.
saravector /
Shutterstock.
com; LovArt /
Shutterstock.
com

to point B' and he would miss his target destination. That's why pilots often compensate for such down winds by aiming for point B", as shown in Figure 4.1.

Just as pilots need to make adjustments to reach their targeted destination, so too must leaders in order for their associates to achieve their vision. Leaders must have the ability to adapt to changing conditions. As Viktor Frankl once said,

> If we take man as he is, realistically, we make him worse due to drifts or detriments in him or his environment. However, if we take him as he should be, optimistically, we help him to become what he can be.[3]

If we apply these words of wisdom to leadership development, then leaders need to elevate their followers' expectations by inspiring them to work together toward a challenging and evocative vision. This requires leaders to aim for the ideal, seek virtue, and promote the greatness that lies dormant in followers who are capable of collaboration and professional development. In essence, this requires leaders to display inspirational motivation.

To better understand the notion of inspirational motivation, think of a time in your life that you were truly inspired by someone or something. Maybe you were inspired by how he overcame a significant challenge in his life. Maybe it was because of the courage he showed under tremendous pressure. Or perhaps it was his idea that resonated with you. Whatever it was, think about what it felt like to be truly inspired. Chances are that when you were inspired, you felt invigorated and energized. You felt enthusiastic and optimistic. You probably were filled with a sense of righteousness in your convictions that gave you a high level of confidence. That's because the word *inspire* comes from the Latin meaning "to breathe into." And when our bodies are refreshed with life-sustaining oxygen, we become energized in our thoughts, words, and deeds.

One of the most important roles you need to play as a transformational leader is to trigger motivation among your followers through inspiration. Inspiration is the heart of transformational leadership and it involves the following three key concepts:

- *Transcendence*—Inspiration is a response to an idea, object, person, or situation. The source of inspiration moves followers through an appreciation of beauty and excellence that allows them to rise above ordinary preoccupations or limitations. Followers experience self-transcendent emotions as they recognize the intrinsic value of what they perceive to be beautiful or excellent, and worthy of emulation, creation or actualization.
- *Evocation*—You cannot force inspiration on someone through an act of will; instead, inspiration is evoked from within or through significant others (e.g., leaders) and their environment. What is evoked within followers adds to the intrinsic value of the source of inspiration as it does with transcendence.
- *Motivation*—Inspiration provides energy and direction that fuels the action of followers. This fueling of followers' action allows them to bring the idea, words, or vision of the inspiring qualities to life. Followers are able to act as the transmission mechanism that extends what was evoked in them to others. Being a vessel of an inspirational vision is extremely enjoyable and meaningful to most people.[4]

These feelings and positive attitudes are commonly associated with the followers of visionary leaders such as Jack Ma of Alibaba Group, Sheryl Sandburg of Facebook, and Richard Branson of Virgin. Each of these transformational leaders knows how to inspire followers in a variety of ways. Since they see a brighter future that no one else sees, they openly challenge their followers by expressing their dissatisfaction with the status quo. But being discontented with the status quo is not enough for these leaders. They are also able to present a viable alternative to the current situation in a way that inspires others to work to achieve their vision. They reinforce their message of change through their language, which is filled with dynamic metaphors and colorful rhetoric (described later).

They also create unique ceremonies and rituals that symbolize their organization's purpose in working to achieve a vision worth pursuing. Such rituals include regularly scheduled "town meetings" that reiterate the company mission, vision, and values. Others include monthly birthday celebrations for staff, company picnics, sporting events, or award ceremonies that recognize employees for their key contributions for working toward the vision. These practices create magnetic imagery that inspires their followers and constituents to make the vision a reality. For example, former Microsoft CEO Steve Balmer once danced wildly around the stage while shouting as he kicked off a company rally. Balmer then stood in front of the podium and said, "I have four words for you. I LOVE THIS COMPANY."[5] His energy and passion inspired the audience of employees. His unconventional CEO behavior illustrates what inspirational motivation is all about.

This chapter shows you how to inspire your associates, teams, and organization to soar to new heights of success. By elevating expectations and boosting collective confidence through the power of teamwork, you can become an inspirational leader. Let's begin to learn about this process by considering the behaviors of inspirational motivation.

Inspirational Motivation: Definition and Examples

Inspirational motivation involves the energy, initiative, persistence, and vision that moves followers to achieve performance outcomes that exceed expectations and develops their leadership potential along the way. This high level of motivation comes from a message that gives meaning to what they aim to accomplish. It makes followers' work important to them because they see how their work contributes toward achieving the vision. Displaying inspirational motivation behaviors is a skill in which Jack Ma excels (see Box 4.1).

Box 4.1 Leader Profile: Jack Ma

How could a former bicycle tour guide who once was turned down for 30 different jobs and rejected ten times by Harvard University ever go on to become a world-famous billionaire, entrepreneur, and technology visionary? Ask Jack Ma, CEO of the Alibaba Group, the world's largest retailer and online marketing company. In college, Ma was trained as a teacher and has used his ability to communicate ideas confidently and effectively in his leadership position.

Ma is well known for his vision of creating an e-commerce company that handles small business sales between importers and exporters in over 240 countries. With Alibaba's market capitalization being $378 billion as of July 2017, Ma has plenty to boast about after surpassing Walmart and Amazon in financial performance. But Ma is more interested in envisioning what workplaces and trade will look like in the future. Ma foresees a decline in the prominence of companies like Apple, Alphabet (Google), and Amazon, with an upswing in small businesses supported by advanced technologies provided by companies like Alibaba. He also envisions great opportunities for American products and manufacturing helping to feed Chinese demand. A cautious champion of artificial intelligence in the workplace, Ma expects the growing adoption of this technology to allow people to work only four hours a day four days a week. He warns that the current technology revolution needs to be tempered by paying more attention to educational systems. By educating people about what machines can do better than people, and vice versa, Ma imagines the quality of life and wellbeing of people being vastly improved.

According to Ma, the secret to his success is a positive attitude, foresight, and tenacity. He uses these traits to hire highly skilled people and enthusiastically unite them under a single goal. The ability to dream and imagine possibilities that others dare not to has helped Ma to create and articulate several visions for his extraordinary success.

Ma's life teaches us the importance of persevering to overcome personal setbacks and having a goal that is worth pursuing. Have the courage to overcome personal and professional challenges, dream big, talk confidently, and act boldly. That's the essence of inspirational motivation.[6]

Like Ma, you need to demonstrate inspirational motivation behaviors to be seen as a transformational leader by your followers. Let's now examine five key transformational leadership behaviors that embody inspirational motivation.

Talk Optimistically About the Future

After losing the 2016 U.S. presidential election to Donald Trump, you'd think that Hillary Clinton would be depressed and lack any kind of optimism about the future. But this was not the case, as Clinton vowed to fight on and champion her political beliefs. She showed her true grit in a speech she gave to the graduating class of Wellesley College in May 2017. In her speech, Clinton highlighted the many issues facing the graduates and challenged them to double-down on their beliefs and stand up for what they believe is right. She began by talking about the many "alternative facts" that sow divisions among us that run rampant on social media. She then linked the ideal of free and open debate back to the days of the Enlightenment and the democratic political beginnings of the United States. She ended her speech with an inspiring challenge:

> Wherever you have set your sights, raise them even higher . . . Do it for truth and reason . . . it's often during the darkest times when you can do the most good . . . Try, fail, try again, and lean on each other. Hold on to your values. Never give up on those dreams.[7]

Her optimistic message added substance to Clinton's style, although some detractors claim that she lacks charisma. According to her supporters, Clinton's effective speaking skills are in part due to her sincere message of hope, perseverance, and a brighter future for the country. In fact, political pundits have remarked that Clinton's achievements conjure up images of great civil and women's rights icons such as Susan B. Anthony, Elizabeth Cady Stanton, and Shirley Chisholm. Clinton's words also build upon a message of optimism echoed by President John F. Kennedy, who once remarked that "The American, by nature, is optimistic. He is experimental, an inventor and builder who builds the best when called upon to build greatly . . ." The core messages of each of these leaders were infused with optimism.[8]

By keeping the message positive and optimistic, transformational leaders motivate their followers through positive psychological states that are intrinsically motivating and satisfying. A message that satisfies intrinsically does not necessary depend upon any tangible outcome or success that followers will get to enjoy. Rather, the knowledge of working toward a noble goal is satisfaction in and of itself. In other words, the gift is in the giving. When people are in pursuit of any goal and what's driving them is internally focused, outcomes are likely to be more successful and effective. This is what academics call intrinsic motivation.

Positive psychological states, such as "being in the zone" or in "flow," generate several beneficial outcomes, such as increased persistence, creativity, and productivity. In addition, research has linked *positive psychological capital*, a related concept that includes hope, optimism, self-confidence, and resilience, to high levels of performance and satisfaction in several business contexts. These

Figure 4.2
The power
of positive
speaking.
Sandra Postel,
director and
founder of the
Global Water
Policy Project,
speaking at
the GreenBiz
Forum in
2017. Image
by Gage
Skidmore.

motivational forces encourage followers to work hard to overcome difficulties and crises. As depicted in Figure 4.2, such significant effort advocated in speeches is often required to change the status quo and perform beyond expectations.[9]

When was the last time that you talked about an exciting future of your team? Have you communicated with your followers about what needs to be done to make your team's future brighter? Have you ever cheered on your team to share your vision and accomplish more? To be an inspirational leader, these are some behaviors you need to practice.

Talk Enthusiastically About What Needs to Be Accomplished

Elaina held the position of chief coordinator of conference services at a large center city hotel. Her position required her to be a liaison with current and potential corporate customers. This was a very demanding, time-consuming, and emotionally laborious role to play. Despite her hectic and challenging schedule, Elaina always found time to get involved in important hotel initiatives such as diversity awareness and promotion of events. Those who knew and enjoyed working with Elaina were amazed by her seemingly eternal enthusiasm. She was always very excited about the work her group was performing. Her exuberance for the challenges her group faced energized the members of her group and created a positive attitude that they shared.

Elaina told us that her enthusiasm came from her difficult childhood. She was the product of a dysfunctional family and suffered as a victim of various types of abuse within her family. Instead of becoming bitter, she worked out any issues that stemmed from her upbringing. She was determined to hold a positive attitude no matter how bad her circumstances were. As if she were living on borrowed time, she resolved to live each day as if it was her last with a *vigorous love of life,*

Figure 4.3
A zest for life.
Inspirational leaders are determined and have a strong will that motivates them to go the extra mile.

as depicted in Figure 4.3. She explained that when you love someone, you are willing to give everything. When you are willing to give everything, you give your all in an enthusiastic and energetic way.

However, there always seem to be people who attempt to extinguish the fire that fuels the enthusiasm of transformational leaders. How can transformational leaders maintain their enthusiasm in the face of difficult people and situations? Elaina answered this question for us by saying that she tries hard to let go of trying to control other people. She only has control over herself—her thoughts, attitudes, and behaviors. She controls her attitude by continuously infusing it with enthusiasm. When Elaina's associates see her enthusiasm, they are inspired to also become enthusiastic about the things that need to be accomplished. Elaina's can-do attitude inspires rather than controls her followers. They rally around challenging work she presents as important and meaningful, rather than a task on a to-do list that needs to be checked off.

Just like Elaina, many transformational leaders are passionate and enthusiastic. Their energy becomes contagious to their followers. Jack Welch once said that to be a successful leader, you need to have "four Es wrapped in P." The first E stands for energy. The second E stands for energizing people. The third E stands for edge to make a decision decisively. The last E stands for execution. All of these Es are surrounded by P, which stands for Passion.[10] So, passion, energy, and enthusiasm are important elements of leadership according to Jack Welch. Based on our research and consulting experience, we can't argue with him.

Articulate a Compelling Vision of the Future
As you read in Chapter 2, leadership is a dynamic system that evolves over time. Leaders who wish to inspire others must link the past with the present and future.[11]

Former U.S. president Barack Obama did this in his 2008 inaugural address, and when he modeled his cabinet after Abraham Lincoln's "team of rivals." In 2017, German Chancellor Angela Merkel paid tribute to former Chancellor Helmut Kohl who spearheaded the unification of East and West Germany in 1990, and today Germany is a powerful force within Europe. Vladimir Putin fashioned his vision for Russia in an old-fashioned European sense infused with strong nationalism. When running for president, Hillary Clinton drew upon her earlier work as former First Lady to fight for the health care and wellbeing of children. Why do such leaders link the past, present, and future?

Fulton J. Sheen, philosopher, theologian, and seminal televangelist, once gave a fascinating talk with implications highlighting the importance of presenting a compelling vision of the future so that followers can understand their place in the larger picture. He began by talking about the notion of time being understood as the relationship between the past, present, and future.[12] Let's examine each element of time in Sheen's lecture to understand its relevance to inspirational leadership shown by many of today's top leaders.

What is the significance of *the past* for leadership? The past is important and should not be ignored. That's because the past is the source of traditions, history, customs, culture, or what organizational scholars call institutional memory. These aspects of the past give leaders and followers a sense of who they are and where they came from. Transformational leaders often remind followers of the great achievements in the past so that they can feel good about themselves and the rich tradition of which they are a part. We often see this in artifacts in collegiate and professional sporting arenas (e.g., the Los Angeles Coliseum), and U.S. military leadership training materials, such as those shown in Figure 4.4. Or, the past can be used as a negative example that a leader can remind people to stay away from or need to overcome. Either way, the past can provide a leader with a base from which he can challenge followers of the present to work toward a brighter future described in the vision.

What is the significance of *the present* for leadership? The present is important because it reflects where leaders and followers are at this point in time. The now has its challenges and opportunities and particular circumstances. To make the most of the now, psychologists often advise people to live in the moment and seize the day. By making the most of the present, we are able to derive intrinsic satisfaction from where we are currently since our future is uncertain and the past is already gone. A challenging present is often needed for inspirational leaders to create and articulate their vision of a better future.

What is the significance of *the future* for leadership? The past and present cannot be comprehended without an understanding of the future. Suppose you are traveling by train from Philadelphia to New York. At any point in time on your journey, the way you describe your travels is in terms of your final destination (e.g., "I'm in Trenton now en route to New York"). The same is true for leadership. The way you describe your leadership goal or destination is with a vision of the future. One reason that makes transformational leadership special and more effective than other leadership styles is that the vision transformational leaders develop is radically different from the status quo (i.e., the present).

28ID History... A short history of a storied & renowned Division

The 28th Infantry Division (28ID) and the PA National Guard trace their lineage back to the militia organized by Benjamin Franklin in 1747 known as the "Associators". Franklin organized artillery and infantry units to defend the city of Philadelphia against French and Spanish privateers. The first meeting of the Associators occurred on November 21, 1747 and on December 7, 1747 the enlistees and officers were formally commissioned by the Provincial Council President, Anthony Palmer. On that day, hundreds of armed Associators presented themselves to Palmer at the Philadelphia Courthouse and he wisely stated their activities were "not disapproved" and duly commissioned all of them.

The 28ID is the oldest continuously serving Division in the United States Army. On March 12, 1879, Governor Henry Hoyt signed General Order No. 1 appointing MG John Hartranft as the first Division Commander of the National Guard of Pennsylvania, and the most storied and renowned Division in the history of the US Army was born. The keystone was prescribed as the designated symbol of the National Guard of Pennsylvania on August 27, 1879.

The Division was mustered into service for the Spanish-American War in 1898, and 3 regiments, 3 artillery batteries, and 3 cavalry troops were deployed for service. In 1916 the Division, then designated the 7th Division, was mustered into service and deployed to El Paso, TX to serve along the Mexican Border.

In response to WWI, the Division was drafted into federal service on August 5, 1917, and trained at Camp Hancock, Georgia. While in Georgia, the Division was reorganized as the 28ID on October 11, 1917. After arriving in France, the 28ID gained fame as a result of its gallant stand on July 15, 1918. As the Division took up defensive positions along the Marne River east of Chateau-Thierry, the Germans commenced their attack with a fierce artillery bombardment. When the German assault collided with the main force of the 28ID, the fighting became bitter hand to hand combat. The 28ID repelled the German forces and decisively defeated their enemy. After the battle, General John Pershing, Commander of the American Expeditionary Force, visited the battlefield and declared that the 28ID Soldiers are "Men of Iron" and named the 28ID his "Iron Division". The 28ID developed a red keystone-shaped shoulder patch, officially adopted October 27, 1918.

History continued on back panel...

History continued from inside ...

The 28ID was mobilized in preparation for WWII on February 1, 1941. The first Soldiers of the 28ID stepped ashore at Omaha Beach on July 22, 1944. On August 29, 1944, the 28ID had the honor of being the first American Division to parade through Paris, and later fought across Northern France into Germany. As the 28ID breached the formidable Westwall of the German defenses in September 1944, SSG Francis Clark from the 109th IN, earned the Medal of Honor. The 28ID fought valiantly in the Huertgen Forest, disrupted the German counter-offensive during the Battle of the Bulge, and eventually liberated Colmar, France from the grip of the German military. The 28ID crossed the Rhine and took up positions in the Ruhr Pocket to stop any German forces driving south, and was in those positions when the fighting in Europe came to an end.

During the Korean War, the 28ID was mobilized and deployed to Europe as a part of the NATO command defending Western Europe from the threat of Soviet attack. The 28ID mobilized on September 5, 1950 and remained in federal service until May 22, 1953.

The Soldiers of the 28ID have continued to make history since September 11, 2001. The Division has conducted operations in places including Bosnia, Kosovo, The Sinai, Kuwait, Iraq, and Afghanistan. Many 28ID Soldiers have made the ultimate sacrifice, and hundreds have been recognized for their dedicated service and valor. The 28ID continues to build on its legacy as the Iron Division and 28ID Warriors take pride in being fit, resilient, and well trained in order to support each other and defend our great Nation.

28ID Song

We're the 28th men and we're out to fight again
for the good old U.S.A.
We're the guys who know where to strike the blow
and you'll know just why after we say:

Roll On, 28th ... Roll On, set the pace
Hold the banners high and raise the cry,
We're off to victory!
Let the Keystone shine right down the line
for all the world to see.

When we meet the foe we'll let them know
we're Iron Infantry,
So Roll On, 28th, Roll On!

28th Infantry Division

MG John L. Gronski
28ID Commanding General

CSM Christopher Kepner
28ID Command Sergeant Major

Iron Division !

Roll On !

28ID Soldier's Creed

The 28ID Soldier can do anything.
There is no challenge that is too great for us.
There is no difficulty that we cannot overcome.
Roll On!

Follow the 28th Infantry Division Online

 http://pa.ng.mil/ARNG/28ID

 www.facebook.com/28thID

 Follow the CG   @28IDCG

Follow the CSM @28IDCSM

28ID Commander's Intent

Purpose: Win when deployed overseas & successfully support DSCA missions here at home.

Key Tasks: We will accomplish this by focusing on nine (9) key tasks (Iron Imperatives) along four (4) lines of effort:

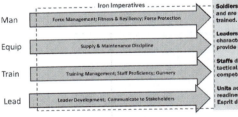

Iron Imperatives

Man — Force Management; Fitness & Resiliency; Force Protection

Equip — Supply & Maintenance Discipline

Train — Training Management; Staff Proficiency; Gunnery

Lead — Leader Development; Communicate to Stakeholders

End State:

Soldiers exemplify Army Values and are fit, resilient, and highly trained.

Leaders exhibit trust, character, competence, and provide direction.

Staffs display technical, tactical, and operational competence.

Units achieve high levels of readiness, camaraderie & Esprit de Corps.

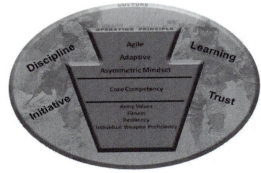

28ID CG Guidance

Every leader is trusted and expected to use disciplined initiative within the commander's intent without wasting time requesting permission. Report up as the situation develops. Request further guidance or support as necessary. *Demonstrating a high level of initiative is worth the risk of making honest mistakes.*

Units will conduct challenging, realistic, battle focused training. Units will train to deploy, fight, sustain itself, and win against complex state and non-state threats in austere environments and rugged terrain (expeditionary mindset).

Mitigate risk by ensuring Soldiers are well trained, rather than implementing artificial measures a Soldier would not encounter in the operational environment.

All Soldiers will train in their core competency based on their MOS or position at least 50% of the time over the course of a training year.

28ID CSM Guidance

The Iron Division Soldier is a fit, resilient, and well trained professional that is ready to deploy, dominate, and win decisively in a complex operational environment.

Non Commissioned Officers are obligated to keep our Soldiers safe; we do that by enforcing standards.

Non Commissioned Officers are the primary trainers of our Soldiers.

Non Commissioned Officers and Soldiers are trained at the appropriate level of NCOES before they are promoted.

Non Commissioned Officers are everywhere our soldiers are; we will take back the barracks.

Non Commissioned Officers will not allow suicide or sexual harassment/assault to happen in our Division, our Brigades, our Battalions, our Companies, our Platoons, our Squads, and our Teams.

The Iron Division Non Commissioned Officer is a standards based professional who enable fit, resilient, and well trained soldiers to dominate and win decisively in a complex operational environment.

For example, Pope Saint John Paul II presented a very compelling vision of Poland transcending the ills of Communism. His vision included restoring traditional Polish values that had been taken away by the Communists. It also contained spiritual, social, and economic elements that improved upon the past.[13] He wanted his followers to embrace the future, while respecting the past.

However, some people reject the past and future and focus on getting the most out of the present. According to Sheen, they want to maximize their pleasure by intensifying the present through short-term rewards or "getting kicks." Their mentality is that the past is useless and the future is too uncertain. Only the present matters. We believe that this present-obsessed attitude is sadly too common today in many companies. We've seen it in the failures of Lehman Brothers, Bearn Stearns, Merrill Lynch, and Fannie Mae.[14] But perhaps this was best exemplified by the way Enron executives lived their corporate and personal lives, which was illustrated well in the documentary entitled *Enron: The Smartest Guys in the Room.*[15] The constant competition among Enron employees in the workplace to outperform each other was due to a survival of the fittest culture (a form of Social Darwinism) where the least effective employees are fired. The Enron philosophy was that there is no need to focus on the future since the present is so ecstatic, and the present is the only thing that matters. This phenomenon is intensified by corporate myopia on maximizing short-term profits and satisfying the analysts on Wall Street.

So, what kind of vision do you have for your team or organization? Is it compelling enough for your team members to accept it willingly? How will you share your vision in a way that excites them? To make your vision more appealing to your followers like the one in Figure 4.4, consider the following points. First, visions must be inspirational and contain shared values that are important to followers. For example, the values of innovation and collaboration have always been ideals that Steve Jobs promoted at Apple. Second, visions need to be challenging enough to stretch followers out of their comfort zones, but also achievable to have motivating power. Third, the language describing visions must use superior imagery that touches followers' emotions. Fourth, the vision must be well articulated. It is one thing to draft a brilliant speech. It is another to be able to deliver it in a passionate and sincere way that moves people. We will discuss this topic in more detail later.

Provide an Exciting Image of What Is Essential to Consider

Inspiring your followers to work together toward a common vision is quite challenging. That's because they possess different personal agendas and strong egos. One way to find common ground among such followers is to focus on the content of the vision and make it evocative and appealing to followers. Richard Branson has effectively used this behavior over his career. Despite some setbacks, Branson has continued to challenge a group of scientists and engineers to help achieve the vision of Virgin Galactic: to provide affordable suborbital space tourism for the first time in history. In February 2016, they unveiled their new SpaceShipTwo, named the VSS Unity.[16]

What an amazing spaceship and exciting and bold vision! Branson's vision for Virgin Galactic is thrilling because it demonstrates a revolutionary change in our

Figure 4.4 (opposite) Major General John L. Gronski's command philosophy. Notice the linking of values, vision, mission, and expected leadership behaviors. Image by John L. Gronski and Christopher Kepner. Reprinted with Permission.

perception of space travel. Traditionally, we have thought of space travel as being limited to NASA or government agencies. Branson has extended the boundaries of our perception of space travel to include ordinary citizens. According to theoretical physicist Stephen Hawking, Branson is "a man with the vision and persistence to open up space flight for ordinary, earth-bound citizens, [who has] made it his mission to make space flight a reality for those intrepid enough to venture beyond the boundaries of the Earth's atmosphere . . . If I am able to go – and if Richard will still take me, I would be very proud to fly on this spaceship."[17]

Who wouldn't want to be part of the team working to attain this exhilarating vision? Nevertheless, leading a team of brilliant professionals working on this project will be a challenge given human nature's competitive drive and innate self-interest. Fortunately, human nature also has the capacity for altruism, collaboration, and self-sacrifice. Therefore, you need to find a way to energize followers so that you can tap into the positive aspects of human nature. Transformational leaders inspire followers by pointing out what is most important and essential for achieving the vision, as shown in Figure 4.5.

There are many competing goals and objectives in organizations today. There are many projects that you and your followers often find on your plate. This can cause stress, lack of direction, and conflicts over limited resources within work groups. To be effective, leaders must prioritize what tasks are most important for followers to work on and explain to them why their completion is essential to achieving the overall vision. An evocative vision that is described in a colorful and appealing way will convince followers what they should focus on at the present. Such focus is essential for completing important tasks.

The tasks at hand at Amazon include providing home services in addition to products, enabling homes connected to the internet with Amazon Echo and Alexa, offering Prime Air and drone delivery of their products, and delivering fresh

Figure 4.5
Let's focus on this. Inspirational leaders show followers what is essential to achieve by clearly communicating the organizational vision.

groceries and specialties from local stores. The vision of Amazon's founder, Jeff Bezos, is to empower consumers to seamlessly integrate their online and offline lives through his reinvention of e-commerce. Bezos is known for his no-nonsense, tough style of leadership. Many of his followers find his style too challenging to tolerate. But he uses his compelling vision to compensate for his toughness and motivate his followers to meet any challenges. So far, Bezos' vision has Amazon's employees focused and their customers wondering what other exciting experiences will come next.[18] So, the important questions you need to ask are: What is most important for your followers to focus on now in your organization? How can you convince them of its importance? What can you do to sharpen their focus?

Express Confidence That Goals Will Be Achieved

When you communicate a compelling but challenging vision with your followers, the next important step is to assure them that goals will be achieved through collective effort. Otherwise, your followers will not even try to attain your vision. Therefore, it is very important to raise your followers' perception of their ability to meet any challenges and attain your vision. This self-perceived confidence a person possesses in the ability to perform a specific task is called *self-efficacy*. When this confidence is shared among members of a group (e.g., "We can do this"), it is called *group potency*, which describes the group's collective perception of its general effectiveness.[19] Transformational leaders build these important motivational forces for their followers, as shown in Figure 4.6.

One important reason that you should increase collective confidence among your followers before or while you work on achieving a challenging vision is uncertainty. No matter how well you articulate your vision for the future, it will entail lots of uncertainty and resistance because it is radically different from the

Figure 4.6
We can do it. Potent teams possess a can-do attitude and put effort into their tasks to get the job done.

status quo. Achieving a vision is all about motivating people to step out of their comfort zone and work toward a better future. When a leader displays such personal confidence, it helps followers get over their fear of navigating unknown and unchartered paths.

Thus, successful transformational leaders try to elevate the confidence levels of their followers and work groups in three different ways. First, they provide followers with experiences that demonstrate their effectiveness. Such experiences may be small tasks or projects that get progressively more complicated. Achieving small victories can boost confidence and performance on more difficult tasks. For example, Brian is a sales manager at Cisco Systems. Brian shared with us a series of emails he sent to Matt, an associate he was coaching for a big presentation to senior management. In his emails, Brian reminded Matt of the important tasks he would have to successfully complete in preparation for his presentation. Brian sent follow-up emails congratulating Matt as he completed each task. The practice and words of encouragement and congratulations boosted Matt's confidence as he prepared for presentation.

Second, leaders try to build confidence through vicarious experiences where they point out examples of similar people who were successful. Vicarious experiences involve trying to boost a follower's self-confidence by saying something like "if Tom can do this project, so can you!" If you use this process, make sure that you highlight the similarities between the exemplar and the person you are trying to persuade. Brian also used this approach in his emails. Brian described for Matt several similar situations he experienced and the presentation and reasoning approaches Brian had successfully used in the past. This sharing of experience and knowledge boosted Matt's confidence and ability.

Third, leaders build confidence by using rational arguments to persuade followers and groups that they can be successful. Brian carefully described for Matt the reasons why he would be prepared for the presentation. Brian backed up his statements with evidence of Matt's prior successes on the small tasks and prior presentations. He pointed out that Matt's strengths were exactly those required for the upcoming presentation. Brian then told Matt that he was learning the best strategies for success. In the end, Matt wowed the audience with an exceptional presentation that generated a profitable contract with the customer. Most importantly, Brian was there for Matt during and after the presentation to see the results of his inspirational motivation. By continually expressing the confidence that goals can be achieved, you too can inspire your followers to focus on the task and direct their energies toward achieving your organization's vision.

Rationale for and Effects of Inspirational Motivation

Now that we've introduced the concept of inspirational motivation to you, we'd like you to understand why it is important and what effects it can have on your followers. Inspirational motivation is important because it helps mobilize followers' efforts to work on something important and achieve much more than they normally do. In other words, it energizes your followers to accept and share your vision and values. The joy that is derived from a meaningful task related to an organization's vision is highly satisfying. If followers view their work as fun-filled sources of learning, they may joyfully view their tasks as less work and more play. This experienced joy can enhance aspects of followers' psychological wellbeing including positive emotions, life satisfaction, zestful living, and self-actualization. People who are inspired often work with high levels of efficiency and productivity. Such personal effectiveness in work tasks can contribute to the overall effectiveness of the organization. So, the extent to which you can create an environment that blends inspiration, work, play, and learning can help followers to be better contributors to your organization.[20]

Inspirational motivation can produce several positive effects on followers. The intrinsic value of the work required to attain the vision makes followers more willing to try harder when performing their tasks. Because they are inspired, followers see themselves as transmitters of the inherent values of truth, beauty, and goodness that they consider the vision to encompass. Inspirational motivation also makes followers willing to exert extra effort at work. This elevated level of motivation comes from the sense that one is contributing to a worthwhile collective goal that transcends the self. So, inspiration and effort, both required for attaining a vision, can reinforce each other in an upward spiral of positive emotion.[21]

Charisma as an Important Foundation of Inspirational Motivation: Pros and Cons

When it comes to inspiring people, we oftentimes think of charisma. So, let's now consider charisma as a form of delivering inspirational motivation. Followers who are inspired and motivated by charismatic leaders become mesmerized by their words, images, and actions.[22] These followers see their leader as possessing a great amount of charisma. When most people hear the word *charisma*, they conjure up images of a strong leader possessing personal charm and having a way with words that makes people feel special. In fact, some people think that charisma is a gift from God that resides in the leader. That's because one of the first places we find the word *charisma* is in the New Testament (1 Corinthians 12:8–10). Here, St. Paul talks about the spiritual gifts of wisdom, knowledge, faith, healing, miracles, prophecy, discerning of spirits, speaking in tongues, and interpretation of tongues. These gifts represented extraordinary abilities bestowed unto the disciples of Jesus Christ. As a result of these gifts, the disciples gained new courage and confidence in their mission during the early days of the Church.

However, this notion of charismatic gifts residing in the leader is not consistent with current thinking on the topic. Sociologist Max Weber pointed out that charisma does not reside solely in the leader. Instead, charisma depends on the followers as well as the leader and can be intensified in times of crisis. The locus of charisma is in the leader and his emotional relationship with the follower during times that demand change. What matters most is how the followers feel about the leader and what special qualities they attribute to the leader. Charisma does not reside in traditional or formal authority or in ordinary exchange relationships with followers, but in followers' perceptions of the leader as being special. Thus, charisma is in "the eye of the beholder" when followers endow an extraordinary or magical quality, popularity, or celebrity status to the leader. Think about the amount of charisma associated with Clint Eastwood, Marlon Brando, Ed Harris, Denzel Washington, Meryl Streep, Angelina Jolie, or George Clooney in the arts and entertainment field. These charismatic leaders shape their image and emotional bond with the followers through their own energy, self-confidence, assertiveness, ambition, and seizing of opportunities.

Charismatic leadership often comes about in times of great distress. Followers look for a leader who can make sense out of stressful situations and crises. Charismatic leaders emerge with a radical vision offering a solution to these dilemmas. Their solutions attract followers who believe in the vision, especially if they experience some early successes in overcoming the crisis and make progress toward attaining the vision. As a result, followers come to perceive the leader as extraordinary. The bigger the crisis, the more the disturbance becomes emotional, and the more such emotionality can be invested in the charismatic leader who is perceived as "the savior."[23] Remember, a leader's self-confidence will play a big role in eliminating fear among followers while they are pursuing the leader's challenging vision. Charisma will surely add more confidence in this process.

Indeed, charismatic leaders yield immense influence and get strong emotional reactions from people. People either love them or hate them. That's why so many assassination attempts have been carried out on charismatic leaders over the years (e.g., John F. Kennedy, Robert Kennedy, Martin Luther King Jr., Malcolm X, John Lennon, Yitzhak Rabin, Saint Pope John Paul II, and Benazir Bhutto).

Therefore, you can think of charisma as a form of influence exerted on a follower's emotional involvement and commitment. Charismatic leaders are known to inspire their followers because they present themselves as being dominant, self-confident, having a high need for power, and possessing strong convictions in the moral rightness of their beliefs. The presentation of this image in turn arouses followers' motives for achievement, affiliation, and power. It also increases followers' intrinsic motivation by linking the followers' self-concept with the mission advocated by the leader. This strong influence causes followers to go the extra mile for charismatic leaders, albeit sometimes down a path that should not be taken.

Unfortunately, charisma can also bring about negative outcomes. First, being in awe of the leader reduces the number of good suggestions offered by followers. This makes followers dependent on the leader and can promote an unhealthy group-think mentality within the organization. As psychologist Irving Janis pointed out, group-think occurs when emphasis is placed on maintaining solidarity within the group at the expense of quality of the discussion.[24] You have probably seen this emerge during meetings at work where subordinates use ingratiation tactics to "butter up" the boss, speak only when spoken to, and never disagree with the boss in meetings. What long-term effects do you think this has on followers and the leader?

Second, the desire for being accepted by the leader inhibits any criticism that followers may have for the leader. A lack of appropriate criticism can fuel the narcissistic flames of charismatic leaders with hubris and a sense of invulnerability. Such excessive confidence and optimism on the part of the leader and followers can blind the leader to real dangers that lurk in the environment. Narcissistic leaders who carry on unchecked can quickly turn into monsters as well.[25] How many times have we witnessed a situation where followers who inhibited their criticism of a narcissistic leader in public spend many hours privately venting about the leader, only to waste time and help fan the flames of the dysfunctional culture that they were trying to extinguish? What is the price followers pay for a desire at all costs to be accepted by a charismatic leader?

Third, many charismatic leaders take complete credit for their organization's successes. This can alienate some key followers who are essential for creating the real success. Followers like to be recognized for their contributions to the collective achievements. When they are denied such recognition, they grow resentful of the leader and dissent starts to emerge within the ranks. For example, Carly Fiorina, the charismatic former CEO of Hewlett-Packard and Republican presidential candidate, was faulted for her self-promotional style of leadership and excessive careerism. Followers viewed her message as "all about Carly and not about HP." What can you do to ensure that you share the credit with your followers so that you do not fall victim to the perils of charismatic leadership?

Fourth, the impulsive nontraditional behaviors associated with being a charismatic leader can create enemies as well as supporters. Consistency of words and actions with organizational traditions and culture can inspire followers to work to achieve the mission. However, when charismatic leaders stray too far asunder from traditions and customs, they can fall out of favor with some less accepting colleagues. It is human nature to like those who are similar to us and be suspicious of those who are different. This is what happened in the case of minister and human rights activist Malcolm X, whom some claim was assassinated by his former associates within the Nation of Islam. According to this view, the top leadership of the Nation of Islam became jealous of Malcolm X's immense popularity and his unique way of communicating messages about current events (e.g., likening the assassination of John F. Kennedy to "chickens coming home to roost"). Members of Malcolm X's own fold became his enemies and had him gunned down as he spoke at a gathering in Manhattan in February 1965.[26]

Finally, dependence on the leader holds back the development of competent successors and eventually creates a leadership crisis. When followers become so dependent upon the leader to make all decisions, their ability to learn on the job and expand their own leadership knowledge base is stifled. When the time comes that the organization needs a suitable replacement for the leader, the talent pool may be empty. That's because the followers will lack the independence and good judgment that can only come through proactive coaching and mentoring from the leader. Instead of perpetuating the dependence of your followers, why not work to promote their independence from you and interdependence among their colleagues in the organization and professions?

In summary, charisma is like a double-edged sword. It can mobilize people and bring about a tremendous amount of positive change for organizations. But when its power is controlled by the leader and used for self-serving reasons, it can unleash terrible destructive forces on people and organizations. Therefore, all of the earlier examples of destructive outcomes teach us to both *be aware* of and *beware* of charismatic leadership. At one point or another in your professional and personal life, you may have come in contact with a "little Hitler" running amok, bullying you and others in your organization. It's important not to get caught up in deceptive images and words that at first may inspire, but later only intimidate. By knowing the circumstances that give rise to these villains and their characteristics, you can identify, isolate, and eliminate them before they inflict fatal damage to your organization. To learn what to look out for, consider the contrast between two famous charismatic leaders of World War II profiled in Box 4.2.

Box 4.2 Two Different Faces of Charisma: Winston Churchill vs. Adolph Hitler

When Winston Churchill (shown in Figure 4.7) assumed his leadership of Great Britain in 1940, Hitler's armies were rolling across Europe. Nation after nation was overtaken by the Nazis. After France fell, the survival of Great Britain was in great jeopardy. Churchill's "Blood, Sweat, and Tears" speech, given on May 13, 1940, helped inspire his country to instill confidence in his new government and to carry on in the struggle against the Nazis despite formidable odds. In this speech, Churchill presented his vision:

> I have nothing to offer but blood, toil, tears, and sweat . . . You ask, what is our aim? I can answer in one word . . . Victory at all costs—Victory in spite of all terrors—Victory, however long and hard the road may be, for without victory there is no survival.[27]

Figure 4.7
Winston Churchill in 1948, realizing his vision after World War II.

Churchill's words were grounded in the virtues of justice and national sovereignty as a just cause for Great Britain's fight for survival. The moral foundation for Churchill's vision was built upon just war theory, a notion originated by philosopher and theologian Thomas Aquinas in *Summa Theologicae*. This idea has been discussed by philosophers of the Scholastic and Jurist schools, and more recently in writings by Michael Walzer, Thomas Nagel, and others in the advent of the Al-Qaeda terrorist attacks on the United States on September 11, 2001.[28]

While Churchill was somewhat abrasive and insensitive in one-on-one interactions with his followers, his charm came from the content of his message and his personification of Victorian values and established English traditions. Churchill was inspiring because he was perceived by his followers as a tough bulldog fighting to save civilization from the evils of Nazi Germany. Churchill's tenacity of purpose was reassuring during the merciless German bombing of London and other cities during the Battle of Britain. Churchill reiterated this purpose time and time again as he challenged his nation to "never, never, never give up." As a result of his inspiration of the British people, Churchill gained the respect and admiration of people all over the world. Churchill's legacy is one of relevance and timelessness, especially in these dangerous days of threats against free nations posed by fundamental and extremist terrorist organizations such as ISIS or Al-Qaeda that challenge our way of life. His inspirational leadership and words remind us that "courage is rightly esteemed the first of human qualities . . . because it is the quality which guarantees all others."[29]

In contrast, Adolph Hitler's legacy is a cautionary tale that warns us of the potential for charismatic leadership to run amok and produce disastrous results. It teaches us what we need to look out for, so we can catch it before charismatic leadership becomes destructive. What we need to look out for is the same thing that the German people failed to see through, that is, dramatic presentations high on style and emotion, and low on substance and reason. Hitler's drama amplified the effects of fear, intimidation, and excessive aspirations that strangled the reasoning ability of his countrymen.

Hitler was an evil master showman who excelled at creating an impression of power, righteousness in his beliefs, and superiority of his nation over all others. This message was quite appealing to the German people after their humiliation from losing World War I, their unfair treatment in the Treaty of Versailles, and the poor economic conditions of Germany during the Great Depression. All of these circumstances undermined collective self-esteem significantly among Germans. As Hitler entered the scene, he presented the German people with a vision to restore Germany's greatness by addressing their problems, righting their perceived wrongs, and in the process, elevating their collective self-esteem.[30]

What is fascinating about Hitler's leadership is that he was able to connect emotionally with the German people—a traditionally rational people known for their engineering and philosophical prowess. However, the majority of Germans failed to use their logic to question Hitler's leadership. They became mesmerized by his emotionally charged rhetoric that was high on passion and relatively low on reason. He spoke at rallies that were staged with the precision of a Hollywood movie production. In fact, Joseph Goebbels, Hitler's minister of culture and propaganda, was a huge fan of Hollywood movies. Goebbels worked with the top film producers of the day, such as Leni Riefenstahl, to create propaganda films such as *Triumph of the Will*.[31] He employed many of the film production techniques of the time to stage these events, which created a sense of awe in the audience members. Those who attended these rallies saw searchlights pointed to the sky marking the event, warm-up speeches given by key Nazi propagandists, immaculately dressed SS guards, torches, and neatly arranged seats filled with captivated audience members. Much detailed planning went into these events, which magnified Hitler's charismatic delivery and the emotional content of his speeches.[32]

Consider an excerpt from a speech Hitler delivered in the German Reichstag on January 30, 1937:

> The main plank in the National Socialist program is to abolish the liberalistic concept of the individual and the Marxist concept of humanity and to substitute therefore the folk community, rooted in the soil and bound together by the bond of its common blood.[33]

While his rhetoric is highly charismatic in its content (note the emphasis on building collective self-esteem among Germans with words like *community* and *common blood*), it contains several flaws in reasoning. First, there is a difference between the concepts of "the individual" and "the person." The concept of the individual is considered to be an interchangeable element subsumed within a collective. However, a truly humanistic view considers the person to be unique and of special value. That's because every person has a unique personality, spirit, soul, and dignity; it cannot be substituted for another as one would with individual components subsumed within a collective.

This kind of thinking was not part of the philosophy of the Nazis or the Soviets. Like Charles Darwin, they both emphasized the survival of the species or collective over the survival of the individual. Hitler's obsession was the survival of the Aryan race (and elimination of other races), with no concern for the German individual. Similarly, Joseph Stalin's and other Communists' goal was the survival of the social class, with no concern for the individual worker. In their minds, workers are mere individuals, not persons.

Second, Marxism and its Communist application in the Soviet Union and other countries did not emphasize humanity as Hitler stated in his speech. Rather, it emphasized the importance and superiority of a common social (i.e., working) class or collective over the individual. Third, Hitler's obsession with maintaining the purity of racial species is inconsistent with contemporary trends of interracial marriage, globalization, and diversity—current realities that Hitler failed to foresee.

Despite his charisma, Hitler lacked a vision rooted in reality and ethics. His vision was full of biases, hatred, and manipulation. In the end, Hitler committed suicide in a Berlin bunker in April 1945 while his German nation was devastated by Allied bombing and overrun by Soviet forces entering from the East. For a German nation that fell victim to the fatal attraction of Hitler, his legacy is one of dangerous demagogue and personification of evil, only admired by neo-Nazis, radicals, thugs, and criminals.

Putting Inspirational Motivation into Practice

So far, you have learned what it means to display inspirational motivation, why it is important, and how it affects followers. You are now ready to practice inspirational motivation as part of your leadership system. Recall that every leadership system is different. So you need to decide upon the best ways to practice inspirational motivation for your team or organization given your situation. This section presents suggestions that you may find useful in displaying inspirational motivation and developing your full leadership potential.

Display the Behaviors Described in This Chapter

This chapter presented five behaviors associated with inspirational motivation. These behaviors focused on the importance of being optimistic and enthusiastic about the future, and presenting an exciting vision of the future to your followers with a great deal of self-confidence. Choose any of these behaviors you feel most comfortable practicing consistently and authentically. Before you know it, your followers will think about that behavior and it will become part of your leadership system.

That's what Barry "Buck" Jones, a current doctoral student and former high school administrator at the award-winning Downingtown STEM Academy, found out after he completed his FRLD course at Penn State University. Always an intelligent and caring person, Buck used the examples of the transformational leaders he studied in class to identify those that influenced his own career in education. From his observations of these role models, he resolved to make transformational leaders of the students at the high school. He spoke to the students with optimistic hope about their futures. He expressed sincere care and stress-reducing humor that helped them to build their confidence and group potency. With collaboration technologies and training, Buck worked to transform the group structure at the school to a team structure that creates synergy and interdependence among the student members who now work together with shared leadership responsibilities. These talented and inspired students are a wonderful legacy for Buck. Their collective success at the Downingtown STEM Academy has provided Buck with a deeper understanding of how to help other educational institutions in his doctoral work.[34]

Boost Your Self-Confidence

As a leader, the image you present to others is essential to the conclusions they draw about you. Therefore, you must project an image of confidence to your followers in order to gain their commitment to you and the vision you share with them. When it comes to self-confidence, there is a plethora of advice available. Here are a few tips that can boost your self-confidence.

First, make sure that you have fully committed yourself to a vision or idea you are about to communicate with your followers. If you have not, you won't appear to be confident and they will see it. The key question you have to ask yourself is, "Do I believe in the message, vision, and/or values I'm trying to strongly communicate to my followers?" If your answer is anything less than a "firm Yes," then you have to find something you strongly believe in first. Second, walk briskly and with a purpose. Instead of dillydallying, be sure to put some pep in your step. That can increase your energy level and give the impression that you are full of vitality. You can also learn some gestures such as Yoga Mudras that will enhance your image as someone who is full of energy.[35] Third, be sure to maintain good posture when you walk or are seated. "Stomach in, chest out, shoulders back"—typical military counsel—is good advice to heed. Fourth, make eye contact with those with whom you speak. This builds trust and projects an image of poise. Fifth, speak up. Make it a point to interject at least one positive comment or probing question during meetings or gatherings. Those who speak first or frequently are often perceived as leaders who emerge within groups.[36]

We've seen all of these tips illustrated every time Susan Wojcicki presents YouTubes' new services and technologies. With her high level of self-confidence, wit, and carefully crafted speeches, her employees and customers believe that there is an exciting future for YouTube serving as a platform for media companies today and in the future.

Write Mission and Vision Statements for Your Organization

One of the best ways to put inspirational motivation into practice is to lead a group effort to create the mission and vision statements for your organization. Most organizations hold annual strategic planning sessions. During these sessions, groups of organizational stakeholders (e.g., managers, employees, customers, suppliers, shareholders, business partners) meet to determine the purpose, values, objectives, and performance metrics of the organization. These exercises can put you in tune with what your organization stands for, and its purpose and greater role in society. This increased understanding provides information that can be used in the content of your speeches and to identify the organizational values to shape your organizational culture.

If you are not involved in such strategic organizational activities, be sure to position yourself so that you have the opportunity to get involved. No matter what role you play, whether it is key participant or member of a small focus group, the information you gain can provide a deep understanding of the opportunities, threats, strengths, and weaknesses facing your organization. This knowledge can help you imagine an inspiring future to describe in your vision, one that is realistic and links the present to both the past and the future. That's the kind of vision that can energize your associates and induce commitment and greater meaning to your mission.[37]

Study the Rhetoric of Inspirational Leadership

Transformational leaders inspire their followers through their words and their deeds. In Chapter 3, you learned how to inspire your followers with your deeds using idealized influence. Let's now spend some time exploring how to inspire followers with your words. To illustrate the content of inspirational messages, consider Dr. Martin Luther King's "I Have a Dream" speech, one of the most influential orations of the 20th century. This speech is available on video streaming websites such as YouTube.com or educational websites such as www.americanrhetoric.com/speeches/mlkihaveadream.htm.

What is admirable about this speech? What can we learn from the content of this speech? Dr. King's speech provides several tips on creating an inspirational message. First, transformational leaders use inspirational messages to frame or reframe the big picture for followers. Their vision presents an appealing overarching end goal. The vision clarifies what the future state of affairs should look like by contrasting the future with the status quo. This typically involves demonstrating some revolutionary change that alters the present landscape. For example, Dr. King's speech contrasted the practices of segregation, discrimination, and injustice with an appealing vision of unity and equality. His compelling vision and well-articulated speech aimed at uniting the American people regardless of their gender, ethnicity, social status, and political parties. One important condition for a vision to be effective is that it has to be relevant and important to people you try to inspire. In Dr. King's speech, we find the values of freedom, fairness, kindness, and love. These qualities inspire the best in humanity.

Second, transformational leaders use words with content that stirs up the emotions of followers. Individuals are moved by their deep desires to be affiliated with noble causes, to strive toward significant achievements, and to exert influence over others. Although Dr. King's vision was a great idea for humanity, he chose the word *dream* instead of *idea*. To say "I have an idea" has too much of an ordinary overly rational sound to it. In contrast, "I have a dream" conjures up positive images that can tap into followers' needs for affiliation with the worthy civil rights cause. This language has the same effect as when one listens to Beatle John Lennon's classic song entitled "Imagine." That song just wouldn't have the same impact if it were entitled "Think."

Third, transformational leaders inspire their followers not only by what they say, but also by how they say it. They use special presentational techniques that can dramatically evoke deeply held values. *Metaphors*, or language that compares seemingly unrelated topics that have something in common, can provide a visual depiction of the message. Dr. King contrasted Mississippi's "heat of injustice" with "an oasis of freedom and justice."[38] *Analogies*, or the contrast of two things to show their similarities, provide a standard of comparison to clarify a complex message. For example, Dr. King proclaimed that "we will not be satisfied until justice rolls down like waters, and righteousness like a mighty stream." By using these rhetorical devices, transformational leaders, like Dr. King, display confidence, poise, and a commanding professional presence. They also use simple visuals to support the message they want to get across to others. These visuals can be quite effective because a picture is worth a thousand words.

Transformational leaders who inspire followers speak with a captivating tone, appropriate inflection, and proper emphasis of key words. They may start off calm and somewhat monotone, but as they continue, they vary their intensity and build up to an emotional and dramatic climax. Their words come across as crisp and refreshing and seem to dance within their followers' hearts and minds. It's almost as if their words are beautiful music to the ears of their followers.

Jesse Jackson's speech to the National Convention of the Democratic Party in 1988 is another good example of delivery of an inspirational speech. Using all of these delivery techniques, Jackson's speech included references to hope and faith by linking the past (e.g., Dr. King) with the present by including 14 references to dreams and dreaming, and encouraged followers to "keep hope alive." Jackson's speech also included verbal persuasion to raise his followers' level of self-efficacy ("never surrender" and "you can make it") and to reinforce the collective efficacy and unity among members of his Rainbow Coalition (e.g., farmers, workers, women, students, African Americans, Hispanics, gays and lesbians, conservatives and progressives, right-wingers and left-wingers). To make an emotional connection with this disparate group of supporters, Jackson shared emotional stories of his disadvantaged upbringing. By presenting himself as a "working person's person," he was able to transcend the differences within his support base and get this diverse voter group to identify with him ("As I make it, so you can make it. You must never surrender to make America get better").[39] Practice using these rhetorical tactics in your next important speech.

Work to Improve Your Public Speaking Ability

Numerous executive coaching firms and consultants provide training and development services designed to improve your public speaking ability. Such programs include the Dale Carnegie course (www.dalecarnegie.com/) or Toastmasters International (www.toastmasters.org/). These programs teach skills that make you feel more comfortable and confident in your speaking. Because command of language and its effective use are extremely important to the leadership influence process, your followers' perceptions of you as an inspiring leader depend very much on your public speaking ability.

The Toastmasters International website, noted in the preceding paragraph, presents ten helpful tips for public speaking that can enhance your ability to inspire your followers. This organization encourages you to:

1. *Know your material.* The content of your speech should contain material that is inspiring to your followers. Be familiar with it. When you use humor and speak from the heart by sharing personal stories, you can get people to identify with you as a leader they will follow anywhere.
2. *Practice over and over again.* Practicing out loud allows you to fine-tune your speech in terms of content, delivery, and timing. The more you practice, the easier it will be to deliver an inspiring speech. If possible, practice in front of a group of your colleagues. This will allow you to receive objective feedback and is an opportunity to observe others.
3. *Know the audience.* Make a personal connection with audience members by greeting them before you begin. They will look upon you as a familiar face rather than a stranger. Be sure to gather general information about them so that you can tailor aspects of your speech to their beliefs, desires, motives, and values. That's one way charismatic leaders connect with their followers.
4. *Know the room.* By arriving early and testing your equipment, you will be better prepared for any unexpected events. You will also feel more comfortable and engaged in your speaking role. This advice is similar to the need for leaders to understand the situation in which they are embedded, as discussed in Chapter 2.
5. *Relax.* A slow and relaxed start to a speech can convert nervous energy into enthusiasm that can build up to a positive emotional climax. A funny joke or friendly greeting can go a long way in connecting with the audience, who will be ready to receive an emotional story or two as your speech progresses.
6. *Visualize yourself giving the speech.* Visualization is a tactic frequently used by professional sports figures to boost their confidence. Prior to giving your speech, conduct a mental walk-through with positive imagery of clapping audience members. This is a good way to create optimistic and enthusiastic thoughts that can translate into an inspiring speech.
7. *Focus on the message, not the medium.* Any nervousness you may experience is likely to stem from public self-consciousness. So try not to think about yourself and your appearance once on stage. Instead, focus on the content of your speech and the way you will deliver it with appropriate volume, inflection, tone, and emphasis.
8. *Realize that people want you to succeed.* This is another tip that can boost your self-confidence. The audience is there because they want to learn from you and be inspired. That can only happen if you are successful. And that's an outcome you're both hoping for.
9. *Don't apologize for being nervous or any mistake you may make.* Audience members do not know what you were planning to say or do while you speak. Move forward in your speech with confidence and enthusiasm.
10. *Gain experience.* The more speeches you give, the more experience you gain. The more experience you gain, the more inspirational your speeches will become.

Use Storytelling Techniques to Articulate Your Vision

One of the best techniques for giving an inspiring speech is to tell personal stories that illustrate the values underlying the vision. Everyone has a story. When you speak from the heart, your ability to inspire others improves for several reasons. First, your talking points will come naturally to you because they are based on your personal experience. You are very familiar with your experiences. So talking about them should be easy and comfortable. Second, relating personal stories that are important to you is likely to evoke a wide range of emotions in you as you speak. When your followers witness these emotions in you, they too will feel your emotions and be inspired by the effect they have on you. Social psychologists call this phenomenon *emotional contagion*.[40] Third, people are generally interested in stories and the lessons they illustrate. Over the centuries, the great philosophers and teachers have taught their students with parables.

One excellent example of effective storytelling is a speech delivered by Steve Jobs to Stanford University graduates on June 12, 2005. On one hand, his speech was hardly impressive because he practically read his notes throughout the talk. But what made his commencement speech so effective was the use of personal stories to convey his core messages. In his speech, Jobs told three stories. His first story was about connecting the dots. This story was about trusting that the events in one's life are related to one another and will make sense in the long run. His second story was about love and loss. He talked about the importance of finding what you truly love in life and at work and not settling for second best. His third story was about death. This story was about the idea that your time is limited, so don't waste it living someone else's life—follow your heart and intuition. Each of his stories dealt with common life issues. As a result, many of the Stanford graduates and their proud parents in the audience could identify with the topics and with Steve Jobs as a human being rather than just another corporate leader.[41]

There are numerous resources available to aid in your storytelling competence. These resources range from books to articles to internet websites. Spend some time reviewing these resources before you present the vision to your followers. You'll be amazed how inspired your followers will become by what you are teaching them through your personal stories.[42]

Build Consensus Around Your Vision

Once you present the vision to your followers, it is important to obtain their support and get them to share in the ownership of the vision. Nothing is more detrimental to your organization's success than a vision not being shared by its members. One way to do this is to hold formal and informal celebrations of the vision. During these ceremonies, you can recognize the key contributors who are working toward attaining the vision. It's also important to show associates how their work contributes to the progress and success of your organization. For example, most every spring, Penn State Great Valley holds a Leadership in Action event that demonstrates to the public what our Master of Leadership Development program's vision and mission is, what the program means to our students, and how they have applied the knowledge they gained in the program to their professional and personal lives. These events are very popular and successful because they build cohesiveness and solidarity around the vision, and show the business community how the program benefits individuals, teams, organizations, and local and global communities through student initiatives.

While it is beneficial to promote the vision and celebrate success, visions need to be modified to adapt to the changing environment. Sharing information relevant to your organization's vision with followers is important to reinforce their feeling connected to the vision. You need to make sure that every new associate understands the vision and mission of the organization and clarify their role in accomplishing these goals. You should also seek opportunities to communicate and share ideas with people both inside and outside the organization. This communication flow can help in updating the vision by bringing new opportunities and threats to light, as well as strengths and weaknesses of your organization and its competitors. Remember that sharing the vision with followers increases their perception of you as an inspiring leader. It also enhances their emotional commitment to the organization because they see their role in helping attain the vision, which becomes a part of who they are. In the next chapter, we'll turn our attention to building followers' commitment to the organization by using rational means that promote creativity and innovation.

Summary Questions and Reflective Exercises

1. This exercise uses results of your Multifactor Leadership Questionnaire (MLQ) report to assess your level of inspirational motivation behavior. Compare your inspirational motivation ratings with the research-validated benchmarks. How did your self-ratings, ratings from subordinates, ratings from peers, ratings from superiors, and ratings from others compare against the benchmarks? On which specific MLQ items (i.e., questions) did you score highest? Lowest? What can you do to improve on the items where you scored lowest?

2. This exercise also uses results of your MLQ report to assess your level of inspirational motivation behavior. Compare your self-ratings on *inspirational motivation behavior* with ratings provided by subordinates, peers, superiors, and others. Compute the difference score (d) as the difference between your self-rating score and the specific other rating source score of interest. If d is less than .5 and the other rating source score is less than 2.9, then you are considered to be *in agreement/poor*. If d is less than .5 and the other rating source score is greater than 2.9, then you are considered to be *in agreement/good*. If d is equal to or greater than .5 and the self-rating score is greater than the other rating score, then you are an *overestimator* on this dimension. If d is equal to or greater than .5 and the self-rating score is less than the other rating score, then you are an *underestimator* on this dimension. Consider the category under which you fall in terms

of inspirational motivation behavior. What are the implications of this categorization for you? Are there any things you can do to improve in this area?

3. The purpose of this exercise is to develop your inspirational speaking skills. Assemble a team of four members who will assist you in delivering and recording a speech. Assign the following roles to your team members:

    Speaker: You will assume the speaker role.
    Camera person: A technically competent individual who will record the speech.
    Paralanguage specialist: An emotionally intelligent individual who will coach the speaker regarding nonverbal behaviors to be displayed during the speech.
    Visionary writer: A thoughtful individual with foresight who will draft (i.e., outline) the content of the speech using tips presented in this chapter.
    Literary writer: A literary ace and master of metaphors and analogies who will work closely with the visionary writer to embellish the speech with dramatic literary devices to evoke a potent emotional response from the audience.

    Once you have assigned roles to your team members, imagine that your team has been invited by the Public Broadcasting Service (PBS) to draft and deliver a three-minute speech using the rhetoric of inspirational leadership and the power of teamwork. Your message should focus on inspiring positive change in individuals, groups, organizations, and the community. Select one of the following audiences for your speech: Saints Phillips and James sixth grade class (www.sspj.net), Church Farm School (www.gocfs.net/), the Association of Accountants and Financial Professionals in Business (www.imanet.org/?ssopc=1), Big Brothers and Big Sisters (www.bbbs.org/), or Willow Valley Retirement Communities (www.willowvalleycommunities.org). Please tailor your speech to one of these audiences (i.e., where they are in their lives) and spend no more than 30 minutes drafting your speech. Use personal stories like Steve Jobs. Practice it before you deliver it in front of a video or smartphone camera. Then deliver and record your speech. Repeat this process a few times. Before you know it, people will be talking about how inspirational you are!

4. Visit a local chapter of Toastmasters International and attend one of their meetings. For meeting locations and times, visit www.toastmasters.org. Talk with members to learn how to improve your poise when delivering leadership speeches. Share what you learned with your colleagues or leadership learning partners.

5. At your next company meeting, make a presentation on a FRLD topic and use one or two personal stories to make your point. Use personal or organizational values to link your stories to your topic. Your stories should be based on personal experiences that are interesting and relevant to the message you intend to communicate. Follow up with a few audience members regarding the impact of the stories on them and whether they were helpful in influencing them.

Notes

1   Retrieved from https://content.extremenetworks.com/extreme-networks-blog/be-your-agency-s-it-hero-three-steps-to-unlock-federal-it-potential; and http://newsroom.brocade.com/press-releases/brocade-appoints-new-vice-president-of-federal-sales-nasdaq-brcd-1272618#.WWS3w4qQyi4.

2   Retrieved from www.brocade.com/en/backend-content/pdf-page.html?/content/dam/common/documents/content-types/whitepaper/brocade-acg-tco-wp.pdf.

3   Frankl presentation to students viewable at www.youtube.com/watch?v=fD1512_XJEw.

4   Thrash, T. M., & Elliot, A. J. (2003). Inspiration as a psychological construct. *Journal of Personality and Social Psychology, 84*, 871–889; and Thrash, T. M., Moldovan, E. G., Oleynick, V. C., & Maruskin, L. A. (2014). The psychology of inspiration. *Social and Personality Psychology Compass, 8/9*, 495–510.

5   To view the dance, visit www.youtube.com/watch?v=dbCmnRztK1Y.

6   Wei, C. (2014). *Jack Ma: Founder and CEO of the Alibaba Group.* Paramus, NJ: Homa & Sekey Books; and www.cnbc.com/2017/06/21/alibabas-jack-ma-says-people-will-work-four-hours-a-day-in-30-years.html.

7   Retrieved from www.cnbc.com/2017/05/28/hillary-clintons-2017-commencement-speech-at-wellesley.html.

8   Lawrence, J. (2017, June 5). Dear Hillary Clinton, please stop talking about 2016. *USA Today.* Retrieved from www.usatoday.com/story/opinion/2017/06/05/hillary-clinton-get-over-2016-election-jill-lawrence-column/102485326/; Lewis, E., & Rhodes, R. (1967). *John F Kennedy: Words to remember.* New York: Hallmark Editions; and Traister, R. (2017, May 26). Hillary Clinton is furious. And resigned. And funny. And worried. *New York.* Retrieved from http://nymag.com/daily/intelligencer/2017/05/hillary-clinton-life-after-election.html.

9   Csikszentmihalyi, M. (2003). *Good business: Leadership, flow, and the making of meaning.* New York: Viking; and Newman, A., Ucbasaran, D., Zhu, F., & Hirst, G. (2014). Psychological capital: A review and synthesis. *Journal of Organizational Behavior, 35*(S1), S120–S138.

10 Tredgold, G. (2016, March 3). What are the 4E's of high performance leadership? *The Leadership Network.* Retrieved from https://theleadershipnetwork.com/article/creative-leadership/4es-high-performance-leadership.

11 Shamir, B. (2011). Leadership takes time: Some implications of (not) taking time seriously in leadership research. *The Leadership Quarterly, 22*(2), 307–315; and Shamir, B., House, R. J., & Arthur, M. (1993). The motivational effects of charismatic leadership: A self-concept based theory. *Organization Science, 4*(4), 1–17.

12 Sheen, F. J. (1988). *The psychology of the rat race; psychology of temptation* [Videocassette]. Victor, NY: Sheen Productions.

13 Weigel, G. (1999). *Witness to hope: The biography of Pope John Paul II*. New York: HarperCollins; and Weigel, G. (2010). *The end and the beginning: Pope John Paul II — The victory of freedom, the last years, the legacy*. New York: Doubleday.

14 Bair, S. (2011). Lessons of the financial crisis: The dangers of short-termism. *Harvard Law School Forum on Corporate Governance and Financial Regulation*. Retrieved from https://corpgov.law.harvard.edu/2011/07/04/lessons-of-the-financial-crisis-the-dangers-of-short-termism/; and Beer, M. (2009, September 14). The lesson of Lehman: Do the opposite. *Forbes*. Retrieved from www.forbes.com/2009/09/14/lehman-strategy-failure-leadership-managing-risk.html.

15 Gibney, A. (Producer/Director), & McLean, B., Elkind, P., & Gibney, A. (Writers). (2005). *Enron: The smartest guys in the room* [Documentary film]. New York: Magnolia Pictures.

16 Burton, C. (2017, July 5). After the crash: Inside Richard Branson's $600m space mission. *GQ*. Retrieved from www.gq-magazine.co.uk/article/richard-branson-virgin-galactic; and www.virgingalactic.com/press/sir-richard-branson-unveils-virgin-galactics-new-spaceship-named-vss-unity-by-professor-stephen-hawking/.

17 Retrieved from www.virgingalactic.com/press/sir-richard-branson-unveils-virgin-galactics-new-spaceship-named-vss-unity-by-professor-stephen-hawking/.

18 Hallam, S. (2017, January 10). Amazon's business strategy: 6 examples of the latest trends in ecommerce. *Hallam*. Retrieved from www.hallaminternet.com/amazons-business-strategy-new-developments/.

19 Bandura, A. (1997). *Self-efficacy: The exercise of control*. New York: Freeman; and Guzzo, R., Yost, P., Campbell, R., & Shea, G. (1993). Potency in groups: Articulating a construct. *British Journal of Social Psychology, 32*(1), 87–106.

20 Ackoff, R. L., & Addison, H. J. (2011). *Ackoff's F/laws: The cake*. Axminster, UK: Triarchy Press; and Thrash et al. (2014). As cited in Note 4.

21 Bass, B. M., & Avolio, B. J. (1990). *Full range leadership development: Basic workshop*. Binghamton, NY: Center for Leadership Studies/SUNY-Binghamton; and Thrash et al. (2014). As cited in Note 4.

22 Jung, D. I., & Sosik, J. J. (2006). Who are the spellbinders?: Identifying personal attributes of charismatic leaders. *Journal of Leadership and Organizational Studies, 12*(4), 12–26.

23 Conger, J. A., & Kanungo, R. N. (1998). *Charismatic leadership in organizations*. Thousand Oaks, CA: Sage; and Weber, M. (1947). *The theory of social and economic organizations* (T. Parsons, Trans.). New York: Free Press.

24 Janis, I. (1972). *Victims of groupthink*. Boston, MA: Houghton-Mifflin Co.

25 Mayo, M. (2017, April 7). If humble people make the best leaders, why do we fall for charismatic narcissists? *Harvard Business Review*. Retrieved from https://hbr.org/2017/04/if-humble-people-make-the-best-leaders-why-do-we-fall-for-charismatic-narcissists; and Sosik, J. J., Chun, J. U., & Zhu, W. (2014). Hang on to your ego: The influence of destructive and constructive narcissism of charismatic leaders on follower psychological empowerment and moral identity. *Journal of Business Ethics, 120*(1), 65–80.

26 You can learn more about Malcolm X and his tremendous charisma by viewing various video clips on YouTube.com. Additional information can be found in Bassey, M. O. (2005). *Malcolm X and African American self-consciousness*. Lewiston, NY: Edwin Mellen Press; Helfer, A. (2006). *Malcolm X: A graphic biography*. New York: Hill and Wang; and Marable, M. (2011). *Malcolm X: A life of re-invention*. New York: Penguin.

27 Retrieved from www.historyplace.com/speeches/churchill.htm.

28 Fascinating reading on just war theory can be found in Brough, M. B., Lango, J. W., & van der Linden, H. (2007). *Rethinking the just war tradition*. Albany, NY: SUNY Press;

Nagel, T. (1995). *Moral questions*. Cambridge, UK: Cambridge University Press; and Walzer, M. (1977). *Just and unjust wars: A moral argument with historical illustrations* (4th ed.). New York: Basic Books.

29 Best, G. F. (2001). *Churchill: A study in greatness*. London: Hambledon & London; and Roberts, A. (2002). *Hitler and Churchill: Secrets of leadership*. London: Weidenfeld & Nicholson.

30 Bullock, A. (1964). *Hitler: A study in tyranny*. New York: Harper & Row.

31 Riefenstahl, L. (1934). *Triumph of the will* [Videocassette]. Novi, MI: Synapse Films.

32 Roberts (2002). As cited in Note 29.

33 Retrieved from http://research.calvin.edu/german-propaganda-archive/hitler1.htm.

34 Jones, B. (2015). *Leadership development plan for Barry Jones* [LEAD 555]. Malvern, PA: Penn State Great Valley; www.dasd.org/STEM; and www.usnews.com/education/best-high-schools/pennsylvania/districts/downingtown-area-sd/downingtown-stem-academy-145298.

35 For more information on the connection between speech, gestures, and energy, see www.azulfit.com/hand-mudras-power-and-meaning/, and www.scienceofpeople.com/2015/08/how-to-speak-with-your-hands/.

36 Burton, N. (2016, December). Building confidence and self-esteem. *Psychology Today*. Retrieved from www.psychologytoday.com/blog/hide-and-seek/201205/building-confidence-and-self-esteem.

37 Sosik, J. J., Jung, D. I., Berson, Y., Dionne, S. D., & Jaussi, K. S. (2004). *The dream weavers: Strategy-focused leadership in technology-driven organizations*. Greenwich, CT: Information Age Publishing.

38 Retrieved from www.americanrhetoric.com/speeches/mlkihaveadream.htm.

39 Shamir, B., Arthur, M. B., & House, R. J. (1994). The rhetoric of charismatic leadership: A theoretical extension, a case study, and implications for research. *The Leadership Quarterly, 5*(1), 25–42.

40 Hatfield, E., Cacioppo, J. T., & Rapson, R. L. (1993). *Emotional contagion: Studies in emotion & social interaction*. Cambridge, UK: Cambridge University Press; and Sy, T., Côté, Stephane, & Saavedra, R. (2005). The contagious leader: Impact of the leader's mood on the mood of group members, group affective tone, and group processes. *Journal of Applied Psychology, 90*(2), 295–305.

41 Retrieved from http://news.stanford.edu/2005/06/14/jobs-061505/.

42 The following references provide excellent overviews of how storytelling is used to benefit leaders and their followers: Adamson, G., Pine, J., Van Steenhoven, T., & Kroups, J. (2006). How storytelling can drive strategic change. *Strategy & Leadership, 34*(1), 36–41; Bai, M. (2005, July 17). The framing wars. *New York Times Magazine*, pp. 38–45, 68–71; Denning, S. (2005). Transmit your values: Using narrative to instill organizational values. In *The leader's guide to storytelling: Mastering the art of discipline of business narrative* (Chap. 6, pp. 121–148). Edison, NJ: Wiley; and Orr, K., & Bennett, M. (2017). Relational leadership, storytelling, and narratives: Practices of local government chief executives. *Public Administration Review, 77*(4), 515–527.

Chapter 5

Intellectual Stimulation

The Rational Side of Transformational Leadership

Imagine that you were tasked with helping children who have been affected by or infected with HIV/AIDS. You'd soon realize that these children suffer not only from physical symptoms that vary daily, but also from many emotional and social wounds inflicted by being labeled by their peer group and shunned by society. Imagine what it would be like if your children or children you loved either were infected with HIV/AIDS or were in a position where they had to care for someone living with this cruel disease. How would they feel? Could you empathize with them? What would you do to give them back their human dignity and precious childhood moments that this devastating disease takes away? How could you reach out in a way to help address this social problem?

Patty Hillkirk and a team of compassionate and imaginative transformational leaders committed their hearts and minds to the task of answering these questions. In August 1996, they established Camp Dreamcatcher (www.camp-dreamcatcher.org/) in Kennett Square, Pennsylvania, to address this issue. The camp's mission is to challenge society's views on HIV/AIDS and its effect on the lives of their campers. Camp Dreamcatcher is a unique organization because it is the only weeklong free therapeutic camp on the U.S. East Coast that offers a camping experience for HIV/AIDS-infected or -affected children between the ages of 5 and 17. Contrary to conventional wisdom, Camp Dreamcatcher assumes that these children can participate in and enjoy a full week of summer camp, just like healthy kids. That's because a talented team of experienced medical and counseling professional volunteers create a safe environment for the campers. Under proper supervision and leadership, the campers enjoy a wide variety of support group, recreational, training, and educational activities.[1]

Camp Dreamcatcher's success under Patty Hillkirk's leadership is well known. Media reporters and politicians have recognized that she gives children coping with HIV/AIDS both hope and an environment where they can develop socially, mentally, and spiritually within the physical limitations imposed upon them by their disease. Patty's efforts have been documented in *Tiny Tears*, a film produced by Robert Corna that examines the lives of AIDS orphans across the globe.[2]

Students in Penn State's Master of Leadership Development (MLD) program have worked with Patty and Professor Barrie E. Litzky (currently of Drexel University) to write a business plan for Camp Dreamcatcher because they want to purchase property and get accredited. Together, they have developed a strategy for accreditation in the American Camping Association. They have identified lists of potential collaborating organizations, HIV/AIDS organizations, and groups that may use the camp. They have also calculated Camp Dreamcatcher's social return on investment using metrics such as pre- and posttest surveys to campers and their parents/guardians measuring what they have learned in the camp, repeat attendance at the camp, and donations and fund-raisings to support the camp. These measures are factored into an innovative calculation of the camp's value to society based on activities that determine the camp's ultimate social outcomes (see Figure 5.1).[3]

Patty Hillkirk's intellectually stimulating leadership is a noble response to political scientist James MacGregor Burn's call to use transformational leadership to address the world's social problems and help people pursue happiness.[4] She is shifting society's views on HIV/AIDS from focusing on helping patients who are "dying from" to "living with" the disease. The traditional view of HIV/AIDS is that it represents a worldwide health crisis. By recognizing that the Chinese word for crisis includes both "opportunity" and "danger" at the same time, Hillkirk has seen the opportunity for Camp Dreamcatcher to "foster an atmosphere of tolerance, compassion, respect and understanding through volunteer opportunities,

Inputs	Activities	Outputs	Outcomes
• Volunteer's time	• Recreational	• Medicine tolerance	• Improved emotional health of campers
• Fund-raising/donations	• Health/Wellness	• Return enrollment	• Increase awareness & tolerance of HIV/AIDS to local, national, and global community
• Year-round camp facility	• Educational programs	• Parental satisfaction	• Improved awareness of medical regimes by campers
• Medical equipment	• Therapeutic programs	• Increased fund-raising/donations	• Increase in # of infected/affected children having a real camp experience
• HIV/AIDS literature	• Social/entertainment	• Family support and advocacy	• Increase HIV/AIDS awareness programs in middle- and high-schools
• Recreational equipment	• Retreats	• Community outreach	
• Therapeutic equipment	• Reunions	• Knowledge of life skills	
	• Support groups	• Trained junior counselors	
	• Teen speaker bureau		
	• Documentary film "Tiny Tears"		

Figure 5.1 **Return on social investment. Camp Dreamcatcher uses these metrics to assess how resources and activities impact their organizational stakeholders and contribute to society.**

services and expanded community outreach," as stated in its mission statement. Hillkirk's reframing of crisis as an opportunity is an example of intellectual stimulation. This behavior is often used by transformational leaders when they try to find innovative solutions.

This chapter shows you how to get your followers to think in unconventional ways about solving important leadership problems that face your organization and society, like Patty Hillkirk and Sundar Pichai (see Box 5.1) did. By showing your followers how to think for themselves, instead of relying solely on "tried and true" policies and procedures, you too can become an intellectually stimulating leader. You need to get your followers involved in work and decision-making processes because you alone can't possibly keep up with all of the fast-paced changes in the world that are happening all around you.

Box 5.1 Leader Profile: Sundar Pichai

Sundar Pichai, CEO of Google, was born in a middle-class family in Chennai, India. His father was an electrical engineer and his mother worked as a stenographer. Together they lived in a humble two-room apartment. Gifted with mathematical abilities, Pichai went to the Indian version of the Massachusetts Institute of Technology called the Indian Institute of Technology and continued his higher education at Stanford University where he studied engineering. After earning his MBA at the University of Pennsylvania's Wharton School and briefly working as a consultant at McKinsey & Company, he landed a job at Google. There, he began developing a very successful career and was instrumental in launching a number of important services such as Google's search toolbar, Chrome, Android, and Chrome OS. Pichai's years of hard work paid off and he was appointed as the new CEO of Google in August 2015.

Pichai's story illustrates a new era where success cannot be achieved alone in innovation-driven business environments. Together with his employees, he was instrumental in initiating many of Google's innovative technologies and services that we use today. However, Pichai isn't the type of leader who barks a marching order to his employees and enjoys the spotlight of being "center stage." Instead, he is a quiet leader who likes to remain in the background. He doesn't tell his employees what they need to do and try to control their work processes. Instead, he challenges them by asking questions. For example, when Google was still a default option for internet searches along with Microsoft Internet Explorer, he challenged his associates by asking "what problems we might have to face if and when Microsoft decides to further develop their own internet search engine?"

Pichai's example shows what it takes to be a successful leader in today's innovation-based economy. Back when efficiency was the main principle of competition, the "Be quiet and follow me" type of leader was successful if he was able to set the right direction and execute organizational strategies. However, the changes in technology and customer preferences that we face today are much too complicated and fast paced for a single leader to handle. Therefore, we believe that you need to tone down your urge to control everything and instead begin thinking about how you can encourage the participation of your followers and utilize their collective wisdom. This is where intellectual stimulation, such as that shown by Pichai, becomes useful. Challenge your followers to look at the problems they face from different angles. Ask questions of your followers to get rid of any unnecessary or outdated assumptions they might have regarding their work processes. The important point is that you don't need to be a CEO of a world-class company like Google to use intellectual stimulation. This rational side of transformational leadership is equally important in many smaller for-profit and not-for-profit organizations at all organizational levels.[5]

Intellectual Stimulation: Definition and Behavioral Examples

To develop breakthrough strategies and champion innovation like Sundar Pichai and Patty Hillkirk, you need to display intellectual stimulation behaviors. That's because *intellectual stimulation* involves rational thinking, creativity, and the freedom to fail. These concepts allow followers to think for themselves in ways that challenge conventional wisdom and seek innovative solutions. Displaying intellectually stimulating behaviors might also help you create a billion-dollar business like Neil Blumenthal, Dave Gilboa, Andy Hunt, and Jeff Raider did (see Box 5.2).

Box 5.2 Leader Profile: Founders of Warby Parker

If you wear eye glasses, you probably agree that they are too expensive and inconvenient to buy because you have to drive to an optometrist's office or retail shop to try out a new pair. One of the reasons that the eyewear industry hasn't seen a lot of innovation and customer-friendly prices and service is because it has been dominated by a single company. Neil Blumenthal, Dave Gilboa, Andy Hunt, and Jeff Raider, who studied together at the University of Pennsylvania's Wharton School of Business in 2010, began thinking about challenging these nonsensical assumptions. When one of them lost his eye glasses during a backpacking trip, he had to endure an entire semester of demanding MBA courses without glasses due to the high cost of replacing them. When the four MBA students were in a lab working on a project, an important question was raised: "Why are glasses so expensive?" This question led them to investigate the eyewear industry and the answer seemed fairly clear. A single company owns about 80% of the licenses for big fashion brands such as Prada,

Ray-Ban, and Oakley *and* the retail outlets such as LensCrafters and Pearle Vision.

After investing about a year and a half of their time on this issue, their idea became a reality. They developed a new business model in which customers can navigate through thousands of eye glasses and select five frames on a website. Their company, named Warby Parker, mails eye glasses to customers for free and customers have five days to try them out. Customers can even take the five frames to work and have their colleagues provide feedback on them. After making their choice, customers can place their order online and they will be sent a new pair. They simply return the five frames to the company with a prepaid return envelope. The new business offers customers an opportunity to buy eye glasses in a fun and convenient way. What's even better is that customers can buy a pair of eye glasses for about $95 instead of $500!

When the former MBA students came up with this innovative and simple way to buy eye glasses, their customers responded with enthusiasm. Warby Parker exceeded their first year's sales targets during the first three weeks of their inception. They sold 20,000 pairs of glasses during the first year of their business. Sales skyrocketed to 100,000 pairs in 2013 and one million pairs in 2014. *Fast Company* ranked Warby Parker #1 in their Most Innovative Companies of 2015 List, even outperforming Apple which was ranked second. As of April 2015 (only five years after their inception), the company was valued at $1.2 billion.

Warby Parker and its founders' story teaches us to live life with a sense of curiosity and imagination that knows no bounds. We must always question the status quo and ask ourselves, "Why do things have to be like this?" This leader profile reminds us of the words of Lieutenant General Willard W. Scott Jr.: "Any fool can keep a rule. God gave him a brain to know when to break the rule."[6]

Like the founders of Warby Parker, you can demonstrate intellectual stimulation by practicing behaviors that challenge the status quo. Let's now examine six key transformational leadership behaviors that allow you to display intellectual stimulation.

Reexamine Critical Assumptions to Question Whether They Are Appropriate

After working on our job for a few years, we tend to develop several assumptions and/or practices we take for granted. These assumptions might come from our own experiences (especially successful ones) and advice from other people. Think about how this applies to you. Once you become comfortable with these assumptions, chances are you will never challenge them unless someone asks you to think about them. Then, all of a sudden, you might realize how you became so blindsided and never tried to look at your job from a different angle. We believe that one of your most important jobs as a leader is to challenge yourself and your followers, like we have seen with one brave soul in the health care field.

Think about the last time you or a member of your family was in need of health care. Whether you visited your doctor or the hospital, you probably experienced some agitation over the way you were treated during your wait and perhaps during your treatment. And don't forget about the hassles associated with your health care insurance and its reimbursement rules. Our life experiences seem to teach us that we must accept our flawed health care system as it is and simply go with the flow. Some of us may also assume that we should take a passive approach to our health and react only when something goes wrong. Some doctors may presume that they are independent sources of knowledge and information on healing, and that their contact with us is "episodic, high intensity, and low touch."[7]

The U.S. health care system has been based upon these assumptions for many years, but not all doctors have accepted them. Consider Hunter "Patch" Adams, the maverick medical doctor and social activist portrayed by actor Robin Williams in the film *Patch Adams*. While in medical school, Adams began to question the basic assumptions underlying the way health care is provided to patients. He asked himself and others why things could not be different.

Over his 42-year career, Adams has championed developing compassionate connections with patients. His philosophy is to use humor and the natural environment to forge a bond between the patient's physical, emotional, and spiritual wellbeing. Adams has always felt that a patient's wellness can be enhanced by the natural environment. Pending sufficient funding, Adams and his colleagues are completing the Geshundheit! Institute. This promises to be much more than a nontraditional hospital. The vision for this facility is to create a sustainable system including a free full-scale hospital, health care eco-community, center for the arts, nature, agriculture, and recreation with a focus on holistic medicine and overall personal wellbeing. Indeed, the Geshundheit! Institute seems to be a kind of Walt Disney World of holistic medicine and healing.[8] For a virtual tour of the Geshundheit! Institute, visit www.patchadams.org.

In many leadership courses and workshops we've conducted over the years, we've used Patch Adams to illustrate the power of questioning critical assumptions underlying strategic initiatives, work processes, company policies and practices, and cultural norms. As shown in Figure 5.2, you can achieve major breakthroughs in innovation and continuous improvement by questioning such basic assumptions with your coworkers and followers. When elements in the leadership context change (see Chapter 2), the basic assumptions underlying policies and practices may no longer be valid and may require an organizational change in policies, practices, and people. When changes are made to basic assumptions, new models for organizing and operating can be developed. These new models can lead to innovative solutions to pressing problems. In your next team meeting, be sure to challenge some basic assumptions your associates seem to have regarding the way work gets done.

Figure 5.2
Imagine it this way. Team members brainstorm ideas that question traditional ways of completing job tasks.

Seek Different Perspectives When Solving Problems

Another way to intellectually stimulate your followers is to look to others for different ways of doing things. For example, most high jumpers used a technique called the straddle jump before the 1968 Summer Olympic Games in Mexico City. With the straddle technique, the jumper crosses the bar facing down, with both legs straddling it. This gave the jumper a mechanical advantage over previous jumping techniques since it allowed the jumper to cross a bar that is higher than jumper's center of mass. So, most elite jumpers used the straddle technique and thought it as the best way of crossing a bar.

Then an American athlete named Dick Fosbury began thinking about a better way to perform that task. Fosbury wondered, "Is there any better way to cross the bar?" He tried many different approaches and was openly ridiculed by other jumpers. But he never gave up. He soon realized that it would be more effective to turn his body around a few steps before the bar and use a lower center of gravity as a stronger source of energy. Everyone laughed at Fosbury for his strange way of crossing a bar, until he won a gold medal at the 1968 Summer Olympic Games. Soon after his remarkable achievement, most jumpers adopted Fosbury's approach and began calling it "The Fosbury Flop."[9]

So, when complex problems face your group or organization, it is a good idea to challenge your followers by asking "Is there a different way we can solve this problem?" Your job as a leader is to encourage your followers to think out of the box and approach a problem from different perspectives.

Get Others to Look at Problems from Many Different Angles

Katrina leads a group of instructional designers in a large manufacturing company. She is well known for being a creative and insightful problem solver. Her reputation comes from a positive outlook on life that appreciates unique and quirky natural and man-made objects. Given her talent for appreciating beauty and excellence, Katrina has always been interested in artwork and photography and has taken up these activities as hobbies in her spare time. Over the years, she has taken several university-sponsored photography classes that have allowed her to use her talents to produce an impressive gallery of photos. Katrina is always ready with her camera in hand to snap an interesting shot of nature, family gatherings, or work events.

Photography has taught Katrina several important lessons about intellectually stimulating leadership. Katrina's photos often capture her subjects from an unusual angle that reveals interesting details that would have gone unnoticed if not for her insightful positioning of the camera. This has taught her to consider leadership problems from different angles as well. These slants on perceiving leadership problems include considering short- and long-term implications of problems, most and least likely scenarios, best and worst case situations, and nuances in the behavior patterns of group members. Katrina also considers issues of lighting, timing, and framing of the subjects of her photography using unorthodox approaches or unexpected situations. These unconventional tactics often produce behavioral snapshots rich in meaning from which personality characteristics of her human subjects can be gleaned. Applying this skill to her leadership at work, Katrina has learned the importance of hearing from individuals whom most people would likely pass up when gathering information. These people can provide advice that adds value to the decision-making process.

The easiest way for you to get others to look at problems from many different angles is to promote as much diversity as possible in your work groups and organization. People tend to look at things based on different values, personalities, culture, etc. Even if they face the same problem, they often come up with

Figure 5.3
What do you think? Intellectual stimulation includes the sharing of perspectives on new ways to address pressing issues in organizations.

different solutions, which oftentimes lead to creativity and innovation. So, one way to create intellectual stimulation is to involve a diverse group of members in the decision-making process, as shown in Figure 5.3. Diversity doesn't just mean different members of your organization. It also means involving customers, suppliers, and even competitors, who can add value to the issue being considered. The varied perspectives that each member brings to the group can spark the intellectual stimulation needed to produce a creative and effective solution.

While producing these solutions, sometimes you can get this information from the least likely people. You never know where you will find your next source of intellectual stimulation. Try looking at someone or something from a different angle, perhaps outside of the role that organizations or society stereotypically place upon them. And be open-minded and listen to others' views on your issues. Allow them to share their perspective on your issues. No matter how many good ideas you have or how many leadership workshops you've attended, unless you are open to embracing drastic and fundamental changes in the way you and your followers work, practicing your own intellectual stimulation may be a challenge.

Suggest New Ways of Looking at How to Complete Assignments

Corporations are notorious for benchmarking and prescribing methods for their employees to use to complete tasks. Managers will frequently say, "But we've always done it this way." Procedure manuals often spell out in excruciating detail how work should be performed, and supervisors often monitor its compliance. This approach stifles creativity and force fits people into procedural boxes that may not be natural for them. It assumes that all people are the same and possess the identical skillsets and preferences for completing assignments. However, research on diversity has shown us that this is not always true, and that people prefer choice and variety in the way they perform tasks.[10]

One way to use this preference to spur creativity and innovation is to suggest new ways to complete assignments and tasks, as shown in Figure 5.4. Such suggestions can identify steps in the process that do not add value and can be eliminated to streamline the method and add efficiency. Or it can simply make the process more fun and encouraging of creativity. We know that freedom of choice regarding how to complete tasks is associated with creative outcomes in business, education, and entertainment.[11] Freedom of choice may also increase employee engagement, which is known to be an important foundation of innovation.

One of the most creative popular musical albums ever produced was the *Smile* LP, finally released in 2004. This musical masterpiece was the brainchild of the Beach Boys' leader and musical genius Brian Wilson and his lyrical collaborator, Van Dyke Parks. Instead of writing songs in the traditional way (e.g., in the office or studio, or at home), Wilson had a large sandbox installed in his living room with a baby grand piano placed in it. Wilson invited his collaborators to sit in the sandbox to compose songs with him for the *Smile* LP. The idea was to create a feeling of being at the beach and to inspire melodies atypical of the Beach Boys'

Figure 5.4
Let's try it this way. Engaging followers by allowing them to freely explain their ideas often leads to the intellectual stimulation of others.

California sound. According to Wilson, several of the essential songs on *Smile* were written in the sandbox to the delight of the lyricists.[12]

This new approach to completing the assignment of songwriting for an album illustrates how intellectual stimulation can be used to create an environment that facilitates creative thinking and behavior. The next time your associates are planning the completion of a project, suggest that they consider alternative locations for or approaches to completing their work. A novel, amusing, or refreshing method may spur the creativity required to produce a project that is a hit with senior managers and customers alike.

Encourage Nontraditional Thinking to Deal with Traditional Problems

If you want to increase creativity and innovation in your organization, you need to encourage your employees to use nontraditional thinking to deal with on-going problems. People tend to stick with old and comfortable ways to work on their job. But we believe that it is an essential part of your job as a leader to promote nontraditional thinking in the workplace.

When it comes to nontraditional thinking, Sir James Dyson is second to none. He has invented a multitude of consumer electronic products that are not only more convenient than traditional ones, but also revolutionary in terms of technology. It is well known that he tried 5,127 times until he perfected a vacuum cleaner which doesn't lose its suction power based on cyclonic separation technologies. He is also known to challenge his employees to look at problems in ways that they've never thought about.[13] No wonder why Dyson keeps churning out innovative products such as a fan without external blades and a hair dryer that has a motor in the handle for compact sizes. As a result, Dyson products have millions of loyal fans and enjoy premium prices without much resistance from customers.

In addition to *nontraditional thinking* which involves thinking outside of the traditional frames of reference, you can also use *contrarian thinking* in which you play the devil's advocate and take a position that is totally opposite to the generally accepted beliefs of the organization. While contrarian thinking may make you come across as difficult or annoying to some coworkers, it certainly can help stem group-think problems and lead to higher-quality decisions that may have been overlooked under tried-and-true problem-solving approaches. Finally, you can also try *lateral thinking* which allows you to look at the problem from a point of view that differs from the norm. To sum up, no matter what kinds of thinking approaches you may want to use, you need to encourage nontraditional thinking to identify new and more innovative solutions for success.

Encourage Rethinking Those Ideas That Have Never Been Questioned Before

When it comes to creativity at work, John had an amusing experience in the early stage of his career as an accountant. Prior to entering academia, he worked as an internal auditor and financial analyst in industry. He can clearly remember his first day of work. As a newly minted CPA-MBA in a brand-new job, he was very excited and looked forward to applying what he had learned in school to improve his company's operational systems and work processes. However, his enthusiasm was quickly diminished by Ted, his first supervisor. Ted's idea of employee orientation was to have John sit in a cubicle and read policy and procedure manuals all day "until new job assignments are assigned to us by the boss." By the end of the day, this lack of interpersonal interaction and intellectual stimulation prompted John to meet with Ted. John asked him questions about the department's auditing and systems policies and procedures. John's questions (Q) and Ted's responses (A) went something like this:

Q: Why do we limit our functions to only internal auditing?

A: Because that's what corporate headquarters defines as the mission for its internal auditing units and it's our job to go by the book. After all, we're accountants!

Q: But as internal auditors, we're often seen by the people we audit as cops looking for mistakes or ways to eliminate their jobs. Why can't we provide other services that help them when we aren't assigned our audits?

A: Because we speak only when spoken to and we don't want to "stir the pot." Besides, that's the way internal auditors have always and will always be seen. You've got to learn how to play the game and go along to get along. John, your idea is not all that bad. . . . Let me think about presenting it to the boss at the right time.

Q: These policies seem to apply to large units like our bakeries or corporate headquarters in New Jersey. Why not try something different here?

A: If it's not broken, don't fix it. It's not our job to worry about these things.

We follow and enforce rules and do as we're expected and told. By the way, you ask too many questions.

Q: So, how have I been doing so far today? How about some feedback?

A: I'll let you know if you screw up. I got to get back to reviewing Joe, Rose, and Grace's working papers. See you tomorrow morning.

Talk about passive management-by-exception leadership! What a wasted opportunity! Ted could have used this opportunity to give his best intellectual simulation to this newly minted and highly engaging employee. But instead, he did the opposite thing, and it turned out as a big turnoff for John. As Don later quipped, "No wonder John eventually changed careers and became an intellectually stimulating leadership professor!"

According to fellow leadership scholars Bruce Avolio and Fred Luthans, moments matter when it comes to leadership.[14] Every interaction you have with your followers provides an occasion to teach, inspire, role model, or challenge them. It offers the chance to move them out of their comfort zones. It provides them with the opportunity to grow. For example, the interaction between Ted and John could have formed the foundation for new directions for the department and more positive attitudes toward internal auditing from internal customers. Despite this missed opportunity, Ted and the department manager eventually did question and reevaluate the role of the department. As a result, they expanded its role beyond audits to creating personal computer and mainframe systems that made the jobs of employees more enjoyable and efficient. And when the internal audit team visited colleagues in the other departments, they greeted them with a friendly smile instead of the look of suspicion. Intellectual stimulation made even an audit team likable!

Figure 5.5 **All points considered. Experienced leaders emphasize intellectual rigor. They concentrate intently as they apply problem-solving methods to perform a group task. Image by Fil J. Arenas, Ph.D. Reprinted with permission.**

When was the last time that you raised an issue that has never before been questioned? By encouraging your followers to rethink ideas that have never before been questioned, you too can steer your group in the right direction. This intellectually stimulating behavior gets followers to rationally evaluate old ideas and strategies that may need to be revised or totally eliminated. As shown in Figure 5.5, intellectual stimulation trains your followers to think critically and systematically. That allows them to use their reason and logic to address important issues and concerns. It also provides you with a wellspring of ideas that you can use to deal with problems that have been plaguing your organization.

Rationale for and Effects of Intellectual Stimulation

Now that we've introduced the concept of intellectual stimulation to you, we'd like you to understand why it is important and what effects it can have on your followers. Intellectual stimulation is important because it allows followers to engage their rational minds in problem-solving activities, participate more fully in the leadership system, and build a strong organizational learning culture. Followers, especially those in the technical fields such as engineering and computer science, typically enjoy problem-solving activities that intellectual stimulation encourages. Such enjoyment is likely to increase employee engagement, creativity, and innovation initiatives. Followers, especially those of the Millennial Generation, expect to participate in leadership initiatives that intellectual stimulation encourages. Intellectual stimulation is also important because it encourages the development of a growth mindset culture, where followers are not afraid to make mistakes and learn from them with much passion and practice along with increased levels of psychological wellbeing. The pursuit of any great accomplishment requires much deep thinking, trial and error, dedication, and effort that the challenges of intellectual stimulation foster.[15]

We believe that a leader's intellectual stimulation might be the best way to develop followers' leadership potential over time because it helps them to exert cognitive (i.e., thinking and perceptual) energy to find better ways to perform their jobs or solve organizational problems. If you are a leader who has a strong desire to practice transformational leadership, we believe that intellectual stimulation is an excellent way to get started because it is easier to execute and more practical than other dimensions of transformational leadership.

Intellectual stimulation can produce several positive effects on followers and organizations. By displaying such behaviors with followers, they become more willing to think, generate creative and innovative ideas, and develop new perspectives about people, processes, and projects. Such behaviors and thought processes are essential aspects of innovation and operational capabilities in organizations and strategic alliances, which are fostered with both transformational leadership and transactional contingent reward leadership.[16] As part of this mix of leadership behaviors, intellectual stimulation changes your followers' assumptions about people, ideas, and work flows. It shows them that you value their intellect and the power of their imagination by asking them to constantly challenge old ways of doing things. As a result, they are more likely to question the status quo, introduce change, champion innovation, and use reason along with the emotion you invoked with inspirational motivation. This powerful combination of effects helps develop followers' perceptional, cognitive, and intuitive skills that are required to become effective leaders.

Intellectual stimulation also makes followers feel fascinated with and curious about their work and challenged by their tasks. It summons them to think in unconventional ways that moves them out of their comfort zone. This deep level of thinking comes from a willingness to question basic assumptions, policies, and procedures that may no longer be valid due to changes in business contexts. It makes followers feel comfortable experimenting with new ideas, technologies, or management tools because they can try out new things without being viewed as undermining authority or being foolish.[17]

Intellectual stimulation can also have some negative effects on followers. The questioning of assumptions and asking followers to rethink their ways of doing things can come across as critical carping or petty faultfinding. The introduction of critical comments into any form of idea generation can make followers reluctant to share their ideas, inhibit their participation in discussions, and stifle their creativity. For these reasons, it is essential that you first build a strong level of trust with your followers by fostering a learning and growth mindset culture before using intellectual stimulation with them. Such an approach should put your followers at ease and change their perception of intellectual stimulation from critical carping to constructive criticism required to reach levels of performance excellence.[18]

Putting Intellectual Stimulation into Practice

Display the Behaviors Described in This Chapter

This chapter presented six behaviors associated with intellectual stimulation. These behaviors emphasized the importance of seeking different perspectives and ways of analyzing problems, questioning assumptions that may no longer be valid, suggesting new ways to complete assignments, encouraging nontraditional thinking, and rethinking ideas that have never been questioned in the past. But before you can put them to use, you must set the stage for intellectual stimulation so that your followers and organization are ready for them.

Identify and Remove Roadblocks to Intellectual Stimulation

Before attempting to display intellectually stimulating behaviors, it's a good idea to identify (and then work to remove) any potential stumbling blocks that may get in the way. Displaying intellectual stimulation without considering potential stumbling blocks, or without building trust, can actually have negative effects on group creativity.[19] So you need to be more strategic about the content and timing of your intellectual stimulation because it may trigger resistance from several sources. These sources of resistance include your organization, leader, followers, problem orientation, and yourself. For each of these sources shown in the next sections, think about the following items that describe them and the degree to which they describe your organization. Keep track of the items that are true for you and your organization.[20]

Your Organization

What do you think might prevent you from using creative thinking processes and practicing intellectual stimulation in your organization? For example, the policies, procedures, and practices that define your organization's culture and structure may present huge barriers to your ability to display intellectual stimulation. How many of the following items are true for your organization?

- Being a creative thinker is risky in my organization.
- Most new ideas don't get implemented in my organization.
- In the past, people in my organization have not been given credit for their innovative ideas.
- In my organization, there are standard rules and procedures for doing the work that must be followed.
- My organization doesn't provide enough support for new ideas to be initiated.
- My organization frowns on mistakes, so innovation and creativity are to be avoided.[21]

If your organization's structure, practices, and policies are a stumbling block, you must work with your colleagues to mobilize support to make appropriate changes. This involves developing an innovation-oriented organizational learning culture, building reward structures that support innovation, hiring creative people, and enlisting top management to identify and remove these roadblocks. What stumbling blocks do you need to get rid of? Who can you rely on when you initiate such changes? What can you do to jump-start such changes in your organization?

Your Leader

Your leader may put the brakes on your ability to display intellectual stimulation. How many of the following items are true for your leader?

- My leader expects everyone to think as he or she does.
- My leader believes only the leader is responsible for developing new ideas.
- My leader is unreceptive to new ideas.
- If I want to get ahead in my organization, I must avoid acting smarter than my leader.
- My leader discourages me and my staff when I try to be more creative.
- My leader often makes fun of other peoples' ideas.[22]

If your leader is a major stumbling block, short of a coup d'état, you must find ways to work around any roadblocks he or she presents. This involves engaging others to show how championing innovation leads to success, creating interest in problem-solving processes, creating demonstration projects to test out new ideas, and educating your leader about the folly of inhibiting creativity and innovation. What can you do to work around the roadblocks your leader builds?

Your Followers

Your followers may get in the way of your ability to display intellectual stimulation. How many of the following items are true for your followers?

- My staff relies on me to develop new ways for them to do their jobs better.
- My followers would feel silly if they were asked to brainstorm new ideas.
- My staff members avoid taking intellectual risks.
- My followers rarely initiate new ideas on their own.
- Most of my staff is afraid to show what they don't know.
- People who work for me lack creativity.[23]

If your followers represent a stumbling block, you can always train and reward them for displaying creative behavior. You can do this by matching their talents and skills with appropriate work. Teach them the intellectually stimulating behaviors described in this chapter. Enroll them in problem-solving and creativity courses offered through universities or consulting firms. Use traditional or electronic brainstorming (described later). Don't forget to "catch them being creative" and reward them for it. Lastly, if you believe that creativity and innovation are really an important part of your success, you need to restructure your hiring criteria to screen out people who are not open to new ways of working on their jobs. Which of your followers can you work with to change their attitude toward creativity?

Yourself

Jack Paar, a famous U.S. radio and television talk show host, once said, "All of life is an obstacle course, with myself being the chief obstacle." Indeed, so many of the wounds that maim or kill intellectual stimulation are self-inflicted. To assess your level of self-mutilation, count how many of the following items you agree with:

- It makes me uncomfortable to question other people's assumptions.
- Usually there is only one right solution to a problem.
- Sitting around trying to generate new ideas is a waste of time.
- When I do something well, I stick to the basic ideas that support my approach.
- If I have the time, I can be far more creative on my own than with my followers.
- I will continue to use old methods that work for me.[24]

Again, the more items with which you agree, the more you are blocking your own ability to intellectually stimulate others. But of all the sources of roadblocks, this one is the easiest to fix (if you really want to change). All it takes is a positive attitude toward creativity and the habit of practicing the behaviors and tactics described in this chapter every day. Your learning partner can also help you a great deal by monitoring and reinforcing your practice of intellectual stimulation.

Use Pragmatic/Problem-Solving Leadership

Problems are a part of everyday life. Leaders are responsible for developing creative and useful strategies for generating solutions to problems based on the functional needs of their organization. For example, Bavarian Motor Works (BMW), the world-famous German manufacturer, is known for its engineering prowess in producing high-performance luxury vehicles. BMW's executive leadership has a long tradition of challenging their engineers to create innovative yet practical cutting-edge designs that address important issues such as fuel efficiency and ecology-friendly emissions. They do this by stimulating the thinking of their employees, as described in Box 5.3.

Box 5.3 Leadership Profile: BMW's Harald Krüger and Technology Leadership

BMW, a company famous for manufacturing high-performance automobiles, can add another feather to its cap. It is now partnering with some of the world's greatest thinkers to spread intellectual thoughts throughout the world in the hope of shaping a better future for all of its citizens. Under CEO Harald Krüger's leadership, BMW is working with Japanese firms who are on the vanguard of self-driving car technology, and reaching out to today's youth who understand the demands of connectivity, electrification of products and services, and the need for autonomy. Krüger constantly challenges his engineers to find the right balance between innovation and tradition, and artistic style and functional substance. For many years, BMW has used several of the intellectually stimulating tactics discussed in this chapter to spur groundbreaking innovation. For example, BMW structures its work processes using network-based cross-functional teams that constantly discuss ideas and projects, both intensely and relentlessly. BMW realizes that the knowledge base for innovation resides in networks of workers, and that leadership is needed to meld their brainpower through intellectual stimulation.

Through cross-functional teams, lateral thinking and communication, balancing hierarchy and discipline within chaordic organizational structures, BMW has created an experimental learning-oriented environment where ideas come first and old-school rigidity is passé. According to BMW's top leadership, engineers working in this environment are exposed to a variety of rich information that allows them to perceive problems in new ways, and frame ideas more accurately. The speed and agility in creativity and problem solving that comes from this environment helps BMW to shift strategy so it can meet changing market demands.

BMW has also joined forces with the TED (Technology, Entertainment, Design) Conference to share their belief that ideas can address many of the world's most pressing problems, such as global warming, poverty, sustainability, prosthetics, war, violence, alternate energy sources, and disease. Each year, over 1,000 great thinkers and performing artists are invited to

TED. Speakers have included Al Gore, Tony Robbins, Simon Sinek, Jill Bolte Taylor (stroke survivor), philosopher Daniel Dennett, and concert violinist Sirena Huang, among many other of the world's thought leaders. Through BMW-produced short movies and website distribution, TED provides people all over the world with intellectual stimulation. This form of mental exhilaration can drive the intersection of technology and social systems toward positive outcomes, just as a BMW can provide its customers with the ultimate driving experience.[25]

BMW's practical approach to innovation is consistent with theory on pragmatic leadership. In Chapter 1, you read about pragmatic or problem-solving leadership theory and how it relates to Full Range Leadership Development (FRLD). Now, let's consider how intellectual stimulation can be used to support pragmatic or problem-solving leadership.

In their conceptualization of pragmatic leadership, Michael Mumford and his academic colleagues proposed that outstanding leadership does not always have to involve inspirational and idealized leadership (i.e., charisma), but instead may be associated with a more practical and functional search for solutions to problems confronting individuals and their organizations. Thus, pragmatic or problem-solving leadership is a process of collecting and using knowledge from problems, people, and their organizations to build and leverage higher levels of wisdom, experience, and perspective-taking capacity.[26]

Knowledge gained from problems is obtained through four processes: (1) defining the problem, (2) gathering information, (3) formulating understanding, and (4) generating trial solutions. You can use the intellectually stimulating behaviors described earlier to support these processes. Considering the problem from many different angles and perspectives can lead you to uncover hidden problems that are more fundamental to the situation and problem. Questioning deeply rooted opinions and assumptions can produce a solid understanding of the problem and alternate solutions. So, we strongly recommend that you ask the right questions, rather than keep asking for the right solutions.

Knowledge gained from people is obtained through three processes: (1) communicating, (2) initiating structure, and (3) implementing and revising plans. You also can use the intellectually stimulating behaviors described earlier to support these processes. Seeking different perspectives and challenging basic assumptions and premises can enrich the quality of the communication process. Intellectual stimulation can "establish a pattern or framework to explain a flow of events to reduce the complexity and diversity of those events,"[27] thereby providing structure to tasks followers must complete. Encouraging followers to revisit problems and reexamine assumptions can support the implementation and revision of plans.

Knowledge gained from organizations is obtained through four processes: (1) protecting outcomes and reactions, (2) identifying restrictions and requirements,

(3) garnering support, and (4) formulating plans/visions. Displaying intellectually stimulating behaviors can help as well. Questioning deeply rooted opinions and assumptions can point out restrictions and requirements needed to solve problems successfully. Seeking varied perspectives can help to ensure that all opinions are communicated thoroughly so that consensus can be achieved more readily than if these perspectives were omitted or ignored. Imagining alternative states, considering absurd assumptions, and widening, shrinking, and splitting the leadership context can assist in formulating an evocative and compelling vision.

Use Brainstorming

When you challenge followers the way BMW CEO Harald Krüger does, you expand their capacity to generate creative ideas together. The more ideas with which they have to work, the greater the base of raw material they have to build innovative solutions to their problems. One method for producing such a large range of ideas is *brainstorming*, a group creativity technique designed to generate a great number and variety of ideas. Traditional face-to-face brainstorming was developed in the 1930s by Alex Osborn, a marketing executive interested in enhancing the creativity of his staff. Today, many organizations use *electronic brainstorming* (EBS), which uses special software to encourage participation through anonymity, file sharing, and simultaneous input of comments from group members.[28] Or, you might consider using online chatting features within Facebook or Google as an informal means to implement brainstorming.

Whether you choose face-to-face or electronic brainstorming methods, be sure to remember to apply the rules of brainstorming:

- *The more ideas, the better.* Encourage your group to produce as many ideas as possible because quantity is assumed to be related to quality.
- *No criticism is allowed.* There are no wrong or bad ideas in brainstorming. It is important for you to separate idea generation from idea evaluation because judgment of ideas by others can stifle creativity.
- *The wilder the ideas, the better.* The goal of intellectual stimulation is to encourage nontraditional thinking and ideas that are "off the wall." Some seemingly crazy ideas can actually lead to innovative breakthroughs. Remember when American Motors Corporation introduced the unsightly Pacer in the 1970s or when Toyota introduced the unusual Prius in 1997 in Japan? Both cars were funny looking when we first saw them. But with the high cost of fuel and social pressure for sustainability these days, Toyota is laughing all the way to the bank.
- *Build on others' ideas.* By combining, modifying, and improving upon ideas offered, you can produce a wide variety of alternative solutions, some of which may be judged as useful when your group meets in a subsequent idea evaluation session.[29]

Brainstorming is a fun and effective way to intellectually stimulate your followers. For example, Pixar is known for using brainstorming as a basis for their work ranging from the story building stage to editing stage of their creative process. Their phenomenal record of success suggests that brainstorming could provide your company with an effective tool for innovation. Give brainstorming a try and be sure to record all ideas generated by your group members either manually or automatically via EBS software. You should then evaluate, rank, and fine-tune all ideas on the list in a future meeting to transform the raw material of the brainstorming session into an action plan.

Promote the Use of Fantasy

The witty Beatle John Lennon once quipped, "Reality leaves a lot to the imagination." Intellectual stimulating leaders, like Lennon, give themselves and their followers a reason to daydream and imagine an ideal situation or world. One way to encourage this is to promote the use of fantasy prior to or during decision-making meetings. *Fantasy* involves portraying in the mind something positive that is not the case or not present at this time. Many of the great inventors, such as Thomas Edison and Louis Pasteur, or famous movie directors, such as Steven Spielberg, Tim Burton, and Spike Lee, imagine pleasant but unlikely events to jump-start their creativity. Fantasy is also used in corporate strategic planning methods such as *scenario planning*, in which alternative futures are envisioned as a way to give free rein to imagination.[30] We also find fantasy in role-playing exercises often seen in corporate training programs.

Fantasy provides us with several outcomes that can benefit our creative thinking. It can supply an experience that is optimal and free from real-life constraints and limitations that bind our ability to generate creative solutions. It allows us to try out various modes of action as potential solutions to problems without cost or risk. It can be a rejuvenating distraction from the daily pressures and stresses of life. It also allows us to get away from it all via a "mental vacation." Even a brief respite can rejuvenate the mind and lead to more creative forms of thinking. In addition, fantasy allows us to dream in ways that are not allowed free expression in our real lives. Fantasy permits us to transcend these boundaries in ways that gain access to deeply stored information in the human psyche. This information can influence and create interest in problem-solving processes.[31]

Fantasy was used by the creators of the Educational Concern for Hunger Organization (ECHO) located in North Fort Meyers, Florida. ECHO uses science and technology to help feed the world's poor in 180 countries. By transcending traditional assumptions about agriculture, ECHO's founding leaders fantasized about and then developed a 50-acre farm that demonstrates how tropical food plants and innovative agricultural techniques can be applied to solve the real problems of world hunger and resource allocation. They do it by providing three services. They educate and train people through internships and workshops. They solve problems by sharing solutions through their bulletins and website, technical response unit, and seed bank. And they build networks of international community development workers through their annual conference and website. Next time you are in South Florida, visit this exemplar of intellectual stimulation that seeks "hunger solutions for families growing food under difficult conditions."[32]

Imagine Alternative States

Fantasy is helpful for intellectually stimulating your followers because it allows you to imagine alternative states. Many of our solutions are not optimal simply because we get bogged down in describing the current situation (and framing our problem) as things are or according to what we're used to, instead of how they *should be*. Rather than describing the current state of affairs, try envisioning the future state you are seeking for your problem solution.

Robb Most of Mind Garden, Inc. is excellent at imagining alternative future states. We often meet Robb at national academic conferences on leadership and organizational psychology. He always updates us on cutting edge ideas for leadership development. Robb is a visionary who excels at seeing possibilities and opportunities through syntheses of ideas, people, processes, and technologies. Rather than seeing things as they are, Robb sees things as means for creating positive ends through alternative futures.

For example, as Robb showed us his latest iPhone, he talked of the possibility of running Mind Garden through his exciting new technology "toy." Robb also mentioned the need for intellectually stimulating leaders to step back and listen to the collective wisdom and life experiences that followers bring to the table. Robb has envisioned internet-based tools to provide multiple self-surveys and assessments that can be administered to such leaders. Multiple observers could rate the leaders. Significant positive and negative events in the leaders' life context could be rated. All of these ratings could be repeated over time to track leadership development. By maintaining the focus on the leader, an unfolding of continuing understanding develops. With this information, a report could be generated and give leaders a comprehensive view of their beliefs, behaviors, feelings, and life context, and how these have changed over time.

Guided by ideas from his staff, Robb also imagined setting up web pages based on Wikipedia that could capture the ideas and experiences of aspiring leaders and their followers. These web pages could be used to illustrate FRLD concepts using unconventional media such as photography, music, art, and movie clips, along with commentary explaining their application. What a fun way to learn more about FRLD! How can you imagine alternate states in your leadership contexts?

Learn to Think Differently

International Business Machines (IBM) originated in Endicott, New York, only a few miles away from the Center for Leadership Studies at SUNY-Binghamton, where we earned our doctorate degrees. IBM Endicott served as corporate headquarters for many years and was home to its education and training activities in the "IBM Schoolhouse." Employees trained at the IBM Schoolhouse were reminded every day of the importance of thinking differently. As they entered into the schoolhouse, they walked up "the five steps of knowledge." Below each step, one of the following words was engraved: read, listen, discuss, observe, and think.[33]

Why? Because reading allows us to expand our knowledge base and exercises the mind. Listening allows us to enlarge our perspective by learning about different points of views and gaining knowledge from the world around us. Discussing things permits us to exchange ideas and fine-tune our thought processes. Observing lets us learn by watching what other people do. Thinking allows us to synthesize all of this information into useful strategies and actions. By espousing these intellectual processes, IBM was teaching its employees that people learn and think differently and that this diversity is required to maximize the effects of intellectual stimulation. Without a doubt, IBM's learning-oriented culture and respect for diverse thinking has been one of the most fundamental reasons for its prolonged success. As an intellectually stimulating leader, you should be aware of several different approaches to thinking that you can use to influence followers.

Rationally oriented thinking uses logic and deduction to develop and articulate reasonable arguments supported by evidence. Use this form of thinking to convince followers by appealing to their reason, or when dealing with individuals who are more transactional in nature, such as colleagues from accounting, finance, and engineering, or with philosophical individuals.

Empirically oriented thinking uses data-gathering processes to weigh the evidence and test propositions offered by the self and others. Like rationally oriented thinking, empirically oriented thinking may be linear in nature and follows a systematic procedure of collecting and analyzing data to test the appropriateness of one solution at a time. Use this form of thinking with scientifically oriented people or technical types to justify your proposition or position developed through data-based decision-making.

Idealistically oriented thinking bases its standards of evaluation on consistency with cherished virtues, values, and principles generally accepted by the community. If you value intellectual stimulation, you may have to adapt your standard of evaluation to include perspectives held outside of your community and those that change over time. Use this form of thinking to influence people who are ideological and find comfort in traditions and customs.

Existentially oriented thinking attempts to synthesize a variety of different perspectives and solutions through informal interactions with others. Because you are dealing with diverse opinions, you may have to use your intuition to access deeply held organizational assumptions, values, symbols, and emotions that you've learned through experience. Use this form of thinking when group consensus is important to moving your agenda forward.[34]

Ask Challenging Questions

Your followers and associates are more educated and technology-savvy than earlier generations. They enjoy being challenged intellectually. Another way to intellectually stimulate them is to ask what they find fascinating and what challenges them intellectually at work and in the community. Once they provide you with answers, you can ask them how they can respond to these challenges with your support.

Asking people challenging questions is something Google likes to do. Google utilizes this form of intellectual stimulation in many of their operations ranging from recruiting new employees to developing innovative technologies and services. Here are some examples of questions they ask job candidates to test their creative thinking capacities.

- How many golf balls can fit in a bus?
- How much should you charge to wash all the windows in Seattle?
- How many piano tuners are there in the world?
- Why are manhole covers round?
- How many times a day does a clock's hands overlap?[35]

Don't these questions sound somewhat confusing and challenging? These questions are not designed to solicit one correct answer. Instead, they are designed to test how people answer ambiguous questions using creative and nontraditional perspectives. So, the next time you sit across from job candidates, consider asking your own version of Google's interview questions to test their creative capacity.

In conclusion, we firmly believe that one of the biggest problems among many leaders today (even the successful ones) is that they do not fully utilize followers' intellectual capacity and creative potential. We have found that this failure is due in part to the leaders' arrogant thinking that they cannot get anything useful and creative from their followers. If you share their viewpoint, this constant underutilization of creative potential among employees will eventually compromise your success as a leader and ultimately undermine the prosperity of your organization. But you can avoid these failures by putting the intellectually stimulating behaviors described in this chapter into practice every day that you lead. Let's now turn our attention to individually considerate behaviors needed to further develop followers into leaders in the next chapter.

Summary Questions and Reflective Exercises

1.   This exercise uses results of your Multifactor Leadership Questionnaire (MLQ) report to assess your level of intellectual stimulation behavior. Compare your intellectual stimulation ratings with the research-validated benchmarks. How did your self-ratings, ratings from subordinates, ratings from peers, ratings from superiors, and ratings from others compare against the benchmarks? On which specific MLQ items (i.e., questions) did you score highest? Lowest? What can you do to improve on the items where you scored lowest?

2.   This exercise also uses results of your MLQ report to assess your level of intellectual stimulation behavior. Compare your self-ratings on *intellectual stimulation behavior* with ratings provided by subordinates, peers, superiors, and others. Compute the difference score (d) as the difference between your self-rating score and the specific other rating source score of interest. If d is less than .5 and the other rating source

score is less than 2.8, then you are considered to be *in agreement/ poor*. If d is less than .5 and the other rating source score is greater than 2.8, then you are considered to be *in agreement/good*. If d is equal to or greater than .5 and the self-rating score is greater than the other rating score, then you are an *overestimator* on this dimension. If d is equal to or greater than .5 and the self-rating score is less than the other rating score, then you are an *underestimator* on this dimension. Consider the category under which you fall in terms of intellectual stimulation behavior. What are the implications of this categorization for you? Are there any things you can do to improve in this area?

3. When you meet with your associates, ask them the following questions, develop an action plan based on their responses, and then solicit their feedback before implementing the plan:

   a. Is there any work/procedure we should change or eliminate for faster implementation?
   b. What would be an important trend we need to examine for next year's strategy and operation?
   c. What do you think customers want from us in terms of products, services, and experiences?
   d. What do you think our competitors would do if we implement the new strategy (or marketing plan)?

4. Identify and adapt a popular game/toy or TV game show from the days of your youth to teach your associates about FRLD. For example, we often use the task of building an airplane with LEGO® building blocks to show FRLD training course participants how leadership styles influence group processes and outcomes. We assign this task to four groups, each guided by a leader displaying either laissez-faire, passive management-by-exception (MBE-P), active management-by-exception (MBE-A), or transformational leadership styles. Participants are amazed how different their planes turn out based on their group's leadership. How can you illustrate the differential effects of FRLD on group processes and outcomes in a fun-filled and intellectually stimulating way?

5. This exercise teaches you how to apply intellectually stimulating and inspirationally motivating behaviors to solve a problem you are facing at work. Assemble a team of four or five associates and describe a problem that you have been working on together as concisely as possible. Start out by talking about the nature (not solution) of the problem with your team. Pay attention to differences in assumptions and perspectives of each team member and note them. Then apply methods of intellectual stimulation to help your team to:

- Envision the *future state* you are seeking for your problem solution. What would it be like if the problem were solved? How would you and your followers feel? How would they benefit?
- Consider the problem's *current state* (i.e., the way you see the problem). You can begin discussing whether any of you have an intuitive or gut feel about the right ways to handle the problem.
- Based on your analysis of the problem, generate and list as many solutions as you feel are appropriate. In this brainstorming of solutions, be sure to list all of your ideas without censoring or evaluating any team member's ideas.
- Establish the criteria you will use to rank the solutions. Then modify and combine any solutions that you can and rank your solutions in the order of quality. Your criteria for ranking might include "It's doable" or "It has the greatest payoff."
- Record the insights and discoveries from using intellectual stimulation and inspirational motivation to solve your problem.[36]

Notes

1   Foote, A., Enterline, T., Egolf, P., & Kline, C. (2008). *Camp Dreamcatcher business plan.* LEAD 582: Social entrepreneurship and community leadership final report. Malvern, PA: Penn State Great Valley.

2   Film information is available at www.imdb.com/title/tt1428083/plotsummary?ref_=tt_ov_pl. For a short trailer of the film, visit www.youtube.com/watch?v=O1uBjLKN8RI.

3   Foote et al. (2008). As cited in Note 1; and Global Social Venture Competition *Social Impact Assessment Guides.* Retrieved from http://gsvc.org/competition/social-impact-guidelines/.

4   Burns, J. M. (2003). *Transforming leadership.* New York: Atlantic Monthly Press.

5   Bhanver, J. S. (2014). *Pichai: Future of Google.* Gurgaon, India, Hachatte; and D'Onfro. (2016). The incredible rise of Sundar Pichai, one of the most powerful CEOs in the world. *Business Insider.* Retrieved from www.businessinsider.com/sundar-pichai-about-2016-2.

6   Denning, S. (2016, March 23). What's behind Warby Parker's success? *Forbes.* Retrieved from www.forbes.com/sites/stevedenning/2016/03/23/whats-behind-warby-parkers-success/#551557b8411a; www.fastcompany.com/company/warby-parker; and www.warbyparker.com/history.

7   Retrieved from www.well.com/~bbear/assumptions.html.

8   Adams, P. (2010). *House calls: How we can all heal the world one visit at a time.* Brandon, OR: Robert D. Reed Publishers; and Adams, P., & Mylander, M. (1998). *Gesundheit! Bringing good health to you, the medical system, and society through physician service, complementary therapies, humor, and joy.* Rochester, VT: Healing Arts Press.

9   Farrow, D., & Kemp, J. (2006). *Why Dick Fosbury flopped: And answers to other big sporting questions.* Crows Nest, Australia: Allen & Unwin.

10 Bell, S. T., Villado, A. J., Lukasik, M. A., Belau, L., & Briggs, A. L. (2011). Getting specific about demographic diversity variable and team performance relationships:

A meta-analysis. *Journal of Management, 37*(3), 709–743; and Dreachslin, J. L. (1996). *Diversity leadership*. New York: Health Administration Press.

11 Amabile, T. M., Conti, R., Coon, H., Lazenby, J., & Herron, M. (1996). Assessing the work environment for creativity. *Academy of Management Journal, 39*, 1154–1184.

12 Priore, D. (2005). *Smile: The story of Brian Wilson's lost masterpiece*. London: Sanctuary Press; and Wilson, B. D., & Greenman, B. (2016). *I am Brian Wilson: A memoir*. Boston, MA: De Capo.

13 Dyson, J. (2000). *Against the odds: An autobiography*. New York: Texere.

14 Avolio, B. J., & Luthans, F. (2005). *The high impact leader: Moments matter in accelerating authentic leadership development*. New York: McGraw-Hill.

15 Dweck, C. S. (2006). *Mindset: The new psychology of success*. New York: Random House; and Sosik, J. J., Chun, J. U., & Koul, R. (2017). Relationships between psychological wellbeing of Thai college students, goal orientations, and gender. *Psychology in the Schools, 54*(7), 703–717.

16 Schweiter, J. (2014). Leadership and innovation capability development in strategic alliances. *Leadership and Organizational Development Journal, 35*(5), 442–469.

17 Bass, B. M., & Avolio, B. J. (1990). *Advanced workshop: Full range leadership development*. Binghamton, NY: Center for Leadership Studies, SUNY-Binghamton.

18 Sosik, J. J., Avolio, B. J., & Kahai, S. S. (1998). Inspiring group creativity: Comparing anonymous and identified electronic brainstorming. *Small Group Research, 29*, 3–31.

19 Sosik et al. (1998). As cited in Note 18.

20 Bass & Avolio (1990). As cited in Note 17.

21 Adapted from Bass & Avolio (1990). As cited in Note 17.

22 Adapted from Bass & Avolio (1990). As cited in Note 17.

23 Adapted from Bass & Avolio (1990). As cited in Note 17.

24 Adapted from Bass & Avolio (1990). As cited in Note 17.

25 DeMattia, N. (2016, December 6). BMW CEO Harald Krüger talks youth, innovation, and our future. *BMW Blog*. Retrieved from www.bmwblog.com/2016/12/05/bmw-ceo-harald-kruger-talks-youth-innovation-future/; and Edmondson, G. (2006, October 16). The secret of BMW's success. *Business Week Online*. Retrieved from www.bloomberg.com/news/articles/2006-10-15/online-extra-the-secret-of-bmws-success.

26 For a comprehensive overview and case study of pragmatic leadership, see Mumford, M. D. (2006). *Pathways to outstanding leadership: A comparative analysis of charismatic, ideological, and pragmatic leaders*. New York: Psychology Press; Mumford, M. D., Zaccaro, S. J., Harding, F. D., Jacobs, T. O., & Fleishman, E. A. (2000). Leadership skills for a changing world: Solving complex social problems. *The Leadership Quarterly, 11*(1), 11–35; and Mumford, M. D., & Van Doorn, J. R. (2001). The leadership of pragmatism: Reconsidering Franklin in the age of charisma. *The Leadership Quarterly, 12*(3), 279–309.

27 Bass & Avolio (1990, p. 12.8). As cited in Note 17.

28 Sosik, J. J., Kahai, S. S., & Avolio, B. J. (1998). Transformational leadership and dimensions of group creativity: Motivating idea generation in computer-mediated groups. *Creativity Research Journal, 11*(2), 111–121. One such effective tool for electronic brainstorming is available at https://thinktank.net/.

29 Hoever, I. J., van Knippenberg, D., van Ginkel, W. P., & Barkema, H. G. (2012). Fostering team creativity: Perspective taking as key to unlocking diversity's potential. *Journal of Applied Psychology, 97*(3), 982–996; and Paulus, P. B., & Nijstad, B. A. (2003). *Group creativity: Innovation through collaboration*. New York: Oxford University Press.

30 Sosik, J. J., Jung, D. I., Berson, Y., Dionne, S. D., & Jaussi, K. S. (2004). *The dream weavers: Strategy-focused leadership in technology-driven organizations*. Greenwich,

CT: Information Age Publishing; and Wade, W. (2012). *Scenario planning: A field guide to the future*. Hoboken, NJ: Wiley.

31 Glassman, E. (2017, May 6). Creativity in action: How to use fantasy creativity triggers at work. *The Times of Israel*. Retrieved from http://blogs.timesofisrael.com/creativity-in-action-how-to-use-fantasy-creativity-triggers-at-work/; and Maccoby, E. E. (1954). Why do children watch television? *The Public Opinion Quarterly, 18*(1), 239–244.

32 American Automobile Association. (2017). *South Florida tourbook* (p. 113). Heathrow, FL: AAA Publishing; and www.echonet.org/.

33 www-03.ibm.com/ibm/history/exhibits/vintage/vintage_4506VV2081.html.

34 Bass & Avolio (1990, p. 12.9). As cited in Note 17.

35 Carlson, N. (2009, November 9). 15 Google interview questions that will make you feel stupid. *Business Insider*. Retrieved from www.businessinsider.com/15-google-interview-questions-that-will-make-you-feel-stupid-2009-11/#how-many-golf-balls-can-fit-in-a-school-bus-1.

36 Adapted from Bass & Avolio (1990). As cited in Note 17.

Chapter 6

Individualized Consideration

The Nurturing Side of Transformational Leadership

According to a survey conducted by *Inc.*, one leadership responsibility that becomes more important today, especially when working with younger generations of associates, is to find a way to unlock their hidden potential.[1] This is because young professionals want to grow quickly and leaders who are willing and able to fulfill their strong need to grow tend to attract top-notch talent. Another interesting trend to consider is highlighted in a recent report published by Deloitte, the global HR consulting firm. They surveyed approximately 7,700 Millennials from more than 20 countries about their plans for career development and attitudes toward their current job and company. It may come as a surprise to older generations of managers that 25% of Millennials have a specific plan to leave their current employer to join another company or to do something different. What's even more surprising is that a whopping 66% of them plan to quit their current employer over the next five years.[2] Think about this situation as a HR manager or team leader would. You now realize that two thirds of your people might have the mentality that "if I don't like my job here, I will quit anytime and move on." This sounds like a nightmare for a leader like you.

But wait, you still can look at this situation from a positive perspective. Here is your cloud's silver lining: the remaining 34% of the respondents who said that they did not have any plan to quit their current job suggests that the most important reason for their strong loyalty is because they feel that their leader or organization has a strong interest in their leadership development and career growth. Therefore, it seems reasonable to conclude that these young people consider leadership development or personal growth as a very important priority. They want to grow. And if you are willing to spend your time to help them grow and develop their leadership potential, then you will become a very attractive leader who can command strong loyalty from your young followers. That's what one of our MBA graduates found out as he helped a new associate who was uncertain about his abilities and organizational role.

As a business improvement manager at global industrial gases company Air Products, John Frinzi is frequently challenged with motivating Millennials. When a position came open in his team, Frinzi went with his gut feeling by selecting Neil, an unknown, outside candidate who did not have specific industry experience. Frinzi took a lot of flak from colleagues who preferred to fill the position with internal candidates that knew the company culture, had specific experience, and could further their career at Air Products by filling the position. But Frinzi sensed that Neil had a strong potential for growth, despite his lack of demonstrated confidence and role certainty. Based upon Neil's rapid progression during his first few months on the job and his Millennial-minded potential to "jump ship" to another company, Frinzi decided to actively engage and personally mentor Neil. They met and discussed Frinzi's assessment and intention of mentoring Neil. Frinzi then invited Neil to accompany him on a customer visit in Manhattan. This close interaction enabled Frinzi to further engage Neil in discussions during their travel.

Frinzi specifically chose a customer in Manhattan so that they could stop in Neil's hometown for lunch. This route created a relaxed environment for Neil and allowed them to get to know each other on a more personal basis. During their lunch meeting at Neil's favorite hometown Italian restaurant, they enjoyed pizza, talked, and compared life experiences. Their previous work roles, backgrounds, and family experiences revealed that they had similar alignment in their thinking and strategic tactics. Although they had different industry experiences, their identified similarities enabled Frinzi to mentor Neil and bridge his learning gap within the industry. Frinzi set high goals for Neil and told him that he would replace Frinzi when he moves on, or that Neil would eventually become one of Frinzi's regional counterparts. After observing Neil's work progress, listening intently to his goals, and comparing their management approaches, Frinzi felt very confident in setting high expectations for Neil. Over the next week, they collaboratively drafted a plan that included assigning Neil to an SAP project and scheduled to have him backfill managers on vacation at work sites within the region.

As a result of observing Neil's abilities, carefully listening to his career ambitions, setting of challenging goals, and developing an action plan with him, Frinzi noticed an immediate positive response and increased energy on Neil's part. Neil responded by providing a detailed matrix of how he planned to learn each work site and gave a comprehensive list of key stakeholders that could assist him in his journey. He even purchased a GMAT test preparation book and identified a potential date to complete the exam so that he could earn an MBA, just like Frinzi. Neil also participated more on conference calls and volunteered to do root cause analyses on challenging issues that the team faced. Frinzi's display of individualized consideration provided Neil with additional confidence and motivated him to higher levels of achievement and career development.[3]

John Frinzi's story teaches us that individualized consideration recognizes the importance of followers to the success of the leadership system. Individualized consideration allows us to look at leadership from the followers' perspective, rather than just our own perspective. When you look at your leadership from their viewpoint, you will see things that you have never seen before. The goal of individualized consideration is to make this change in your perspective and thus increase the engagement level of followers by providing necessary coaching and mentoring for their personal development. This approach allows followers to actively take part in their personal and professional development, while they contribute to achieving organizational goals. Individualized consideration gets followers to become active participants in the leadership system, as described in Box 6.1.

Box 6.1 Recognizing the Types of Followers

Leadership researcher Barbara Kellerman identified a follower's engagement level as a way to classify followers who either contribute or detract from leadership systems. According to Kellerman, followers who detract from leadership systems are called isolates or bystanders. *Isolates* are followers who are completely detached from their work and organization. *Bystanders* go along to get along, but they do not actively participate in organizational initiatives.

In contrast, followers who contribute to leadership systems are participants, activists, and diehards. *Participants* are engaged in their work in ways that benefit them. *Activists* possess a strong emotional connection to their job and organization and are eager to contribute to almost all organizational activities. *Diehards* are zealots who are so enamored with their leader that they are willing to sacrifice themselves for the cause espoused by the leader.[4] John Frinzi's follower could be classified as developing from a bystander to a participant, and with time he may evolve into an activist. Therefore, your comprehension of the individualized consideration component of FRLD should begin with identifying your followers' level of engagement and motivation. By understanding where your followers are in terms of their level of engagement, you can better understand how to apply individualized consideration to help them reach their full leadership potential. Doing so also helps you enhance your organization's performance since individualized consideration is the component of transformational leadership most predictive of organizational effectiveness.[5]

This chapter shows you how to appreciate and tap into the unique variety of knowledge, skills, abilities, and engagement levels your followers bring with them to work every day. You will also learn how to develop your followers' talents into strengths that contribute to your organization's success. By coaching and mentoring your followers into transformational leaders themselves, instead of keeping them as your very own dependent underlings, you too can become a leader who builds a long-lasting relationship with your followers. But that involves learning about a nurturing approach to leadership as described in the case of one of the most successful coaches in the history of college basketball (see Box 6.2).

Box 6.2 Leader Profile: Pat Summitt

In her quest to continue the legacy of a coaching legend, Holly Warlick, head coach of the Tennessee Lady Volunteers, often asks herself two questions. What does it take to accumulate 1,098 wins and 8 national championships over a 38-year coaching career? What leadership behaviors must you display to earn the title of "all-time winningest coach in the history of NCAA basketball"? Pat Summitt, Warlick's predecessor and mentor, knew the answers to these questions because she lived the principles of Full Range Leadership Development (FRLD) almost every day of her life prior to her untimely death in 2016 from early-onset Alzheimer's disease.

Over her magnificent career, Summitt coached some of the greatest athletes in women's college basketball, transforming them from maverick high school superstars into team players who went on to success in professional basketball, coaching, business, and life. Many of Summitt's recruits were "diehard" enthusiasts committed to their own personal agendas. Summitt broke them down and rebuilt them into team players. They came to appreciate that success depends on interdependence rather than independence. Her legacy is not so much about the titles, trophies, or tournaments she has won, but the vast number of players who have achieved personal success in their own careers as a result of her magic touch. That's the true developmental power of transformational leadership.

How did she do it? Summitt devised a leadership system that identifies the raw talents that players bring to the team and transformed them into strengths through a series of processes and principles she called "the Definite Dozen." Actually, these methods are personal values that can be applied as life skills and include respect, responsibility, loyalty, discipline, hard and smart work, teamwork, positive attitude, competition, change, and humility.[6] Many of these values are aspects of idealized influence that Summitt ingrained into her players to guide their behavior on and off of the court. So, the first thing Summitt did was to teach and role model these values so that her players had clear expectations regarding what drives success. These expectations served as important guidelines for their behavior and personal development.

Once Summitt set these expectations, she then used individualized consideration to pay special attention to each player on and off of the court. The heart of individualized consideration lies in treating each and every follower as a unique person, each with different needs and aspirations, and providing different development plans based on their strengths and talents. Thus, she did not treat all of her players the same. She administered personality tests to her players to learn how to best motivate each of them. She scrutinized their behavior and playing styles at practice and studied game tapes to point out areas for development. She frequently met one-on-one with her players to review their progress and make suggestions for improvement. She gave her players feedback that was both timely and direct. Because she was passionate about the game of basketball, Summitt used a form of tough love on her followers. She constantly challenged them to improve and grow into team players. As a result, some players found her ways too demanding. In fact, she's been likened to retired American coach Bobby Knight, her cantankerous counterpart in the men's collegiate game.[7]

Summitt's exemplary mix of individualized consideration and idealized influence shows that transformational leadership is not "feel good" or "touchy-feely" leadership. Many people have the misconception that transformational leadership is a soft form of leadership. This is not true. Rather, transformational leadership gets followers to move out of their comfort zones to develop to their full potential. Like exercise and weight training, this process can be painful or exhilarating, depending on the methods used and the attitude and maturity of the individual willing to make the effort. That's why transformational leaders often provoke strong emotional responses from their followers. During this process, individualized consideration can mitigate followers' burden of accepting the leader's risky vision and performing their role in unconventional ways. It also makes followers feel that their relationship with the leader is more personal, nurturing, and compassionate, and less unconventional and demanding. As Pat Summitt once observed, "It's OK to let down your guard and allow your players to get to know you. They don't care how much you know until they know how much you care."[8]

Individualized Consideration: Definition and Behavioral Examples

Like any great coach in sports, you too can develop your followers into high-performing transformational leaders by displaying individually considerate behaviors. That's because *individualized consideration* involves dealing with others as individuals and considering their needs, abilities, and aspirations as you work together to further their development. Individualized consideration means being empathetic toward the follower, understanding what he or she is about, and investing time in their professional growth. In essence, individualized consideration allows you to transfer your leadership capacity to the next generation of leaders. This action perpetuates your leadership development cycle and legacy.

Individualized consideration is what makes transformational leadership more developmental and sustainable than other types of leadership. As another example of these results, think about how displaying individually considerate behaviors comes naturally to David Novak, the former CEO of Yum Brands (see Box 6.3).

Box 6.3 Leader Profile: David Novak

When David Novak was appointed as the new CEO of Yum Brands, a company spun-off from PepsiCo in 1997, a lot of people were skeptical about the future of the company. Critics argued that his new company didn't have any chance of success. That's because Yum Brands includes brands such as Kentucky Fried Chicken (KFC), Taco Bell, and Pizza Hut that many people try to avoid due to health-related reasons. Who would want to eat fried chicken and pizza when there are abundant choices of healthy alternatives available today?

Despite these gloomy predictions, Novak turned Yum Brands into one of the largest and most powerful restaurant companies with over 43,500 restaurants in more than 135 countries. They employ more than 1.5 million people across the globe. Under Novak's leadership, Yum Brands doubled in size to 41,000 restaurants and its stock price grew 16.5% every year since 1997. With his remarkable accomplishments, Novak was recognized as "2012 CEO of the Year" by *Chief Executive* magazine, one of the "30 Best CEOs" by *Barron's*, and one of the "100 Best-Performing CEOs in the World" by *Harvard Business Review*.

While these recognitions and kudos are impressive, Novak's more important accomplishment lies somewhere else. He leveraged his employees' collective strengths as a powerful force of diversity to build effective teams. He built a company where people were recognized based on their strengths and their knowledge, skills, and abilities were respected. For example, his office was covered with framed photos on every square inch of wall space and even on the ceiling. They were not pictures of Novak with famous movie or sports stars, but with his employees who performed exceptionally well and were given special awards.

He awarded his employees for excellent customer service. Now Novak's former critics considered him to be the business world's ultimate team builder. He developed a company culture that valued nurturing and developing people into leaders and recognized their contributions and achievements. He even personally created a leadership development program called "Taking People with You" in which he taught a three-day workshop with a small group of managers. He taught about 4,000 managers with this program until he retired in 2016. This program teaches managers how to turn people from being focused on themselves to being focused on the team, recognize associates' potential and strengths, celebrate their achievements, truly listen, tap into people's pride, and lead positively.[9]

Like Novak, you can help people develop their full potential and become transformational leaders by practicing behaviors that show care, concern, and empathy for your followers. Let's now examine six important leadership behaviors that allow you to display individualized consideration.

Consider Individuals as Having Different Needs, Abilities, and Aspirations from Others

We believe that the best way to start practicing individualized consideration is to recognize that your followers are not just a bunch of people who were hired to do their work. Instead, you need to realize that they have different needs, expectations, and aspirations. For example, John had an amazing teacher when he was in middle school who showed him what individualized consideration was all about, and that experience had a big impact on his life.

When John was in seventh grade, he transferred from public school to St. Vincent's parochial school in Plymouth, Pennsylvania, because he wanted to attend a private Catholic high school. It was easier for students to gain admittance to this high school if they came from a parochial middle school. After settling into his new school, John quickly mastered the academic subjects and found time to join the basketball team. He enjoyed the fun and camaraderie of training with his friends and classmates and learned much about leadership and teamwork along the way. Unfortunately, John's athletic abilities on the basketball court did not equal his academic prowess in the classroom. In class, he was "the one with all the answers," but on the court, he was an average player, far from being "the answer," like National Basketball Association (NBA) legend Allen Iverson, or today's superstars like LeBron James and Stephen Curry.

John's basketball team was coached by Anthony Saraceno, who was also his seventh and eighth grade science and math teacher. Mr. Saraceno was very demanding during practice and drilled each player based on what they needed to know to develop their playing skills. One day after practice, he came up to John and said he wanted to talk to him before school the next morning. "Oh no," John thought, "he must be cutting me from the team or will make me do more grueling drills." John dreaded coming to school the next day and worried about their meeting.

The next morning, with a sense of impending doom hanging over him, John approached Mr. Saraceno's office and slowly entered. Much to John's surprise, Mr. Saraceno did not lead him down to the gym or even mention the word *basketball*. Instead, he led John to the school's science supply room and asked if John would be willing to help him with a project. He wanted to inventory all of the materials (e.g., beakers, scales, microscopes, chemicals) stored in the supply room. Their job was to determine what materials and supplies could be salvaged or restored for use in teaching science and math topics in class. To a 13-year-old, entering this room was like coming into a mysterious cave filled with ancient artifacts and treasure chests. Many of the supplies dated back more than 50 years, to the school's inception. For a kid who loved history, being in this room was like going back in time through a magic time machine. The chance to bring these artifacts back to the present was both fascinating and motivating to John.

One day, while John was working on the project after school, Mr. Saraceno asked him a question: "John, do you know why I asked you to help me with this project?"

"Is it because you can count on me to get it done?" John asked in response. He replied,

No, because I want you to realize that you, like everyone else, have different talents and skills that can be your ticket to a better life. For a very few, it will be basketball. In your case, education, not basketball, will be your ticket out of here because you have a love of learning, a keen mind, and the heart to persist. Recognize the gifts you were blessed with and work hard to make them stronger, just like we run drills to improve our basketball skills. But always remember that your priority should be your education. People who don't focus on the right priorities in life will end up like the old dusty beakers and chemicals that we're going through . . . useless and irrelevant.

Looking back now, John realizes that Mr. Saraceno was demonstrating individualized consideration with him. He recognized that John was a transfer student who wanted to fit in with the crowd by being on the team. More importantly, he took the time to recognize John's curious mind and need to learn and grow through education. By getting John involved in his special project, he leveraged John's unique talents and strengths and used them to set him on the path that would ultimately lead to his academic career. He also encouraged one of John's teammates to pursue his athletic aspirations. He recognized the different needs, abilities, and aspirations that his students all possessed and through his actions was able to help shape their futures in a significant way.

As leadership researchers, teachers, and consultants, we have come across many successful leaders over the past 20-plus years. To us, it is quite interesting to find that there is a story like John's behind every single successful leader. No one can grow and succeed alone. We need to have someone who can recognize our strengths and give us a sense of hope and confidence at the beginning of our life's journey. Do you have a story like this? Be sure to pass this tradition down to your followers by building upon their story or creating one for them. By treating your followers in your organization as having different needs, abilities, and aspirations, you can make an equally profound impact on their life and career. As shown in Figure 6.1, you can assign them challenging tasks and high-visibility career

Figure 6.1
Go for it. Individually considerate leaders assign challenging tasks appropriate for developing followers' potential to excel.

assignments that are a good fit with their innate talents and skills. By focusing on developing their talents into strengths, you can give them the confidence to become their best possible self. When they become the best version of themselves, they can contribute to the best of their ability. Their contributions can help your organization achieve its collective goals by leveraging the uniqueness and special value that every human being possesses. You don't have to be a CEO of a Fortune 500 company like Dave Novak to practice individualized consideration. You simply need to start practicing individualized consideration today.

Treat Others as Individuals Rather Than a Member of a Group

Kristina works in the human resource department of television home shopping company QVC as a trainer. She is responsible for developing and delivering training modules on corporate leadership and culture. The employees who attend her training workshops come from a variety of functional areas, including accounting, finance, marketing, sales, information technology, and operations. Each group possesses its own leadership challenges, subcultures, and project requirements. They demand much of Kristina and often challenge her regarding training material content and the way she presents it to them.

Several participants complained to Kristina that her training was "too vanilla" and did not apply to their specific problems at work. Under the guise of fairness, she was treating all of her participants the same by force fitting her curriculum on them. Kristina soon realized that her use of an "average leadership style"[10] on all participants was like a one-size-fits-all product offering or Henry Ford's ancient "any color you'd like as long as it's black" approach to marketing. This approach does not work today. With the increased diversity and educational levels of today's followers, leaders and managers must realize that they need to treat their followers as unique individuals rather than as just a group of people.

Kristina came to this realization by thinking about all of the ways her participants differed. After pondering this for some time, she recognized critical differences, such as cognitive abilities, moral development, self-confidence, attitudes, preference for teamwork, technology skills, task engagement, and developmental readiness among her participants. Some enjoyed learning and thinking about new ideas, while others liked to do the same old thing and test what they already knew against what she taught them. Some were interested in doing the right thing and developing character, while others considered such topics as condescending and preachy. Some possessed a positive attitude about their coworkers, jobs, and life in general, while others had a misanthropic view of humanity. With all this diversity, it is no wonder Kristina's training was not being well received.

Once Kristina grasped the nature of their differences, she created an action plan to start treating them as individuals and not simply as a bunch of training participants. She asked them to complete a survey that assessed the earlier-mentioned factors and list their leadership challenges and expectations regarding her training sessions. She then asked them to identify a specific work-related problem that they would turn into a class project and solve using the knowledge, skills, and abilities she imparted upon them in her training. Based on ideas she learned in graduate school, she began to follow a set of principles that she shared with her training program participants:

- *Rule 1: Rattle your righteous mind.* Introduce new ideas that challenge your worldviews and the way you are used to doing things. While we may believe that we are righteous and think accordingly, we may fall victim to self-righteousness that can only be cured with a healthy dose of diverse thinking.

- *Rule 2: Believe.* Believe in yourself. Believe in your team. Believe in your leader. Believe in God. Research has revealed positive relationships between self- and group confidence and performance. So, believing leads to performing well, and can help to reduce the amount of stress and anxiety in our lives.[11]

- *Rule 3: Attitude is everything.* A negative attitude is poisonous and contagious. It ruins not only your life, but also the lives of those around you. It often ruins your day and makes you miserable. It makes your associates miserable. Fortunately, life is all about choices. You can choose to be positive! Next time you fall victim to negativity, stop to talk with a person who is in failing health or is dying. Chances are, they will tell you that every day is a gift and that we have the choice to perceive things either positively or negatively. Life is 10% of what happens to us and 90% of how we choose to react to it. Make the positive choice, and you will be happier and more successful.

- *Rule 4: There is a* me *in* team. Some people will tell you that there is no *me* in *team*. We believe this is false. Anyone can see that the letters *m* and *e* appear in the word *team* and that they spell *me*. However, notice what happens to the word *me* that is part of *team*. The *m* gets separated from the *e*. The *me* is changed when it is part of *team*. And that's what happens when you become part of a team. A part of you changes when you join a team. You start to lose some, but not all, of your egocentric ways as your individual qualities are melded into the collective force of the team. But it is your unique individual qualities that complement those of other team members and help to build high-performing teams. This is what leadership scholar Bruce Avolio meant when he talked about the vital forces within teams and the way that individualized consideration is required to reconcile the power of diversity with the collective synergies produced with inspirational motivation.[12]

- *Rule 5: Break out of your virtual prison and start talking.* Organizational researcher Phil Bobko was once asked how he solves faculty conflicts that often arise over issues of curriculum development or resource allocation. Phil responded by saying that the first thing he does is to move people away from email communication and get them talking face-to-face. How many times have you felt imprisoned by the unnatural pace and stress that our technology-driven society places upon us? Have you noticed the propensity for people to argue more forcefully and "flame" others when they communicate through email? Phil recommends taking time to talk things out until the conflict is solved. If such talking takes a lot of time, so be it. As shown in Figure 6.2, the relationships that you save by solving the conflict are priceless compared to the cost of the time it takes to talk.

- *Rule 6: That which does not kill you makes you stronger.* Kristina often shows her students a clip from the *Rocky Balboa* film (2007, Columbia Pictures). In the clip, Rocky shares a life lesson with his son. Rocky tells him that life is tough and will knock people down often. Successful people get knocked down as much as those who are less successful. But the difference is that successful people keep getting back up and trying again. They never give up. They never stop believing. Life's hard knocks often teach us the most important lessons. We often learn more from our failures and disappointments than from our successes. So, whenever you feel that life just betrayed you, go back to Rule 3 and rejuvenate yourself with a positive attitude.

- *Rule 7: Become the best version of yourself.* Master of Leadership Development (MLD) alum Jay Wischum recommended to Kristina and us one of his favorite authors, a talented motivational speaker and writer named Matthew Kelly.[13] We were intrigued by his work because it paralleled findings that we reported in a series of studies on the self-concept and positive forms of leadership.[14] Kelly's message is that your true purpose in life is not about what you do (e.g., teach at a university) or what you have (e.g., a red BMW and big new house). Rather, it should be about *what you become* over your lifetime. In other words, your purpose in life should be to grow into your best hoped-for possible self through constant self-improvement. Individually considerate leaders use this philosophy when they build upon each follower's unique talents and strengths and encourage them to grow through inspiration, character development, role modeling, perspective taking, and coaching and mentoring.

Figure 6.2
Let's talk it over. Talking one-on-one helps leaders treat followers as unique individuals rather than members of a group. This makes followers feel special and appreciated.

Listen Attentively to Others' Concerns

Let's return to the case of the former CEO of Yum Brands described in Box 6.3. Soon after David Novak became CEO of the failing company, one of the troubles he found was that there was a great deal of animosity between staff at headquarters and franchisees. Many franchise owners blamed headquarters for a lack of support and unrealistic expectations on sales targets and profits. Headquarters blamed franchise owners for not following company policies and guidelines. Novak decided to change that hostile culture. So, he began visiting franchise restaurants across 50 different states whenever he could. During his visits, he listened to franchise owners about their concerns and frustrations. He also asked for any best practices they acquired while running their restaurant.

After recognizing Novak's humble attitude and willingness to listen to their concerns, franchise owners began opening their minds and making a number of invaluable suggestions. Some shared special recipes they developed and tested in their own restaurant. Some offered more efficient ways to prepare foods. They never thought that the CEO of their company would be willing to travel to their own restaurant and listen to their ideas and concerns. Novak's open-minded attitude and respect for their expertise and experiences were able to open franchise owners' hearts and a more collaborative culture was born.[15]

Why bother with such griping sessions, either in corporations or other leadership contexts? Why should we care about hearing what is on the minds of others? The answer is simple: we need to listen because followers and others, such as customers, competitors, and suppliers, are part of the leadership system described in Chapter 2. They provide important sources of information and serve as partners that facilitate the operation of the leadership system. Simply put, they want to be heard by their leader, and as a leader, you have the responsibility of listening to them.

That is one of the first things that Lou Gerstner did when he joined IBM as its CEO in the early 1990s, during perhaps the biggest crisis they ever experienced; he visited key customer accounts and listened to their concerns. He realized that customers are an important part of the leadership system. By meeting with customers, Gerstner was able to detect changes in customer preferences and demand, areas for product and service improvement, and information about competitors. By displaying individually considerate behavior with his customers, Gerstner was able to jump-start one of the greatest corporate turnarounds in history.[16]

When you attentively listen to followers' concerns, you are able to empathize with them. You can recognize their state of mind and emotion, as shown in Figure 6.3. You are able to "put yourself in their shoes." This can make your communication very effective. Most of the time, we're so busy that we ignore what followers say. Or we pretend to listen to them, but we're really thinking about something else. Other times, we listen only to what we want to hear and screen out the rest of the message. But when we practice individualized consideration with active listening, we devote our full attention, and our heart and mind, to what they have to say. This allows us to achieve what leadership consultant Stephen Covey identified as one of the seven habits of highly effective people: "Seek first to understand, then to be understood."[17]

Figure 6.3 **I'm listening. The individually considerate leader listens empathically to the concerns of the follower by cuing in on her emotions and the subtext of her message.**

Help Others Develop Their Strengths

A team of MLD students once interviewed American entrepreneur, sports team executive, and television personality Pat Croce. In the Philadelphia area, Croce is a celebrated maverick leader whose adventurous lifestyle has made him an entertainment and business icon. He has led companies ranging from physical therapy firms to internet start-ups to the Philadelphia 76ers NBA team. One visit to his Twitter webpage (@pat_croce) or website (www.patcroceandcompany.com/) shows the wide range of business initiatives and community events that Croce leads. With his high-energy and charismatic personality, Croce provided the students with an up close and personal view of inspirational motivation and individualized consideration.

One of the questions they asked Croce was whether he focuses on identifying and developing followers' strengths or aims to eliminate their weaknesses through training and development. Croce bemoaned that some of the internet technologists (i.e., programmers) in his companies have no personality, but their strengths come into play when you put them in front of a keyboard and they are "wickedly good." Or a receptionist may have a great personality. She can welcome customers in the front door,

> but she can't add two and two together. So, what you do is that you expand on the strengths and you pair her weakness with someone who is strong in her area of weakness because it takes too much time and energy to try to make her weakness strong. I'd rather take someone and match them up instead of saying "you can't add, so I'm going to send you to a math class." Nah. Tell her, "You just make sure you smile and tell that person 'hello,' bring them in, book them, make sure the date's right, but you make sure your next-door neighbor here does all the billing" . . . you spend too much time and energy training to train people who don't already have the talents and skills . . .[18]

Once Croce identifies strengths in his people, he puts them in jobs and assignments that build their strengths to the level of champions. Then he spends time getting to know about their likes and dislikes and what they find motivating. He finds out about their passions and what they need to accomplish their "game plan." Some need reminders to stay positive. Some need to unlock their minds and think differently. Some need to be reminded that if you don't ask, the answer will always be no. Others need to do more listening and less talking. By providing motivational feedback along the way, Croce stretches his people to develop their innate talents into strengths. And he encourages them to stretch their muscles with his daily exercise routine that he calls "freakin' fitness."

You may not be as extreme as Pat Croce, but you also can demonstrate individualized consideration when you help others develop their strengths. Sometimes, your followers may not have any clue as to what their strengths are. Or, they are not confident enough to believe that they are talented. You have to help them identify their strengths and utilize them. This takes a lot of encouragement and assurance from you. By helping them to accentuate the positive, you build your organization's collective skillset and can match them up with other team members whose skills can complement each other. As shown in Figure 6.4, those actions make for a potent one-two punch when tackling complex and difficult tasks. They also build a high degree of mutual respect because followers typically appreciate the time and effort you expend investing in their personal and

Figure 6.4
Bringing out the best. The speaker is receiving elocution tips from the individually considerate leader.

professional development. We present a four-step coaching approach in Box 6.5 that you can easily follow to identify your followers' strengths and develop their full potential.

Spend Time Teaching and Coaching

In early 2009, Google began an important project identifying common behaviors associated with their top performing managers. They called this *Project Oxygen* since they considered people as the life blood for their company. They analyzed the results from performance reviews, survey feedback, and data collected for nominations of leadership awards, etc. Based on this comprehensive dataset, they identified the following top behaviors of high-performing managers (based on their importance):

- Be a good coach
- Empower your team and don't micromanage
- Express interest in team members' success and personal wellbeing
- Don't be a sissy; be productive and results-oriented
- Be a good communicator and listen to your team, and
- Help your employees with career development.[19]

Out of the six listed behaviors that top performers exhibit at Google, how many behaviors can you identify as an example of developing people? We can see at least four behaviors in the list that have something to do with growing people. Notice what sits at the top of this list. "Be a good coach" is not only an important component of individualized consideration, but also an absolutely required behavior to be a top performer at Google. But, you don't have to be a Googler to practice the coaching of your associates. Coaching is an important skill to develop no matter where you work, if you want to be a successful transformational leader. To illustrate this point, let's consider the case of MLD alumnae Ashley Schneider-Wilson.

Prior to founding DirectHirePharma in 2014, Ashley Schneider-Wilson worked as a global study manager at GlaxoSmithKline Pharmaceuticals. On account of her unusually astute and critical mind, Ashley often reported to multiple bosses from several cross-functional teams. She was frequently called upon to bring new team members up to speed on new drug trials and product tests. Due to her extensive background in research methods and experimental design, Ashley spent a majority of her time teaching colleagues about the benefits and drawbacks of new statistical procedures and designs that they could use. These teaching sessions were typically delivered one-on-one on an ad hoc basis. Ashley enjoyed the deep level of understanding she gained by teaching others the concepts she has learned. However, proper training takes time, and Ashley faced many demands for training from all levels of the organization.

Based on her experience, Ashley has developed a few tactics that make teaching and coaching more efficient across organizational levels. She still uses these tactics today in her role as CEO of her company today. First, she explains

Figure 6.5
Just a few
pointers.
Individually
considerate
leaders spend
time teaching
followers
about work
processes and
procedures.
They are good
coaches and
mentors.

why the topic is important to the trainee and the organization. Second, she asks a lot of questions and uses the Socratic method to probe the trainee's level of comprehension. Third, she uses colorful diagrams to illustrate difficult concepts. And she makes herself available for follow-up tutoring sessions or to answer any questions they may have. All of these tactics enhance trainees' level of interest, comprehension, and ability to quickly apply their new knowledge, skills, and abilities.

When you take the necessary time to teach and coach others like Ashley, you expand your power base as you influence others. As shown in Figure 6.5, you become a trusted source of knowledge and information as you share your wisdom with others. You also contribute to the organization by passing on essential wisdom and knowledge. Indeed, an essential aspect of transformational leadership is the development of followers into leaders themselves. So, it seems that this individually considerate behavior may be mandatory for effective transformational leadership.

Promote Self-Development

Prior to her career advancement at IQVIA, Endo Pharmaceuticals and QuintilesIMS, Aimee Firth-Maggs, MLD was responsible for managing a large group of associates in the revenue analytics department at DaVita, one of the largest kidney-care companies in the United States. Aimee is a strong advocate of promoting the self-development of her staff. While at DaVita, Aimee met with each of her 11 teammates on a biweekly basis or once a week if they were new to the team. During their meeting time, they explored their successes and challenges since their last meeting, and Aimee provided them with coaching and support. She also promoted self-development and encouraged her teammates to pursue stretch assignments that would help them to develop their career opportunities. With teammates who have a great interest in self-development, she worked with them on creating and working on an individual development plan (IDP). By crafting and following up on their IDP, Aimee's teammates could focus on specific behaviors or attributes associated with high performance and identify ways to develop in identified areas.

Aimee still feels that building on strengths is important, but ignoring areas of weakness can blindside associates down the road. She quipped,

> You can ignore your weaknesses and fail to address them, but I guarantee that your competitors or adversaries will not ignore them. They will exploit them. That's why it's important to build on your strengths and address your weaknesses through transformational leadership.[20]

Aimee's comment reminds us of the concept of *confident vulnerability*[21] discussed by leadership scholar Bruce Avolio and alluded to by Mother Theresa, who said that "we must come to terms with the hole in our heart." All of us have holes in our heart, mind, and soul that we need to recognize and mend in the spirit of continuous personal improvement in order to become the best version of ourselves. What vices do you and your followers possess that are puncturing your heart, mind, or soul? How will you eliminate them?

Promoting self-development involves getting your associates to possess a love of learning. They must become enthralled by the process of learning from feedback from others, self-reflection, and discussions with others who also value self-development. Feedback from surveys such as the Multifactor Leadership Questionnaire (MLQ) promotes self-development because it points to strengths and areas for development in specific areas. As shown in Figure 6.6, self-reflection

Figure 6.6 **Some quiet time. Individualized consideration motivates followers to study and reflect on their own as they discover a love of learning.**

promotes self-development through quiet time and thinking deeply about leadership issues in a setting devoid of external stimuli, noise, and interruptions. Discussions with others can enrich and expand understanding of strengths and areas for development through stories and life experiences that bring humanity back into the leadership process. Isn't that what individualized consideration is all about?

Rationale for and Effects of Individualized Consideration

Now that you've been introduced to the concept of individualized consideration, we'd like you to understand why it is important and what effects it can have on your followers. Individualized consideration is important because it allows you to develop the next generation of leaders who can play a critical role in filling the leadership pipeline of your organization. According to a recent study of 100 largest companies in America conducted by *Forbes*, about 86% of CEOs were promoted from within their company.[22] If you don't have a healthy stream of young talent being developed into leaders, your organization may not have a sustainable competitive edge of leadership in the future. That's why many successful leaders have emphasized a leader's role as a people developer. For example, Jack Welch, the famous former CEO of General Electric (GE), said that he spent about 30% of his time on developing people. He went to GE's leadership center at Crotonville twice a month and spent a minimum of three hours teaching leadership because GE places a high value on leadership development (as described in Chapter 2).

Individualized consideration is also important because followers feel respected and valued when leaders treat them as human beings with a different set of needs and aspirations from other followers. And since the role of followership is increasingly important today in maximizing the effectiveness of an organization's leadership system, it makes sense to leverage followers' differences so that they can make important contributions. Think about this claim by putting yourself in your followers' place. Imagine that your boss is looking at your leadership profile and trying to identify your strengths and weaknesses for professional development. Based on that assessment, you are given a job that utilizes your abilities and experience. How would that kind of leadership make you feel?

You might feel that this is the person you want to work with for a long time. This approach is what A. G. Lafley, who served twice as Proctor & Gamble's CEO, was famous for using. As CEO, Lafley had a routine of sitting down with his chief human resource officer on Sunday afternoons so they could talk about their top talent and how to best develop them. His willingness to invest a major part of his personal time for employee development made a difference for the careers of many top-notch talented associates at P&G. As a result, Lafley was able to create a group of highly committed young managers.[23]

As these examples suggest, individualized consideration can produce several positive effects on followers and organizations. By displaying such behaviors with followers, they often become more willing to initiate self-development activities, engage more actively in their followership role, and participate more effectively in discussions with their leaders and associates. They are more likely to express their individuality, learn to enjoy the process of continuous personal improvement, and eventually develop into transformational leaders themselves. That's because individualized consideration makes your followers feel empowered and desire to grow as professionals and persons. It also makes them feel valued because you are paying special attention to them. It encourages a two-way exchange of ideas and personalizes your relationship with them. It also encourages individualism, which is required to promote creativity and prevent group-think that may occur from too much inspirational motivation or blind obedience to the leader.[24]

Individualized consideration can also have some negative effects on followers depending on the leadership context or situation. The encouragement of too much individualism stemming from individualized consideration is at odds with the values of collectivistic cultures that encourage egalitarianism (i.e., all people are equal and deserve the same treatment, resources, and opportunities) and subordination of individual interests to community interests.[25] In collectivistic countries such as Korea, China, or Thailand, leaders who pay too much attention to a specific follower may be viewed unfavorably by other followers. For this reason, we recommend that you temper your display of individualized consideration in such leadership contexts, or add inspirational motivation to your display of individualized consideration so followers can see how they each contribute to the collective plan to achieve your organization's mission.

Another danger of individualized consideration (when coupled with idealized influence) is the potential to create co-dependent followers rather than empowered followers. When followers receive specialized treatment and careful attention from a leader whom they deeply admire, they can become dependent on the leader rather than empowered. *Empowerment* occurs when followers develop into confident and capable independent-minded leaders in their own right, who may or may not share exactly the same ideals, values, and beliefs as the leader. In contrast, *dependency* occurs when followers become emotionally attached to the leader in a way that they cannot separate themselves from the image and ideals of the leader. Therefore, be careful not to get too close to followers when using individualized consideration. Be cognizant of excessive levels of dependence that followers may develop and place upon you as a leader. And be sure to encourage their independent thinking.[26]

Putting Individualized Consideration into Practice

Display the Behaviors Described in This Chapter

This chapter presented six behaviors associated with individualized consideration. These behaviors emphasized the importance of (1) recognizing and appreciating the different needs, abilities, and aspirations followers possess; (2) personalizing interactions with followers; (3) being an active listener with followers; (4) developing followers' talents into strengths; (5) effectively coaching, counseling, and mentoring; and (6) promoting self-development and love of learning. In order to properly display these behaviors with your followers, you first need to understand two core concepts of individualized consideration.

Individuation

When leadership scholar Bernard Bass first conceptualized the idea of individualized consideration, he identified two main subcomponents: individuation and mentoring.[27] *Individuation* refers to the process of recognizing important individual differences in followers that can influence their levels of motivation and performance and promote their development. This process is perhaps more important than ever given the increased workforce diversity in organizations today.

One diversity trend is that women are assuming more leadership positions in U.S. corporations than ever before. According to the Catalyst Organization, 46.8% of the total workforce in the U.S. consists of women.[28] While we have made some progress in terms of gender equality in the workplace, we have a long way to go. For example, women held less than 6% of CEO positions at Standard & Poor's 500 companies and made up 20.2% of corporate board seats of the Fortune 500 companies in 2016. If we consider the global workforce, the situation becomes even worse for women. While women made up 49.6% of the total global workforce in 2015, the global average annual earnings for women were only $11,000, compared to men's earnings of $21,000.[29] Women held only 12% of corporate board seats globally in 2015. We believe that this situation is not only a social injustice, but also an operational injustice because women tend to be rated by their coworkers as slightly more transformational (especially individually considerate and inspirationally motivating) in their leadership style than men. Furthermore, women are more adept than men in navigating social networks and utilizing teams, both of which are important to effective leadership in today's technologically tethered business environment.[30]

To overcome this injustice, women are working very hard to navigate through their complex labyrinth-like career paths. They are also striving to shatter the glass ceiling, which presents an invisible barrier that blocks women and minorities from top management positions. They do this by exceeding performance expectations, and therefore transformational leadership can help in this regard. They are also developing a leadership style with which male leaders are comfortable (i.e., a blend of transactional and transformational leadership). They are seeking out difficult or challenging assignments through individualized consideration displayed by their leaders. They also benefit from learning from influential mentors.

Another trend that illustrates the need for individuation is the growth of racial minorities in the workforce. According to the Pew Research Center, Americans are more diverse in terms of ethnicity and race than ever before. This trend is projected to be stronger in the coming decades.[31] For example, the United States will not have a single dominant racial or ethnic majority by 2055. In order to deal with this increased level of diversity and reduce the growing charges of perceived discrimination within minority groups, leaders should learn to individuate between followers. This allows for tailoring their leadership styles to followers on a personal basis and addressing issues related to diversity leadership. This will make leadership more appropriate and effective in our highly diversified work environment.

DIVERSITY LEADERSHIP ISSUES

A large number of organizations have established diversity leadership processes to introduce their members to the benefits and disadvantages of diversity (visit www.diversityinc.com for detailed examples). Theories of information processing and decision-making highlight the advantages of diversity. Heterogeneous (diverse) groups use better task-relevant processes that lead to higher-quality decisions and creative or innovative products and services. However, social categorization theory proposes that similarity leads to liking and attraction of group members. Such appeal can lead to fewer interpersonal conflicts, cooperation among members, and cohesiveness in homogenous groups.[32] Diversity also can promote conflict and confusion among group members.[33] So, your focus should be on how to manage diversity properly so that you can enjoy the benefits associated with diversity while minimizing its potential challenges.

Proper management of diversity first requires proper perspective. For example, the melting pot metaphor illustrates the traditional view of diversity. Perhaps you have seen video clips from a popular ABC television series entitled *Schoolhouse Rock!* first televised in the 1970s. One of the classic songs from this show is "The Great American Melting Pot," written by Lynn Ahrens and sung by Lori Lieberman. (Please view this short video clip on YouTube.com.) At that time, diversity was considered to be a form of assimilation where "you simply melt right in" and blend into American "collective" culture. FRLD trainees often chuckle with a mix of nostalgic sentimentality and skepticism every time we play the video clip for this song to illustrate this perspective. With today's emphasis on globalization and political correctness, most people experience a discomfort with focusing on assimilation to describe diversity. They are also uncomfortable with focusing solely on differences. Fortunately, a new paradigm that updates the notion of diversity has gained some attention.

A better and more contemporary approach called "diversimilarity" offers a perspective that can be expressed in the phrase "We are different but we are the same."[34] You can consider this approach as the "Salad Bowl (in lieu of Melting Pot)" view of diversity. This alternative view of diversity recognizes and respects differences between people while highlighting similarities. To understand diversimilarity and practice it through transformational leadership, we must first review several layers of diversity that represent individual differences in followers.[35]

We can individuate between followers and associates by considering four layers of diversity: personality characteristics, internal dimensions, external dimensions, and organizational dimensions.[36] In terms of personality, there are many ways we can understand an individual's social reputation and innate nature. However, most individuals vary greatly on the degree to which they possess the Big 5 personality characteristics: openness to experience, conscientiousness, extraversion, agreeableness, and neuroticism/emotional stability.[37] Among these traits, extraversion and agreeableness were most consistently associated with transformational leadership and leadership emergence and effectiveness across a range of studies.[38] Another important personality trait that transformational leaders leverage and work to strengthen is a follower's *self-efficacy*, which refers to a person's belief that he or she is capable of performing a specific task. Research indicates the higher a follower's self-efficacy, the better his or her performance.[39] Followers can increase their self-efficacy levels by learning from past experiences and celebrating their success on similar tasks. Behavior models, such as leaders who display idealized influence and individualized consideration, boost followers' self-efficacy levels. Verbal persuasion and encouragement from leaders also make followers feel more efficacious. Followers can also raise their level of self-efficacy by assessing their physical and emotional states and working to improve them.

Beyond individual differences in personality, diversimilarity recognizes other internal dimensions that can represent differences or similarities. These include age, cognitive/emotional intelligence, sexual orientation, physical ability, ethnicity, and race. Individually considerate leaders appreciate the unique talents, knowledge, and experience that both older and younger followers bring with them. They tailor their interactions and motivational approaches to match followers' level of intelligence and emotional states. They respect individual differences in followers' sexual orientation. They accommodate and are kind to individuals with disabilities, both physical and mental. They also appreciate and celebrate the traditions and values of the race and ethnicity of their followers.

Diversimilarity extends beyond internal dimensions to reflect dimensions outside of the workplace. These external dimensions include followers' geographic location, income level, personal and recreational habits, religion, educational background, work experience, appearance, and parental and marital status. Individually considerate leaders learn about where their followers came from, where they live, and their cultures. They recognize that followers differ in their socioeconomic status; some must work to make ends meet, while others work to derive enjoyment or express themselves. They find out what followers like to do in their spare time, how they relax, and what their hobbies are. They are sensitive to followers' right to practice the religion of their choice and exercise their religious obligations. They find out where followers went to school and how their university degrees can help them better contribute to the organization. They talk to followers about their prior work experience so they can match them in appropriate jobs. Within reason and organizational policy limitations, they tolerate differences in appearances in terms of dress codes and personal expression. They also recognize and facilitate work–family balance for followers with and without families.

Diversimilarity also considers differences and similarities that organizational structures, policies, and culture place on individuals. These include followers' functional area, work content or field, division/department/unit or work group, seniority, work location, and management status. Individually considerate leaders are aware of the functional area in which their followers work, such as accounting, finance, human resources, marketing, or operations. They learn about the professional fields of their followers. They know where followers fit on the organization chart in terms of their business unit or work group. They track followers' tenure with the organization by recognizing work anniversaries. They know the geographic work locations of followers. They also recognize differences in whether followers are management, professional, or staff. In this regard, they do *not* practice "rankism," in which they give individuals at a higher rank more respect or perks than individuals lower on the organizational totem pole.[40] By considering the many ways followers can differ (or be similar), you can become more sensitive to followers and adapt your leadership behaviors to better fit the motivational and developmental needs of today's diverse workforce.

CREATING CULTURES OF DIVERSITY LEADERSHIP

Diversity and health care management scholar Janice L. Dreachslin developed and taught a popular course in Penn State's MLD program based on her research on diversity leadership. Dreachslin sees diversity as multidimensional, including all of the similarities and differences that we previously discussed. She identified a five-part transformation process that organizations and their members must follow to move from awareness to understanding to action on diversity leadership:

- *Step 1: Discovery.* Hold events that grow awareness of diversity as an important leadership and organizational strategic imperative. This step helps individually considerate leaders be alert to the individual needs of followers.
- *Step 2: Assessment.* Systematically review the organization's culture, climate, and practices from the perspective of diverse stakeholders. This step assists individually considerate leaders to recognize differences among people in their strengths, weaknesses, likes, and dislikes.
- *Step 3: Exploration.* Deploy targeted and ongoing training and professional development, including executive coaching, to build on the strengths and address the challenges identified through the assessment phase. This step helps individually considerate leaders provide learning opportunities for followers.
- *Step 4: Transformation.* Introduce fundamental change to people, policies, procedures, culture, and climate to better address the needs of a diverse workforce and customer base. This phase establishes a pattern of incremental successes for elements of the leadership system.
- *Step 5: Revitalization.* Pursue continuous renewal of the organization's commitment to diversity leadership as a distinctive competence and strategic imperative. This phase institutionalizes diversity leadership into the organizational culture.[41]

Consider following these steps to create and sustain a culture of diversity leadership and individualized consideration in your organization.

Mentoring

Transformational leaders are not created by accident. They are oftentimes nurtured by a positive role model who cares about their personal and professional development. For example, Silicon Valley legends Bill Hewlett and David Packard, who started Hewlett Packard in a garage, studied under Stanford University professor Frederick Terman. Whenever they struggled with technical or business issues, Terman gladly spent time with the two young entrepreneurs. Terman was later dubbed as "The Father of Silicon Valley" for his active role as a mentor of aspiring entrepreneurs. Similarly, the two founders of Microsoft, Bill Gates and Paul Allen, were inspired by personal computer inventor Ed Roberts to start their own company and often sought his advice. More recently, one of Google's cofounders, Larry Page, said that he drew much inspiration from Michael Bloomberg and Steve Jobs for business ideas and leadership.[42] The list of famous mentor–protégé relationships seems endless. Nevertheless, what this means is that you cannot establish and run a successful organization alone. Even the brightest people need someone to lean on for advice and leadership development.

These examples suggest that mentoring represents the other major subcomponent of individualized consideration. *Mentoring* occurs when a more knowledgeable and senior individual (i.e., mentor) shares wisdom and experience with a more junior individual (i.e., protégé) for the purpose of advancing the junior individual's career and professional development.[43] Think about the relationships you have been in at work over the course of your career. Who were your mentors? Who have you mentored? What did you think was an effective way to be mentored? As a mentor or protégé, what did you get out of your mentoring relationship?

BENEFITS AND FUNCTIONS OF MENTORING

Research indicates that mentoring relationships benefit mentors and protégés and their organizations. Individuals with mentors (i.e., protégés) receive more promotions and compensation than individuals without mentors. They also experience higher levels of job satisfaction, career satisfaction, life satisfaction, and commitment than those without mentors. Mentors reap benefits such as feelings of prestige, satisfaction that they are shaping a younger version of themselves, and knowing that they are passing on their legacy to another generation or cohort. In addition, the organization reaps benefits from mentoring relationships, including higher levels of organizational commitment and engagement, retention, better managerial succession planning, institutional memory, perceived justice, and enhanced productivity and performance.[44] These benefits occur through the display of mentoring functions by the mentor and perception of them by the protégé.

To produce these results, mentors provide two main functions: career development and psychosocial support. *Career development* involves several task-related actions that help advance the protégé's career. Examples include sponsoring the protégé in organizational events and championing her cause politically. Providing protégés with high exposure and visibility opportunities gets protégés noticed by top management and sets them up for promotions. Coaching the protégé with performance feedback and strategies for success is another important career development function. Also important is protecting the protégé from nasty organizational politics and advising the protégé of potentially dangerous adversaries in the organization and industry. In addition, providing the protégé with challenging and intellectually stimulating assignments can develop skillsets and knowledge bases essential for career advancement.[45] All of these career development mentoring functions use tasks and information to develop the full potential of the protégé and therefore reflect aspects of individually considerate behavior.

In addition to career development functions, good mentors provide *psychosocial support* to address the psychological and emotional needs of protégés so that they stay satisfied and engaged in their careers. These functions address the personal needs of the protégé. They include role modeling of idealized influence behavior by the mentor so that the protégé can emulate appropriate behavior for career success. Mentors also provide acceptance and confirmation behaviors when they complement and encourage protégés to continue along despite struggles and challenges. When needed, mentors counsel protégés on the best approaches for dealing with setbacks or failures. Most importantly, mentors form friendships with the protégé. As time progresses, the mentoring relationship often evolves from a teacher–student association to a collegial association, and ultimately to the protégé's independence from the mentor.[46] All of these psychosocial support mentoring functions use relationship building and diversimilarity concepts to develop the full potential of the protégé and therefore reflect aspects of individually considerate behavior. Learn to enjoy the process of mentoring and you will become a more individually considerate leader.

Become Interested in the Wellbeing and Character Strengths of Others

Individually considerate leaders show real care and concern for their followers and associates. Consider the example of Lieutenant General Stephen L. Kwast of the United States Air Force (USAF), who John met during his Fall 2017 sabbatical visit to Maxwell Air Force Base in Montgomery, Alabama. At that time, Kwast was Commander and President of Air University which provides education, research, and outreach on the art of war and profession of arms through academic degree granting, professional military education, and professional continuing education to more than 170,000 USAF and allied international officers, enlisted and civilian personnel each year.[47]

Kwast is well-known for showing great interest in the concerns, career goals, and character strengths of his Airmen. At the close of business each work day, Kwast opens his home for one hour to Airmen who want to visit and share their concerns and ideas on improving Air University and the USAF. He listens to their ideas so that he can get to know his junior Airmen. Their ideas also assist his organization to adapt more rapidly to the demands of our rapidly changing world. He often talks about the importance of the USAF's mission of controlling violence as a way of bringing rule of law, protecting our civilization from those who seek to destroy it, and uplifting the dignity of human beings from all cultures. At his meetings, Kwast pays special attention to the unique character strengths of his Airmen, often pointing out those that connect with USAF values of humility, integrity, moral courage, empathy, selfless service, and continuous improvement. As described in Box 6.4, these character strengths reflect malleable traits that Airmen bring to life through various transformational and transactional behaviors they display in their operational experiences while they work to achieve tactical and strategic missions. Kwast's concern for his Airmen and appreciation of their unique character strengths illustrates a powerful application of individualized consideration by a top military leader who, with his Airmen, are committed to collectively uplifting the human condition.

Box 6.4 Appreciating the Character Strengths of Officers at Maxwell Air Force Base

Recognizing and appreciating the unique character strengths of followers and how they manifest in leadership behaviors is an essential component of individualized consideration. This is a potent tool for leadership development, especially if the character strengths align with organizational values. In the USAF, integrity (acting honestly and humble beyond reproach), moral courage (standing up for what is right in the face of opposition), empathy (showing compassion and understanding of the feelings of others), and willpower (exercising self-control to do what is right, refrain from doing wrong, and desiring what is good) are valued character strengths. In focus group interviews we conducted at Maxwell Air Force Base,[48] we observed several interesting examples that may help you better understand how to recognize or appreciate such strengths as catalysts for leadership behavior:

- *Integrity*: A Judge Advocate General (JAG), an officer representing the legal branch of the USAF, noticed inconsistencies on how legal policies were being applied. This created a great deal of confusion and some disillusionment among the JAGs. She raised the issue and framed it in terms of how the community was handling ethics, how rules may be applied inconsistently, and how such inconsistencies were affecting levels of trust within the community. The intent of this intervention was to show her senior leader how such actions look to outsiders and how the news media would view the situation. The JAG's integrity motivated her to apply a blend of idealized influence and MBE-A (active management-by-exception) because the JAG community is typically driven by monitoring of ethical performance of others and sometimes not considering themselves.

- *Moral courage*: A pilot aloft in his aircraft was responsible for watch over an Army Ranger ground unit in peril. Despite a command from his superior officer, the pilot refused to stop supporting the Army Rangers and go support an operation to hunt down a high value individual. The pilot took a poll of his aircrew and told the command and control agency that they would not come off of their watch mission. The direct leadership on the ground eventually supported his decision and senior leadership concluded that this was the right decision. The pilot's moral courage fueled his inspirational motivation and idealized influence. He acted decisively with confidence. He collaborated with his flight crew and harnessed team decision-making. He used USAF values to decide which mission to support. He selflessly acted in the best interest of the Army Rangers.

- *Empathy.* A USAF Company Grade Officer was trying to institute a cultural change in his unit. He was challenged to obtain information to better understand how to interact with Army and allied international units. He took the time to interact with peers in other career fields to learn different perspectives on his tactical issue. This action allowed him to solve his issue and complete his mission without having to inquire of higher ranked officers. His empathy triggered a display of inspirational motivation focused on collective action. When making the change, he involved various groups and sought their cohesion. He also demonstrated intellectual stimulation in seeking different perspectives regarding the proposed change.

- *Willpower.* An Army Ranger under fire with his unit did not totally agree with guidance pushed out by his superior officer. The command simply was not consistent with his experience and certainly not in line with his thinking. Despite his initial uncertainty and grave concerns, the Ranger restrained from overriding the order due to a self-assessed lack of perspective in that situation. As it turned out, his superior provided the correct directive and the unit escaped unharmed. As the Ranger pointed out, "Self-control is tricky because it's not always bad to lose a little control, but can be if you let it overtake you." The Ranger's willpower moderated his display of intellectual stimulation as he yielded to his initial questioning of the assumptions of his superior officer.

We want to challenge you to follow Lieutenant General Kwast's example by looking out for the best interest of your followers. A similar approach can easily be taken in corporate settings. Over the past ten years, Don has asked MBA students in his leadership course to take one of their followers out to lunch and question them as part of course requirements. He then requires his students to write a leadership reflection journal based on their experiences and the answers they provide to the following questions:

- "Do you need any support or help?"
- "What are your strengths?"
- "What kind of career do you envision to develop?"
- "What is your ultimate goal in your career and life?"
- "Do you have any issues in terms of relationships with other people?"
- "How is your family doing?"

Don has identified two important patterns in his students' reflection journals. First, many students wrote that they *thought* they knew a lot about the follower they took out to lunch. But in reality, they realized that they knew nothing about the person and felt ashamed of themselves. Second, many students wrote that they realized that the course assignment was the very first time they had a one-on-one conversation with the follower they took out, even though they had been working together for several years. This also was a sad realization for many students.

What about you? Do you think you can do better than these MBA students? If you want to find out, take one of your followers out for lunch or coffee and ask the earlier-mentioned questions. You may be surprised to know that you are no different than Don's MBA students.

We believe that there is no better way to build trust and rapport with your followers than by getting to know them on a personal basis. After all, how is it possible to build a long-term developmental relationship and trust with followers without knowing their strengths, concerns, aspirations, and personal plans? Let them know that you appreciate who they are and what they do. Talk to them about what is going on in their life. Get to know their challenges and needs. Once you gain this knowledge, you will be able to identify developmental opportunities and resources that you can provide them. Such individualized consideration shows that you care about their wellbeing and character.

Celebrate Diversity

Armando Johnson, MLD is a senior manager of nuclear fuels at a large regional power company. As part of his leadership role, he supervises training for a group of technicians. His associates come from all walks of life, a large range of ages, and several different ethnic and racial groups. Instead of demanding conformance to his directives across the board, Armando realizes that there is an infinite number of ways to do a job. He takes the time to explain to his associates the intent of his objectives. Then he leaves it up to his associates to find the best ways to complete their tasks.

Armando uses personal recognition (just like David Novak did at Yum Brands, as described in Box 6.3) to highlight and share success stories that illustrate his associates' participation in his leadership process. For each individual who gets involved, he celebrates diversity by sponsoring various ethnic food lunches, favorite music genre days, and other cultural events. A similar practice is implemented companywide at Qualcomm, where employees with different ethnic backgrounds take turns hosting a party to introduce their unique culture and cuisine. Through these cultural events, employees learn to appreciate cultural diversity and develop global insights for their work. By making as many people as possible feel comfortable and appreciated, Armando and leaders at Qualcomm are able to highlight the benefits of diversity described previously in this chapter.

Establish Mentoring/Coaching Programs in Your Organization

Whereas mentoring is a process in which a mentor provides advice for career development and personal growth in general, coaching is a process in which a coach provides advice for developing a specific competency or ability to perform a job. Therefore, you can choose either mentoring or coaching to promote your followers' growth, depending on their needs or stage of career development. For example, several students and alumni in Penn State's MLD program are employed as senior managers by the Vanguard Group, a prestigious provider of no-load mutual funds. Lara Dushkewich and Gary Generose established an informal group of MLD students and alumni at Vanguard. The group meets to mentor other Vanguard employees who are interested in becoming better leaders. The group uses one-to-one, peer, and network-based mentoring practices to build the leadership skills of interested associates.

This informal mentoring program, along with Vanguard's formal mentoring program, builds a strong learning community. Promoting a love of learning and culture that embraces change is paying off big dividends for Vanguard. The company is yielding a smarter and more diverse portfolio of aspiring leaders, reducing turnover, and enhancing employee engagement and satisfaction levels. Isn't it time for you to grow your human resources through mentoring programs to maximize your return on investment as well?

If you want to try coaching for more immediate outcomes and specific skill development, you don't need to take a three-month training program on coaching or wait for the benefits of mentoring relationships to emerge. Just follow the simple four-step approach described in Box 6.5. You don't need to have an MBA or MLD degree, or be a leadership genius to provide coaching for your followers. Just begin coaching someone for skill development and your individualized consideration will flourish.

Box 6.5 A Four-Step Coaching Process

When it comes to coaching, we have successfully used the following approach with our clients and students. Take each step one at a time to get the best results.

- *Step #1: Selection and Observation*. Pick one follower with the highest level of potential. Observe that person for one day and document his or her strengths and weaknesses.
- *Step #2: Informal Discussion and Feedback*. Have a friendly informal one-on-one meeting over lunch or dinner. During your meeting, discuss the results of your observations. Be sure to highlight this follower's strengths first, rather than pointing out weaknesses first.
- *Step #3: Developmental Task Assignment and Monitoring*. Assign a developmental task that allows your follower to maximize his or her strengths and that affords a good chance of success. Be sure that the task provides a stretch goal (about 120% of his/her normal performance level). Give any needed support at the beginning of task execution. The purpose of the support and feedback is so your follower will not become overwhelmed and give up in the beginning when the task challenge is high. Once the follower feels confident

---

> to begin working on the task, step aside and begin monitoring task performance.
>
> - *Step #4: Feedback and Reward.* Provide continued feedback on the progress your follower makes and praise the positive outcomes. If your follower goes through this four-step cycle, we believe that he or she can develop a greater sense of self-confidence along with increased knowledge, skills, and abilities.[49]

Create Strategies for Continuous Personal Improvement

Vicki Ferguson, MLD, SHRM-SCP, SPHR, is a human resources business partner at Aon Risk Solutions, a global risk management firm. One of Vicki's jobs is to grow the talent pool at her company. Vicki was successful in this role for many years prior to joining Aon. Part of her sustained success comes from her ability to get associates excited about personal development and continuous improvement of the self. Through reward programs, celebrations, fun events, and relevant training, Vicki created a culture of continuous improvement that senior management supported with resources. With proper organizational support, you, like Vicki, can get your associates in the right frame of mind when it comes to building their best possible self. If you accomplish this feat, you have truly mastered the essence of transformational leadership.

But effective transformational leadership is built upon a solid foundation of transactional leadership to satisfy both the intrinsic and extrinsic needs of your followers. We turn our attention to this essential element of FRLD in the next chapter.

Summary Questions and Reflective Exercises

1. This exercise uses results of your Multifactor Leadership Questionnaire (MLQ) report to assess your level of individually considerate behavior. Compare your individualized consideration ratings with the research-validated benchmarks. How did your self-ratings, ratings from subordinates, ratings from peers, ratings from superiors, and ratings from others compare against the benchmarks? On which specific MLQ items (i.e., questions) did you score highest? Lowest? What can you do to improve on the items where you scored lowest?

2. This exercise also uses results of your MLQ report to assess your level of individualized consideration behavior. Compare your self-ratings on *individualized consideration behavior* with ratings provided by subordinates, peers, superiors, and others. Compute the difference score (d) as the difference between your self-rating score and the specific other rating source score of interest. If d is less than .5 and the other

rating source score is less than 2.9, then you are considered to be *in agreement/poor*. If d is less than .5 and the other rating source score is greater than 2.9, then you are considered to be *in agreement/good*. If d is equal to or greater than .5 and the self-rating score is greater than the other rating score, then you are an *overestimator* on this dimension. If d is equal to or greater than .5 and the self-rating score is less than the other rating score, then you are an *underestimator* on this dimension. Consider the category under which you fall in terms of individualized consideration behavior. What are the implications of this categorization for you? Are there any things you can do to improve in this area?

3. Select a high-potential associate in your organization who you would feel comfortable coaching. Follow the four-step coaching process we presented in Box 6.5. Prepare a coaching journal and write down your observations and reflections. Repeat this process for other followers. Receiving coaching from one of your bosses could be an excellent learning experience for yourself as well.

4. Establish the practice of holding a weekly or monthly "town meeting" with your staff. At this meeting, be sure to share the group's accomplishments and allow each member to report on activities since the last meeting. Then ask them to voice any concerns or questions they might have. Be sure to concentrate on listening empathetically to their issues. Take note of their concerns. Work diligently to identify potential solutions to their issues and continue this process to strengthen your individually considerate leadership.

5. With permission of top management, establish a Diversity Action Council (DAC) in your organization. The mission of DAC should be to create a more inclusive culture and educate your associates about the concepts of diversity, diversimilarity, and individualized consideration. Hold meetings and events to inform your associates of culture, history, individual differences, and the benefits of diversity for your organization. Introduce intellectually stimulating concepts such as Robert Fuller's notion of rankism (http://breakingranks.net). Be sure to hold discussion sessions after these events so that others can learn from the DAC events. Report your activities to others interested in leadership development.

6. Imagine that you have four employees in your work group. Your four employees are:

Miles—Miles is out for himself. He always seeks to maximize his personal goals, regardless of whether they are at the expense of others. His goal is to become the youngest manager in the history of your company to be promoted to director of a business unit. Miles thinks of people as either those who can help his cause or those that will get in his way. He sees people as having motives similar to his and therefore judges people on that basis. Miles is a very effective manager, but he has a hard time cooperating with others, unless it advances his own personal agenda.

Flint—Flint likes to please other people. He considers the personal interests and attitudes of others and recognizes that the needs of others are different from his own. He attempts to coordinate his needs with the needs of others. Flint is well known for sacrificing his personal needs and goals to maintain good relations with his coworkers. He generally has high regard and respect for his associates. Flint's problem is that he has trouble taking a hard stand on issues. He walks away from the tough fights that need to be dealt with at work. It's not his style to confront or challenge others. He's afraid of hurting the feelings of others.

Sam—Senior management considers Sam to be a high-potential manager and future top-level director. He likes to place others in challenging assignments that stretch them to the limits of their capacity. Sam believes in stretching people, rewarding them for their performance, and working with them toward a common goal. He is highly motivated to do his best on every job. People who work with Sam place a great deal of trust in his ability to overcome difficult challenges. Sam has a high level of energy that gets others to work harder. When you work with Sam, you feel like he gives you his undivided attention and that you really matter to him.

Perry—Perry has worked for your company for over 15 years but has become increasingly alienated and unengaged in his work. He only puts in the minimum amount of effort to slide by on his job because he feels like the organization owes him. He has not kept up on changes in technology and is the last one to get up to speed on changes in new performance standards. He could care less about learning new and better ways to perform his work. Perry was once a very capable manager when he was promoted into management many years ago. Today, Perry's skills have deteriorated to a point where he is not very effective. Perry thinks that if he stays within the minimal bounds of acceptable performance he will not lose his job.[50]

Due to budget constraints, you can only select one of the four employees to develop through delegation. Your objective is to *maximize the amount of transformational leadership in your work group*. Who will you choose? What tasks will you delegate to this person to raise his level of moral development and performance? Why? What will your preliminary performance improvement plan look like for this person? Which three employees will you *not* choose to develop through delegation? Why?

Notes

1   Yankowicz, W. (2014, January 28). 3 leadership trends of 2014. *Inc.* Retrieved from www.inc.com/will-yakowicz/leadership-trends-of-2014.html.

2   Deloitte. (2017). *The Deloitte Millennial survey 2017.* Retrieved from www2.deloitte.com/global/en/pages/about-deloitte/articles/millennialsurvey.html.

3   Frinzi, J. (2015, April 1). *Leadership experiential exercise post [LEAD 555].* Malvern, PA: Penn State Great Valley.

4   Kellerman, B. (2008). *Followership: How followers are creating change and changing leaders.* Boston, MA: Harvard Business School Press.

5   Most, R. (2008, September 11). Personal communication.

6   Summitt, P. H., & Jenkins, S. (1998a). *Reach for the summit: The definite dozen system for succeeding at whatever you do.* New York: Broadway Books; and Summitt, P. H., & Jenkins, S. (1998b). *Raise the roof: The inspiring inside story of the Tennessee Lady Vols' undefeated 1997–98 season.* New York: Broadway Books.

7   Smith, G. (1998, March 2). Eyes of the storm. *Sports Illustrated, 88,* 88–106; and Towle, M. (2016). *I remember Pat Summitt: Personal memories, insights, and testimonials about the legendary Tennessee Lady Vols basketball coach.* Henderson, TN: Fitting Words LLC.

8   Summitt & Jenkins (1998a). As cited in Note 6.

9   Colvin. G. (2013, July 25). Great job! How Yum Brands uses recognition to build teams and get results. *Fortune.* Retrieved from http://fortune.com/2013/07/25/great-job-how-yum-brands-uses-recognition-to-build-teams-and-get-results/; and www.lead2feed.org/about/david-novak/.

10 Dansereau, F., Graen, G., & Haga, W. J. (1975). A vertical dyad linkage approach to leadership within formal organizations: A longitudinal investigation of the role-making process. *Organizational Behavior and Human Performance, 13*(1), 46–78; and Wallis, N. C., Yammarino, F. J., & Feyerherm, A. (2011). Individualized leadership: A qualitative study of senior executive leaders. *The Leadership Quarterly, 22*(1), 182–206.

11 Peterson, C., & Seligman, M. E. P. (2004). *Character strengths and virtues: A handbook and classification.* New York: Oxford/American Psychological Association.

12 Avolio, B. J. (1999). *Full leadership development: Building the vital forces in organizations.* Thousand Oaks, CA: Sage.

13 Kelly, M. (1999). *The rhythm of life: Living every day with passion and purpose.* New York: Fireside Books; and www.facebook.com/Matthew-Kelly-217042751666054/.

14 Koul, R., Sosik, J. J., & Lerdpornkulrat, T. (2017). Students' possible selves and achievement goals: Examining personal and situational influences in Thailand. *School Psychology International, 38*(4), 408–433; Sosik, J. J., Jung, D. I., & Dinger, S. L. (2009). Values in authentic action: Examining the roots and rewards of altruistic leadership. *Group & Organization Management, 34*(4), 395–431; Sosik, J. J., Avolio, B. J., & Jung, D. I. (2002). Beneath the mask: Examining the relationship of self-presentation attributes and impression management to charismatic leadership. *The Leadership Quarterly, 13*(3), 217–242; and Sosik, J. J., & Dworakivsky, A. C. (1998). Self-concept based aspects of the charismatic leader: More than meets the eye. *The Leadership Quarterly, 9*(4), 503–526.

15 Colvin (2013, July 25). As cited in Note 9.

16 Gerstner, L. V. (2002). *Who says elephants can't dance? Inside IBM's historic turnaround.* New York: Harper Business.

17 Covey, S. R. (1989). *The seven habits of highly effective people: Restoring the character ethic.* New York: Simon & Schuster.

18 Interview with Pat Croce conducted February 5, 2008, by Brian Kovatch, Andrea Laine, Robert Eidson, and Shawn Minnier.

19   Morrison, M. (2012, August 22). Google's Project Oxygen—8 point plan to help managers improve. *RapidBi*. Retrieved from https://rapidbi.com/google-project-oxygen-8-point-plan-to-help-managers/.

20   Firth-Maggs, A. (2009, April 16). Personal communication.

21   Avolio (1999). As cited in Note 12.

22   Williams, D. K. (2016, December 12). How to grow leadership from within your organization. *Forbes*. Retrieved from www.forbes.com/sites/davidkwilliams/2016/12/12/how-to-grow-leadership-from-within-your-company/#fd6795f11293.

23   Hashemipor, G. (2016. June 13). A. G. Lafley: A look back at the career of the most successful CEO in P&G history. *Chief Executive*. Retrieved from https://chiefexecutive.net/g-lafley-look-back-career-successful-ceo-pg-history/.

24   Bass, B. M., & Avolio, B. J. (1990). *Basic workshop: Full range leadership development*. Binghamton, NY: Center for Leadership Studies, SUNY-Binghamton.

25   Jung, D. I., Bass, B. M., & Sosik, J. J. (1995). Bridging leadership and culture: A theoretical consideration of transformational leadership and collectivistic cultures. *Journal of Leadership Studies, 2*(4), 3–18.

26   Cheong, M., Spain, S. M., Yammarino, F. J., & Yun, S. (2016). Two faces of empowering leadership: Enabling and burdening. *The Leadership Quarterly, 27*(4), 602–616; and Kark, R., Shamir, B., & Chen, G. (2003). The two faces of transformational leadership: Empowerment and dependency. *Journal of Applied Psychology, 88*(2), 246–255.

27   Bass, B. M. (1985). *Leadership and performance beyond expectations*. New York: Free Press.

28   Catalyst (2017, August 11). *Knowledge center: Statistical overview of women in the workplace*. Retrieved from www.catalyst.org/knowledge/statistical-overview-women-workforce.

29   Catalyst (2017, August). As cited in Note 28.

30   Vinkenburg, C. J., van Engen, M. L., Eagly, A. H., & Johanbesen-Schmidt, M. C. (2011). An explanation of stereotypical beliefs about leadership styles: Is transformational leadership a route to women's promotion? *The Leadership Quarterly, 22*(1), 10–21.

31   Cohen, D., & Caumont, A. (2016, March 31). 10 demographic trends that are shaping the U.S. and the world. *Pew Research Center*. Retrieved from www.pewresearch.org/fact-tank/2016/03/31/10-demographic-trends-that-are-shaping-the-u-s-and-the-world/.

32   Thompson, L. (2000). *Making the team: A guide for managers*. Upper Saddle River, NJ: Prentice Hall.

33   Pearsall, M. J., Ellis, A. P. J., & Evans, J. M. (2008). Unlocking the effects of gender fault lines on team creativity: Is activation the key? *Journal of Applied Psychology, 93*(1), 225–234.

34   We wish to thank Sandi L. Dinger-Zeljko for introducing us to diversimilarity in discussions held in 2006 and 2015. For more details on this concept, see Ofori-Dankwa, J., & Julian, S. D. (2004). Conceptualizing social science paradoxes using the diversity and similarity curves model: Illustrations from the work/play and theory novelty/continuity paradoxes. *Human Relations, 57*(11), 1449–1477; and Ofori-Dankwa, J., & Reddy, S. (2007). Diversity management using the diversimilarity paradigm: A case study of a major Mid-West food retailing and distribution company. *Journal of Diversity Management, 2*(2), 61–66.

35   Bass, B. M. (1997). Does the transactional/transformational leadership paradigm transcend organizational and national boundaries? *American Psychologist, 52*(2), 130–139.

36   Gardenswartz, L., & Rowe, A. (1994). *Diverse teams at work: Capitalizing on the power of diversity*. New York: McGraw-Hill; and Hajro, A., Gibson, C. B., & Pudelko, M. (2017). Knowledge exchange processes in multicultural teams: Linking organizational diversity climates to teams' effectiveness. *Academy of Management Journal, 60*(1), 345–372.

37 Barrick, M. R., & Mount, M. K. (1991). The Big Five personality dimensions and job performance: A meta-analysis. *Personnel Psychology, 44*(1), 1–26.

38 Judge, T. E., & Bono, J. E. (2000). Five-factor model of personality and transformational leadership. *Journal of Applied Psychology, 85*(5), 751–765; and Judge, T. E., Bono, J. E., Ilies, R., & Gerhardt, M. W. (2002). Personality and leadership: A qualitative and quantitative review. *Journal of Applied Psychology, 87*(4), 765–780.

39 Bandura, A. (1997). *Self-efficacy: The exercise of control.* New York: Freeman.

40 Fuller, R. W. (2004). *Somebodies and nobodies: Overcoming the abuse of rank.* New York: New Society Publishers.

41 Dreachslin, J. L. (1996). *Diversity leadership.* Chicago: Health Administration Press.

42 Huspeni, A. (2012, July 11). Meet behind-the-scenes mentors of 15 top tech executives. *Business Insider.* Retrieved from www.businessinsider.com/meet-the-mentors-behind-the-visionaries-of-tech-2012-7?op=1/#id-hoffman-of-linkedin-turns-to-mark-zuckerberg-and-a-slew-of-other-people-for-advice-7.

43 Kram, K. E. (1985). *Mentoring at work: Developmental relationships in organizational life.* Glenview, IL: Scott, Foreman & Co.

44 Eby, L. T., Turner, D. T., Allen, T. D., Hoffman, B. J., Baranik, L. E., Sauer, J. B., Baldwin, S., Morrison, M. A., Kinkade, K. M., Maher, C. P., Curtis, S., & Evans, S. C. (2013). An interdisciplinary meta-analysis of the potential antecedents, correlates, and consequences of protégé perceptions of mentoring. *Psychological Bulletin, 139*(2), 441–476; and Wanberg, C. R., Welsh, E. T., & Hezlett, S. A. (2003). Mentoring research: A review and dynamic process model. *Research in Personnel and Human Resource Management, 22*, 39–124.

45 Kram (1985). As cited in Note 43.

46 Bouquillon, E. A., Sosik, J. J., & Lee, D. Y. (2005). It's only a phase: Examining trust, identification and mentoring functions received across the mentoring phases. *Mentoring and Tutoring, 13*(2), 241–260; and Kram (1985). As cited in Note 43.

47 U.S. Air Force biographies webpage—Lieutenant General Stephen L. Kwast (2017, October 4). Retrieved from www.af.mil/About-Us/Biographies/Display/Article/108470/major-general-steven-l-kwast/.

48 A multi-year research project conducted by J. J. Sosik, J. U. Chun, Z. Ete, F. J. Arenas, and J. Scherer focused on better understanding how character strengths are transmitted through leadership behaviors, and how they relate to the performance and psychological wellbeing of USAF and Allied captains and the moral development of their subordinate Airmen. The focus group interviews were conducted by J. J. Sosik, F. J. Arenas, and Air University colleagues in 2017. This stream of research has been highlighted in a USAF video podcast discussion (www.dvidshub.net/video/553924/character-day-2017-maxwell-afb) produced as part of Character Strength Day 2017 (https://twitter.com/globalcharacter?lang=en).

49 Our review of the coaching literature identified several different coaching approaches ranging from three-step to eight-step models. Since we prefer parsimonious and intuitive models for leadership development, we distilled these approaches into a simplified and practical four-step model. Excellent references for learning more about the coaching literature include Blakely, J., & Day, I. (2012). *Challenging coaching: Going beyond traditional coaching to face the FACTS.* Boston, MA: Nicholas Brealey-Hodder & Stoughton; Lancer, N., Clutterbuck, D., & Megginson, D. (2016). *Techniques for coaching and mentoring* (2nd ed.). Abingdon, UK: Routledge; and Lyons, P., & Bandura, R. P. (2017). Management coaching with performance templates to stimulate self-regulated learning. *European Journal of Training and Development, 41*(6), 508–518.

50 Adapted with permission from Bass and Avolio (1990, pp. 6.21–6.22). As cited in Note 24.

Chapter 7

Contingent Reward and Management-by-Exception Active

The Two Faces of Transactional Leadership

The Vanguard Group was founded in 1975 by John C. Bogle, a visionary on corporate social responsibility.[1] As CEO, Bogle helped Vanguard to become one of the largest investment companies in the world with more than $1 trillion of assets under management. They focus on selling no-load mutual and index funds where the buyer pays no sales commission. Our students who work at Vanguard tell us that they offer a very small number of socially responsible funds because they are expensive to run. Vanguard's strategy is to be a low-cost investment management company that provides products and services based on what their clients desire. As clients become increasingly committed to a more balanced approach to corporate success (profit + people + planet issues), we suggest that Vanguard use its well-established goals, action plans, and reward systems that harness returns from more socially responsible and environmentally sustainable investments. Such action would be consistent with their signing on to the United Nation's Principles for Responsible Investment agreement and public statements championing efforts to fight climate change.[2]

Vanguard is well positioned to make this strategic move based on its goal-setting and reward systems. Vanguard strives to accomplish these goals through a two-pronged approach to goals. There are goals that relate to employees' personal development that are reviewed on a semiannual basis. And there are strategic goals around what top management wants to achieve as a business. These are also set on a semiannual basis and discussed monthly. Their senior leaders meet at least once every other week with each of their direct reports. They talk about what they're doing and how they're getting things done. They also talk about development opportunities and where things are headed. This helps to prevent big surprises by the time year-end rolls around, when they discuss bonus rankings or merit pay increases. We believe that this mentoring-based developmental approach gives direct reports a more meaningful opportunity to learn something important and relevant to their growth compared to a more traditional program-based approach.

Vanguard's strong work ethic culture and reward systems can also help. In the Vanguard culture, it is assumed employees come to work with the expectation that they will work hard every day. That expectation gets even stronger the higher one is in the company. For associates in the upper echelons of the company, it is expected that they are going to work very hard, and that will yield positive results because they're in the office, more available, and giving maximum effort. At lower levels of the organization, associates look for some type of reward, something to satisfy those who say, "What's in it for me to work harder?" That's where reward systems are vitally important and Vanguard continually explores both monetary and nonmonetary ways to reward their associates. They have reward and recognition mechanisms in place to motivate their associates on a wide range of initiatives. And when senior leaders see their associates step up and do a great job, they reward them for meeting performance expectations.[3]

As the Vanguard case illustrates, people are better motivated when they know what they are expected to accomplish clearly, how their performance is going to be evaluated, and what they will get for their efforts and outcomes. Even if leaders spend a lot of time emphasizing the importance of vision as discussed in earlier chapters, when it comes to "getting things done," these transactional motivation issues become equally important in reality. This chapter shows you how to use goal setting and contingent rewards to pave a path for your followers to reach their performance goals. It also shows you how to actively monitor and control your followers' performance and redirect their focus and effort when they step off the path to success. By monitoring their progress and exchanging contingent rewards for their achievement of agreed-upon goals, you can become a leader who is very instrumental in helping followers attain expected levels of performance. Let's start learning about this transactional approach to leadership by considering Box 7.1 which profiles one of today's most powerful CEOs.

Box 7.1 Leader Profile: Ginni Rometty

When Ginni Rometty assumed the helm at IBM as its CEO in 2011, she had big shoes to fill. Her CEO predecessor Sam Palmisano had a knack for focusing IBM's workforce on meeting quarterly sales goals and rewarding them when they reached their goals. But now in 2017, after failing to meet Palmisano's swan-song revenue goal, and with 20 consecutive quarters of earnings declines, Rometty is busy engineering a downturn for IBM. The former computer and electrical engineer turned CEO is now setting corporate-wide goals of $40 billion in annual revenue by 2018. And she's also promised to add another $4 billion in corporate acquisitions that create new markets for IBM.

Rometty has also advocated better ways of selecting, developing, and rewarding IBM's talented workforce for introducing more innovative strategies into their culture. These arcane human resource systems have been criticized by IBM's employees on Glassdoor.com. That's because they are based on a normal distribution performance rating system that limits annual raises to only top or above-average contributors, who account for only 20%

of all employees. Some employees felt that IBM's distribution of annual pay increases was an unfair veiled non-contingent punishment and headcount reduction that forced them to seek employment elsewhere. Along with complaints about paltry annual salary increases of 1–2% for above average performers, employee morale has declined due to many of IBM's U.S. and European jobs being moved to India and the Far East. Employees also cite IBM management's lack of direct communication of company and division goals. As a result, some of IBM's most talented employees have moved to other companies that offer more transparent communication of company goals and better compensation packages.

Leading a huge company through a significant transition is never easy. Rometty and her top management team are addressing these issues by implementing a system called *Checkpoint*. It provides better and more frequent feedback on job performance, improved coaching practices, and redesigned review processes that move away from stacked rankings based on the normal distribution rating approach to another contingent reward system. The new system was designed with IBM employee input from divisions located all over the world. Managers are trained to better acknowledge and reward the contributions of IBM's talented workforce. That's an asset base that Rometty must continue to attract and retain, so IBM can continuously innovate, meet its challenging revenue growth targets, and gain vital strategic business market share in the fiercely competitive technology industry.[4]

Contingent Reward: Definition and Behavioral Examples

Like Ginni Rometty, you too can pave a path for your followers to reach their performance targets by displaying contingent reward leadership behaviors. That's because *contingent reward* involves a constructive transaction between the leader and the follower. It is constructive because the leader sets goals for followers that clarify expectations for what needs to be achieved to meet desired levels of performance. It is also constructive because it uses rewards to reinforce the positive behaviors followers must display to meet performance targets. Followers typically like receiving rewards because they are positive affirmations of their value as a professional and good organizational citizen.

Over the many years we have been teaching Full Range Leadership Development (FRLD), one *inaccurate* perception we have found over and over again among our MBA students and even executive audiences is that transformational leadership is the only positive way to lead. Some have wrongly concluded that transactional leadership based on contingent rewards is inferior to transformational leadership and therefore should be discouraged. Don once read a column in a business newspaper in which the writer urged people to avoid transactional leadership because it is a very calculative and inhumane form of leadership! However, past research has consistently found that contingent reward can be an equally effective and powerful way to motivate people because it creates consistent expectations between the leader and followers.

Contingent reward is based on an implied transaction between the leader and the follower. Think of contingent reward as a type of contract. A contract spells out what is expected for the parties involved in the transaction. With a constructive transaction, the leader's side of the deal involves setting goals, identifying potential pathways for meeting the goals, and supporting followers for meeting performance expectations. The follower's side of the deal involves performing the tasks required to meet the goals and reaching those goals. When the follower does this, the leader then completes the deal by providing an agreed-upon extrinsic reward to the follower for her satisfactory performance. *Extrinsic rewards* come from outside of the follower, such as a bonus or recognition provided by the leader. These are financial, material, or social rewards given by the leader or organization to the follower. In contrast, *intrinsic rewards* come from inside of the follower from performing a task without external incentives. These are self-granted or psychic rewards internally given by the follower.[5]

Contingent reward leadership establishes instrumentality and valence for followers. It suggests for followers how they can achieve their targets. By clarifying what management wants to achieve and values, followers become well positioned to achieve what's deemed important by their organization, which will create more meaningful and relevant outcomes. Through these processes of clarifying mutual expectations, followers can focus on their tasks, which typically creates higher levels of trust and commitment toward their leaders and organization. This is how contingent reward leadership becomes an important foundation of effective leadership (sometimes as much as transformational leadership) as shown by Ginni Rometty in Box 7.1.

Like Rometty, you can display contingent reward leadership by practicing behaviors that guide, monitor, and reward your followers. Let's now examine four important contingent reward behaviors that allow you to establish a constructive transaction with your followers.

Set Goals for and with Followers

Daniel is department manager of a training group within a corporate university. His staff consists of trainers and support staff. Every April he asks his staff members to complete an activity report. This report summarizes their achievements in terms of the number of courses they have taught and developed and the ratings and comments they received from participants in their courses. It also includes a list of job-related goals for the upcoming year as well as a comparison of last year's goals to their actual performance achieved during the current year. After staff members complete these reports, Daniel meets with each of them to review their goals for the upcoming year. They discuss how the individual goals fit into the overall goals for the department. Daniel often revises his staff's goals to direct their attention to the most important goals that will contribute to the department. He also uses "stretch goals" that elevate his staff's performance expectations because some of his staff members get lazy and set goals that can be easily achieved.

As shown in Figure 7.1, setting goals with your followers individually is an important aspect of contingent reward leadership because it directs followers' attention to what needs to be achieved. If they know what to shoot for, they can regulate the amount of effort they exert. Goals motivate followers by increasing their persistence to try and try again. Goals also get them to search for task-related knowledge and to strategize ways to best achieve the objective or develop action plans to meet their target.[6]

Do you play golf? The sport of golf is a great way to understand the power of goals in motivating your followers. When you tee up your shot at the beginning of a hole, you know the par for the hole. *Par* represents the normal or standard number of shots it takes to hit the golf ball into the hole. Therefore, par is a type of goal. The par tells you what you need to achieve for the hole. With this knowledge, you can strategize how many shots you'd like to take and which golf clubs you will use to achieve par. You get a good sense of the amount of effort you need to put into your shots. Even if you don't make par, knowing what par is gives you the incentive to make par next time you play that golf course. Ever wonder why 60 million people spend a fortune to buy expensive golf clubs, practice countless hours, play golf in hot and humid summer weather, and still enjoy it? Think of the power of goal-setting processes.

Whatever your golf game is, you can win the "master's cup of leadership" by setting goals with your followers and encouraging them to be more persistent. This helps you to reframe their perspective of work into a challenging game. This change in perspective will increase their focus, drive, and commitment to achieving desired results because they, like you, love to be a winner.

Figure 7.1
Mapping it out. A mother sets a travel goal with her child to clarify the expected destination of their planned trip.

Suggest Pathways to Meet Performance Expectations

Setting goals is one thing. But knowing how to accomplish them is another. Followers often want some ideas on how they can attain the goals they agree to achieve. That's why clarifying your expectations by suggesting ways to accomplish tasks is important to initiate a constructive transaction with your followers. This contingent reward leadership behavior is something that Ken practices every chance he gets.

Ken's daughter Sally has Asperger's Syndrome. Sally's condition presents her with challenges in responding to social situations and thinking on her feet in unique situations with unfamiliar people. For example, she gets flustered during phone conversations when people ask her questions she does not understand. Sally's social awkwardness takes its toll on her self-esteem. Concerned by his daughter's challenges, Ken's goal was to raise Sally's self-esteem and confidence in handling future social challenges.

So Ken asked Sally to complete two phone conversations. First she had to call Wells Fargo regarding her investments. Then she had to call the bursar to register for an upcoming college course. Ken displayed transactional leadership by outlining a basic strategy for Sally: anticipate what might be asked, gather the information needed, and have a Plan B or alternative strategy. Prior to the Wells Fargo call, Ken rehearsed the steps with Sally. With information at hand, she placed a speakerphone call to the representative. When Sally was unsure what was requested or made a mistake in her answer, Ken pointed to the computer screen or paper where it was displayed. The Wells Fargo call was successful. There were no hang-ups, no tears, and no miscommunication. The call to the bursar provided Sally a chance to practice this strategy on her own, without Ken's intervention and no speakerphone. When Sally completed the call to the bursar Ken said, "Good job! Success, and no tears!" Ken was proud of his daughter when she concluded her call to the bursar. She demonstrated success and gained increased self-confidence in communicating over the phone. And he realized that a simple task for some may not be a simple task for others.[7]

This example shows that followers need support from their leaders and organization to meet their goals. By suggesting ideas and providing resources to attain the goal, you can provide the well-defined pathway followers need to reach performance targets. This contingent reward leadership behavior helps to initiate a structure that supports followers' efforts to be successful. Meeting performance expectations is an increasingly difficult task because expectations from organizational stakeholders are higher than ever. We believe that most of your followers will do their very best, as long as, in return, you support them through the many trials and tribulations they face in working to achieve their goals. So, have you sat down with each of your followers to set up goals individually and talked about how you will provide support for them to meet these objectives?

Actively Monitor Followers' Progress and Provide Supportive Feedback

As we saw with Ken, parenting is one of the noblest but also most challenging forms of leadership. One great benefit of FRLD is that almost everything you learn in this book can be applied to your role as a parent. That's what Jackie Sharifi did when she used a combination of transactional and transformational leadership on her 21-year-old son, Oliver. Like many children his age, Oliver is at a crossroads in his life where he is reluctant to leave adolescence and move into adulthood. Jackie has been watching the progress Oliver is making in transitioning into a new chapter in his life. She took the time to write a supportive letter to provide him with feedback on where he is in life, where he needs to go, and how she will help him get there.

Jackie told Oliver that he is now a man and that he is facing some daunting challenges that she is confident he will overcome. She emphasized her intent of helping him with some tools that he can use to succeed in whatever it is that he chooses to do in life. She went on to praise him for his friendship with Sam:

> You have been spending a lot of time with your friend Sam, which is a terrific example of reaching out to a friend for help and advice. Sam has set some goals for himself, has a vision of what he wants to become, and a plan for how he is going to achieve his goals. You don't have to follow Sam's path but you can use some of his strategies to get you going in the direction you want to go, like envisioning your future a year or two from now and setting goals to get there and maybe even keeping a daily log of your progress.[8]

In her letter, Jackie outlined six suggestions for Oliver to consider in successfully transitioning into adulthood. These included meeting with her to consider his options for a career, reading a book on career paths for college graduates, studying money management topics, identifying a mentor or life coach for him, reflecting upon Coach John Wooden's "pyramid of success"[9] as an inspirational guidepost, and watching a video of Steve Jobs' speech at the 2005 Stanford University graduation ceremony. Jackie gave her son these suggestions as specific guidelines for what needs to be done to succeed in life. Oliver read the letter and told his mother that it was motivating when they sat down to talk about it. When we checked back with Jackie in July 2017, she told us that she continues to monitor her son's progress and provide him with supportive feedback for all of life's challenges and opportunities. What a great leader Jackie is!

Whether in the role of parent (like Jackie) or leader at work, it is important for you to monitor your followers' progress toward goals proactively, and provide resources that empower them physically, psychologically, and intellectually. Don't let your followers think that once you gave out goals, you became absent in the process. Your role here is to be supportive—to catch them if and when they fall. Be careful not to be too overbearing or controlling. The only time you should look down on them is to help them back to their feet. By doing this, you are building a base level of trust with transactional leadership. Remember that transactional leadership is an important foundation before you can practice transformational leadership.

Provide Rewards When Goals Are Attained

Exchanging extrinsic rewards and recognition for meeting performance targets is the hallmark behavior in contingent reward leadership. As illustrated in Figure 7.2, this is the payoff that followers expect from leaders when they follow through on their side of the deal. And they expect rewards that they value and find personally appealing. That's why it is important to personalize the type of reward you use to the follower's needs and preferences.

For example, Vicki likes the finer things in life and loves to show off her material possessions. With this in mind, Ernie (the boss) rewards her with salary increases or stock options when she meets her sales targets. In contrast, Pierre is financially secure from wise investment of some "old money" from his family. But his financial security fuels his big ego. Therefore, Ernie rewards Pierre with compliments and public recognition that make him feel special and important to the company. Ernie also recently assigned Betty, his gregarious project manager, to a nice corner office after she successfully sealed an important deal. He used this type of extrinsic reward because she spends a lot of time at work and is responsible for building relationships with many people both inside and outside of the company. After Ernie gives his followers their rewards, he often hears them say, "Now, that's what I like!"

Such extrinsic rewards can also enhance the level of intrinsic rewards your followers perceive. For example, when your followers are promoted, get recognition, or get a pay increase, they will feel pride in themselves, a sense of accomplishment and joy in their jobs. These feelings are likely to increase their self-esteem. There are also many people who enjoy their job or service even without a high level of salary or public recognition. Such people include social activists,

Figure 7.2
Making the grade. Parents can set goals for their children's academic achievement and reward them for getting good grades. Image by Karen Norheim. Reprinted with permission.

nonprofit or social service workers, artists, poets, "starving" musicians, or painters. However, some researchers argue that extrinsic rewards diminish intrinsic motivation and rewards. Nevertheless, we believe that if you don't use extrinsic rewards properly and in moderation, intrinsic rewards might have limited effects on employee motivation in the long run. Therefore, you have to remember that reward systems need to allow followers to grow and develop as people, but at the same time realize the power of pay and benefits as strong forces for motivating action. Be sure to give rewards to your followers only when they are deserved. That way your followers will view their distribution as fair and contingent upon outcomes. Remember that the distribution of rewards (and punishments) are frequently observed and reacted to by other followers, so perceptions of how fair you are when distributing rewards are often tested.[10]

Management-by-Exception Active: Definition and Behavioral Examples

We now turn our attention to a more severe face of transactional leadership. If contingent reward leadership is the cordial and civil face of FRLD, then *management-by-exception active* (MBE-A) is its stern face. The MBE-A leadership style seeks to monitor and control followers through forced compliance with rules, regulations, and expectations for meeting performance standards and behavioral norms. It is based on an old concept of exception management dating back to Fredrick Winslow Taylor and the scientific management school. This school of thought aims to improve organizational efficiency through structured systems, detailed instruction, careful observation, and active supervision. One of their tenets suggests that leaders should focus their attention on the special cases (e.g., noncompliant people or processes, inaccurate data, mistakes, poor performance) that need to be addressed because they deviate from normal business operations, expectations, or performance.[11] Based upon this philosophy, MBE-A leadership behavior actively seeks to find and eliminate exceptions prior to or immediately after they occur.

MBE-A leadership aims to keep people and processes in control. Leaders can use elements of control to harness their followers' willingness to contribute and achieve performance goals. At the strategic leadership level, such systems can reduce strategic uncertainties, avoid unnecessary risks, and ensure that important goals are being achieved. For individual followers, control systems can reduce uncertainty about purpose, reduce temptations to shirk duties or act unethically, refocus attention to what needs to be achieved, and define opportunities to meet performance objectives.[12]

MBE-A leadership behavior involves a *corrective transaction* between the leader and the follower. It is corrective because the leader tends to focus on deviations from predefined standards. In other words, the leader swiftly fixes the problem whenever the follower's performance deviates from standard. If used only occasionally or in critical situations, we believe that MBE-A is OK because it allows the leader to control risks and deal with potential problems proactively. However, if used too frequently or inappropriately, followers will despise your

MBE-A leadership behaviors because they focus on what is wrong (punitive), rather than what is right (developmental). Followers will also see you as an annoying micromanager who meddles in everything. This focus can be de-motivating, disheartening, or unfair to followers if it is repeated over time, applied out of context, or used non-contingently as Jamie Dimon found out at JPMorgan Chase (see Box 7.2).

Box 7.2 Leader Profile: Jamie Dimon

Digging into the details is something that JPMorgan Chase Chairman, President, and CEO Jamie Dimon considers essential for effective leadership. After being flabbergasted when presented with trading positions causing the landmark $2 billion trading loss for his company in 2012, Dimon solidified his appreciation of the importance of detailed-oriented processes (and people) in leadership systems. As a son and grandson of stockbrokers, Dimon was taught the importance of finances and management as well as working closely with people to achieve financial goals. This knowledge sparked his interest in economics and psychology, so he went on to earn undergraduate degrees in those fields and an MBA from Harvard University. Prior to assuming the top leadership position at JPMorgan Chase, Dimon worked at American Express as its CFO. His finance and accounting background fueled his obsession with detail-orientation and management-by-exception leadership tactics.

Over the years, Dimon has publicized his leadership philosophy in both interviews and corporate press releases. He sees leadership as requiring active involvement that avoids complacency and mistakes that can hurt employees, customers, clients, and entire markets. This means going to source data that has not yet been analytically finessed by other associates. He believes in documenting most everything, streamlining and monitoring processes, and testing protocols for accuracy and integrity. He also sees leadership as requiring fortitude to take action when needed, high standards of performance that must be monitored and met, and the ability to face the cold-hard facts. For Dimon, dealing with the facts means focusing on negative outcomes and finding ways to improve them. The fixing of problems in a transparent, direct, and honest manner is one way Dimon is able to boost followers' morale because people appreciate integrity and fairness. A staunch advocate of pay-for-performance, he still believes that compensating followers for achieving performance goals counts as an important source of motivation. He has seen many people get upset when they feel that they have not been fairly compensated for their contributions to the company compared to their peers both inside and outside the organization. But Dimon also realizes that judging performance in organizations is not easy (as has Ginni Rometty of IBM as described in Box 7.1). In Dimon's industry, performance is not just about meeting sales goal metrics. It also involves measures of character, teamwork, selection and training of competent associates, and building of sustainable systems and products that add value to the organization. All of these hallmarks of Dimon's leadership philosophy illustrate aspects of transactional leadership that are of critical importance to profit-seeking organizations.[13]

Like Dimon, you can display MBE-A leadership by aggressively searching for errors, micromanaging, and correcting problems before they occur. Let's now examine three important leadership behaviors that allow you to establish a corrective transaction with your followers.

Closely Monitor Work Performance for Errors

Herman delivered the interoffice and postal mail at a financial service center of an international foods company. Although Herman was not one of the most efficient workers, coworkers loved him because of his outgoing personality. During his daily mail delivery runs, Herman would stop and chat with almost anyone. He could ably strike up a conversation on a wide variety of topics, such as how well Major League Baseball (MLB) teams were playing, what was on television the night before, office gossip, and even the quality of food at local church bazaars and festivals. These conversations brightened many days for his coworkers and boosted their morale. When the long conversations ended, Herman would cheerfully meander to his next stop in the office.

One day, Herman's manager, Kim, returned from a seminar on "management-by-walking-around."[14] Kim was a well-respected manager and, at the time, the only woman in the upper echelons of company management. As such, she felt compelled to exceed performance expectations and instill a high level of motivation in all of her employees. She pondered how she could apply what she learned at the seminar to satisfy her compulsion. After thinking about this for some time, she identified Herman as an obvious target.

The next day, Kim snuck behind a cubicle and watched Herman as he lollygagged along, philosophizing about how the New York Yankees are the most overpaid MLB team. After listening to five minutes of Herman's sermon, Kim sprang into action and shouted, "Aha! Is that how you add value to our company, Herman? By working at a snail's pace while the rest of us have our nose to the grind? You better get cracking!" Scared half out of his wits, Herman picked up the pace and started chanting "Speedy delivery! Speedy delivery!" as he moved to the next mail drop. Herman's exclamation conjured up images of Mr. Speedy McFeeley (David Newell), the nervous mailman on the classic PBS television show *Mr. Rogers' Neighborhood*, in the mind's eye of a nearby group of coworkers. They broke into laughter as they witnessed the hilarity of the situation.

Kim used management-by-walking-around to closely monitor Herman's work performance for errors, and he certainly gave her a lot of material with which

Figure 7.3
**Waiting
to strike.
Eyeglasses
lowered, this
manager spots
an employee's
error that
she will soon
address.**

to work. This type of MBE-A behavior motivates followers through intimidation. Because they fear the repercussions of not complying with standards, they typically will change their behavior to get back in line. Their behavior modification is often swift and may be effective in the short run. However, it is unclear whether these changes are long lasting. What Kim got from Herman was mere compliance, not commitment—she needs to create sustainable motivation. By monitoring the work of your colleagues as shown in Figure 7.3, you can help to control their work habits, eliminate deviations from work processes, and improve your organization's efficiency.

Focus Attention on Mistakes, Complaints, Failures, Deviations, and Infractions

Mickey loved his job as executive director of corporate training. His position gave him the power and opportunity to control almost everyone in his department. A born problem solver and control freak, Mickey enjoyed fixing as many problems that he could find with his staff and telling them what to do. He did this with information gathering sessions veiled as social gatherings, interrogations of associates, and heavy-handed approaches to micromanaging his direct reports. Even though he was an executive responsible for building relationships with his clients, Mickey spent most of his day in the office monitoring email, editing copy for print ads, and even editing the email grammar of coworkers. Mickey's frequent display of MBE-A behavior led others to believe that he had a "God complex."

One morning Mickey sat at his desk drinking coffee from his cup that read "He who must be obeyed." As he sipped from the cup, he thought about his approach to leadership. Always a pragmatic type, he reasoned that leadership is all about solving problems for others. He felt confident that he was helping others by "fixing what was wrong with them." After all, a little tough love never hurt anyone. Right?

Wrong! Contrary to his self-perception, people will see Mickey as a spy who snoops around the office and looks for an opportunity to smack down his subordinate for a mistake, not a problem solver. This example teaches us that there is a fine line between the pragmatic problem-solving approach to leadership described in Chapter 1 and focusing your attention on mistakes, complaints, failures, deviations, and infractions to the excess, like Mickey did. Mickey's tough love approach to leadership, when used too frequently, can have extremely negative consequences on followers, such as anxiety, inhibition, and damage to self-esteem and self-efficacy. When you break people down as much as Mickey did, some never are able to come back. Instead, why not build people up when they are broken? The only reason you should look down on people is because you are going to pick them up.

When you actively focus on exceptions, you need to quickly turn the negative message to a positive one by framing it as a developmental experience. Mickey missed out on a great opportunity to use intellectual stimulation to help his followers solve their own problems instead of dictating to them what is wrong and how they should go about fixing their problems. By moving from the display of MBE-A to the display of intellectual stimulation, Mickey could have created a great mentoring moment for many of his followers. Learn a lesson from Mickey and temper your focus on exceptions with transformational leadership. That way you will not end up being the one who must be obeyed due to fear and retaliation, but instead the one who must be respected and admired.

Arrange to Know If and When Things Go Wrong

Janet is a big believer in systems as sources of control because they let people know if and when things go wrong. Coming from the Information Technology (IT) department, Janet felt confident in her ability to use various IT systems, such as time trackers, keystroke recorders, and web browsing monitors, for designing policies and practices to "keep her people in control." Her philosophy stems from the accounting and auditing profession's emphasis on using a system of *internal controls* to keep an organization on track toward meeting its objectives and minimizing the risks that things will go wrong. The purpose of internal controls is to keep people and things in control because of what can happen when things get out of control. Fraud, deception, and financial loss are just some of the outcomes that Janet wanted to avoid.[15]

Janet uses a variety of control activities to monitor employees and ensure that the strategic initiatives set by the senior leadership team are efficiently executed. First, her staff conducts performance reviews of the operational and financial aspects of the departments within her organization. For example, her staff reviews monthly reports comparing budgeted to actual dollars spent and activities performed by the department. They investigate any unusual differences or deviations from standards and ensure that department managers take corrective action. Second, she reviews IT systems to ensure that the accounting and reporting of financial transactions are accurate. She also leads her staff in protecting physical assets and records through inventory counts and reconciliations to records. Third, she makes sure that a segregation of duties exists by assigning different individuals to the recording of transactions and physical custody of the actual assets. This helps to reduce the risk of fraud.[16]

Like Janet, you also can establish a system of internal controls to know if and when things go wrong. By consulting with your associates in the accounting and IT departments, you can leverage auditing knowledge and the power of technology to provide you with the information to monitor and control the people and processes in your department. A solid understanding of organizational policies and their clear communication to your followers helps them understand what you are policing through MBE-A leadership. Using IT to monitor employees for deviations and potential problems makes the policing process routine and consistent rather than emotional and subjective.

Rationale for and Effects of Transactional Leadership Behaviors

Now that you've been introduced to the constructive and corrective forms of transactional leadership (contingent reward and MBE-A), we'd like you to understand why they are important and what effects they can have on your followers.

Contingent Reward: Justification and Expected Outcomes

Contingent reward leadership is important because it provides the foundation upon which transformational leadership behaviors can be most effective. That's because contingent reward leadership directs followers' attention to working toward well-defined short-range goals and satisfies their lower order needs for safety, security, and sustenance through the provision of rewards. These lower-order needs must be satisfied before followers can concern themselves with higher order needs for love/belonging, esteem, and self-actualization that transformational leadership satisfies. So, goal setting and rewards are the essential components that make contingent reward leadership an effective base for transformational leadership.[17]

When leaders set goals for their followers, they must make the goal attractive to followers *and* increase the amount of effort they exert toward attaining the goal. Master of Leadership Development (MLD) program graduate Neil Bryant, who is vice president of sales and development U.S. and Canada at Carestream Health, excels at both of these tasks. Neil makes goals attractive to his followers by illustrating to them how attaining the goal will have a positive impact on their professional and personal development. He does this by explaining how their success in achieving the goal is one small step toward where they want to be in a year or two in their career. He shows them how they can attain personal goals in their life by successfully achieving the tasks required to meet the goal at hand. This helps them to see that the outcome they are striving for is valuable to their growth and success in the future and maintains a balance and connection between professional and personal objectives.

To increase the amount of effort his followers put into their work, Neil raises their expectations of attaining performance goals if they work hard. He does this by pointing out other colleagues who have achieved their goals by working hard and tells them how alike they are. He also points out similar situations where followers were successful in the past and how their success was based on exerting a high level of effort. Another important element is challenging an employee to create her plan for how to achieve objectives within the larger goals so that individual creativity and commitment are ensured. Neil also gets his followers to work harder by increasing their perception of the attractiveness of reaching the performance goal. He does this by highlighting the prestige associated with reaching the goal for followers with a high need for achievement or big egos. For those with a high need for affiliation, he emphasizes the professional and social connections that can come from attaining the goal. And for those with a high need for power, he calls attention to the influence they can exert on others by hitting their target. In essence, Neil makes the goals attractive to his followers by showing them how, by reaching their goals, they can satisfy their personal needs.[18]

Regardless of how you practice goal-setting processes, it is very important to do it consistently. Otherwise, your followers will get confused. Be as persistent as you can be. That's why Neil constantly emphasizes discipline and persistence, knowing followers will face challenges, by embracing a philosophy of "adversity does not build character—it reveals it!" How persistent are you and your followers when you face difficult situations?

One of the most important aspects of successfully using goal setting in contingent reward leadership is holding high expectations for followers. This is what psychologists call *self-fulfilling prophecies* and the Pygmalion effect. In ancient Greek mythology, Pygmalion was a lonely sculptor who carved a statue of a woman out of ivory based on his expectations of the perfect woman. The statue was so beautiful that he fell in love with it. He offered it as a gift as he prayed to the goddess Venus, who brought the statue to life because she pitied him. This myth is the basis for George Bernard Shaw's famous play in which Professor Henry Higgins refines a lower-class flower girl named Eliza Doolittle into a society lady. Both of these stories show us that the power of expectations cannot be overestimated.

These stories are supported by a growing base of research that indicates that your high hopes for another person can result in high performance and that a person's self-expectations can also lead to high performance. In leadership contexts, a leader's high hopes coupled with supportive leadership can increase a follower's positive self-expectations. High hopes that followers self-impose make them more persistent and oftentimes lead to superior levels of performance, which in turn reinforces followers' positive self-expectations and those of the leader. Over time, this sequence of events can spiral into higher and higher levels of confidence and performance.[19] So, follow the suggestions described in Box 7.3 based upon the research of Edwin Locke and Gary Latham, and your goal setting will be much more powerful and effective.

Box 7.3 Making Goal Setting Relevant and Impactful for Followers

- Develop high hopes for your followers and communicate them actively. These expectations fuel their positive expectations and performance and, over time, can allow them to top their previous achievements. However, if you don't communicate your high expectations to your followers, they won't know anything about them.
- Find out what your followers want in their personal and professional lives. Then link their current work to these outcomes so that they will see value in achieving the goals.
- Build your followers' confidence levels by pointing out their previous success stories and identify good performance so that they can connect the behaviors they used to meet their goals with the value you both place on achieving the goal.
- Set moderately difficult goals for followers rather than telling them to "do your best." People rarely perform well when told to "do your best" because they have no standard against which they can compare their effort and outcome.
- When leading your followers, emphasize the importance of reaching the goal for both their career and organizational success. Justifying the goal this way makes followers more committed to the goal, and exert more effort and persistence in working toward the goal.[20]

Goal setting is a method that works well with contingent reward leadership. But not all goals are effective motivators. The most effective goals meet the characteristics that spell out the mnemonic SMARTER that are described in Box 7.4.

Box 7.4 Making Goals SMARTER

The next time you have to create a budget, strategic plan, or action plan for a project, create goal statements that possess these qualities:

- *Specific*: Goals need to be precise and clear. "To purchase a BMW Z4" is a specific goal, while "To purchase a vehicle" is not.
- *Measurable*: Goals need to be matched with metrics to assess the degree to which they are attained. "To increase my sales results by 20% as measured by the Pipedrive sales tracking system" is preferred to "I'll do my best and see what happens."
- *Attainable*: Goals need to be difficult, but not impossible to meet. "To decrease my MBE-A score by 1" is attainable, while "To decrease my MBE-A score to 0" may be unattainable in an auditing department.

- *Results focused*: Goals need to focus on outcomes, not processes. "To increase my annual sales dollars generated by 20%" is results oriented, while "To increase my level of concentration during interactions with customers by 20%" is not because it focuses on processes used to achieve a sales goal.
- *Time-bound*: Goals need a specific time period that they cover so that deadlines can be set. "To increase my annual sales dollars by 20% by fiscal year-end 2019" is a good example.
- *Evaluated*: Goals need to be reviewed to determine the extent of progress made toward their attainment. Hold an evaluation session in which you provide candid and constructive feedback about progress toward goals.
- *Rewarded and shared*: Recognize and reward those who meet your goals. Share the results of your successful goal-setting outcomes with all followers so that best practices can be learned.[21]

Once goals are set and followers work toward attaining the goals, transactional leaders shape followers' subsequent behaviors which lead to positive outcomes. Such behavioral shaping is based on a tenet from educational psychology that people tend to repeat behavior that has favorable consequences or is rewarded, as with contingent reward leadership. In contrast, they tend to avoid behavior that has unfavorable consequences or is punished,[22] as with MBE-A leadership. Rewards and punishments are an effective way to shape a follower's behavior by systematically reinforcing each successive step that moves her closer to the desired action. Such reinforcement may be required to change a follower's behavior, similar to the training shown in Figure 7.4.

In general, *positive reinforcement* (e.g., providing rewards or recognition) strengthens positive behavior. This makes the behavior occur more often by contingently presenting something positive. *Negative reinforcement* (e.g., withdrawing a negative condition) also strengthens positive behavior. This makes the behavior occur more often by contingently withdrawing something negative, such as nagging or hazing. *Punishment* (i.e., administering a negative consequence) weakens or eliminates negative behavior. This makes the behavior occur less often by contingently presenting something negative (e.g., MBE-A) or by contingently withdrawing something positive.[23] To make your contingent reward behavior more effective, choose among these three approaches (positive and negative reinforcement and punishment) carefully depending upon your situation. Apply them as soon as possible so your followers see the connection between their actions and the application of these approaches in accordance with organizational policy.

These approaches to shaping your followers' behavior provide a wide array of possible actions you can use with transactional leadership. But one critical issue that you should always remember is that you need to reward and punish

Figure 7.4
Good going.
Rewards and
punishments
used to shape
followers'
behavior
are based
on the same
premise as
seen in animal
training.
Because Bella
was rewarded
for her hard
work, she is
likely to repeat
her positive
behavior in the
future.

your followers *contingently* upon their performance. In other words, you need to reward them for successful attainment of an agreed-upon goal consistently. And you should punish them contingently only when appropriate and in a consistent manner. If you don't reward people consistently, they will not be able to make the connection between the effort they put into their work and their performance. They will also fail to see the connection between their performance and the outcomes that you value.[24]

It is even worse if you punish your followers (with MBE-A) for no reason at all. Were you ever the victim of noncontingent punishment? What did it feel like to be on the receiving end of this kind of punishment? How did it affect you and those around you? Did you ever dole out punishment for no reason at all? If so, what happened to you and your followers as a result? It probably caused much confusion in the minds of those punished. It may have caused them to dislike or even hate you. As a result, there might have been total breakdowns in communication and the destruction of trust in your relationship. Because punishments affect not only those punished but also observers, groups of followers might have gossiped about the unfair sanctions and their morale probably dropped. That's why it is important for you to use reinforcers contingently and consider the timing of their application. We believe that you now have a potentially powerful tool in contingent rewards and punishments (via MBE-A), but the potency of such a tool is totally dependent upon how you use it. Think carefully and use it wisely if you want your followers to become more willing to exert the effort needed to attain goals, become focused on their work, understand what is expected of them, and be satisfied with your leadership.

MBE-A: Justification and Expected Outcomes

MBE-A leadership is important because organizations have critical systems, policies, processes, and rules that must be maintained and kept under control. No one is perfect. People make mistakes. Some mistakes are serious and create big problems for employees, customers, suppliers, and other organizational stakeholders. The selective attention to deviations and correction of problems when they are detected helps prevent such misfortunes and gets things back on track. As a result of MBE-A, followers become more focused on what leaders pay attention to and control any maverick impulses. They also develop a more cautious attitude and take corrective actions to bring their work back in line with organizational norms and policies.[25]

After reading about MBE-A, you may not particularly care for this style of leadership. After all, MBE-A also results in followers not taking risks and not implementing new ideas that could fail.[26] We agree with you that MBE-A is not the most effective way to lead people. Few people enjoy working for a micromanager. And fewer can constantly deal with MBE-A leadership that dwells on fixing problems. Does this suggest that there is no place for MBE-A leadership?

Actually, MBE-A leadership can be quite effective in a number of situations. When working on tasks or in industries that are regulated, such as the accounting, banking, or pharmaceutical industries, MBE-A is essential for ensuring compliance with rules and regulations. MBE-A can be most effective and even critical in some functional areas in a company. Consider the IT group in your organization. IT systems are critical for the collection and analysis of organizational data and knowledge and for our basic means of communication these days. These systems cannot go down. The same is true in manufacturing sites were a small deviation or problem can cost millions of dollars. For example, there was a small mistake made by an employee working for Samsung Electronic several years ago and it stopped the whole semiconductor operation in Suwon, Korea for a few minutes. But, it cost Samsung $5 million! MBE-A leadership may be required to ensure that such systems are up and running. Another place where MBE-A leadership is appropriate is in life-and-death situations. Military operations often rely on MBE-A to support the command and control function that protects the lives of soldiers. Individuals managing nuclear power plants use MBE-A to ensure safe operations and prevent meltdowns or accidents such as those we witnessed at Three Mile Island in Pennsylvania, Chernobyl in Russia, or Fukushima in Japan. Even Jeff Bezos, the charismatic CEO of Amazon, uses a degree of MBE-A to control human resource and operational processes, but his use of MBE-A has resulted in some unfortunate side effects as described in Box 7.5.

So, you need to figure out what are appropriate situations in which you can selectively practice MBE-A. It's interesting to note that there is a fine line between MBE-A and intellectual stimulation. Both use rational decision-making to solve problems. Both take an active approach to solve problems. These similarities give you a great opportunity to quickly shift from MBE-A behavior to the more effective intellectual stimulation behavior. Once you identify problems to fix, why not *collaborate* with your followers to solve the problem, instead of *commanding* them to do as you say. The difference here is subtle, but the outcome in terms of

Box 7.5 Leader Profile: Jeff Bezos and Amazon's Control Systems

Jeff Bezos is one of the most demanding and controlling corporate leaders of our time. Even as a child, Bezos showed great interest and ability in applying science and technology to achieve his goals while keeping people in check. He once designed an alarm system that kept his younger brother and sister out of his room. After graduating from Princeton, Bezos worked on Wall Street in the computer science field before starting Amazon.com in 1994.

Over the years, Bezos has developed a peculiar leadership style that combines his charisma and penchant for data-analytic control systems with the dream of making Amazon the first trillion-dollar retail company. He assesses his employees on 14 leadership principles or rules that must be memorized and put into practice. He holds his employees accountable for "unreasonably high" (e.g., working 80–85 hours per week) and continually rising performance goals. Amazon's culture of continuous improvement is reinforced with a communication system that promotes sniping and sneaky competition. Employees send secret feedback to other employees' bosses via the Anytime Feedback Tool. The goal of this system is to make employees "self-critical" and constantly strive for improvement in a Darwinian survival of the fittest culture. In the style of Fredrick Taylor's scientific management, a labyrinth of detailed instructions document job processes, performance standards, and high-tech electronic monitoring of employee job performance with a multitude of performance metrics. This data-driven management system is based on a continuous performance improvement algorithm aimed at creating "Amabot" employees who are integrated parts of the Amazon organizational system, like cogs in a colossal corporate wheel.

Employees who fail to meet standards or hold the "Amabot" mindset must face brutal feedback in punishing performance reviews. They endure debates among managers concerning the effectiveness and value of employees. They also withstand stressful team meetings where peer feedback is often worse than feedback from bosses. The unfortunate employees who do not fare well on these assessments are fired. While these control systems have helped Amazon to achieve tremendous growth over the past ten years, they have come with an exorbitant cost to employees' physical and psychological wellbeing. These costs include exhaustion, emotional breakdowns on the job, workaholism, self-doubt, hyper-competition and infighting among coworkers, total male domination of the top management team, perceptions of unfair treatment of employees, and high levels of turnover. Bezos and his "Amabots" do not consider these costs to be evidence of the failure of his control systems, but rather the by-products of producing the most efficient and effective employees determined to achieve total world domination of retail marketing.[27]

followers' commitment and attitude toward their work will be significantly different. Therefore, before practicing MBE-A, be sure to assess your leadership system or work context and determine what type and level of MBE-A would be optimal.

Putting Transactional Leadership into Practice

To be fluent in FRLD, you should be able to apply both corrective and constructive forms of transactional leadership. To establish the corrective form of transactional leadership, apply MBE-A behavior to the situation. To establish the constructive form of transactional leadership, apply contingent reward behavior to the situation.

Applying Contingent Reward Leadership

Display the Behaviors Described in This Chapter

This chapter presented four behaviors associated with contingent reward leadership. These behaviors emphasized the importance of (1) setting goals for and with your followers, (2) suggesting pathways to meet performance expectations, (3) actively monitoring followers' progress and providing supportive feedback, and (4) providing rewards consistently when goals are attained. Choose one subordinate you like to work with and go through these four steps and reflect upon your experience. Repeat this process with other employees.

That's what a vice president of customer service at Verizon did. This executive told us that goal setting starts at the strategic level by looking at different areas of the market. At Verizon, they do this geographically as well as by looking within market segments while maintaining reliable service goals. They then align these goals with departmental goals. Each employee needs to understand the part he or she plays in reaching these goals. Verizon conducts a series of planning sessions for both individuals and teams so that their efforts are well aligned toward accomplishing organizational objectives.

When it comes to rewards, top management at Verizon spends a fair amount of time thinking about how to recognize and reward people. Each year they find more creative ways to do that. They are careful not to always reward people just for doing their job because this creates an unhealthy sense of entitlement. But sometimes this is necessary, especially with Verizon's employees right out of college. Verizon gives out free lunches or other small rewards to those who meet their performance goals. This helps to keep up good morale with employees. This example teaches us that goal setting coupled with contingent rewards is an effective way to provide leadership.[28]

Provide the Resources Needed by Followers to Reach Their Goals

Transactional leaders physically empower their followers by giving them the time and resources at their discretion to get the job done. This practice sets followers up for success. Consider the example of Kirk Fleming, who is a training manager working in a team in a large, global pharmaceutical company. Kirk's operating company is responsible for drug safety and regulatory reporting of adverse events possibly related to his company's products. His team is tasked with introducing and training flexible standards that meet the needs of the over 200 independent operating companies, while also promoting the efficient processing of events on time and within quality standards. The team also monitors and assesses complex medical situations.

Much of what Kirk's team does is to promote organizational change. But most people do not like change and are stuck in their ways. That's the case with Sally, who Kirk has spent much time with establishing a plan to help her adapt to change. Sally says that she wants to try new things at work, but she does not take any action to make any change. She spends much of her time saying that she will "have to take a look at the possibilities and make a plan." She gets spurts of energy to investigate possibilities and asks Kirk for advice, but never gets beyond information gathering. Sally is frustrated that her efforts so far to help shape organizational culture have either been dismissed or generated hostile reactions from other colleagues.

Kirk addressed Sally's need for leadership by highlighting the talents and strengths that she possesses. Then he offered her specific support and advice for goal setting to take action. He discussed in specific terms what Sally needs to accomplish, suggested some ways she could meet her goals, and got her to agree with their objectives. Kirk complimented Sally along the way as she took small steps toward acting on her plan. This example illustrates that effective leaders balance the energy they spend on building both transactional and developmental relationships with others to create positive outcomes.[29]

Use Rewards to Support Six Sigma and Total Quality Management Initiatives

Quality is not a trend. It is a much-valued characteristic of individual, team, and organizational effectiveness that will never go out of style. The U.S. National Institute of Standards and Technology established the Malcolm Baldrige National Quality Award to support quality initiatives in manufacturing. This award was the U.S. government's attempt to use contingent rewards to jump-start the quality movement. Over the years, award winners have come from a wide variety of types and sizes of organizations, ranging from Lockheed Martin Missiles and Fire Control to the PricewaterhouseCoopers Public Sector Practice to the Charter School of San Diego.[30]

Today, many organizations are using Six Sigma programs and other quality initiatives to improve the quality of their products and services. These initiatives are a natural application for contingent reward leadership because they rely heavily on goal setting, planning, and measuring progress toward goals. These goals include customer satisfaction relative to competitors, customer retention, and market share gains. Building and maintaining organizational and technology systems to reach these goals requires clarification of effective pathways for desired outcomes and the exchange of rewards and recognition for their accomplishment.

Contingent reward leadership can provide a foundation for supporting these requirements by rewarding with bonuses followers who have the lowest error rates in production, or best supporting continuous, employee-driven, customer-focused improvement. Be sure to make continuous improvement an everyday matter, not a daylong event. Listen to and learn from customers and employees. Use teams to foster cooperation, trust, and mutual respect. And reward associates for doing it right the first time to eliminate costly rework. What opportunities for improving quality through constructive transactions lie dormant in your organization?

Applying MBE-A Leadership

Display the Behaviors Described in This Chapter

This chapter presented three behaviors associated with MBE-A leadership. These behaviors emphasized the importance of (1) closely monitoring work for performance errors; (2) focusing attention on mistakes, complaints, failures, deviations, and infractions; and (3) arranging to know if and when things go wrong. When appropriate, apply one or two of these behaviors, but be sure to shift your emphasis to contingent reward and intellectual stimulation behaviors as your followers learn from their mistakes.

Results from our research support what the Verizon executive told us about his experience with MBE-A leadership. At Verizon, employees and managers alike know that people are accountable for their own actions. We've found that a lot of managers in technology-driven companies use MBE-A as a way not to meddle with their highly educated subordinates' work processes.[31] They use MBE-A to step in only when necessary. Managers and individuals need to make sure the tasks are clear. If this turns out to be a problem, corrective action is taken. Warnings for failing to comply with policies and procedures are given as often as necessary. Many discussions take place in the human resource department concerning how such corrective action needs to be done and what rules need to be enforced. This is one way Verizon keeps things in control.

Set Standards

Transactional leaders use benchmarks to set standards for followers' performance. These predetermined standards allow leaders to assess the level of effectiveness and efficiency in their organization. When standards are not met, leaders can coach followers to adjust their behavior or increase their efforts to meet the standard. Over time, leaders typically raise these standards to reflect best practices and encourage continuous improvement.

Consider how Leah sets standards for her faculty's performance in teaching and research as department head in a public university. In evaluating teaching effectiveness, Leah collects teaching evaluation scores, rated on a seven-point scale, for both course quality and instructor quality. She collects these data for each course her faculty members teach. She then computes a departmental average for both metrics and uses them as standards to compare against scores for each faculty member. In evaluating research effectiveness, Leah counts the total number of faculty publications and computes a departmental average. She uses this average as a standard to compare against each faculty member's output. She also assesses the quality of the faculty's journal publication based on its impact factor and reputation. Her faculty has commented that they are now aware of what constitutes unsatisfactory versus satisfactory performance in the department. Leah's example illustrates how MBE-A's focus on standards can promote efficiency and effectiveness in your employee's work processes.

Emphasize Accountability and Responsibility

Transactional leaders guide their followers along the path to achieve expected results by clearly communicating mutually accepted expectations. Leaders do the guiding while followers do the work. This implies that you must ensure that your followers understand how their actions impact the organization and that they are being held accountable for making progress toward achieving their goals. A sense of accountability often motivates followers to be conscientious and dedicate focused attention to their jobs. These motivational effects often lead to desired levels of performance. For these reasons, take the time necessary to clearly communicate expectations to your followers regarding the awesome responsibility that comes with the prized position power of their job. While communicating with your followers, be sure to spell out your expectations in terms of "who," "what," "when," and "why" so that they are perfectly clear about their assignment.

Assess Risk and Be Alert

Transactional leaders identify ahead of time any threats that can seriously affect individual, team, and organizational performance. They actively monitor events inside and outside of their organization and work to assess and minimize risk. Once identified, these leaders use MBE-A to pick up quickly on these risks and take steps to mitigate their effects. As a result, followers pay attention to activities, processes, and performance metrics that leaders monitor.

After returning from his auditing seminar, Andy became worried about the volatile economic and business environment. He reasoned that the constant changes in the market can introduce uncertainty and risk in his company. Being risk averse, Andy needed some strategies to help him keep things in control. He needed ways to keep up on the trends and changing events so he could reduce the amount of his perceived risk.

The auditing seminar provided Andy with some ideas on how to deal with such risk by being alert to things that might create any risk-related concerns. First, competition and regulation often introduce unforeseen changes in customer demands and business processes. To successfully field these changes, Andy set up a task force that uses environmental scanning techniques to identify and monitor important trends and create strategies for dealing with them.[32] Second, rapid growth can strain an organization's workforce and internal controls. New staff members, who are unfamiliar with corporate values and expectations, also present a potential liability to the organization. Andy tasked his internal audit group with periodically assessing workload demands and the effectiveness of internal controls. Third, new technologies and revamped IT systems are often saturated with problems that can destroy operational efficiency and productivity. To stem these potential disasters, Andy met with his director of IT services to develop several automated controls, systematic testing plans, and disaster recovery plans. Andy's efforts to use MBE-A leadership to assess risk have helped him to maintain more control in his organization and get a better night's sleep as well.[33]

Like Andy, if you use MBE-A wisely, it will substantially reduce your vulnerability as a leader. However, we firmly believe that absolute control is unattainable. Trying to attain it relentlessly with MBE-A leadership can break down your followers, who might develop a feeling of helplessness. Such helplessness comes from a situation where people are under constant tight control and think that there is nothing they can do about the way they work. Therefore, be sure to temper your corrective transactional leadership with a healthy blend of constructive transactional leadership and empowerment. If you fail to do so, your followers may perceive your leadership to be "hyperactive leadership on steroids." They will stress or burn out and leave you for greener pastures where they perceive leadership to take on a more passive role. In the next chapter, we turn our attention to more passive forms of leadership that are sometimes needed.

Summary Questions and Reflective Exercises

1. This exercise uses results of your Multifactor Leadership Questionnaire (MLQ) report to assess your levels of contingent reward behavior and MBE-A behavior. Compare your contingent reward and MBE-A ratings with the research-validated benchmarks. How did your self-ratings, ratings from subordinates, ratings from peers, ratings from superiors, and ratings from others compare against the benchmarks? On which specific MLQ items (i.e., questions) did you score highest? Lowest? What can you do to improve on the items where you scored too low or too high?

2. This exercise also uses results of your MLQ report to assess your level of contingent reward behavior. Compare your self-ratings on *contingent reward behavior* with ratings provided by subordinates, peers, superiors, and others. Compute the difference score (d) as the difference between your self-rating score and the specific other rating source score of interest. If d is less than .5 and the other rating source score is less than 2.9, then you are considered to be *in agreement/poor*. If d is less than .5 and the other rating source score is greater than 2.9, then you are considered to be *in agreement/good*. If d is equal to or greater than .5 and the self-rating score is greater than the other rating score, then you are an *overestimator* on this dimension. If d is equal to or greater than .5 and the self-rating score is less than the other rating score, then you are an *underestimator* on this dimension. Consider the category under which you fall in terms of contingent reward behavior. What are the implications of this categorization for you? Are there any things you can do to improve in this area?

3. Write or revise five goal statements for your work unit or personal leadership development plan. For each goal statement, be sure that the goal is SMARTER—specific, measurable, attainable (but difficult), results oriented, time-bounded, evaluated, and rewarded and shared. For each of the goal statements, identify an appropriate measure or metric to assess whether the goal is attained. Present your goals and their measures to your learning partner or a colleague for their feedback. Determine the validity and reliability of the measures you have identified. A valid measure assesses what it is supposed to assess, while a reliable measure provides a consistently true score across situations and time. How is this process helpful in providing feedback to you and your colleagues?

4. Work with your superior or human resource department to identify the types of rewards you can use to motivate your staff to achieve your goals. Make a list of these rewards. Which of these goals are intrinsic motivators? Which of these goals are extrinsic motivators? Match the rewards shown on this list with the names of individuals in your work group who would respond well to the reward. What motives, needs, or personal characteristics should you consider when matching each type of reward to these individuals?

5. Make a list of staff members whose performance or attitude requires monitoring. Pay special attention to these individuals and work to ensure that they improve their problematic performance or attitude toward work and the company. Note which employees respond favorably and unfavorably to your MBE-A leadership behavior. Determine which situations in your work unit are appropriate for displaying MBE-A leadership behavior.

Notes

1 Bogle, J. C. (2005). *The battle for the soul of capitalism*. New Haven, CT: Yale University Press; and Long, H. (2017, March 8). 10 things on legendary investor Jack Bogle's mind. *CNN Money*. Retrieved from http://money.cnn.com/2017/03/08/investing/vanguard-jack-bogle-interview/index.html.

2 GreenAmerica. (2016, September 14). *Corporate hypocrisy on climate change*. Retrieved from www.greenamerica.org/blog/corporate-hypocrisy-climate-change#sthash.hHOzKxvH.pglFG2p9.dpbs.

3 Adapted from interview with Robert Snowden conducted by Gary Generose, July 1, 2002.

4 Bort, J. (2015, February 26). Ginni Rometty just set a big goal for IBM: Spending $4 billion to bring in $40 billion. *Business Insider*. Retrieved from www.businessinsider.com/ibm-ceo-sets-big-40-billion-goal-2015-2; Ogg, J. C. (2017, May 5). How Warren Buffett's IBM sale hurts the Dow and hurts Ginni Rometty. *24/7 Wall Street*. Retrieved from http://247wallst.com/technology-3/2017/05/05/how-warren-buffetts-ibm-sale-hurts-the-dow-and-hurts-ginni-rometty/; and www.glassdoor.com/Reviews/IBM-Reviews-E354.htm.

5   Deci, E. L., & Ryan, R. M. (1985). *Intrinsic motivation and self-determination in human behavior.* New York: Plenum.

6   Locke, E. A., & Latham, G. P. (2002). Building a practically useful theory of goal setting and task motivation: A 35-year odyssey. *American Psychologist, 57*(9), 701–717.

7   Anonymous (2015, November 8). *Leadership Experiential Exercise Post* [LEAD 555]. Malvern, PA: Pennsylvania State University, Great Valley School of Graduate Professional Studies. For further reading on Asperger's Syndrome, see Rosen, H. (2014, March). Letting go of Asperger's. *The Atlantic.* Retrieved from www.theatlantic.com/magazine/archive/2014/03/letting-go-of-aspergers/357563/; and www.webmd.com/brain/autism/mental-health-aspergers-syndrome#1.

8   Sharifi, J. M. (2008). *Analysis of Leadership Potential Assessment Center.* Malvern, PA: Pennsylvania State University, School of Graduate and Professional Studies at Great Valley.

9   Retrieved from www.woodencourse.com/woodens_wisdom.html.

10 Podsakoff, P. M., Bommer, W. H., Podsakoff, N. P., & MacKenzie, S. B. (2006). Relationships between leader reward and punishment behavior and subordinate attitudes, perceptions, and behaviors: A meta-analytic review of existing and new research. *Organizational Behavior and Human Decision Processes, 99*(2), 113–142; and Ryan, R. M., & Deci, E. L. (2000). Self-determination theory and the facilitation of intrinsic motivation, social development, and well-being. *American Psychologist, 55*(1), 68–78.

11 Drucker, P. (1974). *Management: Tasks, responsibilities, practices.* New York: Harper & Row; and Dumas, M., La Rosa, M., Mendling, J., & Reijers, H. (2013). *Fundamentals of business process management.* Berlin: Springer Verlag.

12 Downes, D., Rock, P., & McLaughlin, E. (2016). *Understanding deviance: A guide to the sociology of crime and rule breaking* (7th ed.). Oxford, UK: Oxford University Press; and Simons, R. (2008). *Control in the age of empowerment: How can managers promote innovation while avoiding unwelcome surprises?* Boston, MA: Harvard Business School Press.

13 Crisafulli, P. (2009). *The house of Dimon: How JPMorgan's Jamie Dimon rose to the top of the financial world.* Hoboken, NJ: Wiley; Dimon, J. (2017). *What makes a good leader.* Retrieved from www.chase.com/news/111614-jamie-dimon-hallmarks-of-a-good-leader; and Schrage, M. (2012, May 23). If you're not micromanaging, you're not leading. *Harvard Business Review.* Retrieved from https://hbr.org/2012/05/if-youre-not-micromanaging-you.html.

14 Peters, T. J., & Waterman, R. H. (1988). *In search of excellence: Lessons from America's best-run companies.* New York: Harper & Row; and Tucker, A. L., & Singer, S. J. (2015). The effectiveness of management-by-walking-around: A randomized field study. *Production and Operations Management, 24*(2), 252–271.

15 K2 Enterprises. (2016). *K2's small business internal controls, security, and fraud prevention and detection.* Philadelphia: Pennsylvania Institute of Certified Public Accountants; and Thompson, R., & Letcher, G. E. (2007). *Ethics and the attest function: A practical update for CPAs in public practice 2007.* Philadelphia: PICPA Foundation for Education and Research.

16 Thompson and Letcher (2007). As cited in Note 15.

17 Bass, B. M. (1985). *Leadership and performance beyond expectations.* New York: Free Press; Maslow, A. (1970). *Motivation and personality* (2nd ed.). New York: Harper & Row; and Seltzer, J., & Bass, B. M. (1990). Transformational leadership: Beyond initiation and consideration. *Journal of Management, 16*(4), 693–703.

18 Maslow (1970). As cited in Note 17; and Vroom, V. H. (1964). *Work and motivation.* New York: John Wiley & Sons.

19　Eden, D. (1990). *Pygmalion effect in management: Productivity as a self-fulfilling prophecy*. Lexington, MA: Lexington Books; Eden, D., & Sulimani, R. (2013). Pygmalion training made effective: Greater mastery through augmentation of self-efficacy and means efficacy. In B. J. Avolio & F. J. Yammarino (Eds.), *Transformational and charismatic leadership: The road ahead 10th anniversary edition (monographs in leadership and management* (Volume 5, pp. 337–358). Bingley, UK: Emerald Group Publishing; and Shea, C. M., & Howell, J. M. (2000). Efficacy-performance spirals: An empirical test. *Journal of Management, 26*(4), 791–812.

20　Locke & Latham (2002). As cited in Note 6.

21　McAleer, B. (2014). *Setting goals using the SMARTEST method*. Bloomington, IN: Xlibris; and O'Neil, J., & Conzemius, A. (2005). *The power of SMART goals: Using goals to improve student learning*. New York: Solution Tree.

22　Thorndike, E. F. (1913). *Educational psychology: The psychology of learning*. New York: Teachers College Press.

23　Podsakoff et al. (2006). As cited in Note 10; and Smith, D. L. (1992). On prediction and control. B.F. Skinner and the technological ideal of science. *American Psychologist, 47*(2), 216–223.

24　Podsakoff et al. (2006). As cited in Note 10.

25　Bass, B. M., & Avolio, B. J. (1990). *Full range leadership development: Basic workshop*. Binghamton, NY: Center for Leadership Studies/SUNY-Binghamton.

26　Bass & Avolio (1990). As cited in Note 25.

27　Kantor, J., & Streitfeld, D. (2015, August 15). Inside Amazon: Wrestling big ideas in a bruising workplace. *The New York Times*. Retrieved from www.nytimes.com/2015/08/16/technology/inside-amazon-wrestling-big-ideas-in-a-bruising-workplace.html?partner=rss&emc=rss&_r=0; Stone, B. (2015). *The everything store: Jeff Bezos and the age of Amazon*. Boston, MA: Little, Brown & Company; and Wartzman, R. (2017, June 26). Amazon and Whole Foods are headed for a culture clash. *Fortune*. Retrieved from http://fortune.com/2017/06/26/amazon-whole-foods-corporate-culture-clash-jeff-bezos-john-mackey/.

28　Interview with key executive at Verizon, conducted April 29, 2003 by Michelle Dearwater.

29　Fleming, K. D. (2008). *Analysis of Leadership Potential Center (LPAC)*. Malvern, PA: Pennsylvania State University, School of Graduate and Professional Studies at Great Valley.

30　Retrieved from http://patapsco.nist.gov/Award_Recipients/index.cfm.

31　Sosik, J. J., Jung, D. I., Berson, Y., Dionne, S. D., & Jaussi, K. S. (2004). *The dream weavers: Strategy-focused leadership in technology-driven organizations*. Greenwich, CT: Information Age Publishing.

32　Sosik et al. (2004). As cited in Note 31.

33　K2 Enterprises. (2016). As cited in Note 15.

Chapter 8

Management-by-Exception Passive and Laissez-Faire

Inactive Forms of Leadership

Lisa was never one to give up on a vision she was passionate about. Even after her idea for car sharing was nixed back in 2010, Lisa moved on to other ideas of interest. After attending a sustainability conference in Philadelphia in 2017, Lisa was bristling with excitement as she drove north along Interstate 81 through the beautiful Endless Mountains region of Pennsylvania. She was returning home to Binghamton, New York, after hearing about Philadelphia's Greenworks framework for sustainability built around eight visions for a more environmentally friendly and efficient city. The visions foresee (1) healthy, affordable, and sustainable food and water, (2) healthy air quality, (3) affordable clean energy, (4) carbon pollution reduction, (5) parks, trees, storm water management, and healthy waterways, (6) safe, affordable low-carbon transportation, (7) neighborhood cleanliness and reduced waste, and (8) sustainability education, employment, and business opportunities.[1] This ecologically sound and financially smart business opportunity caught Lisa's attention when she discussed potential ways to increase awareness of ecologically sound businesses in the triple cities of Binghamton, Johnson City, and Endicott with her community group. Students and others in the academic community at Binghamton University were doing their part generating great ideas with the new Koffman Southern Tier Incubator.[2] By now it was time for yearlong residents to make their contributions.

Lisa was quite impressed with the environmental movement that Greenworks promises. According to the Greenworks Dashboard, Philadelphia is making progress toward attaining the visions it has laid out in its plan.[3] Philadelphians have embraced Greenworks as part of their city's culture and its government initiatives. Based on Philadelphia's success, Lisa wondered, why couldn't she work with community leaders to establish a similar vision in her community? This idea inspired her as she took the Conklin/Kirkwood exit off I-81 and headed straight for the home of Pat, who was still the most prominent community leader in her group due to political connections.

Once at Pat's home, Lisa made a compelling case that the status quo of green initiatives in Broome County needed a jump-start. Lisa argued that with the information gained from her trip, they now had a viable model to introduce a great set of ideas to their own community. They might even join the growing list of organizations that have received the New York State's Department of Environmental Conservation Excellence Awards for their efforts to promote sustainability in Broome County.[4] To Lisa, doing good things for people and the planet, while providing good government, is something that made a lot of sense.

After sharing some beverages, Nirchi's pizza, and spiedies[5] with Lisa, Pat sat quietly and grinned after thinking about what Lisa told him. Pat then advised Lisa to wait until there was more of a call from local officials to address the environmental issues. Pat argued that Binghamton does not have the infrastructure or environmental problems that big cities do, and therefore it would be premature to establish a plan like Greenworks in Broome County. He also claimed that no prominent political figures are calling for such an idea at the present time. In Pat's opinion, it was a decent idea, but the time wasn't right to put it into action in their region. It wouldn't hurt to be just a bit more safe and careful. As Pat reached for another slice of pizza, he told Lisa that things are fine just the way they are. After their visit was through, Lisa left his house feeling dejected.

Have you ever felt like Lisa after someone continually rejected ideas you were excited about? Have you ever tried to introduce positive change only to be dismissed by somebody higher up who prefers the status quo? Ever been frustrated by someone who likes to take a passive approach to leadership? On the other hand, were there times when you acted like Pat and saw your followers react like Lisa? Take a few minutes to reflect upon the causes and consequences of such passive forms of leadership based on your life experiences.

Chances are your experiences with passive leadership were not positive. Leadership is about action rather than inaction. It's about change, not maintaining the status quo. It's about being there to give any support followers need. Nevertheless, we've found that there are times when taking a passive approach to leadership is more appropriate. In fact, in our previous research, some leaders in top executive positions told us that there are times when they prefer *not* to take action and simply let things settle naturally.[6] Their leadership experiences suggest that you should understand when and how to display passive forms of leadership selectively. However, when this inactive form of leadership becomes a habit or normal pattern of your behavior, chances are that you will not be able to motivate your followers and become an effective leader.

This chapter presents the pros and cons of passive leadership. It shows you how to let things settle naturally and take a passive approach to leading by avoiding unnecessary actions. It also shows you how to passively monitor and control your followers' performance and enforce corrective action when necessary. By reacting to mistakes and refraining from intervening in your followers' work initiatives, you may be able to keep things quiet and in order. However, we do want to emphasize that *passive leadership is generally not a good thing*, but it is sometimes necessary. Let's start learning about this passive approach to leadership by considering some of the most inactive leaders in history.

The Legacy of Lazy Leaders

Inactive forms of leadership, while sometimes appropriate, often result in predictable and negative consequences. Consider the following examples:

- King Louis XVI of France lost his head for spending most of his time tinkering with clocks and ignoring France's social and economic problems. During the 1792 French Revolution, he was arrested, found guilty of treason, and executed by a guillotine.
- America's 30th president, Calvin Coolidge, was reported to have slept 11 hours a day while in office. "Silent Cal's" passive presidency prompted a subsequent movement away from laissez-faire government styles of the 19th century.[7]
- Zappos CEO Tony Hsieh, famous for his company's unconventional and creative culture, committed a big blunder in 2016. He eliminated all bosses and reorganized his management structure into a passive *holacracy*, where authority and decision-making are shared within networks of self-managed teams. While this may sound like a good idea, the reorganization flopped because the lack of any hierarchy led to inaction, confusion, infighting, and a 29% staff turnover in just one year.[8]
- United Airlines CEO Oscar Munoz learned that a leader's lackluster response to a serious issue can result in a public relations disaster. In April 2017, United Airlines employees violently dragged a passenger off of a plane for refusing to give up his seat when it was announced that the flight was overbooked. Instead of providing an unconditional apology for this unfortunate incident, Munoz tweeted out a cold and callous statement apologizing only for having to re-accommodate passengers. His tepid response drew the ire of customers and the public. Ironically, United was once known for its motto of "Fly the friendly skies," which was one of its core values. Munoz's passive leadership teaches us that actions (and inactions) speak louder than words, and can severely damage a company's reputation.[9]
- During the summer of 2017, New Jersey Governor Chris Christie closed several of his state's beaches because of a government shutdown. Then he showed up on one of the closed beaches with his family and was photographed lazing around on a beach chair—while state police were turning residents away from the beaches. When the photo went viral and provoked widespread criticism from taxpayers, Christie gave a flippant reason for his private holiday, "That's just the way it goes. Run for governor, and you can have a residence." When asked about his meager 15% approval rating, he responded, "Poll numbers matter when you're running for something. When you're not running for something, they don't matter a bit. And I don't care."[10]

These examples teach us that leadership requires conscious efforts and proactive actions. A lack of effort on the part of the leader typically results in a lack of effort from followers, which leads to lousy results. As the old saying from the information technology (IT) field goes, "garbage in, garbage out." When leaders take a passive approach to their roles and responsibilities, they often leave situations behind that are worse than when they first arrived on the scene. Even if leaders produce some positive outcomes during their tenure, people tend to remember the negative things they did. They let memories of bad events overtake the good. That is human nature. When leaders fail to take the initiative to actively manage situations and proactively introduce positive change, followers have no incentive to forgive and forget. When leaders are too passive, things can quickly get out of control. Therefore, you need to carefully consider if and when you should display passive leadership. The benefits of doing so are small, but the detriments and risks from things getting out of control can be devastating to your reputation and the future of your organization.

Management-by-Exception Passive: Definition and Behavioral Examples

After considering the earlier-mentioned examples of passive leadership, you probably would never want things to get as out of control as in these situations. Fortunately, you can rely on organizational processes and systems to help you keep things in control. But if you believe that the active form of management-by-exception (MBE-A) will create nothing but an image of a micromanager for you or result in the negative effects described in Chapter 7 (see Box 7.5), management-by-exception *passive* (MBE-P) might be a good alternative. With MBE-P, you choose to sit back and wait for things to go wrong before taking action. The MBE-P leadership style allows you to intervene only if standards are not met because of the controls you have in place. It permits you to hold the attitude "if it ain't broke, don't fix it" and refrain from taking action until absolutely necessary. This was the case with U.S. President Abraham Lincoln, who used it sparingly during the Civil War (see Box 8.1).

Box 8.1 Leader Profile: Abraham Lincoln

Most people who have seen Steven Spielberg's critically acclaimed film entitled *Lincoln* (2012, Twentieth Century Fox) walk away thinking that surely Abraham Lincoln was the greatest American president in history. Many political scientists agree, ranking him among the top three along with George Washington and Franklin Delano Roosevelt. Lincoln's iconic stature stems from the application of his keen intelligence, tremendous willpower, and deeply humanitarian values. These personal attributes originated from his well-known background of poverty and loss of family members, heroic self-education and accumulation of wisdom gained from the school of life, and clear purpose-in-life of an important destiny to fulfill. Lincoln was motivated by these traits as he evolved as a leader. Despite being an introvert, he developed outstanding communication skills as an orator. Because of his personal hardships, he showed extraordinary empathy and compassion for people. In spite of the difficulties that surrounded his country, he imagined and communicated revolutionary visions such as the Emancipation Proclamation, social mobility for the betterment of all races, and government support for education, industry, and banking to offer opportunities for prosperity and wellbeing for all citizens. For these reasons, most scholars

---

consider Lincoln to be a visionary transformational leader. He displayed idealized influence through his impeccable integrity and deep faith in God. He showed inspirational motivation that consolidated political factions with his vision for the nation. His intellectually stimulating ideas challenged a nation to abolish slavery. He demonstrated individualized consideration when he frequently visited Union troops near the front lines.

Whereas political scientist James David Barber classifies Lincoln as being an active leader very much involved in military and political affairs during his presidency, other political scientists and historians suggest that Lincoln may have used passive forms of leadership from time to time. Lincoln believed in constitutionalism, a form of government based on crafting and enforcing formal procedures, rules of law, and due processes that echo the philosophy of MBE-P. Constitutionalism required a leader's self-restraint to step back as not to overreach authority or misuse presidential power. He formed his cabinet with several competing factions and empowered them to assist with decision-making. In his Second Inaugural Address, Lincoln stated that "The Almighty has His own purposes . . ." based on a belief that events were predestined by God and man could do little to influence them. He took no significant action to arrange security when faced with several death threats. On April 14, 1865, John Wilkes Booth entered Lincoln's box at Ford's Theater and assassinated him.

Lincoln's martyrdom, exemplary transformational leadership, and legacy of visionary social change will live on throughout the ages. His example teaches us that even iconic leaders who lead actively and effectively sometimes must rely on a bit of passive leadership due to the situations that surround them.[11]

Although most leaders are not nearly as iconic as Lincoln, they do sometimes display MBE-P leadership by practicing behaviors that wait for deviations from policies and then react aggressively to mistakes that are made. Let's now examine four leadership behaviors that allow you to set standards, wait until things go wrong, and then spring into action to get things back in control.

Intervene Only If Standards Are Not Met

A dean at a small college was notorious for his MBE-P leadership style. He would hold two faculty meetings per year—one at convocation (in September at the beginning of the academic year) and one at graduation (in May at the end of the academic year). This is unusual since most college faculties meet once a month during the nine-month period. At the end of the first meeting, the dean would quip, "See you at graduation." For the most part, he would remain in his office during this time. He would emerge only if there was a serious problem that needed to be addressed. This caused his faculty and staff to become anxious every time they saw him. They became conditioned to fear him because they linked his appearance with some punitive action that awaited them. Whenever he came around, they smelled trouble.

The dean relied on systems of controls to monitor student enrollments and faculty performance in the areas of teaching, research, and service. These systems were based on notions of control employed by the finance and accounting industries. Controls represent policies, procedures, and activities designed to make sure an objective is achieved. They are created so that functions and processes run smoothly according to a plan. Some are created to prevent fraud or errors from occurring. Others are set up to detect fraud or errors that have already taken place.[12] The dean displayed a leadership style that focused on deviations from norms, substandard performance, and irregularities. By displaying this MBE-P leadership behavior, he felt confident that he could run a tight ship.

However, the faculty viewed the dean as passively maintaining the status quo, focusing only on what was wrong, and failing to recognize what was going right in the school. He was correct in considering systems of controls as useful in monitoring critical processes and outcomes. However, the dean failed to recognize that *people are the most important part of any organizational system*. People require active attention, direction, coaching, support and development. To be successful, you must learn a lesson from the dean's blunder. Rely on control systems to manage processes, but use them sparingly with people. Instead, work on building the true "internal controls" within your followers that we discussed in the chapters on transformational leadership—trust, value congruence, and commitment.

Wait for Things to Go Wrong Before Taking Action

Stephanie worked as an internal auditor at Crowley Foods, a U.S. East Coast producer and distributor of dairy products. She was comfortable with her company's system of controls that indicated the time to take action to prevent financial fraud and errors. Her comfort level was high because her director of internal audit made effective monitoring systems a priority. Senior leadership emphasized the importance of control in Crowley's production and distribution systems. Their human resources staff worked hard to place the right people in the right jobs. HR was quick to communicate any deviations from standards to their associates. They let associates know when things went wrong and insisted on prompt remedies to fix any problems. Any time a change or variation was introduced into their systems, they managed the change effectively by introducing a new standard or by fixing the problem that led to the deviation. In other words, they focused their attention on areas of change. This gave Stephanie the opportunity to wait until the time was right to introduce more proactive change with transformational leadership.

Waiting for problems to arise before addressing them sometimes allows leaders like Stephanie the opportunity to develop followers. Do you remember when and how you grew professionally? Perhaps it was when your boss waited for you to try out different approaches without too much intervention. An MBE-P approach can give your followers a chance to accumulate appropriate experiences

Figure 8.1
**Big brother
is watching.
Leaders who
display MBE-P
behavior
can rely on
computer
systems
to monitor
people and
processes for
compliance
with standards
when things
get out of
control.**

to grow while you can maintain a minimum standard of managing their risks of failure.

However, MBE-P can only work in organizations that have effective monitoring systems and predefined plans for addressing contingencies (see Figure 8.1). Effective monitoring systems integrate controls with their operations. They use data analytic tools to sift through statistics and determine important trends in customer preferences, competing products, and operational issues. They provide objective process and performance measures. They include associates who understand how their systems work. They use feedback from their systems to improve processes. And they communicate control issues efficiently and effectively. If you decide to use this form of MBE-P leadership, be sure that the size of your organization is not large and the complexity of your operational processes is not high. Relying on controls as a foundation for your MBE-P leadership in these cases can place you and your organization at a level of risk that is unacceptable to your organizational stakeholders.[13]

Believe That "If It Ain't Broke, Don't Fix It"

Howard and Al anxiously awaited the big local high school football game between the Binghamton Patriots and their long-time rivals, the Union-Endicott Tigers. In their mind, it was going to be a classic. Snow was in the forecast as the temperature plunged through the 30s. Al quipped, "This is what *Friday Night Lights* is all about." They got to the game early to buy hot chocolate and get good seats to see Al's nephew quarterback for the Patriots. Their expectations were met as the first half of the game was a knockdown drag-out brawl, with the Patriots leading by only a field goal. But in the second half, Al and Howard noticed that the Patriots were on to something. Coach Mike Ramil realized that if his offense kept running the ball to the left side, they could make at least six yards per carry. So, the Patriots kept running sweeps or traps to the left. "If it works, keep doing it!" yelled Al. With a wink of the eye, Howard smiled and replied, "If it ain't broke, don't fix it. Sounds like good old MBE-P leadership from our training sessions at the Center for Leadership Studies. Ha!"

As the coach realized, there are times for leaders to take a passive stance and let things settle naturally by maintaining the status quo. This type of MBE-P behavior rests on the assumptions that there is no evidence of a problem with the current system, and trying something new would not result in a better outcome. In these cases, it is better to not waste followers' time and energy trying something new that would result in some fruitless outcomes. Leaders with this attitude believe that change is necessary only when a better and surer alternative becomes available or when the processes they use no longer work. We believe that this attitude is appropriate only when proper monitoring and control systems are in place, and they allow leaders to sense potential trouble early. You can rest assured in these assumptions only when (1) your control systems operate effectively; (2) you can identify changes in people, processes, and situations that put you at risk; (3) your control and leadership systems can manage change as needed and produce intended results swiftly; and (4) independent appraisals of your control systems confirm their effectiveness.

React to Mistakes Reluctantly

Chances are you have worked for or with someone with a hands-off approach to leadership. We certainly have. Consider the example of Betty, who was director of academic affairs for a small college. Betty rose through the ranks to her current position because of her friendly disposition and "go along to get along" attitude. In mentoring sessions with junior faculty, she advised her protégés to "learn to play the game" and "know what it takes to keep *everyone* happy." Unfortunately, Betty's closest friend was Trent, a tenured faculty member who had a reputation for bullying the untenured junior faculty. Trent would use a combination of threats, uninvited office visits, innuendo, and slander to intimidate junior faculty not to publish more than he did and not to create new courses. Michael was one victim of Trent's misbehavior.

Then one day, Michael had enough of Trent's antics, hired an attorney, and told Betty to tell Trent to knock it off and threatened legal action. Betty responded by saying that she didn't want to come across as being heavy-handed. She intended to sit back and not get involved in the situation. It was not until Michael told Betty that legal action would implicate her and bring her down as well that she agreed to intervene. She reluctantly told Trent to knock it off and ordered human resources to resolve the conflict with a face-to-face meeting between the two opponents. If it were not for Michael's threat to bring Betty into the fray, she would have looked the other way and allowed Trent to continue misbehaving.

Betty learned the hard way about the perils of being reluctant to take timely actions or respond to inappropriate behavior displayed by followers. As a leader just beginning to understand the key tenets of FRLD, Betty realized that sometimes the challenges she must meet involve how to find an optimal balance between active and passive forms of leadership. To meet her challenge, Betty has now established and uses a control system to set key objectives for being successful. Then she works with her followers to identify any risks that might get in the way of achieving these objectives. They prioritize risks that will have the most adverse effects on their school. For each risk, they have designed appropriate policies with responses to reduce their likelihood of occurring and mitigating their negative effects if undetected. They now take a more active approach to monitoring their processes and procedures, especially when it comes to creating a more collegial culture. They communicate the importance of creating a collegial culture and the policies they created to take corrective action to bring things back in line. Betty now pays much more attention to what matters most—her followers and their development.[14]

Laissez-Faire: Definition and Behavioral Examples

Leaders who display MBE-P behavior enforce corrective action when mistakes are made. However, they can become complacent with their monitoring systems and grow to accept a wide range of errors and deviations. This complacency prompts them to police any actions that rock the boat, and therefore followers maintain the status quo. If MBE-P behavior leads to complacency, then laissez-faire behavior is a catalyst for outright indifference. When leaders display laissez-faire behavior, they really don't care whether or not followers maintain standards or reach performance goals. That's because they are rarely involved in their followers' work. They avoid taking a stand on issues and evade solving pressing problems at all costs. They are often absent from important meetings and sometimes find excuses to circumvent their daily work responsibilities. Therefore, laissez-faire leadership behavior is not really leadership at all. It is the absence of leadership since it involves absolutely no exchange between the leader and the follower.

Research has shown that laissez-faire behavior is associated with the lowest levels of follower, team, and organizational performance. Followers become confused over their roles. Their confusion often leads to conflicts with their coworkers and the leader. Eventually, followers become totally detached from their leader and work as much as (or even more than) their leader is detached from them. Some may view their leader more as an idiot than a source of influence. Some may develop cynical attitudes toward their leader. In desperation, followers may make up for their leader's laziness by substituting for his leadership with their own knowledge, skills, abilities, and professional experiences. They may also look to others to provide them with guidance and support. In the end, they become frustrated, and this leads to low levels of satisfaction with the leader, their job, and organization. Some even leave the organization for better job opportunities elsewhere.[15]

Consider Imelda Marcos, who seemed to care more about collecting shoes and real estate properties than caring for the social and economic problems of the Philippines. Her laissez-faire approach to leadership is described in Box 8.2. Be careful not to hold an attitude toward leadership like Imelda Marcos did. It's easy to become complacent and direct your attention to the wrong things. Let's now examine four key aspects of laissez-faire leadership that you should typically avoid.

Box 8.2 Leader Profile: Imelda Marcos

Ferdinand Marcos and his wife, Imelda, ruled the Philippine islands from 1966 until 1986, when they were ousted following the People Power Revolution led by Corazon Aquino. One of the first things Aquino did as president of the Philippines was to investigate and restrict the amazingly large amount of wealth that the Marcos family had amassed during their administration.

Imelda played a central role in governing the Philippines during her husband's dictatorship. Even in her early days, Imelda always possessed a sense of entitlement. After graduating from college, Imelda gained prominence as a beauty queen in several pageants in the Philippines. She desired the finer things in life and loved to accumulate prized possessions of the rich and powerful. Her husband's position as supreme leader of the Philippines helped satisfy her needs.

Imelda and Ferdinand led an extravagant lifestyle and accumulated their vast fortune at the expense of their citizens. Imelda was known for her $5 million shopping trips in New York and Rome, her purchases of multimillion-dollar sky rises in Manhattan, 508 gowns, 888 handbags, and 1,060 pairs of shoes. As a ruler of an impoverished nation, her lifestyle seemed most selfish and inappropriate. She justified her profligacy by saying that the poor in the Philippines needed her to be a role model of success and point the way for them.

Imelda lived this lifestyle while her husband used intimidating and heavy-handed approaches to leadership. When uprisings occurred, he would wait until the right moment and intervene with brutal force to crush the opposition. The Marcos regime worked to preserve the status quo. This afforded them with a gold mine of funds derived from natural and labor resources sold abroad. But ultimately, their passive and self-centered approach to leadership led to their eventual exile to Hawaii where Ferdinand died in 1989. After her husband's death, she was allowed by President Aquino to return to the Philippines along with her net worth which grew to an estimated $5 billion as of 2017. Imelda then served three terms as a congresswoman in the Philippines and contributed to the Marikina City Shoe Museum. But she was plagued by lawsuits concerning funds she and her husband had allegedly pilfered over the years from national storehouses. If only they had used their fortune to address the Philippine's economic and social problems, their legacy may have been positive.[16]

Avoid Getting Involved, Making Decisions, or Solving Problems

Oliver was manager of the internal audit group of a financial service center within a large manufacturing company. His beautiful mahogany desk and cabinets were always impeccably clean. They were stacked with neatly piled working papers to give the impression that he was very busy with work. However, Oliver would delegate all tasks and meeting responsibilities to the department's supervisor. This allowed Oliver to sit with his back to the door reading the *Wall Street Journal* and keeping track of his personal handgun inventory on a spreadsheet.

Oliver's staff came to know this because the department shared a computer printer. They sent their documents to this printer so they could get hard copies of their work. However, this particular kind of Hewlett-Packard printer required pressing the form-feed button. If someone forgot to do this, the last page of the printout would remain in the printer. When Oliver sent his spreadsheet list of handguns to the printer, he forgot about this requirement and the last page of his printout stayed in the printer. It was later discovered by two of his staff members. Talk about shotgun management!

Oliver's followers reacted in a way that is typical for followers of laissez-faire leaders. If Oliver didn't get involved in work-related events and instead put his personal pursuits ahead of the department's, then why should they? Performance levels dropped. Staff became disengaged from their work and started using their time at work for personal matters. The department took on an atmosphere of a country club. There was little overtime and most associates left the office by 4:30 p.m.

Oliver's laissez-faire behavior created a wide range of negative outcomes in his department. This story teaches us that followers look to the leader as a role model whose words and actions guide their own behavior at work. As shown in Figure 8.2, you need to be very careful not to be perceived as indifferent or

Figure 8.2
Plugged in and tuned out. On "Casual Friday," this supervisor is ignoring his associates' request for help in the privacy of his own office. It's only a matter of time before his laissez-faire attitude will result in negative consequences.

uninvolved in decision-making and problem-solving processes. If you are not actively engaged in your work, your followers may reduce their own commitment toward work and the organization.

Be Absent When Needed

Jack was not looking forward to getting back to the office. But his department had a 10:00 a.m. Monday morning meeting with the boss. They had to review a presentation for a big client. Presenting at this meeting held little appeal to Jack. It was far less interesting than the four golf games at the En-Joie Country Club that Jack played with his clients over the past two weeks. Not to mention his recent trip to the Technology, Entertainment and Design (TED) conference in Hawaii. It certainly was back to reality for Jack.

Then his direct reports started sending him a flurry of emails and text messages. They had no idea what was required for the meeting because he didn't keep them in the loop during his frequent absences over the last two weeks. As Jack started to panic, Laura, his ace salesperson, knocked on his door. She came in and sat down to talk with him.

"What are we supposed to do at today's meeting? I have no idea what to expect. I wish you could have spent some time giving us some guidance, Jack," said Laura.

Ah, well . . . we've certainly been out of town a lot lately. And we've got too many irons in the fire. Look, Laura, just follow my lead and work off of this canned template sales presentation we made last time. Things will work out just fine. Don't worry, be happy. By the way, Laura, could you whip up the PowerPoint slides for me in the next hour? Thanks!

responded Jack. Laura left the room looking both angry and defeated.

How well do you think Jack and Laura will fare at the meeting? Chances are they will not do well because they are not at all prepared. Jack is absent physically and psychologically. His frequent absences affected Laura's attitude and expectations in a negative way because he is supposed to provide the support she needs to perform her job effectively. Jack's work habits and interaction with Laura teach us that leaders need to be present, prepared, and care about what needs to get done.

Delay and Fail to Follow Up

During his graduate school days, Don lived in a nice apartment complex in Johnson City, New York, just north of the local shopping mall. It provided comfortable accommodations and was generally well maintained. From time to time, there were minor problems with heating or plumbing that required the attention of the maintenance staff. The winter weather in the southern tier of New York gets very cold and snowy. Problems with heating or plumbing can cause big headaches for tenants.

After one long and hard day on campus, Don looked forward to relaxing at home listening to some music on radio station 680 WINR. As he drove home around the Johnson City traffic circle, Don turned on the radio and smiled as he heard Andy Williams sing "The Most Wonderful Time of the Year." Don couldn't wait to spend time at home with his family during the upcoming holidays.

But when he got home, there was no heat, despite the fact that it was a freezing cold day in December. His wife called the office repeatedly during the day, but every request for service seemed to be ignored. The maintenance man waited until almost 5 p.m. to come to look at the heating system. Finally, by 6 p.m., the heat was back on and restored to its normal operation. But the damage was already done because Don's family suffered through the cold day with no heat. They were frustrated, tired, cold, and angry from the lack of appropriate and timely response.

This is a problem that almost everyone might have experienced in the past. A one-hour delay means one hour more pain to somebody. For example, have you ever tried to navigate through government red-tape, only to find many more documents to be filled out and having to deal with non-responsive government officials or clerks? Some leaders just do not realize how their inaction or delayed reaction might hurt their followers. Consequently, leaders (and followers) who delay in responding to requests or fail to follow up on issues get similar reactions. A lack of proper attention and timely response to issues shows a lack of respect and is de-motivating. It destroys trust. It decreases the credibility that you must develop as a leader. And it demonstrates a lack of caring and concern for others. Followers require attention and feedback so they can adjust their level of effort and approach to work. Whenever possible, respond to followers' inquiries and requests as promptly as possible and always with the highest level of sincerity, lest you be perceived as laissez-faire, like Don's old maintenance man.

Avoid Emphasizing Results

Jack Welch, the iconic former CEO of General Electric, once wrote a column in a business magazine about lousy leadership.[17] One of the awful leaders he bemoaned was what he called "the wimp." These are leaders who can't make a hard decision. They are the consensus builders who avoid emphasizing results. They are unwilling to give candid and rigorous performance evaluations. They give everyone the same "good job" review regardless of their actual performance results. This does little to differentiate the star performers from the mediocre ones, and offers little developmental feedback and improvement opportunities for followers. What feedback they do give is vague and meaningless.

Have you ever noticed how most politicians, when asked questions about tricky issues, purposely keep their responses vague? They provide little details on what their position is on the issue or how they plan to achieve the results people are hoping to achieve. That's because they want to maintain "political correctness" for fear of losing people's votes if they speak up on unpopular opinions. Or, they simply don't want to be held accountable for failing to meet predefined goals.

Some leaders are even worse. They avoid emphasizing results. They fail to set standards for key financial performance measures such as sales growth, market share, net income, or return on investment. Likewise, they avoid any responsibility for achieving these results. Their lack of responsibility allows them to loaf around and do their own thing. The illusion that they are not responsible for outcomes persuades them to persist in being passive.

Unlike leaders who display contingent reward leadership, laissez-faire leaders are not motivated by goals. They actually try to avoid setting specific goals due to a fear of not achieving them. They also believe that they can always delegate or dump their responsibilities on their followers. They may be working behind the scenes to advance their personal agenda or next career move. They have already checked out of their current leadership position. Have you ever avoided your leadership responsibility? What was a consequence of your inaction? What did your followers gain from your avoiding the emphasis of results?

Rationale for and Effects of Passive Leadership Behaviors

Now that you've been introduced to MBE-P leadership and laissez-faire nonleadership, we'd like you to understand why they are important and what effects they can have on your followers.

MBE-P: Justification and Expected Outcomes

MBE-P is important because time is a precious resource and leaders must decide how they spend it with their followers and organizational stakeholders. We have come across many leaders who seem to believe that they are super heroes who deal with every single issue directly. This is a game to be lost! There are only so many hours in a day. Therefore, it may be wise for you to focus on important priorities and use MBE-P to deal with other issues as described in Box 8.3. Some processes should be automated, monitored, and addressed only when they need to be corrected. For example, organizations depend on human resource policies and systems to control and guide their employees. They also use IT systems to control communication, production, service, and other processes. Such policies and systems need to be monitored and controlled through exception reporting (i.e., paying attention only to what went wrong after the fact and ignoring what went right), so MBE-P may be a good choice in these cases.

But MBE-P is often associated with a wide acceptance range of deviations and ineffective monitoring which may result in a number of suboptimal outcomes. When leaders wait for problems to arise and only then intervene reluctantly, followers tend to maintain the status quo (unless they are relentlessly challenged as described in Box 7.5's Amazon example). Maintaining the status quo can lead to certain failures in today's ultra-competitive and fast-paced global business environment. Paying attention to fixing what went wrong while ignoring what went right (and what can be done right in the future) can be highly de-motivating to followers, who may feel that their work is never good enough. A better approach is to communicate the negative feedback along with some positive outcomes produced

---

Box 8.3 The Case for "Lazy Leadership"

Why would a leader be motivated to "let it be" instead of "get it done"? This question puzzled us when we came across an emerging school of thought while writing the second edition of this book. A few practitioners have become proponents of passive forms of leadership, like MBE-P and laissez-faire behavior, in their recent writings on lazy leadership and followership. They argue that leisure is a good thing rather than a waste of time because being busy working on meaningless tasks is *the* real waste of time. Citing Michael Lewis, the author of *Moneyball*[18], and other best-sellers, they point out that being too active or focused on tasks lowers creativity and leads to missed opportunities of working on truly important and game-changing projects. Lewis uses a lazy approach to filter out what stories don't need to be told and zero in on those that do. That way he knows he is working on impactful stories.

Lewis' attitude about lazy leadership has been extended to followers. These writers denigrate the age-old virtue of diligence and venerate the vice of laziness displayed by employees. They argue that industrial-age jobs required workers to "act first and think second" so that processes and policies can be diligently followed. But in these authors' view, today's information-age jobs require workers to "think first and act second." A lack of action can allow employees to see alternative ways to work effectively, instead of working hard. This lazy approach is said to allow workers to engage in blue-sky thinking, brainstorming, and contemplation that fuel creativity and find ways to simplify jobs and work processes.

A similar line of reasoning being advocated by other lazy leadership enthusiasts concerns efficiency. By avoiding busy work, leaders and their followers can find easier ways to perform their work. This efficiency gain can free them up to focus on envisioning better futures, creating innovative products and services, and avoiding the perils of perfectionism such as self-doubt, depression, and being a slave to success. Although some people are born with lower levels of motivation than others and the brain can be naturally lazy (as shown in research conducted by psychologist Daniel Kahneman), it is more likely that laziness is a mindset that people choose to possess because of fear of failure, complexity and ambiguity of tasks, or negative moods and attitudes. So, we urge you to think twice about embracing the so-called merits of lazy leadership, given the tremendous volume of studies demonstrating that it often leads to the lowest levels of performance and satisfaction for individuals, teams, and organizations.[19]

---

by the follower being corrected. That approach is likely to boost the follower's confidence and self-esteem instead of feeling bad about himself.

MBE-P can also result in followers feeling disconnected from their organization. The constant monitoring and focus on negative outcomes can cause followers to consider their workplace to be full of incivility. Because followers hold these negative perceptions and attitudes, they may be less likely to identify with their company and share the same goals and values. And they will be less likely to go out of their way to help other followers and be good organizational citizens. Research has also found that such passive leadership can result in reductions in workplace safety and increased injury rates.[20]

With all these negative outcomes, you might be wondering "when and why would a leader choose to display MBE-P leadership?" We did too. So, we once asked a group of executives in high-tech firms the following interview questions: "How often do you prefer not to take action and let things settle naturally?" and "Can this policy be effective sometimes?"[21] We were somewhat surprised to find several top leaders making a case for displaying passive leadership from time to time. But most executives said they use passive leadership only in moderation. For example, a top executive at the San Diego-based wireless telecommunication innovator Qualcomm told us:

> It depends on the individual and the circumstances. It can be effective with motivated employees and the challenge of orienteering their way out of a tough spot. Orienteering is the use of a map and a compass. Some people like the freedom to come up with the full draft document with the full analysis. We can't always do that because of schedules and needs that may not allow that. . . . I don't really believe in being passive. If you want a passive boss, I'm not the guy to work for. At the same time, I'm not a micromanager. I am detailed-oriented and I am a good follow-up person. And a good way to get me off your back is if you could give me specific answers as to when, where, what, who, and how the project is coming along. What are the big issues? How are we approaching them? . . . So, it is always a judgment call, but I try not to be passive in any of the areas I am responsible for.[22]

Research on *substitutes for leadership* supports this executive's response. It suggests that passive leadership may be appropriate when characteristics of the followers, the task, and organization can effectively substitute for the leader's lack of initiative. Regarding followers' characteristics, a passive approach to leadership may be appropriate when the level of ability, training, experience, and knowledge of followers is very high. In addition, followers who like to work alone or those who work in highly regulated professions may not need very active forms of leadership. Similarly, aspects of the task that a follower performs can substitute for leadership. Tasks that are somewhat routine and unambiguous, provide their own feedback, or are intrinsically satisfying are good candidates for MBE-P leadership. Regarding the organization, passive forms of leadership may be OK in formalized or inflexible settings with clear plans, rigid rules, and procedures. When leadership is shared within a team, it may be best for the formally designated leader to take a passive approach and simply provide support when needed.[23] However, it is equally important for you to actively monitor work progress your followers make and be ready to intervene when necessary. And remember that when you want your followers to try out their own ideas and learn from their experiences, MBE-P might be a good choice.

We cannot emphasize enough that you need to be very selective in displaying passive forms of leadership. There is a time and place for everything, but using passive leadership too frequently can be a big turn-off with today's followers who hold high expectations for leaders. Which of your followers, jobs, and organizational units may be able to get by with passive leadership?

Laissez-Faire: Justification and Expected Outcomes

Laissez-faire is important because the delays and absences it affords leaders provides time to devote to developmental or empowerment tasks (if the leaders do not use the time for personal reasons instead). This idea comes from new jaw-dropping writing on *lazy leadership*, the premise of which is for top leaders to detach themselves from the detailed day-to-day task-oriented problems in lieu of working harder to find the right followers to solve the problems (see Box 8.3). Rather than stepping up to do the work themselves, these leaders step back and get busy with search and selection processes to find highly talented followers.[24] As the saying goes, "the people make the place."[25] Of course, this counterintuitive leadership approach of leveraging laissez-faire behavior requires leaders to exercise self-control to resist completing personal projects on company time. It also requires leaders to be good at spotting excellent job candidates, choosing them wisely, and then empowering them to get the work done better than leaders could ever do it.

One thing that we have found in our consulting work is that many successful business people oftentimes get confused between empowerment and laissez-faire behavior. For example, Susan's community group put the issue of global climate change on its agenda. They were convinced that the carbon emissions and greenhouse gases that business and industry produce are ruining our natural environment. They also felt that most corporations can do much more to increase the use of energy-efficient technologies. Invigorated by these beliefs, Susan met with Tim to identify ways to empower a group of community members with information that can help address these issues. Tim assured Susan that at their next meeting he would use his leadership post to empower their group.

One week later, Susan was disappointed by Tim's behavior. As he started the meeting, he said that the new green initiative "is anything that you all want it to be." Then he sat back and said, "I'm hereby empowering you to come up with a plan and do whatever it takes to make it work. I'll never get in your way." Then he turned the meeting over to Susan.

This was not what Susan expected. When she heard Tim use the word *empowering*, she visualized him giving the group more than decision-making authority. She expected an overall mission and vision for the group, along with some key objectives and suggestions for getting started. And she expected Tim to create a short- and long-term timeframe, specific responsibilities assigned to each member, and some metrics to assess outcomes. Where was Tim's encouragement of learning more about carbon emissions? Why didn't he mention the need for better fuel economy or ways they could switch to "green power" or electricity generated by low routine emissions of carbon dioxide? And why didn't Tim offer resources to support their efforts? In Susan's opinion, Tim was more laissez-faire than empowering. And, she believed that Tim either was a lousy leader or did not have a genuine commitment to make their green initiative happen.

Empowerment means much more than shifting decision-making authority to others. It involves the leader getting actively involved in providing resources and support for the ideas that followers generate. It also involves psychologically empowering followers by boosting their confidence levels through inspirational motivation and individualized consideration, as discussed in previous chapters. Tim failed to do all of these things, and Susan and the group viewed his attempt at leadership to be laissez-faire, instead of empowering, as he originally intended.[26]

Susan's reaction to Tim's laissez-faire behavior is similar to what is reported in the literature on outcomes of such passive behavior. In most cases, laissez-faire leaders are not viewed by followers as a source of influence or empowerment. Their followers often fight with each other over what their roles and responsibilities are. As a result, followers may take on leadership roles themselves or look to other sources for direction, feedback, and empowerment.[27] And in some cases, these followers even report bullying and psychological distress due to the lack of concern and attention to task and social interactions displayed by laissez-faire leaders.[28] As we explained in Chapter 2, when leaders are consistently passive, followers respond in kind. Because fairness is something all individuals typically value, followers will seek an equitable behavioral response to their leader's laziness. Two additional typical responses followers working in groups have for their leader's passive behavior are social loafing and free riding.

Consider the case of a group of three employees who were high-performing individuals, but were social loafers when they worked as a group. Every time Steve, André, and Vee Jay got together, they goofed around instead of working hard. *Social loafing* occurs when group members put less effort into their collective work than when they work alone. They are able to hide their inactivity in the group since there is no mechanism for their individual accountability. This causes them to loaf. Followers will loaf when they feel their inaction or lack of contribution can go unnoticed by other group members and more importantly by their leader. Because passive leaders role model loafing themselves, followers typically feel justified in withholding their own effort. In essence, passive leaders create a norm signaling to their followers that it is OK not to take any action.

With MBE-P leadership, followers see little importance in the work they do, except avoiding being corrected by the leader and her systems of control. They also may perceive that there is a chance that their contributions will not be evaluated by the control systems in place. In other words, they think there is a chance that the leader will not catch them loafing. They think they can get away with it. This motivates them to engage in social loafing. The case is even worse with leaders who display laissez-faire behavior. Followers of these passive leaders perceive less of a chance of being detected and don't understand the importance of their task, so they loaf.[29]

Another undesirable result of passive leadership is *free riding*. Unfortunately, we have seen this phenomenon occur when a lazy colleague gets involved in one of our research projects, but contributes little if any effort and value to the

---

Box 8.4 Dealing with Free-Riding Followers

What can you do to prevent your followers from loafing on account of your leadership style? Fortunately, you can evade this undesirable outcome with the following tactics:

- Limit your display of passive forms of leadership (MBE-P and laissez-faire) by monitoring your Multifactor Leadership Questionnaire (MLQ) scores for these behaviors. Spend more time displaying constructive transactional and transformational leadership behavior.
- Increase your followers' level of motivation by getting them involved in performing separate but equally important group tasks.
- Let followers choose what tasks they will perform based on their innate talents, strengths, or preferences.
- Beef up work monitoring system and performance evaluation methods to assure followers that engagement and group work will be properly rewarded.
- Spend time with followers explaining why the tasks they perform are important and how the tasks contribute to the overall goals of the project. Here, a combination of inspirational motivation and contingent reward leadership (goal setting) can do wonders to eliminate any desire to loaf or be a free-riding parasite.

---

published paper. Sound familiar? In many organizations, this can occur when followers substitute for their passive leader's lack of initiative and influence by usurping the leader's role and responsibility. In other words, they pick up their leader's slack. The lazy leader benefits unfairly from the leadership effort exerted by the followers and not his own effort. To use an old metaphor, the leader "hitches his cart to the followers' horse" and catches a free ride to desired outcomes. Once the situation becomes stable or the problem is eliminated, the free-riding leader tends to receive more benefits for his "leadership" than he deserves. However, continued free riding by the leader can create resentment among followers when they get tired of carrying the leader's weight for him.[30] Have you ever had a temptation to get a free ride or take a credit away from your followers? Do you know of any passive parasitic leaders who have used free riding to advance their careers? How did their free riding come to an end? We suggest some tactics to eliminate free riding of followers in Box 8.4. Remember, there is no free riding in cultures built with transformational leadership.

Putting Passive Forms of Leadership into Practice

To be fluent in FRLD, you should be able to selectively apply passive leadership. To react to problems after they occur, apply MBE-P behavior to the situation. To avoid intervening when your leadership is not necessary, apply laissez-faire behavior to the situation.

Applying MBE-P Leadership

Display the Behaviors Described in This Chapter
This chapter presented four behaviors associated with MBE-P leadership. These behaviors emphasized the importance of (1) intervening only if standards are not met, (2) waiting for things to go wrong before taking action, (3) believing that "if it ain't broke, don't fix it," and (4) reacting to mistakes reluctantly. First, you need to determine under what circumstances MBE-P behaviors can be effective. When appropriate, apply one or two of these behaviors, but make a point to shift your emphasis to contingent reward and intellectual stimulation behaviors as your followers learn from their mistakes.

Finding solutions to problems is an outcome that Jason Torrance of the Vanguard Group achieved in a team-building leadership challenge. With his background in accounting and finance, Jason was well-aware of many opportunities at work to use MBE-P behavior. But he got his big chance to use it in a more effective way when Bob was promoted from another department to join Jason's team. Jason's goal was to establish mutual trust with Bob as well as communicate that the responsibilities of safeguarding investment assets is the core purpose of their team. Throughout onboard training, Jason noticed that Bob was making many mistakes in executing tasks. But Jason saw these mistakes as opportunities for learning and development of technical skills and conceptual thinking. So later in the week, he provided feedback on how the tasks should be properly completed.

As a result of these initiatives, Jason noticed that Bob was able to practice what they covered in training on his own to familiarize himself with new technology, systems, and processes. In addition to the extra practice, Jason noticed Bob taking notes during training which he referred to when asked to complete assignments on his own. The team's bi-weekly feedback sessions were used to address strengths, weaknesses, and opportunity areas. These meetings have increased the level of trust and communication between the teammates and promote mutual growth and development. Thanks to Jason's MBE-P approach to training, Bob has made great progress in picking up conceptual ideas without being penalized or embarrassed in front of other coworkers. Jason's good counsel enhanced Bob's ability to perform and made Jason a great role model.[31] Jason's example of enforcing corrective actions when followers make mistakes teaches us that an interesting blend of MBE-P and idealized influence behaviors can sometimes make a real difference in the development of coworkers.

Place Energy on Maintaining the Status Quo
The federal and state budget cutbacks of 2017 brought many challenges to Carl as he assumed a top leadership position at a public high school in a rural part of the state. His school was under increasing pressure to figure out how to make their programs tighter and encourage more students to excel on the state's advanced placement exams in science and math. But his budget was being cut by 10% and enrollments were down. The drop in the earnings power and rise in food prices were hitting families hard. For everyone, it was hard to make ends meet. Given

these conditions, belt tightening and risk aversion became key aspects of Carl's strategic plan. It was time for the school to proceed with caution.

Carl's situation illustrates a time when MBE-P leadership may be appropriate. When it's time to pull in the reins on spending and risk, a passive approach to leadership can be appropriate. That's because it focuses followers' attention on performing within constraints and maintaining the status quo. It also reduces risk because it does not encourage followers to try new things, but to play it safe by complying with rules and regulations. By displaying MBE-P behavior and relying on the professionalism of his faculty, Carl shifted his leadership into a conservative mode that was right for the times. He hopes that when economic conditions improve he can once again display transformational leadership to show his faculty that they can work together to implement growth and change in their school. Carl's combination of MBE-P and transformational leadership illustrates the need to display flexible leadership under tight economic conditions.

Fix the Problem and Get Back to Coasting Along

Leaders who are fortunate enough to have knowledgeable, skilled, or professional followers can rely on them to set and work toward lofty goals, and take appropriate risks as necessary. University settings are a classic example where faculty members with professional training, extensive knowledge and skills, and intrinsic motivation work interdependently. Such empowered professionals typically do not like leaders to get in their way when it comes to creative tasks, weighing pros and cons, and making complex decisions. As shown in Figure 8.3, too much direction can inhibit followers' creativity and entrepreneurial efforts. We have seen some leaders, who after empowering their able followers, support their efforts only if problems arise that the followers don't feel comfortable addressing themselves. When called upon, these leaders use MBE-P behavior to fix the

Figure 8.3
Watch it! Overbearing leaders who display MBE-A behavior too frequently can inhibit their followers' creativity and make them anxious about trying anything new.

problem and then get out of their followers' way. Even Jack Welch practiced this passive form of leadership and admitted it: "My job is to put the best people on the biggest opportunities, and the best allocation of dollars in the right places. That's about it. Transfer ideas and allocate resources and get out of the way."[32]

Sometimes, leaders like Jack Welch spend their time maintaining the systems that support their followers' creative processes. Not all followers and jobs require active forms of leadership. It's up to you to determine when you need to get involved and when you can sit back and assume a support role.

Applying Laissez-Faire Leadership

Please Avoid the Behaviors Described in This Section

This chapter presented four behaviors associated with laissez-faire leadership: (1) avoiding involvement and not making decisions or solving problems, (2) being absent when needed, (3) delaying and failing to follow up, and (4) not emphasizing results. Please note that we *do not* advise you to display these behaviors. But you need to be aware of these passive leadership behaviors so you don't fall victim to their outcomes. And more importantly, you need to make sure that nobody in your department or organization displays laissez-faire behavior and becomes detrimental to their followers' successful performance. When you or anybody around you displays these behaviors, followers' performance will suffer and their satisfaction with your leadership will decline.

Unfortunately, that's what Tom experienced when he hired Perry to help their local library save money by going green. Perry was a recent graduate from a business entrepreneurship program taught at a prestigious private university. There he learned how the university developed and implemented policies, practices, and academic courses that promoted effective sustainability efforts. These included "energy management systems, extensive recycling efforts, organic gardening and composting . . . energy saving contests in residential communities, faculty expertise on watershed management, solar energy, flexible electronics, and environmental policy and biochemical sensors used in environmental studies."[33] While in school, Perry saw these efforts result in ecologically friendly solutions and real cost savings. Perry promised Tom he would generate the same results at the library.

Perry was smart, but he also had a sense of entitlement that made him lazy. He never provided the right guidance to the library staff to implement these programs. He failed to build connections in the community to get volunteers involved. He didn't seem to care about the project. He spent most of his time on social media or chatting up the young ladies in the library. Nothing got done. As a result, Tom lost faith in Perry and reassigned him to the job of maintaining the library's computer systems. Perry could have been a "green giant" of change in the library. Instead, he let his opportunity spoil.

Perry's folly teaches us a valuable lesson: these are the days of our lives. We are given a limited supply of days to make a difference in the world. Spend your days wisely. Never waste opportunities to do great things by being a passive leader when circumstances call for a more active form of leadership. Make a difference in your world one opportunity at a time. This will increase your credibility as a leader. American author John C. Maxwell considers leadership and credibility as pocket change (i.e., coinage). Whenever you do something good for your followers, you are adding one more piece of change to your pocket.[34] Your passive leadership will eventually deplete the change in your pocket and reduce your credibility.

Talk About Getting Things Done, But Let Others Take the Lead

Jay was always quite the talker. He loved to chase big ideas and was sure to tell people about them. He would brag about all of his successes, pontificate about his lofty plans for his department's future, and exude confidence that his vision was the only one to follow. He would boast that he was working on ten huge projects at once. He would always take on more work for his staff without considering their current workload. Yet, when push came to shove, Jay never got involved in the details of the plans he constantly made for others without their consent. He would dump the details of his far-flung plans on his unlucky followers in the name of empowerment. As a result, they performed well below expectations because Jay's plans were just pipe dreams.

Consider this example as a warning to be careful not to assume the role of a pseudotransformational leader[35] like Jay, who, as the saying goes, could sing for his supper, but just couldn't make it. The danger of big talking without active involvement and support is being perceived as nothing more than a laissez-faire leader.

Show Lack of Interest When Things Go Wrong

Every day Barbara drove to work from her home in Kirkwood through a rough section on the south side of Binghamton. The local park where she played as a child had deteriorated into a run-down shambles. It had become a haven for drug dealers and gangs. No one dared to spend much time in the park. Barbara remembered many good times she spent there during its better days. She was amazed how things had changed for the worse. Although Barbara had a special place for the park in her heart, she wrote it off as a victim of urban decay. She had many more important things to worry about in her life. Her lack of interest made Barbara a kind of laissez-faire leader.

One day Barbara gave Sharon a ride to work and commented on the sad fate of the park. Always the community activist, Sharon responded by saying that things didn't have to be that way. She spoke of many examples of urban renewal projects around the country that were changing things for the better. She convinced Barbara to volunteer with her community group to do something about the park. They planned to rally a group of workers and partner with the local police department and university to help restore the park. Six months later, the partnership resulted in significant improvements for the park. Their group picked up the garbage littered around the park. They planted new trees, flowers, and shrubs. They put down new mulch under the swing sets and rides. They painted the walls of the park buildings and installed new security systems and picnic tables. They restored the park to its past glory so that people could take pleasure in it today and also look forward to enjoying it tomorrow.[36]

Barbara's laissez-faire attitude offered no help for the park until Sharon got her to do something about it. Don't look the other way when you see persistent problems like Barbara did. The only way they will go away is if leaders and their followers look at them through the filter of a positive vision and then do something about them. Indeed, the difference between laissez-faire and inspirational leadership is much smaller than you might imagine. You can always develop into a transformational leader if you make the time for change and have support from other people.

Let Things Settle Naturally

Leaders need to carefully decide which issues they will get involved in and which issues they will avoid. For example, a CEO of an IT security company told us when it comes to problems workers have with each other, he lets things settle naturally. He encourages them to get back to the "coffee house" and work it out themselves. But he's not passive in affairs relevant to his turf and job responsibilities. In those areas, he asks his followers to work closely with him. He is quite involved in the company side of what they do. He is less involved in the social aspect of the job. That is an area he doesn't mind being viewed as a slacker. He walks around and asks followers how they are and what's on their mind, but for the most part he deals with things at the strategic level of the company as a whole, and not at the personal or micro level. Learn a lesson from this CEO and choose your battles wisely, especially when dealing with contentious groups of followers with competing agendas.

In such group situations, the potential for destroying followers' trust and commitment is more likely to occur. In groups, it is often hard to promote individual accountability and motivate members with passive leadership. We consider the role of FRLD in influencing group members to share leadership responsibilities in the next chapter.

Summary Questions and Reflective Exercises

1. This exercise uses results of your Multifactor Leadership Questionnaire (MLQ) report to assess your levels of MBE-P and laissez-faire behavior. Compare your MBE-P and laissez-faire ratings with the research-validated benchmarks. How did your self-ratings, ratings from subordinates, ratings from peers, ratings from superiors, and ratings from others compare against the benchmarks? On which specific MLQ items (i.e., questions) did you score highest? Lowest? What can you do to improve on the items where you scored highest?

2. Think of a situation or experience you had in the past where "letting things settle naturally" resulted in a better outcome than getting

involved actively. Then think of three or four similar situations where such an approach might be effective. Are there any common characteristics across these situations in terms of people, work, or resources? Write down a few guidelines for these situations where you might consider practicing passive leadership for better outcomes.

3. Assemble a team of colleagues to review the work procedures or standards in your work unit. Announce to your entire staff that a review team will be conducting a compliance review of a randomly selected area in your work unit. What areas need monitoring? How did your staff respond to your announcement? How motivated were the review team members to conduct the compliance review? How can this form of MBE-P leadership be used effectively in your organization?

4. Leaders who use MBE-P leadership typically apply a wide acceptance range for deviations from the standard. How should you determine the range of exceptions that you are willing to tolerate before taking corrective action in your work unit? How frequently should you revisit the appropriateness of this range?

5. Visit www.youtube.com or www.netflix.com/ and search for scenes from popular television shows depicting life in the office. Or visit your local library to borrow DVDs with episodes of these or similar shows. Identify scenes that illustrate the MBE-P and laissez-faire forms of passive leadership and their effects on followers' motivation and performance. Present these scenes to your staff members as an ice-breaker at your next meeting. Use such video clips to start a discussion about the perils of relying too much on passive forms of leadership. Based on your experience, identify ways that laissez-faire behavior can be mistaken for delegation. How should effective delegation be used to avoid being misinterpreted by others as MBE-P or laissez-faire leadership?

Notes

1 Retrieved from https://beta.phila.gov/media/20161101174249/2016-Greenworks-Vision_Office-of-Sustainability.pdf.

2 Bean, D. (2017). Koffman Southern Tier Incubator: A place where new ideas can thrive. *Binghamton University Magazine, 13*(2), 28–29.

3 For metrics on the progress of Greenworks, see https://cityofphiladelphia.github.io/greenworks-dashboard/.

4 Retrieved from www.dec.ny.gov/public/945.html.

5 Spiedies are a unique regional cuisine originating from the southern tier of New York State. They are sandwiches made of grilled pieces of chicken, lamb, veal, or venison marinated in a special sauce that resembles Italian salad dressing. For more details, see https://whatscookingamerica.net/History/Sandwiches/Spiedie.htm.

6 Sosik, J. J., Jung, D. I., Berson, Y., Dionne, S. D., & Jaussi, K. S. (2004). *The dream weavers: Strategy-focused leadership in technology-driven organizations.* Greenwich, CT: Information Age Publishing.

7   Ebert, J. C. (Director), Bass, B. M., & Avolio, B. J. (Writers). (1992). *The full range of leadership* [Training videotape]. Binghamton, NY: Center for Leadership Studies, State University of New York at Binghamton.

8   Fortune editors. (2016, March 30). The world's 19 most disappointing leaders. *Fortune*. Retrieved from http://fortune.com/2016/03/30/most-disappointing-leaders/.

9   Fielkow, B. (2017, April 18). 5 leadership failures that contributed to the United fiasco. *Entrepreneur*. Retrieved from www.entrepreneur.com/article/292820; and Petroff, A. (2017, April 11). United Airlines shows how to make a PR crisis a total disaster. *CNN Money*. Retrieved from http://money.cnn.com/2017/04/11/news/united-passenger-pr-disaster/index.html.

10 Hutchins, R. (2017, June 20). Christie on 15% approval rating: 'I don't care.' *Politico*. Retrieved from www.politico.com/states/new-jersey/story/2017/06/20/christie-on-15-approval-rating-i-dont-care-112922; and Mullany, G. (2017, July 3). Chris Christie hits a closed state beach, and kicks up a fury. *The New York Times*. Retrieved from www.nytimes.com/2017/07/03/nyregion/chris-christie-beach-new-jersey-budget.html.

11 Barber, J. D. (2008). *The presidential character: Predicting performance in the White House* (4th ed.). New York: Routledge; Crowley, M. C. (2012, November 9). The leadership genius of Abraham Lincoln. *Fast Company*. Retrieved from www.fastcompany.com/3002803/leadership-genius-abraham-lincoln; Donald, D. H. (1996). *Lincoln*. New York: Simon & Schuster; Goodwin, D. K. (2006). *Team of rivals: The political genius of Abraham Lincoln*. New York: Simon & Schuster; McPherson, J. M. (1995, November). A passive president? *The Atlantic*. Retrieved from www.theatlantic.com/magazine/archive/1995/11/a-passive-president/376484/; and Smith, S. B. (2013, February 13). What sort of leader was Lincoln? *The New York Times*. Retrieved from https://opinionator.blogs.nytimes.com/2013/02/13/what-sort-of-leader-was-lincoln/.

12 K2 Enterprises. (2016). *K2's small business internal controls, security, and fraud prevention and detection*. Philadelphia: Pennsylvania Institute of Certified Public Accountants; and Surgent Associates (2016). *Generally Accepted Auditing Standards from A to Z*. Philadelphia, PA: Pennsylvania Institute of Certified Public Accountants.

13 Surgent Associates (2016). As cited in Note 12.

14 Harold, C. M., & Holtz, B. C. (2014). The effects of passive leadership on workplace incivility. *Journal of Organizational Behavior, 36*(1), 16–38.

15 Bass, B. M., & Avolio, B. J. (1990). *Full range leadership development: Advanced workshop manual*. Binghamton, NY: Center for Leadership Studies, SUNY-Binghamton; Harold & Holtz (2014). As cited in Note 14; and Wang, G., Oh, I. S., Courtright, S. H., & Colbert, A. E. (2011). Transformational leadership and performance across criteria and levels: A meta-analytic review of 25 years of research. *Group & Organization Management, 36*(2), 223–270.

16 Ellison, K. W. (1988). *Imelda, steel butterfly of the Philippines*. New York: McGraw-Hill; Escalante, S. (2016, October 1). Imelda Marcos shoe museum: The excess of a regime that still haunts the Philippines. *ABC News Australia*. Retrieved from www.abc.net.au/news/2016-10-02/imelda-marcos-shoe-museum:-the-excess-of-a-regime/7877098; and Mijares, P. (2016). *The conjugal dictatorship of Ferdinand and Imelda Marcos*. Seattle, WA: Create Space Independent Publishing Platform.

17 Welch, J., & Welch, S. (2007, July 23). Bosses who get it all wrong: Blowhards. Jerks. Wimps. How inept leaders can derail a thriving enterprise. *Business Week, 4043*, 88.

18 Lewis, M. (2004). *Moneyball: The art of winning an unfair game*. New York: W. W. Norton & Company.

19 Daws, M. (2017). Eight reasons why being lazy will lead you to great success. Retrieved from www.lifehack.org/254526/8-reasons-why-being-lazy-will-lead-you-great-success;

Gregory, D., & Flanagan, K. (2015, February 23). Why you need lazy employees. *Success*. Retrieved from www.success.com/article/why-you-need-lazy-employees; Kahneman, D. (2013). *Thinking fast and slow*. New York: Farrar, Straus & Giroux; and Zetlin, M. (2017, March 20). Being lazy is the key to success, according to the best-selling author of 'Moneyball.' *Inc*. Retrieved from www.inc.com/minda-zetlin/why-being-lazy-makes-you-successful-according-to-the-bestselling-author-of-money.html.

20   Harold & Holtz (2014). As cited in Note 14.

21   Sosik et al. (2004, p. 243). As cited in Note 6.

22   Interview with Rich Sanders conducted by Don I. Jung in June 2002.

23   Kerr, S., & Jermier, J. M. (1978). Substitutes for leadership: Their meaning and measurement. *Organizational Behavior and Human Performance, 22*(3), 375–403; and Pierce, J. L., & Newstrom, J. W. (2008). *Leaders & the leadership process: Readings, self-assessments & applications* (5th ed.). New York: McGraw-Hill.

24   Schleckser, J. (2016). *Great CEOs are lazy: How exceptional CEOs do more in less time*. New York: Inc. Original Imprint.

25   Schneider, B. (1987). The people make the place. *Personnel Psychology, 40*(3), 437–453.

26   Cheong, M., Spain, S. M., Yammarino, F. J., & Yun, S. (2016). Two faces of empowering leadership: Enabling and burdening. *The Leadership Quarterly, 27*(4), 602–616; and Thomas, K. W., & Velthouse, B. A. (1990). Cognitive elements of empowerment: An 'interpretive' model of intrinsic task motivation. *Academy of Management Review, 15*(4), 666–681.

27   Bass & Avolio (1990). As cited in Note 15.

28   Harold & Holtz (2014). As cited in Note 14.

29   Karau, S. J., & Williams, K. D. (1993). Social loafing: A meta-analytic review and theoretical integration. *Journal of Personality and Social Psychology, 65*(4), 681–706; and Rothwell, J. D. (2004). *In the company of others*. New York: McGraw-Hill.

30   Levine, R. (2011). *Free ride: How digital parasites are destroying the culture business, and how the culture business can fight back*. New York: Doubleday; and Tuck, R. (2008). *Free riding*. Cambridge, MA: Harvard University Press.

31   Torrance, J. (2015, November 7). *Leadership Experiential Exercise Post [LEAD 555]*. Malvern, PA: Pennsylvania State University, School of Graduate and Professional Studies at Great Valley.

32   Slater, R. (2003). *29 leadership secrets from Jack Welch*. New York: McGraw-Hill.

33   Anonymous. (2008). A "green" giant. *Binghamton University Magazine, 4*, 7.

34   Maxwell, J. C. (2007). *The 21 irrefutable laws of leadership*. Nashville, TN: Thomas Nelson.

35   Bass, B. M., & Steidlmeier, P. (1999). Ethics, character, and authentic transformational leadership. *Leadership Quarterly, 10*(2), 181–217.

36   Adapted from Anonymous. (2008). Scholars beautify city park. *Binghamton University Magazine, 4*, 4; and Rubin, J. (2017). Scholars serve in the Binghamton community. *Scholars Magazine*, Spring issue, 8.

Chapter 9

Sharing Full Range Leadership within Teams

A group of people sit down around a table at the local Whole Foods Market and contemplate what items should be on sale during the weekend. They are extremely intent about the data they have regarding the weather forecast, customers' buying patterns, local special events, inventory levels, and even the national economy. Based on these data, they project what items should be "eye catchers"—products that will create lots of foot traffic to their store. The team also decides what products they want to stock in order to meet local customers' demands. The next item on the agenda is to evaluate Jerry, the new guy on the team. Jerry has been working for the team for the past four weeks and it is time for team members to carefully assess his personality, attitudes toward teamwork, work ethic, commitment, and contribution. If a two-thirds majority of team members agree that Jerry is a good fit for the team, he gets to stay. Otherwise, he is out. The last item they need to discuss is the team's performance in relation to other teams in the store and similar teams in charge of the same section in other stores across the country. Their performance is measured by the profit per labor hour and is available to them along with comparative data for other teams. Their bonus is directly tied to these comparative performance data.[1]

The team's decision-making process at Whole Foods Market is quite intense, somewhat like a military operation. Does it sound like a Navy SEALs team working on a special mission? Absolutely! There are a lot of commonalities between how this team at Whole Foods Market and a Navy SEALs team work together with their team members. In both teams, it is all about freedom, accountability, and sharing leadership within the team. Just like a Navy SEALs team, all team members are empowered to make important and mission-critical decisions on their own, instead of those given by corporate headquarters. Even if they have a formally designated team leader, leadership on the team is shared with everyone. This is how Whole Foods Market enables its employees to become profit-conscious and highly empowered self-managing team members. And this is how the company's stock grew almost 3,000% since its IPO in 1992, and averaged an 11% annual growth rate for many years, which was three times greater than the industry average at the time.[2] Although the company has struggled over the last few years due to increased levels of competition in the organic foods sector, its stock price increased 37% in 2017 alone. This achievement is a sign of its resilience. In 2017, Whole Foods Market agreed to be acquired by Amazon for $13.7 billion, thereby providing Amazon with another distribution hub for its products and services as well as a physical retail presence.[3]

Contemporary businesses operate in an era in which work has become too complicated to be performed by single individuals. What's even worse is that the market environment and technological changes are so fast that few people at headquarters can deal with them effectively in a timely manner. That's why collective intellectual capacity and a firm's intangible assets for creativity and innovation count more than tangible assets, such as buildings, factories, and technology in today's business environment.[4] Therefore, a great deal of interest has been generated in the United States and abroad in recent years regarding the utilization of collective intelligence in teams due to the fast-paced changes in the market and technologies. New generations of workers described in Chapter 6 are forcing organizations to find flatter and more flexible ways of working while demanding greater degrees of empowerment and interdependence.

As more and more organizations are becoming team-based, the role of leadership becomes increasingly important. One reason is that the role of leadership in building and maintaining effective teams has often been identified as a common cause of failures in implementing teams in organizations.[5] For example, have you ever witnessed basketball players on the Cleveland Cavaliers, Golden State Warriors, or your favorite NBA team confessing after a losing game that they didn't play as a team due to a leadership failure? Yet, only a few researchers have explicitly considered leadership as one of the determinants of team performance in models of team effectiveness.[6]

Team performance can depend upon an individual's leadership capability. That's why much of the prior research that has focused on leadership in teams has assessed leadership by focusing on a single individual leading the team. However, as employees become more autonomous and empowered, and as self-managing teams like the one described earlier at Whole Foods Market become more prevalent, we believe that collective or distributed leadership *within* teams or leadership *by* teams (rather than leadership *of* teams) becomes more critical to a team's success. Transformational leadership applied in a team context can play an important role in creating that success.

As we have discussed throughout this book, two (i.e., idealized influence and inspirational motivation) of the behavioral components of transformational leadership emphasize the importance of understanding the collective vision and making personal sacrifices for the greater good of the team or organization.[7] When a team leader tries to shift team members' focus from their self-interest to a collective-interest, team members are likely to create a strong collective identity (i.e., the central aspect of each team member's self-concept shifts from "me" to "we" based on common interests, experiences, and social bonding) and begin sharing responsibilities that may not be part of their job description but nevertheless important for high levels of team performance. This is a typical process of sharing leadership in high performing teams we have seen in our consulting work. Recent research conducted by our colleague Jae Uk Chun and John provides empirical support for this phenomenon.

According to this research study, when a transformational leader displays the team-focused transformational leadership behaviors of idealized influence and inspirational motivation to promote collective vision and identity, team members' views of the quality of working relationships with other members increase. The quality of the relationships that a team member develops with other team members is called Team Member Exchange (TMX), which is described in Box 9.1. This research demonstrates that TMX is positively influenced in part by the team leader's focus on a collective (i.e., team) identity, and higher levels of TMX in turn strengthens the effect of team-focused transformational leadership on team performance.[8]

This chapter shows you what team leadership is and how to use transformational leadership and other Full Range Leadership Development (FRLD) concepts

Box 9.1 Team Member Exchange Explained

The effectiveness of team processes is largely a function of three things: communication, roles, and relationships. Communication refers to the frequency, type, and quality of messages and conversations team members engage in while getting work done. As a result, a distinct communication network emerges in which team members with specific roles serve as nodes within the network. Roles can be understood in terms of the functions each team member serves. As on football teams where players have specific positions with roles like quarterback (coordinate the offense, run, handoff, or pass the ball) or lineman (block for running and passing plays), team members in business settings have roles such as project manager, devil's advocate, cheerleader, analyst, or technical expert. How effectively they perform in these roles often determines how well their team performs.

Relationships can be understood in terms of TMX. When leadership is shared within teams, the functional roles of leader become distributed among the team members within the communication network. Leadership emerges within the branches of the network of one-to-one relationships between the members of the team. According to TMX theory, team members assess the extent to which other team members reciprocate in exchanges of communication, resources, trust, and execution of roles required of "team players." TMX quality varies with some relationships being higher quality than others. Teams with a high level of TMX create a collective vision and identity through the perceived achievement of norms, roles, and expectations within the team. In general, TMX captures members' willingness to exert extra effort in their roles, allowing them to perform above and beyond job requirements to help other team members and the team (in general) accomplish its goals. Teams that share a high level of TMX contribute more cooperative and collaborative efforts and find interactions more satisfying and effective.[9]

to develop leadership shared by the team. Let's start learning about team leadership by considering a case about arguably the most famous and influential rock band in history.

Team Leadership Lessons from The Beatles

The Beatles are the most commercially successful and important rock band in the history of popular music. Their music, hairstyles, clothes, interests, and social and political commentary influenced not only those who grew up in the 1960s, but subsequent generations as well. Their music has influenced countless artists over the years, including Bruce Springsteen, Elvis Costello, Oasis, U2, Billy Joel, Lady Gaga, and David Grohl. The Beatles consisted of band leader John Lennon, his songwriting collaborator Paul McCartney, their younger schoolmate George Harrison, and fellow Liverpool musician Ringo Starr. The Beatles are an example of a high-performing rock group whose leadership was first driven by John Lennon, but later was shared by members of the group. They have sold over a billion records worldwide and have been ranked as the number one rock group of all time by both *Rolling Stone* and *Billboard* magazines. Their phenomenal international success has passed the test of time and provides us with at least five lessons for effective team leadership using FRLD.

Carry That Weight

Performing at peak levels of effectiveness can be both exhilarating and exhausting, and The Beatles experienced this firsthand (see Figure 9.1). For team leadership to be effective, the team must consist of the right members whose knowledge, skills, and abilities complement each other. This allows teams to bear the heavy burden of striving for and maintaining success over long periods of time. The Beatles' lasting influence comes from the complementary composition of their group. Lennon's drive, sarcastic wit, playfulness, and imaginative lyrical prowess were perfect foils for McCartney's ego, sentimentality, technical expertise, and ability to write beautiful melodies. Both Lennon and McCartney loved to rock out in the style of Elvis Presley and Little Richard, just as many of today's bands like to imitate The Beatles. Based on their common interests, they frequently shared bits of their own compositions with each other as they collaborated. They valued each other's feedback on demos of each other's songs. In a form of friendly competition, they challenged each other to raise the level of quality for their music.[10] No matter who was the primary songwriter, they always credited the songs as "Lennon–McCartney" compositions. These behaviors show The Beatles using forms of intellectual stimulation and individualized consideration in their creative processes.

The Lennon–McCartney partnership was enhanced by the support of Harrison and Starr. Harrison provided a distinctive lead guitar sound. His interest in Indian culture and religion led The Beatles to use unusual instruments, such as the sitar, in their recordings. Harrison's deep spirituality also influenced the core message of The Beatles' songs: love, peace, and life as worth living. While the introspective

Figure 9.1
The Fab Four's triumphant arrival in the United States at JFK Airport on February 7, 1964. John Lennon, Paul McCartney, George Harrison, and Ringo Starr's stamina and synergy helped them become the most successful rock group in history. Image by United Press International, photographer unknown, via Wikimedia Commons.

Harrison provided a positive musical direction for The Beatles, Starr was a gregarious member who held the band together with his unmistakable drum rolls and his laid-back and friendly personality. Starr was the group's peacemaker, who intervened when tempers flared or members felt unappreciated or out of sync with the others. These examples show The Beatles once again using intellectual stimulation and individualized consideration to move the band forward and flourish under stressful conditions.

Don't Let Me Down

Highly developed teams have members who possess high levels of drive and commitment to achieving their goal. When The Beatles were initially turned down by several record labels, Lennon never gave up. Instead, he rallied the group with a war cry veiled in the question: "Where are we headed, boys?" The other group members would chant in return: "To the toppermost of the poppermost!"—meaning they were aiming for the Top the Pops. In other words, their goal was to be the very best. The Beatles backed up their bravado by working extremely long hours, practicing constantly, and fine-tuning their act. Their talent, passion for their work, and commitment to being the best paid off in 1963 when they made it big in the United Kingdom. By 1964, Beatlemania crossed the Atlantic to America and began to spread around the world. The Beatles displayed inspirational motivation and idealized influence by aiming for and working toward excellence in their music.

Come Together

Members of highly developed teams find common ground in their shared vision. This vision helps them put aside their self-interests and focus on advancing the best interest of the team. By 1969, The Beatles were practically torn apart by internal strife, low levels of drive, conflict between group and personal roles, and individual projects that took them away from the group. The *Let It Be* sessions and film were evidence of the group falling apart. During those sessions, McCartney and Harrison can be seen having a verbal fight. With the interest level of Lennon, Harrison, and Starr waning, McCartney assumed leadership, but he failed to instill the high level of motivation and creativity for which The Beatles were known. It seemed as if The Beatles as a group had breathed their last.

But the band and their producer, George Martin, felt that they had "one more good album in them," and they worked during the summer of 1969 to record *Abbey Road*. They agreed that this would probably be their last recording, so they set aside their differences and decided to give it their all so they could end on a positive note. *Abbey Road* is where Harrison came into his own with his classic songs "Something" and "Here Comes the Sun." Lennon contributed several hard-rocking tunes, while McCartney's beautiful suites of compositions on side 2 added to the album's majestic allure. Even Starr contributed with the charmingly quirky "Octopus' Garden." As producer, Martin did an excellent job integrating these pieces into a comprehensive whole that was greater than the sum of its parts. Here The Beatles created team synergy from Martin's inspirational motivation, and they displayed idealized influence by agreeing to reach for the summit of collective success despite their individual differences.

Tell Me What You See

Highly developed teams use life experiences and ideas from their members to identify exciting new directions for the team. Disillusioned and worn out by touring, The Beatles officially retired from the road in 1966. Later that year, they returned to the studio to begin work on their magnum opus, *Sgt. Pepper's Lonely Hearts Club Band*. McCartney suggested the album's concept for The Beatles to portray fictitious characters in this imaginary band. This approach would allow them the room to experiment with different types of songs and instruments. Each member contributed ideas, thoughts on album cover design, and songs based on their experiences. Starr imagined himself as "Billy Shears" and sang lead vocal on "With a Little Help from My Friends." Harrison contributed Indian culture and music for the album. Lennon wrote "A Day in the Life," based on a newspaper account of an automobile accident. McCartney penned the quaint "When I'm Sixty-Four" that appealed to the older generation. The album was a huge international hit and today is ranked as the greatest album of all time by *Rolling Stone* magazine.[11] This example shows The Beatles using intellectual stimulation and individualized consideration to foster teamwork and create perhaps the most influential rock album of all time.

Within You Without You

Highly developed teams seek leadership from all members and help from others outside of the team. Leadership roles shift between team members, depending on the situation and the tasks at hand. During their rise to fame and fortune coming from Beatlemania, Lennon was the strong driving force within the band. McCartney exerted more leadership influence when Lennon's interests shifted toward Yoko Ono. When things got very tense during the recording of *The Beatles* (White Album), Harrison collaborated with guitar virtuoso Eric Clapton on "While My Guitar Gently Weeps" and contributed this work to the project. Starr briefly left the band during this time and McCartney played drums on several tracks. This is when McCartney took on a more dominant role in the group.

To help ease conflict in the band during the *Let It Be* sessions, Harrison brought in soul musician Billy Preston to play keyboards. To paraphrase Harrison, it is amazing how people change when you bring someone new into a group; "people don't act so bitchy"[12] when they know they are being judged by an outsider. And at different points in time, The Beatles relied on their producer, George Martin, and manager Brian Epstein to make important decisions for them that were outside of their areas of knowledge and expertise. These examples show The Beatles using idealized influence to rise above adversity by allowing the best person, both within and outside of the group, to provide ideas and leadership when necessary.[13]

Team Leadership Defined

The members of The Beatles demonstrated all aspects of shared transformational leadership while they worked together to produce some of the best rock albums in history. One important issue that we would like to emphasize is that the role of leadership shifted from one member to another whenever circumstances were changing. For instance, when Lennon's passion and drive toward music cooled down, other members, such as McCartney and Harrison, stepped up with different qualities and talents to substitute for Lennon's leadership role. In other words, their leadership was shared by the team.

Several attempts have been made by a few scholars to define leadership at the team level in the past. For example, while summarizing the Harvard Laboratory Studies on leadership, Robert Freed Bales, a noted social psychologist, created a new term, *co-leadership*, suggesting that it might be beneficial in groups to allocate the task and relational leadership roles to different individuals based on situational requirements.[14] Another group of scholars headed by Robert Waldersee and Geoff Eagleson found empirical evidence supporting Bale's position, concluding that the implementation of major change programs in hotel settings was more effective when the task and relational roles were divided among two individuals on the change management team.[15] These studies suggest that leadership can extend beyond an individual person to behaviors shared by members of a team, and even top corporate executives like Ren Zhengfei and his associates as described in Box 9.2.

Team leadership can be defined as a form of leadership in which team members share roles and responsibilities of a leader. In other words, in team leadership,

---

Box 9.2 Leader Profile: Ren Zhengfei

An example of executives sharing leadership comes from Huawei, a Chinese telecommunication company founded by Ren Zhengfei in 1987. Zhengfei had a vision of creating a company where everyone becomes a leader and innovation is everyone's responsibility. He believes that no one can lead an entire organization with more than 80,000 employees effectively. Thus, he created a rotating CEO system where three deputy chairmen take turns acting as CEO for six months with the support of the other executives. The person who acts as the CEO is the highest-ranking officer in the company for that period of time. Zhengfei acts as a mentor and coach for the rotating CEOs throughout this process. He implemented this somewhat unusual process of rotating CEOs for two reasons. First, he believes that no one, including himself, is perfect and therefore it is very important to learn from each other. Second, the best way to cultivate C-level leaders is by allowing people to experience the CEO role. Zhengfei wants to develop strong bench-strength in his company's executive-level pipeline while he is still active, so that he can minimize the potential risks associated with the rotating CEO system.

How well does this sharing of the CEO role at Huawei work? It seems to be working quite well because the company has been performing phenomenally. Huawei ranked 83rd on *Fortune*'s 2016 Global 500 ranking, with a revenue of $78.5 billion and a profit of $5.6 billion. Huawei's market share in the mobile phone market has been growing rapidly to 9.8% in the first quarter of 2017. Huawei's market share in China is 22.1%, up by 20% from 2016 results. These results show that shared CEO leadership can yield financial success.[16]

---

leadership roles are distributed among, and stem from, team members as shown in Figure 9.2.[17] Therefore, team leadership is different from traditional top-down leadership or leadership *of* the team in several different ways. The self-managing team at Whole Foods Market we described at the beginning of this chapter is a perfect example of where leadership does not reside in a single person but is shared by the team. Team members in this local supermarket are responsible for revenues and profits of their team, which are independent from the performance of other teams, even in the same store. Let's examine how shared leadership works and how it is different from singular (i.e., individual) leadership.

First and foremost, team members share the responsibility for group performance. In a shared leadership situation, the team leader does not bear the responsibility for team performance alone. Team members are collectively responsible for the team's performance. This is evident in an example we discussed earlier. The four members of The Beatles were responsible for their collective success. It was not their manager or their original band leader, Lennon, who was solely responsible for their success.

Figure 9.2
All together now. Players on this football team huddle and share leadership by planning roles to take and responsibilities for executing a play.

Second, since team members are responsible for their own performance, they are almost always fully empowered to make key decisions that affect team performance. In other words, control over the final decision is always left to the team. While this may create some conflict, which was pretty evident among members of The Beatles, this is a very critical part of creating team leadership. We consider this a "growing pain" during which shared leadership is being developed. To facilitate team leadership development, members should be allowed to make all of the critical decisions that would affect their performance. That's the way teams at Whole Foods Market are empowered to make critical decisions such as hiring/firing new members, selecting/pricing/ordering goods, and promoting different product mixes.

Third, interpersonal processes and interactions become much more prominent in team leadership settings. Since all members are expected to carry out team responsibilities jointly, they are likely to interact with one another much more actively and comprehensively (i.e., display high levels of TMX) than in traditional team situations. They tend to raise expectations not only for themselves but also for the others, as The Beatles did when they worked hard to make it very big. These common expectations held among team members are called *norms*. In a traditional team situation, the team leader oftentimes establishes and enforces team norms. However, members share a collective responsibility to develop and use their norms as a governing mechanism in a shared leadership context. This implies that members should voice their needs and feelings so that they get a chance to understand others and be understood.

Now that we have formally defined team leadership and discussed its unique characteristics, let's turn to some important issues on teams and think about how the FRLD model can be applied to these team concepts.

Differences Between Groups and Teams

Groups and teams do not appear to be much different if one thinks of them causally. After all, they consist of two or more individuals, interacting and inter-dependent, who have come together to achieve specific goals. So, what makes teams different from groups? We can differentiate groups from teams in several ways.

Information and Workflow

Group members merely share information and interact with one another to make decisions, which will help them fulfill their own responsibility. In contrast, team members not only share information but also work together to increase their collective performance. In other words, teams must have shared purposes. Therefore, contingent reward and active management-by-exception leadership would be a more frequent norm in groups.[18]

People are often ready to blame others for lack of performance in groups. Or they become quite transactional in that they are willing to work hard as long as others agree to do so. Group members constantly contemplate whether it would be better off if they jump ship and do things on their own to create a bigger and more positive outcome. In groups, social loafing or free riding is quite common because members are not committed to take their responsibility. Self-interest often supersedes collective interest. This often leads to personal conflicts, and that's why many people generally prefer not to work on things in a group context.

In our consulting work, we have seen the distinction between groups and teams become blurred because the client merely named a particular collection of people a team. But in reality, the behaviors of its members resembled a group. For example, individuals first come together in a disorganized fashion and lack a sense of purpose. They set no clear agenda and do not assign specific tasks to their members. As a result, they experience high levels of conflict within the group and are confused about their responsibilities. In essence, they are an *unstructured group* of individuals with a *laissez-faire* attitude about leadership.

Some individuals work in a *semistructured group* and display *passive management-by-exception* (MBE-P) leadership behaviors. They react to the circumstances that surround them and accept a wide range of deviations from standards before taking action. They wait for problems to arise and intervene reluctantly with each other only when absolutely necessary. They are uncertain about their roles and hesitate to offer ideas.

Somewhat more effective are the *structured groups* that use a combination of *active management-by-exception* (MBE-A) and *constructive transaction* (CR) leadership styles. When in the MBE-A mode, the group closely monitors processes for deviations from standards and takes immediate action to correct problems when detected. Members of structured groups strictly enforce rules to guide their work processes. However, they may be unwilling to take risks and may engage in struggles to influence others. When in the CR mode, the group specifies its purpose, defines roles for each of its members, and recognizes their accomplishments. By taking this active approach to group leadership, members of the structured group create an agenda describing what goals need to be accomplished, and what tasks need to be completed to meet the goals. Members follow up with each other to ensure that tasks are completed as well.[19]

In contrast, teams are designed to achieve collective objectives through a shared purpose. Through idealized influence, team members develop a shared vision for their existence and set clear expectations for themselves. They are ready to sacrifice their self-interest if doing so would facilitate the process of achieving collective objectives. They show an intense commitment to the team's vision. At the individual level, such idealized influence behavior is displayed by a leader, but is shown at the team level in shared team leadership situations. If you want to create a high-performing team, you need to develop a vision or purpose that is shared by all members of your team. In fact, the Forbes Coaches Council, consisting of top business leaders and coaches, states that shared/aligned vision or purpose among team members is one of the 13 most important characteristics of high-performing teams.[20]

Synergy

Another key difference between groups and teams involves the level of synergy. *Synergy* means individual efforts create a level of performance that is greater than the sum of individual inputs, such that $1 + 1 + 1 = 4$. Through inspirational motivation, team members elevate expectations by setting extraordinarily high standards. They show enthusiasm and confidence and constantly emphasize interdependence among members of their team. They achieve synergy by collaborating and committing to reach the highest levels of performance goals, as demonstrated by The Beatles.

Due to personal conflicts present in groups, members are not likely to create an outcome that exceeds even their own expectation. The main purpose of their collaboration is getting things done quickly and efficiently, not necessarily creating a better and bigger outcome. This might be due to the problem of poorly articulated expectations among group members. Since they are transactionally oriented, group members do not get a chance to idealize their influence with one another.

In contrast, team members are keenly aware of their collective and individual sense of purpose, and therefore, they talk about a positive future that they will be able to enjoy by working collaboratively. This message shows their idealized influence within the team. Through inspirational motivation, team members also discuss what needs to be done in order to create synergy and share their collective confidence about achieving their stretched targets. We have emphasized personal confidence called self-efficacy in this book so that you can practice FRLD successfully. Collective efficacy or group potency refers to group members' collective perceptions about how efficacious their group is.[21]

This team-level confidence increases team performance in a variety of settings. The importance of having collective confidence has been demonstrated particularly well in various sports settings, where players and coaches oftentimes attribute their success or failure to the fact that they worked (or didn't work) as a team. For example, team members' collective confidence was positively related to team cohesion among 92 volleyball players participating on elite and recreational teams, which oftentimes would lead to a higher level of team performance.[22]

One example of team members working on a common goal and creating an exceptional level of synergy and unbelievable results is the English soccer team Leicester City. The team was founded in 1884 but had been a losing team for the most of its existence. The best performance they had over the last 130-plus years was second place in the top league in the 1928–29 season.[23] At the beginning of the 2015–16 season, many bookmakers placed the odds of Leicester City winning the championship at 1/5,000 or less, which means it is almost impossible for this team to win the championship. However, they were celebrating their first England Premier League championship ever at the end of the season last year.

How did Leicester City pull off this turnaround? They didn't have any shining soccer stars like Lionel Messi of F.C. Barcelona or Cristiano Ronaldo of Real Madrid. Instead, the secret boiled down to two factors: club manager Claudio Ranieri's leadership that respects players' skills and experiences, and team synergies. In an interview with CNN, former Leicester defender Matt Elliott said that "Of all the factors, the most imperative has been the team spirit. The players don't talk about themselves. It's a collective effort – We've got the spirit and the will to win."[24] In summary, synergies created from team spirit produced what a number of newspapers dubbed the biggest sporting upset ever.

Along with the Leicester City example, the "Herb Brooks and the Miracle on Ice" leader profile shown in Box 9.3 also demonstrates the power of synergy when ordinary team members share a common purpose and are fully committed toward the same goal. Miracles can happen not only in soccer and hockey venues but also in organizations. We believe that the examples we described earlier illustrate the importance of building shared leadership practices in order to overcome challenging odds and win the game. Through inspirational motivation, team members can encourage one another to raise their own expectations and passionately talk about visions of victory. Those behaviors can build a high level of shared leadership and collective confidence in your own team.

Box 9.3 Leader Profile: Herb Brooks and the Miracle on Ice

The Soviet Union's national hockey team's dynasty ended at the 1980 Winter Olympic games in Lake Placid, New York, at the hands of Herb Brooks' novice U.S. team. The timing of this miraculous event was critical. America's collective self-concept was reeling from an array of bad events, including the fall of Saigon, Watergate, President Nixon's resignation, and poor economic conditions. Sensing that the United States needed an event to help restore American pride, the U.S. Olympic commission selected Brooks to coach the American hockey team.

Brooks was a no-nonsense, tough-as-nails taskmaster with passion and dedication to hockey as long and hard as a Minnesota winter. Brooks was born in St. Paul and played hockey for his high school team, which won the state championship in 1955. He went on to play for the University of Minnesota and U.S. Olympic teams. During the 1970s, Brooks coached the University of Minnesota hockey team to three national championships before his glorious moment in 1980. Brooks was on the verge of leading his team to a miracle.

In less than one year of preparation for the games, Brooks transformed a rag-tag group of maverick collegiate players into a disciplined and cohesive team. They exploited weaknesses in the Soviet team by using their speed to stay with the Soviet players and aggressively challenge them. They were proactive instead of reactive. Before the game with the Soviets, Brooks told his players, "You were born to be a hockey player. You were meant to be here. This moment is yours."[25] Brooks got his team to believe in themselves and execute well. His blue-collar work ethic, intelligence, drive, and tough love inspired Team USA to defeat the Soviets and then go on to win the gold medal. Team USA's victory is one of the most inspiring tales of sports team leadership in history. Later, this victory was voted the greatest sports moment of the 20th century by *Sports Illustrated*.[26]

With Brooks' coaching, the players on the U.S. hockey team clearly demonstrated how teams differ from groups and what shared leadership is all about in several ways. First, the U.S. team's sole interest was about how they could work together to beat their Russian opponent. There was no "I" on the U.S. team. It was all about how "we" worked together to beat the best hockey team in the world. They weren't thinking about a fat National Hockey League (NHL) signing bonus they could enjoy after they won the Olympic game. Second, the U.S. team consisted of young collegiate players and amateurs who had limited experiences playing at the international level. In contrast, Russian players were mostly professional hockey players who were serving in the military. Therefore, almost everyone thought that it would take a miracle for the U.S. team to beat the Russians. However, what the U.S. team had was synergy. They became much larger than the sum of individual players. They played as a team, not as a bunch of collegiate and amateur players. The high level of synergy and shared leadership gave them the collective confidence they needed.

Third, each player felt a full responsibility to achieve their collective success. Thus, there was a sense of team accountability, not just individual accountability. Each member was not interested in criticizing the other members for their mistakes. Instead, their interest was in figuring out how they best worked together to increase their team performance. In their minds, there was only "we" and "our" performance.

Fourth, since they weren't superstar NHL hockey players, everyone was interested in developing the skills they needed to win the game. They were also keenly aware of the expected role they should play to increase their collective performance. In contrast, the Russian team had many star players, including one of the best right-wingers in the world and a player considered by many to be the best ice hockey goalie in the world at the time. These famous players were more interested in *their* ways of playing the game rather than thinking about developing complementary skills as a coherent team. Therefore, even if the Russian team had many more talented players, they couldn't generate synergy like their U.S. counterpart. For these reasons, Brooks' miraculous story teaches us to pursue our dreams knowing that passion, dedication, and a strong work ethic can make dreams come true. For those of you who are not familiar with it, we strongly recommend watching the movie entitled *Miracle* or view YouTube. com videos about "the Miracle on Ice." [27]

Individual Versus Mutual Accountability

Accountability lies with individuals in the group, whereas it lies at both individual and mutual levels in the team. Since group members are primarily concerned about their own work in the group, their focus is on how to finish their own work. This self-centered attitude (as in thoughts like "What's in it for me?") along with transactional relationship can lead to tension and personal conflict if they see that all members are not contributing equally. Mutual expectations are rarely examined and articulated in groups. There is little consideration as to how their own work contributes to overall performance of their group. As long as they do their work, group members perceive that their responsibility is over.

In contrast, team members believe that they not only are accountable for their own performance, but also hold mutual accountability for collective objectives. They develop a high level of trust, and every member encourages others to look at their work from a larger perspective. There is no slacker who contemplates how he could maximize his outcome by riding on the coattails of others while goofing around. Instead, team members exhibit idealized influence to challenge one another so that they can exceed their own expectations. Common outcomes of highly developed teams where members share leadership together include a high level of trust and cohesion.[28] We see these team dynamics in high-performing college football teams, such as the University of Alabama, Georgia, and Penn State.

Overlapping Versus Complementary Skillsets

Another difference that distinguishes teams from groups is skills that members bring to the table. Groups are usually put together without explicit consideration given to individual skillsets. In this way, skills of group members tend to be random and overlapping. Group work process rarely becomes an opportunity to learn each other's skills.

In contrast, each team member is fully aware of each other's strengths and weaknesses. Through individualized consideration, team members provide coaching to others so as to develop new skills continuously. They are alert to the needs of other team members and are empathetic about each other's strengths and areas for development. Since they know that these complementary skillsets are vital to their collective success, team members have a genuine interest in each other's development. We illustrate this phenomenon to our students by showing them the movie *Remember the Titans*, starring Denzel Washington. It's a great story of how a coach uses intellectual stimulation to build unity in a football team torn apart by racial strife. When the players finally come together, they recognize that their individual strengths and weaknesses can complement each other and make their team strong.

Through such intellectual stimulation, team members challenge the way that they work together. They encourage imagination and challenge assumptions underlying the team's processes and goals. By questioning assumptions, they expand the boundaries of what is appropriate to discuss. As a result, team members feel free to offer new ideas.

As in the case of The Beatles, team members take turns leading the team whenever their skills and expertise become critical in achieving their goals. Members have enough trust in their current leader to become equally contributing followers. However, there is an implicit assumption that when circumstances are changing, anyone from the team with a different set of skills can emerge as a temporary leader. This makes complementary skills such an important foundation to developing shared leadership. The key differences between groups and teams are summarized in Table 9.1.

Table 9.1 Differences Between Groups and Teams

Group	Team
Strong, clearly focused leader (of the group)	Shared leadership roles (leadership by the team)
Individual accountability	Individual and mutual accountability
Purpose same as that of the broader organizational mission	Specific team purpose reflecting the collective work products the team delivers
Runs efficient meetings	Encourages open-ended discussion and active problem-solving meetings
Individual work products	Collective work products
Measures effectiveness indirectly by its influence on others outside of the group	Measures effectiveness directly by the collective products
Discusses, decides, and delegates task with a "split the work" approach	Discusses, decides, and works interdependently to complete tasks together
Emphasis on "star player" or best individual in group	High level of pride and collective identity in the team
Potential for social loafing and free riding of slackers, off of highest performers in group	Developmental vehicle for all team members

Sources: Belbin, R. M. (2004). *Management teams: Why they succeed or fail.* Oxford: Butterworth/Heinemann; and Katzenbach, J. R., & Smith, D. K. (1992). *The wisdom of teams: Creating the high-performance organization.* Boston, MA: Harvard Business School Press.

Levels of Team Development

The Miracle on Ice described in Box 9.3 illustrates a team at the peak of its performance and development. Research indicates that groups and teams go through various stages of development, and the leadership displayed by their members changes depending upon the stage. These stages of development are also associated with different levels of performance, as shown in Table 9.2.

Table 9.2 **Levels of Team Development**

Stage/Performance Level	Tuckman & Jensen (1977)[29] Concept	Center for Creative Leadership Concept	FRLD Concept (Avolio, 1999, 2011)[30]
Early in group life/ lowest	Forming	Undifferentiation	Unstructured group (LF)
When deadline approaches/low	Storming	Differentiation	Semistructured group (MBE-P)
When deadline is imminent/mediocre	Norming	Integration	Structured group (MBE-A + CR)
Due date/high	Performing	Synergy	Team (IC + IS)
Due date and beyond/excellence	Excelling and then adjourning	Synergy squared	Highly developed team (II + IM)

Social psychologist Bruce Tuckman provided the classic description of the stages of group development: forming, storming, norming, performing, and adjourning.[31] Additional scholars have considered these stages using different labels. In Table 9.2, we highlight models created and trained at the Center for Creative Leadership[32] and by leadership scholar Bruce Avolio to explain the dynamics and leadership styles associated with these stages.

Early in their life, groups form in an unstructured fashion. Members of groups at this stage ask the questions "Why am I here?" and "Do I want to be part of this group?" These questions highlight the members' need to maintain their individuality. They frequently experience excitement, anticipation, and optimism along with confusion over roles, fear about outcomes, and anxiety over how they fit in the group. They take a laissez-faire approach to leadership of the group, and their performance is typically poor.

When the group's deadline for completing its project approaches, group members start to storm through confrontations with each other over expectations and roles. Members of groups at this stage ask the questions "Who are you?" and "Who's in charge?" These questions also highlight the members' need to assert their individuality. They typically begin to argue among themselves, choose sides, and become defensive. They posture for specific roles in the groups and start to become acquainted with each other's strengths and weaknesses. They take an MBE-P approach to leadership of their semistructured groups, and their performance level is typically low.

When the group's deadline is imminent, groups become structured by establishing norms and roles for their members and rewarding performance that meets expectations. The members of groups in this stage ask the question "How will we get the work done?" This question highlights the group members' shift in perspective taking from independence to interdependence and their need to integrate the knowledge, skills, and abilities of their members. They typically define roles more clearly, establish norms, and accept their members as part of the group. They reward each other with compliments and financial incentives when they meet goals. They become more cohesive and communicate more frequently and effectively, but may fall victim to group-think. They use MBE-A and CR leadership behaviors to add structure to their work processes and interactions, and their performance reaches mediocre to acceptable levels.

When the group's deadline arrives, it is "show time." Groups at this stage morph into teams that no longer ask questions, but instead exclaim, "We've got it!" This expression of confidence highlights the synergy and optimal experiences achieved by members because they are part of the potent and cohesive team. These teams are very interactive in terms of both communication and collaboration, and therefore display high levels of TMX. They thoroughly understand each other's strengths and areas for development. They are energized by the team's mission and take great pride in being part of their team. Their team becomes part of who they are as an individual. They take a transformational approach to leadership, and their performance is typically very high and exceeds all expectations.

Rationale for and Effects of FRLD in Groups and Teams

Now that you've been introduced to the concept of team leadership, we'd like you to understand why it is important and what effects it can have on your followers. Team leadership is important because it allows for the exchange of ideas, resources, social support, and communication required to address the complexity and variety of tasks facing today's workforces. It also allows for the building of higher levels of trust among team members due to the increased frequency and quality of interactions observed in teams that possess a healthy amount of TMX supported by the display of idealized influence and inspirational motivation by members. Additionally, team leadership is much appreciated by Millennial generation employees who crave empowerment and participation in decision-making and leadership processes. These employees gain a sense of purpose and confidence when their work allows for a meaningful contribution to a team mission beyond their individual career interests.[33]

Team leadership is also important because it is associated with a sense of cohesion and solidarity among team members who come to better understand their roles in executing a common task. This understanding allows them to be satisfied with their tasks at work. Being satisfied with one's work is one of the characteristics of employee engagement, the feeling that we are emotionally connected to our work. Employee engagement is a highly valued motivational state that many corporations, such as Vanguard, Johnson & Johnson, and Toyota, seek to foster in their employees. High levels of satisfaction associated with task performance can create states of optimal experience or flow that team members experience when they are "in the zone." Flow experiences often yield high levels of engagement, creativity, and innovation valued by many of today's organizations.[34]

Team leadership can result in several additional positive outcomes for leaders and followers in a variety of organizations. Team leadership can result in high levels of team performance and effectiveness in corporate settings. Members of teams that share leadership report high levels of cohesion, trust, and consensus regarding the important issues they face. Research in educational settings has shown shared leadership to result in higher levels of students' achievement and teachers' commitment to their schools. Many of these results may be explained by what researchers call an "internal team environment" comprised of a shared purpose (discussed earlier), social support, and voice. Team members receive social support through the high-quality TMX relationships seen in words of encouragement offered to each other, recognition given for achievements, and expressions of emotional and psychological backing. Members feel that they have voice when they can provide input into what the team's mission should be, and how the team should operate to complete it. Each of these elements of the internal team environment can be created by putting FRLD into practice in teams.[35]

Putting FRLD Into Practice in Teams

Now that you are familiar with team leadership concepts, their importance, and outcomes for followers, teams, and organizations, you need to put them to good use. In order to properly utilize them, you should strive to attain two important goals by applying FRLD behaviors: (1) develop high-performing teams, and (2) share leadership in your teams.

How to Develop High-Performing Teams

While it is very important to share leadership with your team members, it may not be sufficient to create high-performing teams. What else do you need to consider for elevating the performance of your teams? A group of leadership coaches at *Forbes* provided what we believe to be a very helpful guide of 13 recommendations that we want to share with you along with our suggestions on how to put them into practice with FRLD behaviors:

1. Recognize individual strengths: It is very important to constantly utilize different talents that each member brings to the table. Try individualized consideration for this.
2. Focus on hitting goals: Be very specific about what needs to be achieved. Clarifying your expectations and focusing on outcomes can be very instrumental in developing high-performing team. Try contingent reward for this.
3. Alignment: You need to align your team members' values and energy around a shared vision. Try idealized influence for this.
4. Open feedback: High-performing teams have transparent cultures for communion, decision-making, and performance. Be sure to create open and

transparent communication processes that create TMX. Try individualized consideration for this.

5. Integrity: The leadership coaches argue that integrity is the most important characteristic of a high-performing team. Integrity creates a sense of trust and gives assurance to people that everyone on the team will do their best to help. Try idealized influence for this.

6. Kept promises: When people know that other members will do their part and maintain high standards on the team, team members are ready to contribute more. Try a mix of contingent reward and inspirational motivation for this.

7. Interest in learning: High-performing team members never stop learning from one another. Because they have high standards, they continue to seek better ways to perform their jobs. Try intellectual stimulation for this.

8. Over communication: In a high-performing team, communication is placed in top priority because team members work like a "well-oiled" basketball team. They observe one another and adjust their approach. As TMX research suggests, over communication is certainly better than under communication. Try a mix of inspirational motivation, idealized influence, and individualized consideration for this.

9. Psychological safety: You need to cultivate an environment in which members of your team feel safe to speak up or try out different approaches without fear of punishment or embarrassment. Try intellectual stimulation for this.

10. Commitment: Team members need to commit themselves fully into a common objective. So, you need to present a team goal in a way that they view it as being worthwhile. Create a high level of accountability for your team members to contribute more and better. Try a mix of inspirational motivation and contingent reward for this.

11. Collaboration: Without collaboration, your team can't create synergies. Develop a noble goal that excites everyone in your team. Establish a different set of performance criteria that enhances collaboration rather than internal competition. Try a mix of inspirational motivation and contingent reward for this.

12. Trust: Trust is essential in a high-performing team. You need to practice leading-by-example to foster a sense of trust as a leader. Try idealized influence this.

13. Respect: Members of high-performing teams have an elevated level of competencies and professional experience. Instead of the "follow me approach," you need to practice a more hands-on and empowering approach of leadership. Try a mix of intellectual stimulation and individualized consideration for this.[36]

How to Share Leadership in Your Team

Throughout this chapter, we have argued that no one can successfully take on a leader's role alone due to overwhelming rates of change in technologies and markets. So, don't try to come up with your team's strategy all by yourself. Instead, be sure to tap into your team members' skillsets and collective wisdom. Begin sharing your leadership with your team members so that they can develop their own leadership as well. Leadership coach and speaker Marshall Goldsmith suggests the following actions on how to share leadership with your team. We believe that this list provides a good starting point for you and your team:

- Empower the most qualified individuals to develop their strengths.
- Put boundaries on decision-making power.
- Foster an environment in which people are comfortable initiating assignments.
- Let people decide and engage in their tasks and resources and encourage them to use these tools.
- Don't question the decisions of the people you have empowered.
- Provide support and resources instead of managing your people.
- Follow up with meetings to track progress and make corrections if necessary.[37]

In addition to these recommendations, we would like to add the following tips to make your shared leadership processes more successful:

- Take your time when implementing shared leadership processes. You should view this task as a long-term project and be willing to take as much time as needed. One big mistake you can make is to share leadership in your team overnight.
- Sharing leadership is not for everyone. We believe that everyone is different regarding their skills, maturity, and attitudes. Consider categorizing your team members based on their level of competency and attitude. Focus on those who are able and willing to accept this added responsibility. For others, be sure to either change their attitude or develop their skills before sharing your leadership with them.
- If possible, change your selection criteria. If you want to share leadership in your team, you need to control who is brought into your team. Try to recruit people who have a strong desire to grow and become a leader. We have found that assessing and selecting the right group of people proves to be a more cost- and energy-effective way than trying to develop everyone into a leader regardless of their readiness.[38]

Building upon our recommendations regarding FRLD behaviors applied to the development of high-performing teams, we now present specific FRLD behaviors that can help you establish shared leadership. These behaviors include: (1) instill pride in team members for being associated with the team, (2) go beyond self-interest for the good of the team, (3) emphasize the importance of having a collective sense of mission, and (4) help team members to develop their strengths. Although every behavior associated with transformational leadership could potentially help you foster shared team leadership, we believe that these are most relevant and make the process more effective. Let's carefully examine each behavior with some examples.

Instill Pride in Team Members for Being Associated with the Team

Don taught two teams of U.S. Navy SEALs several years ago. SEALs are one of the most elite military units in the world. They distinguish themselves as an individually reliable, collectively disciplined, and highly skilled maritime force. Because of the dangers inherent in their mission, prospective SEALs go through what is considered by many military experts to be the toughest training in the world.[39] By working with the SEALs, Don got to know their beloved creed. We encourage you to carefully read the edited SEALs creed excerpts shown in the following (we italicized passages that we felt are especially relevant) as a way to reflect upon your own team and find a sense of pride associated with that of the SEALs:

My loyalty to Country and Team is beyond reproach . . . We expect to lead and be led. In the absence of orders, I will take charge, lead my teammates and accomplish the mission. I lead by example . . . *The lives of my teammates and success of our mission depend on me . . .* I will not fail.[40]

As the italicized words of the SEALs creed reveal, being a SEAL is all about pride. It is an instilled pride that they are the toughest warriors in the world, the most elite military organization in the world, and that they defend their country at the front line of a battle ground. With the highest pride of being associated with the SEALs, everyone is expected to lead and be led at the same time. We believe that SEALs are an excellent example of shared leadership and pride is at the center of their operation. Do you think that your team members are proud of working in your team? What can you do to increase their sense of pride? When was the last time you tried to instill pride in your team or organization?

Go Beyond Self-Interest for the Good of the Team

Recall the Penn State Nittany Lions football team and their coach James Franklin that we discussed in Chapter 3. What makes the Nittany Lions strong is Franklin's conscious effort to temper individual players' big and strong egos. One way he does this is by eliminating players' last names from the back of their jersey. This kind of de-individuation process is absolutely necessary for a leader to enhance team dynamics. Such symbolic action shifts the attention of team members from their self-interest to the critical needs of the team to succeed.

When people work as part of a team, it is always tempting to maximize their personal outcome by engaging social loafing, as shown in Figure 9.3. When team members observe one or two people on the team doing this, it can create anger and betrayal. Soon, such feelings lead to a very common reaction like, "If he does it, I think I should be doing it too!" Then, it is a matter of time for the team to create a negative norm signaling that it is OK to goof around or get a free ride. Therefore, it is important for you as the team leader to highlight the importance of teamwork and urge team members to put their self-interest behind them and work their hardest for the good of the team.

When team members begin thinking about their self-interest, it is impossible to develop shared leadership. Make the best interest of the team part of your team's culture. If necessary, create an image or event through which team

Figure 9.3 Slacking off. Many hands make the work lighter. But they also make it easier for this team member to kick back and not carry his fair share of the workload.

members are constantly reminded that they should put their self-interest behind them, just like what James Franklin does for his players.

Emphasize the Importance of Having a Collective Sense of Mission

As we have emphasized throughout this book, the best way to describe the current business environment is uncertainty. In times of uncertainty, flexibility and adaptability become more important than extensive planning and controlling. Yet some degree of collective planning and decision-making is required in such ambiguous contexts where the only thing that is certain is the rapid pace of change coming at everyone (see Box 9.4 for an example). Under these conditions, all members of the organization should act as if they are a "boundary scanner" looking for potential opportunities and problems. This means that you need to motivate your team members to stay alert and develop a sense of ownership. Over the last several years, we have concluded that having a collective goal or mission is one of the best ways, if not the best way, to deal with uncertainty and crises. Our realization is consistent with leadership authors James Kouzes and Barry Posner, who argued that a collective mission creates a sense of belonging in the times of uncertainty:

> This communion of purpose, this commemoration of our dreams, helps to bind us together. It reminds us of what it means to be a part of this collective effort. It joins us together in the human family. This sense of belonging is particularly key in tumultuous times, whatever the cause of the tumult.[41]

We are currently living in very tumultuous times. Consider the threats of terrorism, advances in new technologies, political turmoil such as nuclear threats from North Korea, and a variety of natural disasters. When Barack Obama assumed

Box 9.4 Tactics of Shared Leadership in the U.S. Army

A U.S. Army Ranger unit is operating deep in central Africa. Their mission is to eliminate fierce and unpredictable groups of Boko Haram, ISIS, and Al Qaeda insurgents in the region. At the same time, they need to build quality relationships with the local village elders to gather intelligence, establish local police forces, and earn the trust of the villagers. Their operational settings are difficult because they are embedded in neighborhoods among both civilians and insurgents. It is hard to tell the difference between the two groups. To make matters worse, things change constantly, resources and support are limited, and orders from top command often don't square with what they are experiencing on the ground. Based on a new order and intelligence suggesting no resistance, a team of Rangers decide to hunt down a high-value target insurgent. The Rangers are gunned down in an ambush. What went wrong?

The U.S. Army and researchers from the Center for Leadership Studies at the State University of New York at Binghamton and University of Oklahoma are interested in finding answers to such questions. Their research suggests that improvements in soldiers' shared decision-making, TMX, and real-time problem-solving skills may help to prevent such tragic outcomes described in the example at the beginning of Box 9.4. Instead of relying on top-down leadership guidance that can become stale and ineffective, soldiers need to efficiently and effectively collaborate and generate their own ideas on how to determine the intent and viability of their mission and execute their operational tactics. Problem-solving leadership skills (described in Chapter 1), planning and goal-setting behaviors (described in Chapter 7), and collective decision-making competencies need to be honed by entire units of soldiers in order to attain these positive outcomes. For these reasons, shared models of leadership that include such knowledge, skills, and abilities are needed in military contexts as well as in business settings where competition is fierce, stakes are high, and environments are rapidly changing.[42]

presidential leadership of the United States, he was dubbed "the Great Uniter." His success in leading a diverse nation and world during his two terms as president was based upon his ability to create a collective mission.[43] Time will tell if historians will describe U.S. president Donald Trump's navigation of our global web of geopolitical, social, and technological turbulence as either unifying or divisive.

Collective mission was key to the iconic NFL coach Vince Lombardi's success in building a dynasty for his legendary Green Bay Packers. According to Lombardi, "Teamwork is what the Green Bay Packers were all about. They didn't do it for individual glory. They did it because they loved one another." He considered individual commitment to a team effort to be what makes a team, company, society, and civilization work.[44]

How often do you emphasize the importance of having a collective mission when you attend a team meeting? Do you only emphasize personal benefits and interests that your team members will enjoy when their project is completed successfully? When you focus on personal benefits rather than collective benefits and achievements, members are not likely to develop high-quality TMX and shared leadership and put the team ahead of their self-interest. High-quality TMX involves a lot of interaction among team members for them to understand their interdependencies. Likewise, sharing leadership is a time-consuming process to develop as we mentioned earlier, and your team members are not likely to commit themselves if they do not share a common mission and vision. So, next time that you have a team meeting, put aside everything on your personal agenda. Spend time on the collective mission and make sure that all team members are fully committed to it before anyone does anything.

Help Your Team Members to Develop Their Strengths

Leadership icon Jack Welch, the former CEO of General Electric, is well known for his leadership philosophy regarding how to use company talent. He believes that a CEO's most important job is to recruit the best people, give them great opportunities, allocate resources they need to perform their job, and then get out of their way.[45] How could he empower people to the level he did? His belief was that when you are surrounded by A-level employees, all you need to do is to give them lots of opportunities to develop their strengths so that they become self-motivated. We believe that this is a form of shared leadership. When team members identify a set of skills they must develop and are committed to take full responsibility for their collective work, they are leading and being led at the same time, just like the Navy SEALs. Although Jack Welch's strong leadership has been recently criticized due to his harsh ways of handling low performers, we believe that his passion for developing A-level players is still equally important in the 21st century.

How do you go about helping your team members develop their strengths? The trick is to conduct astute observations and identify team members' potential that they may not even realize themselves. Do you remember the science and math teacher who gave John one of the most motivational moments in life when he was in the seventh grade? All he did was to observe John for a while, recognize his strengths and weaknesses, and give John work he would be enjoying and doing well. The rest of the story is straightforward. So, we want to challenge you to do the same with your team members so that you can become the next great teacher and developer of talent in your teams.

When team members have enough skills and talents, are self-motivated through empowerment, and are given the opportunity to work together toward a common goal, your role as a leader is helped significantly. We advise you to become more comfortable with your newly defined role in the context of shared leadership. Forget about a sense of control. Avoid having nightmares that your team project is out of control. Don't panic. The less you have a desire to manage, the greater the chance you can develop shared leadership in your team. Trust your judgment and that of your team members. They will do well. All you need to do is to nurture their strengths. That is essential to practicing FRLD, improving team dynamics, and building shared leadership. It is also essential to using FRLD as a strategic intervention in organizations, which we will discuss in the next chapter.

Summary Questions and Reflective Exercises

1. Think about the best team you ever had or were part of. List three characteristics of the team that were most instrumental in creating its good performance. Discuss these characteristics with other people and ask them about their best team experiences. Then identify common characteristics and compare these with the 13 characteristics of a high-performing team we discussed earlier. What are the similarities? Differences?

2. This exercise uses LEGO™ or similar building block toys to demonstrate how behaviors in the FRLD model influence group/team processes and outcomes. Four groups compete to design and showcase a new jet airplane: the Boeing 777½. First, separate the LEGOs into four bags, each with an equal number of colored blocks. In this exercise, each block has a corresponding price:

   a. Black and white = $0
   b. Red = $1
   c. Blue = $2
   d. Yellow = $3

   Each block (regardless of color) has an additional $1 labor assembly cost. Next, each team has five team member roles:

   Team leader—Each team leader portrays either laissez-faire, MBE-P, MBE-A, or transformational leadership behavior. Leaders should display their appropriate FRLD behaviors based on their personality and preferred styles. For example, the laissez-faire leader should simply hand the bag of LEGOs to the team members and leave the room. The MBE-P leader should sit back and only respond when asked questions. The MBE-A leader should micromanage the task using a drill sergeant style. The transformational leader should energize, challenge, coach, and help the team accomplish its task.

   Accountant—Team member responsible for costing out the final product in terms of labor and materials. A $24 budget restriction has been imposed by the client, although the last plane assembled cost $35.

   Design engineer—Team member responsible for making sure the plane meets certain technical specifications. All planes must have the following parts: two wings, a fuselage, and a tail. The plane must resemble a real airplane and be proportional.

Production engineer—Team member responsible for listing step-by-step assembly instructions to pass on to manufacturing. Directions must be clear enough that anyone could duplicate your plane.

Marketing associate—Team member responsible for creating an attractive advertisement poster for the jet airplane, complete with artwork and a catchy slogan.

Once team members have selected their roles, the teams have 20 minutes to complete their jet airplanes. Once 20 minutes have passed, each team leader makes a formal presentation to the entire group of the team's final product, accounting costs, engineering plan, and marketing advertisement. Team members can then comment on what it was like working under their leader. How did each of the FRLD behaviors used in these teams relate to the quality of the final product and the satisfaction level of the team?

3. Teams that share leadership often begin by committing to a common goal for a project and agreeing on how it will be best achieved. One way to accomplish this is to create a *team charter*. Begin by assembling your team and discussing the nature of the project. Discuss and agree upon the following items that will comprise your team charter:

   a. Define the *mission* or fundamental purpose of your project.

   b. Identify the *shared vision* or image of what your team would like to see happen as a result of your project.

   c. List and define the *shared values* that will guide the key behaviors and work values of your team members.

   d. Agree upon the *shared goal* that the team members would like to achieve as a result of the project.

   e. List the *shared objectives* or important milestones that the team must reach in order to achieve its goal.

   f. Identify the *shared tasks* that need to be performed in order to achieve the objectives and goal.

   g. List the *shared assignments*, identifying who is responsible for completing each task and when each task is due.

   h. *Evaluate* the progress made on the shared assignments by agreeing upon the performance metrics/measures to be used to gauge progress.

Assemble this information and draft your team charter. Share the team charter with the team members for their review. Based on their feedback, revise as necessary. When you reach final consensus, ask each team member to sign their names to the team charter to indicate their commitment to the team project. Be sure to hold them accountable for their compliance with the team charter.

4. Select a movie or film that illustrates shared leadership and/or high-performing team processes such as *Miracle, Remember the Titans, Hidden Figures, Band of Brothers,* or *The Beatles Anthology.* Watch it with your team members. Then have an informal discussion guided by the following questions: "What were important factors contributing to the team's success?", "What was the role that a leader played in the film?", and most importantly "How can we incorporate some of their success factors into our leadership system or situation?" Record and share notes on the important conclusions that your team members drew while answering these questions.

5. Identify and reflect upon the three most significant positive and negative critical incidents that occurred in your group/team during the last three months. What did you learn from each incident? What FRLD behavior influenced the incidents? For each of the negative critical incidents, consider what you would have wanted to occur instead. How can you use FRLD behaviors to create an optimal outcome in the future?

Notes

1   Hamel, G. (2007). *The future of management.* Boston, MA: Harvard Business School Press.

2   Hamel (2007). As cited in Note 1.

3   Thompson, D. (2017, June 16). Why Amazon brought Whole Foods. *The Atlantic.* Retrieved from www.theatlantic.com/business/archive/2017/06/why-amazon-bought-whole-foods/530652/.

4   Motohashi, K. (2015). *Global business strategy: Multinational corporations venturing into emerging markets.* Berlin: Springer; and Schmitt, B. H. (2007). *Big think strategy: How to leverage bold ideas and leave small thinking behind.* Boston, MA: Harvard Business School Press.

5   Katzenbach, J. R. (1997). *Teams at the top: Unleashing the potential of both teams and individual leaders.* Boston, MA: Harvard Business School Press; McChrystal, S. A., Fussell, C., Collins, T., & Silverman, D. (2015). *Team of teams: New rules of engagement for a complex world.* London: Portfolio; and Osherove, R. (2016). *Elastic leadership: Growing self-organized teams.* Shelter Island, NY: Manning Publications.

6   Dirk, K. T. (2000). Trust in leadership and team performance: Evidence from NCAA basketball. *Journal of Applied Psychology, 85*(6), 1004–1012.

7   Kark, R., & Shamir, B. (2002). The dual effect of transformational leadership: Priming relational and collective selves and further effects on followers. In B. J. Avolio, & F. J. Yammarino (Eds.), *Transformational and charismatic leadership: The road ahead* (pp. 67–91). Amsterdam: JAI Press.

8   Chun, J. U., Cho, K., & Sosik, J. J. (2016). A multilevel study of group-focused and individual-focused transformational leadership, social exchange relationships, and performance in teams. *Journal of Organizational Behavior, 37*(3), 374–396.

9   Seers, A. (1989). Team–member exchange quality: A new construct for role-making research. *Organizational Behavior and Human Decision Processes, 43*(1), 118–135; Seers, A., Petty, M. M., & Cashman, J. F. (1995). Team–member exchange under team and traditional management: A naturally occurring quasi-experiment. *Group & Organization Management, 20*(1), 18–38; and Sosik, J. J. (2015). Session 12 – Leadership by the team: How leadership can be shared. *LEAD 555: Full Range Leadership Development Online Course Webpage* (webpage 3). Malvern, PA: Penn State University.

10 Shenk, J. W. (2014, July/August). The power of two. *The Atlantic.* Retrieved from www. theatlantic.com/magazine/archive/2014/07/the-power-of-two/372289/.

11 Retrieved from www.rollingstone.com/music/lists/500-greatest-albums-of-all-time-20120531/the-beatles-sgt-peppers-lonely-hearts-club-band-20120531.

12 Aspinall, N. (Producer), Chipperfield, C, (Producer), Goodley, K. (Director), Smeaton, B. (Director/Writer), Storc, S. (Producer) & Wonfor, G. (Director) (1996). *The Beatles anthology* [Motion picture]. London: Apple/EMI Records.

13 Kane, L. (2016). *When they were boys: The true story of The Beatles rise to the top.* Philadelphia, PA: Running Press; Lennon, J., McCartney, P., Harrison, G., & Starr, R. (2000). *The Beatles anthology.* New York: Chronicle Books; and Turner, S. (2005). *A hard day's write: Stories behind every Beatles song* (3rd ed.). New York: Harper.

14 Bales, R. F. (1954). In conference. *Harvard Business Review, 32*(2), 44–50.

15 Waldersee, R., & Eagleson, G. (1996). *The efficacy of distributed leadership in implementing change.* Unpublished manuscript, Australian Graduate School of Management, University of New South Wales.

16 De Cremer, D., & Tao, T. (2015, November 20). Leadership innovation: Huawei's rotating CEO system. *The European Business Review.* Retrieved from www.europeanbusiness-review.com/leadership-innovation-huaweis-rotating-ceo-system/; and www.huawei.com/en/news/2017/9/Notice-Rotating-CEO-Tenure.

17 D'Innocenzo, L., Mathieu, J. E., & Kukenberger, M. R. (2016). A meta-analysis of different forms of shared leadership–team performance relations. *Journal of Management, 42*(7), 1964–1991; and Pearce, C., & Sims, H. (2002). Vertical versus shared leadership as predictors of the effectiveness of change management teams: An examination of aversive, directive, transactional, transformational, and empowering leader behavior. *Group Dynamics: Theory, Research, and Practice, 6*(2), 172–197.

18 Avolio, B. J. (1999). *Full leadership development: Building the vital forces in organizations.* Thousand Oaks, CA: Sage; and Avolio, B. J. (2011). *Full range leadership development* (2nd ed.). Thousand Oaks, CA: Sage.

19 Avolio (2011). As cited in Note 18.

20 Forbes Coaching Council (2016, October 14). 13 characteristics of a high performing team (and how leaders can foster them). *Forbes.* Retrieved from www.forbes.com/sites/forbescoachescouncil/2016/10/14/13-characteristics-of-a-high-performing-team-and-how-leaders-can-foster-them/#4ceafed1394a.

21 Jung, D. I., & Sosik, J. J. (2003). Group potency and collective efficacy: Examining their predictive validity, level of analysis, and effects of performance feedback on future group performance. *Group & Organization Management, 28*(3), 366–391.

22 Spink, K. S. (1990). Collective efficacy in the sport setting. *International Journal of Sport Psychology, 21*(4), 380–395.

23 Retrieved from www.facebook.com/lcfc/ and www.lcfc.com/.

24 Gres, M. (2016, May 4). Champions Leicester City: 7 reasons why Foxes won Premier League title. *CNN.com.* Retrieved from http://edition.cnn.com/2016/05/03/football/leicester-city-champions-reasons-premier-league/index.html.

25 Bernstein, R. (2003). *Remembering Herbie: Celebrating the life and times of hockey legend Herb Brooks.* Cambridge, MN: Adventure Publications.

26 Retrieved from www.si.com/100-greatest/?q=1-miracle-on-ice.

27 Bernstein (2003). As cited in Note 25; and retrieved from www.herbbrooksfoundation. com/.

28 Avolio (2011). As cited in Note 18.

29 Tuckman, B. W., & Jensen, M. A. C. (1977). Stages of small group development revisited. *Group & Organization Management, 2*(4), 419–427.

30 Avolio (1999). As cited in Note 18; and Avolio, B. J. (2011). As cited in Note 18.

31 Tuckman & Jensen (1977). As cited in Note 29.

32 Retrieved from www.ccl.org/open-enrollment-programs/leading-teams-for-impact/.

33 D'Innocenzo et al. (2016). As cited in Note 17.

34 Csíkszentmihályi, M. (1996). *Creativity: Flow and the psychology of discovery and invention.* New York: Harper; Fleming, J. H., & Asplund, J. (2007). *Human sigma: Managing the employee-customer encounter.* Omaha, NE: Gallup Press; and Serban, A., & Roberts, A. J. B. (2016). Exploring antecedents and outcomes of shared leadership in a creative context: A mixed-methods approach. *The Leadership Quarterly, 27*(2), 181–199.

35 Carson, J. B, Tesluk, P. E., & Marrone, J. A. (2007). Shared leadership in team: An investigation of antecedent conditions and performance. *Academy of Management Journal, 50*(5), 1217–1234; Hulpia, H., & Devos, G. (2010). How distributed leadership can make a difference in teachers' organizational commitment? A qualitative study. *Teaching and Teacher Education: An International Journal of Research and Studies, 26*(3), 565–575; Leithwood, K., & Mascall, B. (2008). Collective leadership effects on student achievement. *Educational Administration Quarterly, 44*(4), 529–561; and Wang, D., Waldman, D. A., & Zhang, Z. (2014). A meta-analysis of shared leadership and team effectiveness. *Journal of Applied Psychology, 99*(2), 181–198.

36 Forbes Coaching Council (2016, October 14). As cited in Note 20.

37 Goldsmith, M. (2010, May 26). Sharing leadership to maximize talent. *Harvard Business Review.* Retrieved from https://hbr.org/2010/05/sharing-leadership-to-maximize.

38 For details on determining team members' readiness for leadership development, see Avolio, B. J., & Hannah, S. T. (2008). Developmental readiness: Accelerating leader development. *Consulting Psychology Journal: Practice and Research, 60*(4), 331–341.

39 Retrieved from https://navyseals.com/nsw/seal-code-warrior-creed/.

40 Navy SEALs creed. As cited in Note 39.

41 Kouzes, J. M., & Posner, B. Z. (2002, p.153). *The leadership challenge.* San Francisco, CA: Jossey-Bass.

42 Ellis, K. (2017). Leadership in the Army. *Reaching Higher: Binghamton University Magazine, School of Management, 8,* 16–19; O'Grady, S. (2017, October 20). What the hell happened in Niger? *The Atlantic.* Retrieved from www.theatlantic.com/international/archive/2017/10/niger-isis-us-soldiers-attack/543531/; and Yammarino, F. J., Salas, E., Serban, A., Shirreffs, K., & Shuffler, M. L. (2012). Collective leadership approaches: Putting the "we" in leadership science and practice. *Industrial and Organizational Psychology, 5*(4), 382–402.

43 Rauch, J. (2016, December). What Obama got right. *The Atlantic.* Retrieved from www.theatlantic.com/magazine/archive/2016/12/leaving-a-clean-desk/505856/.

44 Lombardi Jr., V. (2003). *The essential Vince Lombardi: Words and wisdom to motivate, inspire, and win.* New York: McGraw-Hill; and Maraniss, D. (1999). *When pride still mattered: A life of Vince Lombardi.* New York: Simon & Schuster.

45 Welch, J., & Welch, S. (2015). *The real-life MBA: Your no-BS guide to winning the game, building a team, and growing your career.* New York: Harper Business.

Chapter 10

Full Range Leadership Development for Strategic, Social, and Environmental Initiatives

"Never a dull moment" describes most of Debby's days as Director of Human Resources (HR) for a large U.S.-based not-for-profit, standard setting organization. Debby is part of their top management team (TMT) and also works with their Board of Directors' Executive Compensation Committee, which handles all matters of compensation for top executives. Her HR team is responsible for the entire employment life cycle of the organization's staff as well as its leadership development. So Debby embraced the tenants of transformational leadership as a great resource.

One of Debby's most important challenges came with the arrival of a new CEO. At that time, her team administered a baseline employee engagement survey and the results were not good. They indicated that employees did not trust leadership, and wanted to become more involved in decision-making processes when it affected their work. A lack of trust is a big problem because with websites like Glassdoor.com and Indeed.com, employees may vent their frustrations publicly and ruin a company's reputation.

A year later, against Debby's advice, the CEO thought that things were moving in the right direction and ordered a follow-up survey to be completed to monitor progress on employee engagement. It was not a good idea. The CEO had only a one-year tenure and devoted virtually no time to improve the company's culture. The sobering survey results came back and no significant progress was made. The same two primary issues were identified as still being significant obstacles to employee engagement. Needless to say, the CEO and his TMT were not at all happy with the results and worried about their reputation.

After Debby shared the results with the TMT, they brainstormed what to do about them. They then held a "town meeting" with employees, reviewed the results of the surveys, and asked the employees what they believed were the top three most important things to address. They told the employees that the TMT realizes that the number one priority was to build trust between and among the top leadership and employees. They committed to working on becoming a high-performing TMT while deploying other ideas that the employees thought were important. By publicly humbling themselves and acknowledging the poor results of the survey, the TMT started to gain the trust of their associates. The employees became cautiously optimistic that the TMT might actually deliver on their promises and become a more effective leadership team. While some leaders needed to transition out of the organization, and did so, Debby's HR team engaged an outside consultant to work with the remaining leaders. The team elicited ideas from employees as they requested in the surveys.

As a result, workplace fun and engagement activities were sponsored by an event planning committee, which is comprised of all non-management employees from different departments. They meet monthly to discuss and decide on events to host for employees. For example, a cross-cultural pot luck luncheon was held. This fun-filled event was well attended and fostered an appreciation of diversity. Debby and her CEO learned that leaders need to be inclusive of their followers and leverage the motivation they bring with them to work so that the entire organization can benefit. And the results of the employee engagement surveys have improved, as has the reputation of the company in the eyes of the employees.[1]

Debby's story underscores the belief that an organization's culture and reputation are valuable intangible assets. These assets have to be built through the emotional and psychological commitment from people within the organizations. When employees are committed to their jobs, it is reflected in their attitudes and dedication toward customers, which in turn makes their customers happy and satisfied. When customers are satisfied, they become repeat customers who spread positive word-of-mouth advertising about your organization. When customers do this, they become evangelists for you.

Many successful companies, such as Publix Super Markets, Apple, True Value, and Lexus, know exactly how they can make their customers loyal. For example, Lexus provides luxurious dealerships that treat customers as VIPs and surveys its customers about their experiences during service visits. From a strategic standpoint, this is one way organizations can differentiate themselves from others and stand out as something special.[2] Because emotional and psychological processes are key motivational mechanisms of Full Range Leadership Development (FRLD; see Chapter 2), it makes sense to apply FRLD principles to strategic initiatives in your organization and community. This chapter shows you how to do this. Let's start learning about this process by examining the functions of top executives and their leadership roles in organizations.

Responsibilities of Executives: How FRLD Can Help

Building a strong corporate reputation is a task Mary Barra knows well. In 2014, Barra was hired as CEO by General Motors (GM) to re-organize its operations, boost its profits, and rebuild its reputation. For many years, GM suffered from low quality and a bad brand reputation among customers. Once a proud and reputable industry giant, GM sank to new lows in 2009 with its embarrassing bankruptcy. But Barra and her TMT have worked hard to transform GM into a great company again. She's initiated strategic moves including developing cars with new technologies such as self-driving systems, closing or selling off unprofitable operations around the world, and utilizing data to connect with their customers. GM hopes to re-energize employee engagement and innovation, lower costs, boost profits, and improve their reputation by producing higher-quality vehicles. GM's renewed passion for autonomous and electric vehicles and meeting its renewable energy goals have become an exciting vision that inspires GM's employees.[3]

CEOs like Barra work with their TMT to perform several functions while leading their organizations. As shown in Figure 10.1, these functions involve six primary areas of executive responsibility that we believe can be facilitated by FRLD: (1) planning and visioning, (2) operations and logistics, (3) marketing and public relations, (4) human resources, (5) financial control, and (6) governance.

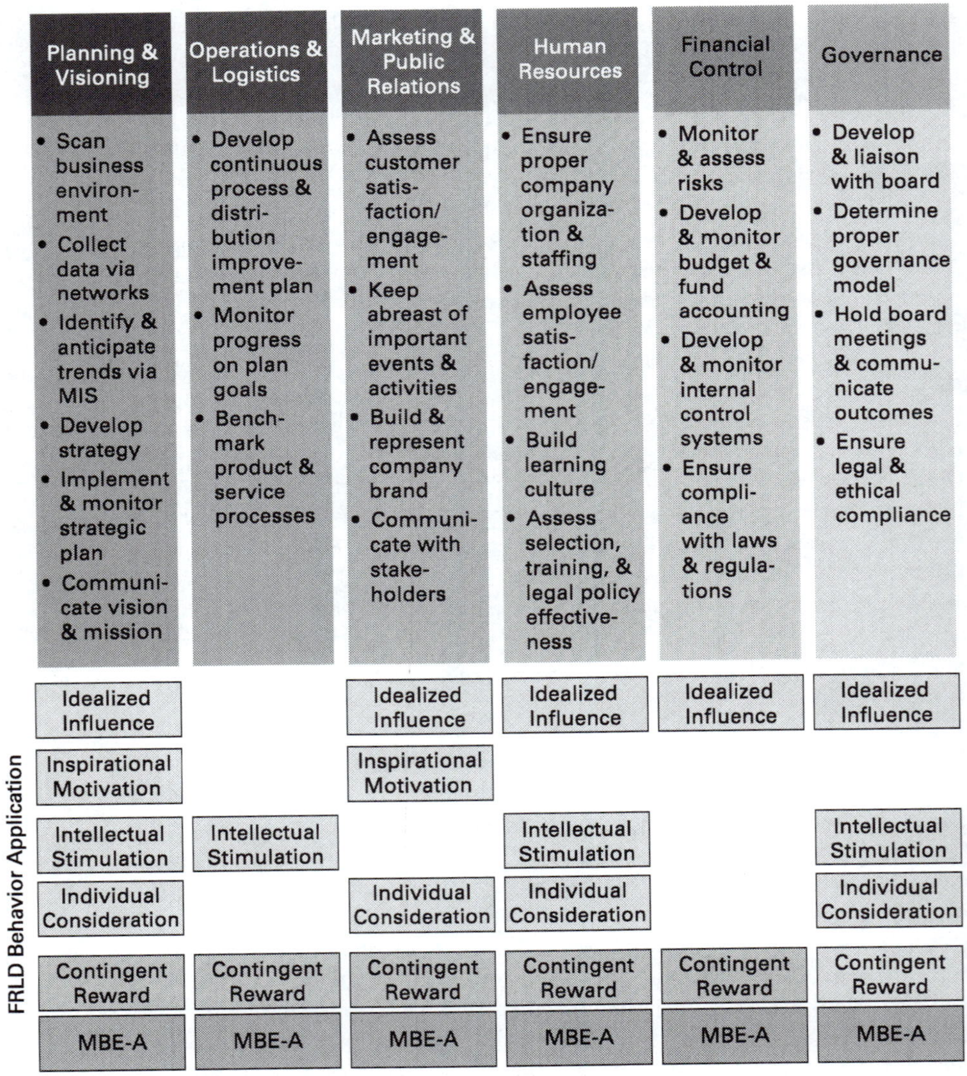

Planning & Visioning	Operations & Logistics	Marketing & Public Relations	Human Resources	Financial Control	Governance
• Scan business environment • Collect data via networks • Identify & anticipate trends via MIS • Develop strategy • Implement & monitor strategic plan • Communicate vision & mission	• Develop continuous process & distribution improvement plan • Monitor progress on plan goals • Benchmark product & service processes	• Assess customer satisfaction/engagement • Keep abreast of important events & activities • Build & represent company brand • Communicate with stakeholders	• Ensure proper company organization & staffing • Assess employee satisfaction/engagement • Build learning culture • Assess selection, training, & legal policy effectiveness	• Monitor & assess risks • Develop & monitor budget & fund accounting • Develop & monitor internal control systems • Ensure compliance with laws & regulations	• Develop & liaison with board • Determine proper governance model • Hold board meetings & communicate outcomes • Ensure legal & ethical compliance
Idealized Influence		Idealized Influence	Idealized Influence	Idealized Influence	Idealized Influence
Inspirational Motivation		Inspirational Motivation			
Intellectual Stimulation	Intellectual Stimulation		Intellectual Stimulation		Intellectual Stimulation
Individual Consideration		Individual Consideration	Individual Consideration		Individual Consideration
Contingent Reward	Contingent Reward	Contingent Reward	Contingent Reward	Contingent Reward	Contingent Reward
MBE-A	MBE-A	MBE-A	MBE-A	MBE-A	MBE-A

FRLD Behavior Application

Figure 10.1 **Areas of executive responsibility, functions, and FRLD behaviors to support them.**

Planning and visioning involves effectively determining and communicating the company's vision, mission, values, and goals set forth in the strategic plan. This responsibility concerns collecting data from outside sources on market situations and competitors, analyzing the business environment for threats and opportunities, determining the company's strengths and weaknesses, and analyzing the data collected so that strategic plans can be created. The TMT uses company management information systems to monitor progress toward the strategic goals. Based on these assessments, the executives modify components of the strategy so that they are in the best interests of the shareholders, employees, customers, and society. As shown in the bottom portion of Figure 10.1, we believe that leadership behaviors ranging from idealized influence through active management-by-exception (MBE-A) can support these initiatives since they serve to inspire, challenge, coach, role model, reward, and control people, processes, and products and services.[4]

Operations and logistics involve the oversight of product manufacturing and service provisions along with the management of the flow of supplies, materials, products, and services from where they originate to where they are ultimately consumed by customers or used by organizations. This responsibility concerns the adoption and use of Six Sigma, total quality management, and continuous improvement initiatives applied to an organization's process and distribution systems. As part of this executive responsibility, the TMT also pays attention to monitoring the organization's progress toward the goals set as part of these initiatives. The benchmarking of best practices and industry standards is another function that TMTs commonly perform to meet this responsibility. As shown in Figure 10.1, the continuous process improvement of products and services can be best supported by executives with the display of intellectual stimulation (to ignite innovation and creativity) and contingent reward (to set improvement goals and reward followers for their attainment). We also believe that the display of MBE-A behaviors is appropriate for supporting the automated control systems commonly found in manufacturing and logistics operations.[5]

Marketing and public relations involve activities that attempt to derive revenue through the distribution of an organization's products and services, as well as positively influencing customers' attitudes toward the organization and its brands by managing the communication channels with organizational stakeholders. This responsibility encompasses the assessment of customer satisfaction and engagement levels to determine the degree to which customers are loyal to company brands. While managing a positive corporate reputation with the public, the TMT stays current regarding important events and activities that can affect the company's image. Making the right impressions through communication channels such as social media and responding to significant criticisms helps to build and maintain a positive organizational brand. So effective and timely communication is an essential function within the marketing and public relations executive responsibility. Inspirational motivation and idealized influence behaviors displayed by executives can go a long way in meeting these communication and impression management functions. A TMT's display of individualized consideration to customers in treating each of them based on their different needs and requirements rather than just a group of customers is critical for increasing customer loyalty and maintaining a strong brand image. Sales goal setting, monitoring of progress toward goals, and rewarding of goal attainment can be supported with the display of contingent reward and MBE-A behaviors.[6]

Human resources involve oversight of the recruitment, selection, compensation, benefits, safety, and employee development along with compliance to laws and regulations governing these activities. This responsibility mandates executives to organize employees into different teams and departments, often depicted in organizational charts with lines of reporting responsibilities delineated so organizations can utilize human talents more effectively. As we saw with Debby's example at the start of this chapter, another important function is the assessment of employee satisfaction and engagement levels with tools such as Gallup's Q12®. Executives who take FRLD seriously would be inclined to advocate learning cultures, where company values, processes, and programs strive to increase the knowledge, skills, and abilities of employees to enhance organizational effectiveness.[7] They would also carefully review the selection, training and development, and legal compliance functions within this executive responsibility.

As organizational scholar Benjamin Schneider once wrote, "the people make the place."[8] So it is imperative that TMT members display leadership behaviors that attract and retain competent and ethical employees. Idealized influence of executives allows them to role model high levels of ethical and performance standards, while their display of intellectual stimulation and individualized consideration can challenge employees and tap into their unique skillsets and personalities to increase collective levels of intelligence and competency. Because pay-for-performance, monitoring employee behavior, and ensuring legal compliance are essential HR policies and processes, we believe that both contingent reward and MBE-A behavior are also required to support the HR executive oversight responsibility.

Financial control involves oversight of an organization's economic resources and obligations including assets, liabilities, and owners' equity, along with the flow of funds into (revenue and investments) and out of (expenses and distributions) the organization as a result of its operations. This executive responsibility consists of monitoring and assessing any financial and non-financial risks and determining the impact they have on organizations. It also includes the development and assessment of annual and monthly financial and operational budgets to determine whether operations are being conducted efficiently and effectively. As described in Chapter 7, systems of internal control represent another financial function to ensure that financial and operational systems are kept in check. An organization's financial transactions and reporting are subject to state and federal laws as well as global standards set by the International Accounting Standards Board, so compliance in these areas is a must. An examination of Figure 10.1 suggests that this area of executive responsibility is quite transactional in nature and would be best supported with transactional leadership behaviors including contingent reward (to set, assess, and reward budget goal attainment) and MBE-A (to monitor deviations from financial goals and legal compliance). We also recommend that executives on TMTs be sure to display idealized influence behaviors.

These behaviors can help them role model ethical leadership to comply with legal obligations associated with financial transactions and reporting.

Governance involves oversight of how the organization is directed and controlled by the CEO, TMT, and Board of Directors through its collection of rules, policies, and practices as well as compliance with laws and regulations established by industry, governments, and the community. Organizations have stakeholders, such as customers, suppliers, employees, management, investors, government, and society, who sometimes have competing values and interests. While striving to achieve a balance among these stakeholders, the CEO and TMT are supposed to act as agents and good corporate citizens who maintain high levels of ethical standards. But this is often not the case as seen in the Lehman Brothers bankruptcy, Wells Fargo's fake customer account scandal, and Fox News' top executive and newscaster sexual harassment of female employees.

Because of the potential self-interests and ethical lapses of top management, corporations create a Board of Directors whose Chairman and committees are supposed to oversee their actions and decisions. One of the executive governance responsibilities of the TMT is to work closely with the board and act as a liaison between it and the organization. The TMT, in cooperation with the board, determines and periodically assesses its governance model. For example, should it be shareholder-centered with the goal of maximizing shareholder wealth, or company-centered with the goal of balancing economic and social wealth with a more meaningful purpose like maximizing the triple bottom line (described later)? To answer this question, CEOs are typically responsible for holding board meetings and communicating their results with organizational stakeholders. Another function of the TMT and board involves ensuring legal and ethical compliance with laws and regulations.[9]

We believe that the governance area of executive responsibility can benefit from the display of a broad range of FRLD behaviors by TMT *and* corporate board members. Idealized influence can help them avoid ethical lapses by focusing on ethical implications of the decisions they make. Intellectual stimulation can leverage new perspectives and expertise required to meet new strategic challenges. And because governance is all about direction and control of the organization, executives would do well by building these transformational leadership behaviors upon a solid base of transactional leadership, namely contingent reward and MBE-A, to ensure the most effective leadership outcomes for the organization. In its support of all areas of executive responsibility and the functions needed to fulfill them, FRLD provides a useful and practical tool to support an organization's strategic leadership.

Strategic Leadership Defined

Top corporate leaders like Mary Barra, Mark Zuckerberg, and Richard Branson are responsible for creating wealth for their shareholders. They do this by increasing profits and stock price and by creating a sustainable growth plan for the future. Of course, they can't do this alone. They have to motivate people within their organizations to create the right set of strategies, resources, processes, and talent pools required to achieve their financial goals. However, these exceptional CEOs possess a special set of perceptional and thinking abilities, along with a vast relevant knowledge base, and excellent interpersonal competencies and leadership. These resources combined enable the most effective leaders to recognize important trends among customers and in the market ahead of their competition and then develop products and services that satisfy these new needs. The capacity to orchestrate complex business processes and to leverage these opportunities into financial rewards for shareholders is called *strategic leadership*. It involves the abilities, skills, behaviors, and processes required to anticipate and prepare an organization for its future and add to its prosperity.

We explained earlier and in our previous research that top leaders often focus on achieving these goals by applying aspects of FRLD.[10] We now explain how top leaders, such as Elon Musk (see Box 10.1), use aspects of FRLD to see important trends and capitalize upon them with innovative products and services. As a result of these leadership effects, their companies become a pioneer in their respective industry and/or create a new market for superb financial performance.[11]

Box 10.1 Leader Profile: Elon Musk

Who has the gall to predict that his car company will someday top Apple's $900 billion stock market capitalization value? No one other than Elon Musk, the brilliant visionary entrepreneur and inspirational leader of a collection of technology-oriented companies with groundbreaking missions. Primarily known for his leadership at Tesla, the automotive and solar energy manufacturer, Musk has been at the helm of Zip2 (web software), X.com and PayPal (online financial services), SpaceX (space exploration), SolarCity (solar power), Hyperloop (high speed transportation), OpenAI (artificial intelligence research), Neuralink (technology to link the human brain to artificial intelligence), and the Boring Company (tunnel boring).

Musk's success in these business ventures stems from his upbringing and unique personality. Severely bullied as a child, Musk found a way to get back at his detractors. Professional success in life would be his revenge. Always highly intelligent and an avid reader, Musk earned undergraduate degrees in physics and economics from the University of Pennsylvania. There he learned the importance of strong willpower, passion, and intellectual stimulation for effective leadership and success. While striving to enhance customer relationships and engagement, Musk demonstrates a strong belief in and love of his brands. His passion comes across to customers through his speeches and the confident way he carries himself. His passion is contagious as people soon become enamored with Musk and his visions. What is so appealing is Musk's enormous ambition to do nearly impossible things, like colonize Mars by 2040 with SpaceX, or "create the most compelling car company of the 21st century by driving the world's transition to electric vehicles" with Tesla.

As an advocate of accelerating employee learning and growth, Musk sets very high standards for his employees. He is famous for having engineers work for days on a project and then redirecting them onto other projects to learn new ways to implement his technological ideas. He constantly pushes his associates to reach their full potential and strive for perfection and innovation in product design. In his quest to improve operational efficiencies at Tesla, Musk shares traits that Steve Jobs possessed—an obsession with products and detail-orientation. Musk is extremely involved in product design and obsesses over the tiniest of details because of his infatuation with his work and the meaning in life it gives him. He encourages his associates to possess an unyielding work ethic fueled by strong willpower. He challenges them to constantly strive for excellence, and never settle for anything less. He is also a strong advocate of mastering the science of robotics in manufacturing and has applied this knowledge in his Tesla factories.

Time will tell whether Musk will achieve his vision of Tesla outperforming Apple and becoming the world's biggest brand. He will need significant investment capital, a growth rate of 50% over a stretch of ten years, a workforce religiously devoted to his vision, and advanced technology to do it. But Musk is already on the right track because he leads by example, holds high performance expectations, constantly innovates, and pushes his people to higher levels of professional development. That sounds a lot like transformational leadership.[12]

Strategic Leadership and the Balanced Scorecard

A useful framework for understanding how FRLD can be applied in strategic leadership initiatives is the balanced scorecard. Management accounting scholars Richard Kaplan and David Norton developed the *balanced scorecard* as a performance management tool to plan, execute, and monitor organizational strategy. It works by encouraging organizations to measure their success from customer, employee, operational, and financial perspectives. Similar to the assumption that leaders are much more likely to influence bottom-line performance indirectly through followers and various organizational processes, the balanced scorecard assumes that organizations should focus on planning for and measuring things that influence financial outcomes over time (e.g., customer engagement, employee engagement, cycle time, waste, production and management efficiency). These factors influence financial outcomes and are called *lead indicators* of performance, while the financial outcomes themselves are *lag indicators* because they are a direct result of the lead indicators.[13]

We believe that strategic leadership should involve identifying and communicating a vision that can be translated into several organizational objectives and more specific goals to be attained. These goals can be measured and monitored by sorting them into the four perspectives of the balanced scorecard:

- *Customer perspective*—Objectives, goals, and measures indicating the quality of relationships with customers and their view of the organization's products and services. Sample measures include market share, market growth, and customer engagement. The Gallup Organization's CE11® survey measures customer engagement by assessing customers' perceptions of confidence, integrity, pride, and passion related to an organization's products or services.[14]
- *Innovation and learning perspective*—Objectives, goals, and measures indicating the quality of relationships with employees and how they view their development of knowledge, skills and abilities, motivation, and commitment. Sample measures include trust, skills inventory, innovation and creativity measures, attitude surveys, and employee engagement. Gallup's Q12® survey measures employee engagement from self-reports of employees' perceptions of what intrinsic rewards they get from their job, what effort they put into their job, whether they belong in their organizational role, and how they can grow in their role.[15]
- *Internal business process*—Objectives, goals, and measures indicating the efficiency and effectiveness of the organization's processes, practices, and manufacturing/service systems. Sample measures include cycle time, waste, and sundry efficiency metrics. As competition relentlessly increases in today's global marketplace, many companies focus on increasing their operational efficiency as a way to compete. For example, warehouse workers at Tesco supermarkets in Europe wear electronic armbands to track their walking speed on the floor and assess who are performing up to company standards. Some companies are even implanting microchips in the hands of their employees as a way to cut the cost of issuing keys! These metrics help managers improve operational efficiency, but certainly raise privacy and potential health issues.[16]
- *Financial perspective*—Objectives, goals, and measures indicating how accountants and financial analysts view an organization's cash flow, financial condition, and investment rating. Sample measures include net income, return on investment, assets, debt, stock price, and economic value-added (EVA™). Companies like Ford, General Motors, and Disney use EVA™, a metric developed by Stern Value Management, to assess after-tax profit less the cost of capital used to generate profits.[17]

We believe that the best starting point for the balanced scorecard process is an organization's vision. Companies differ in their vision. For example, vacation apparel company Life is Good's vision is "to spread the power of optimism." Nike's is to "bring inspiration and innovation to every athlete." Microsoft's is "to help individuals and businesses reach their full potential." Even the engineering department of the Ritz Carlton on Amelia Island, Florida, has a vision: "To go boldly where no hotel has gone before—free of all defects." While all of these visions are interesting and somewhat grandiose, we see them as being pretty vague. This limits their usefulness.

The balanced scorecard process begins by translating the vision into more specific organizational objectives from the perspectives shown in Figure 10.2. Top

Figure 10.2
**Strategic
leadership tool.
Transformational
leaders use a
balanced approach
to strategic planning
that considers
perspectives of
the customer,
employees,
operations experts,
and financiers.**

leaders communicate the vision and its importance to all employees. In developing strategy, a TMT should connect each of the objectives and their specific goals within these perspectives to the organization's vision and its mission. They then drill down these goals through the business units to divisions to departments to teams to individuals. This aligns the goals across organizational levels, encourages coordination and collaboration, and promotes accountability. One thing that CEOs sometimes forget is the importance of *shared* vision. They tend to believe that once they communicate their vision, employees accept and cherish it immediately. However, to make your vision a collective and shared commitment of the overall organization, you must communicate it repeatedly and reinforce it through various means, such as socialization, evaluation, and compensation.

As part of their strategic business planning, the TMT then works with associates to map out *cause-and-effect relationships* between the goals. They create a strategy map in the form of a flowchart. This map charts organizational strategy for achieving the vision, as illustrated in Figure 10.3. The links on the strategy map represent hypothesized relationships between measures within and between the four perspectives of the balanced scorecard. Once appropriate measures are identified for the goals, the TMT collects data from these measures over time. These data can be used in linear regression models to test the causal assumptions in the strategy map. This process allows leaders to examine the validity of their assumptions supporting their strategic initiatives and revise their strategy map whenever necessary.

For example, the TMT may wonder whether employee engagement, depicted in the strategy map shown in Figure 10.3, actually leads to customer engagement and a higher level of employee participation in ideas generation for continuous improvement. Results of the statistical analysis testing relationships between these measures can determine whether money should be spent on improving employee engagement. This process could squeeze speculation out of decision-making processes. Only carefully collected and analyzed data can provide an objective answer to such questions. Therefore, leaders should use data analytics, data-driven decisions, and integrated strategic planning models to align their strategy and vision. This process provides a feedback loop that allows top leadership to learn from the feedback and adjust their strategy appropriately to maximize financial outcomes over time.

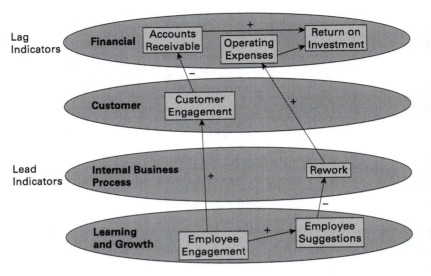

Figure 10.3
Cause and effect. Strategic maps present hypothesized relationships between key metrics within and between the customer, innovation and learning, internal business process, and financial perspectives.

Many organizations including Mobil, Philips Electronics, United Parcel Service, Verizon, and Mutual of Omaha have successfully used this process for strategic planning. According to the late Jack Weekly, former chairman and CEO of Mutual of Omaha, his TMT first talked about what it would require to reenergize the company and attain their vision. As a service company, they identified five key objectives to meet: growth and customer loyalty (customer perspective), profitability and financial discipline (financial perspective), and accountability (innovation and learning perspective). They fleshed out their key objectives with more specific goals and then determined how to measure progress on each of these goals. For example, they partnered with the Gallup Organization to use Gallup's Q12® survey to assess accountability through employee engagement.

Mutual of Omaha's balanced scorecard "was designed so that operating units at all levels with targets and measures could then develop their own scorecards that were in sync with larger corporate goals and objectives." This alignment strategy allowed employees across all business units to see their contributions and responsibility for working toward the overall corporate goals. This helps employees see how their daily work contributes to the overall vision of the company in terms of the five objectives.[18] This strategic process accomplished for Mutual of Omaha what inspirational leaders do when they show followers the importance of their work and contributions. Indeed, FRLD augments strategic leadership in many ways.[19]

How FRLD Enhances This Process

Kaplan and Norton originally designed the balanced scorecard as a performance management and strategy tool that uses principles of management-by-objectives (MBO).[20] This strategic management approach involves aligning a company's objectives at various levels of an organization and monitoring progress toward meeting those objectives. You're probably thinking that this sounds very much like a transactional approach to strategic leadership. If so, you're correct. That's because MBO is based on goal setting (contingent reward leadership) and actively monitoring progress toward achieving these goals (MBE-A leadership). However, transformational aspects of the FRLD model also can be applied to maximize benefits of the balanced scorecard system as a strategic leadership tool.

When you translate the vision into organizational goals, you need to understand what you really want to accomplish to make the translation process more effective. Then, use inspirational motivation and intellectual stimulation to inspire and challenge your associates to define what objectives are most important to achieve as they work toward attaining the vision. Your vision should be about where your company wants to be in the future. It reflects the future environment and works in concert with your organization's mission (i.e., core values, purpose, and reason for existence).

Providing contingent rewards is another great way to motivate associates to begin working hard toward the goal. Contingent reward leadership also provides feedback and learning through a cycle of goal setting, monitoring of results, giving advice derived from results, providing rewards or punishments as necessary, and fine-tuning aspects of strategy, including goals and the actions needed to attain them.

Aspects of FRLD are also helpful in coordinating the people, processes, and resources required to attain objectives and goals across the four perspectives of the balanced scorecard. In regard to the *customer perspective*, you may want to provide perceived value to the most desired customer groups to keep them satisfied and engaged. You can attain this goal via one or some combination of three strategic approaches: operational excellence, customer intimacy, or product leadership. You can promote operational excellence by displaying inspirational motivation behavior that raises the bar on performance levels and contingent reward behavior that compensates associates for meeting elevated performance standards. You can create customer intimacy by encouraging sales staff to display individually considerate behaviors that ask customers what they value in a product or service and use this feedback in improving products or services. You can promote product leadership by displaying intellectually stimulating behaviors that promote creativity and innovation in research and development and deliver new products and services that are cutting edge and cost-effective.

Regarding the *internal business process perspective*, you need to create sustainable processes that develop and deliver your products and services more efficiently and effectively. You can attain this goal by examining all the activities and processes, eliminating those that do not add value to the product or service, and expanding those that do. You should examine the following functional areas: operations management, customer management, innovation, and regulatory/social responsibility. For operations management improvement, you can use intellectual stimulation to question assumptions regarding asset utilization and supply chain management processes. Ask your associates, "What do we need to eliminate to make our operational processes more efficient and effective?" For customer management improvement, you can encourage salespeople to use individually considerate behavior with their customers. For innovation, intellectual stimulation is the obvious choice. And for regulatory and social responsibility initiatives, you can use MBE-A behavior to enforce compliance with laws, and intellectual stimulation to think of new ways to produce and deliver products and services in an environmentally friendly way, like Mary Barra did at GM.

In regard to the *innovation and learning perspective*, you may want to develop the internal skills and capacities required to support your organization's internal business process functions. You can attain this goal via job design, systems development and maintenance, and organizational development (i.e., addressing culture and climate issues). You can promote innovative job design initiatives through individually considerate behavior that identifies talent and fits it into the right role in the organization, and provide coaching and mentoring to turn associates' talents into strengths. Or, you can use intellectual stimulation to redesign jobs to offer more task variety, task meaningfulness, feedback, and autonomy.

You can support systems development and maintenance with a combination of MBE-A, contingent reward, and intellectually stimulating leadership. Intellectual stimulation is helpful when creating new systems and fine-tuning them over time. MBE-A leadership may be necessary to ensure that critical systems do not fail by identifying and correcting problems before they occur. Contingent reward leadership is useful in planning for, monitoring, and rewarding systems development projects that are often burdensome to manage due to their size and lifestyle.

You can help develop a positive organizational culture and climate by displaying idealized leadership that role models high expectations for performance and ethics, inspirational motivation that champions teamwork, and individualized consideration that values diversity and builds a supportive work environment. After all, it's your employees who make most things happen. As Herb Kelleher, charismatic co-founder and former chairman and CEO of Southwest Airlines once said, "Who comes first? The employees, customers or shareholders? That's never been an issue to me. The employees come first. If they are happy, satisfied, and energetic . . ."[21] Kelleher's thoughts teach us that it is *your* responsibility to build a positive culture that values your employees and keeps them happy.

Regarding the *financial perspective*, you may want to see if your strategy and the processes for its execution are indeed creating wealth for your shareholders and a healthy organization to do so. Here the focus is on bottom-line improvement of the organization. But such a focus often comes at the expense of additional goals pursued in the healthier company- centered form of corporate governance—one that also values innovation, strategic renewal, and investment in the company's future.[22] However, you need to consider these outcomes to be long term in nature since they result from the activities described in the customer, innovation and learning, and internal business process perspectives.

Triple Bottom Line

In 2007, the United Nations ratified the notion of a *triple bottom line* as a standard for urban and community accounting. This approach to public sector accounting is a way to expand the traditional notion of organizational effectiveness beyond measures of financial success to include environmental and social measures as well. The triple-bottom-line approach seeks to include measures of success for *people* (e.g., development of human potential; fair and beneficial treatment of labor, community, and region; fair trade; charitable contributions), *planet* (environmental protection and sustainability; resource consumption; waste management; land use), and *profit* (economic benefit via revenue growth and cost reduction) to promote corporate social responsibility.[23] Legislation changes in the United States, United Kingdom, Italy, Australia, and other countries regarding how corporations should measure their success using the triple-bottom-line philosophy have been enacted over the last several years.[24] The triple bottom line offers leaders a new way of defining organizational success and provides many new opportunities to apply FRLD principles.

Many of the world's top companies have embraced the triple-bottom-line philosophy. Consider Patagonia's use of recycled, organic, and environmentally safe materials and vocal advocacy of sustainable farming and water conservation; Google's development of a self-driving automobile; General Electric (GE), with its revenue-boosting Ecomagination green technology; BP's reduction of greenhouse gas emissions from its production processes; or global shipping company DHL's use of bicycle couriers in Europe which is estimated to reduce carbon dioxide emissions by 152 metric tons per year while expanding DHL's market share.[25] These examples teach us that boosting profits while doing something good for the environment are not mutually exclusive. We believe that FRLD can help organizations to boost profits, develop people, and protect the earth.

Full Range Leadership Development as a Strategic and Social Intervention

The advent of the balanced scorecard and triple-bottom-line concepts provides you with many opportunities to do "good business" by applying FRLD to address strategic, social, and environmental issues. In this section, we offer some reasons why social entrepreneurship, organizational safety, and environmental advocacy are excellent contexts for the application of FRLD. As you read on, think about ways you can apply FRLD behaviors to address these issues in your personal leadership situation.

Social Entrepreneurship

Political scientist James MacGregor Burns wrote, "Transforming leadership begins on people's terms, driven by their wants and needs, and must culminate in expanding opportunities for happiness."[26] We believe that expanding opportunities for people's happiness should be one of the most critical missions for today's business enterprises. However, it requires a renewed entrepreneurial spirit that expands its aim beyond the accumulation of wealth to solving the world's most pressing social problems. Entrepreneurship involves starting new business ventures or revitalizing mature organizations based on perceived opportunities to create wealth. Entrepreneurs excel at recognizing opportunities, exploring innovative

Figure 10.4
From dream
to reality.
Visionary
social
entrepreneur
Patty Hillkirk
inspires an
audience as
she explains
the genesis
of Camp
Dreamcatcher.
Image by
Barrie Litzky.
Reprinted with
permission.

approaches, mobilizing resources, managing risks, and building viable, sustainable enterprises. Entrepreneurial skills are just as valuable in the social sector as they are in business because both social and business opportunities involve risk taking and building connections with people. Some entrepreneurs use their skills to craft innovative responses to social needs, such as Patty Hillkirk's work with children with HIV/AIDS described in Chapter 5 (see Figure 10.4). These individuals are called *social entrepreneurs.*

Social entrepreneurs work to improve the world's social conditions while they accumulate economic wealth in the traditional entrepreneurial sense as well. In other words, they do good while they do business. Even during prosperous economic times, numerous social problems remain, and some seem to always get worse.[27] Countless opportunities for social entrepreneurship can be found in helping the homeless, the poverty stricken, the mentally and physically challenged, victims of domestic violence, survivors of natural disasters, troubled children, those suffering from diseases, the elderly, abused animals, gardens lost due to floods, and other disadvantaged groups. Social entrepreneurship, therefore, gives us the opportunity to address these challenges by *connecting with people who are in need and expanding their opportunities for happiness.* We must and can do this, not only through the training of FRLD, but also by role modeling FRLD behaviors in our interactions with others.

These challenges require us to be proactive and innovative social entrepreneurs, who introduce radical positive change to organizations and society, monitor progress toward goals, and avoid being bystanders. FRLD behaviors can help social entrepreneurs to accelerate their social reforms and sustain them over time.[28] You can do these things by creating and communicating a clear entrepreneurial vision (inspirational motivation), providing ample rewards and recognition for socially responsible achievements (contingent reward), and encouraging experimentation, challenges, and education (intellectual stimulation) that promote the entrepreneurial thinking of others.

We feel that FRLD can help social entrepreneurs be more effective in their pursuits by:

- Adding to their practical knowledge of the alternative behaviors and methods for turning good social ideas into viable business options
- Defining new possible roles and strategies with which entrepreneurs and established companies can address social needs and contribute to sustainable development
- Capitalizing upon the social value that can result through the collaborative efforts of businesspeople, government agencies, and educators
- Providing behaviors for interacting with organizational stakeholders, discovering resources for funding, exploring external and internal organizational constraints, setting business goals, and empathically understanding community needs.

Social Entrepreneurship in Action

Our claim is based upon evidence derived from Penn State's Master of Leadership Development (MLD) program, which attracts and educates many social entrepreneurs. Since 2003, MLD and MBA students at Penn State have completed over one hundred social entrepreneurship projects benefiting communities in the United States and abroad. MLD students complete a course in social entrepreneurship and community leadership. This course applies graduate students' accumulated knowledge of FRLD to address the social needs of communities on a local and global scale. MLD students have led teams of high school and undergraduate students as they work on a wide range of social entrepreneurship projects. Examples of such projects include producing marketing plans; planned giving and capital campaigns; brand recognition studies; strategic planning and strength, weaknesses, opportunities, and threats (SWOT) analysis; product development processes; product pricing studies; publicity campaigns; public relations assistance; feasibility studies; fund-raising research; and documentation of leadership strengths of women. By providing such business services to social entrepreneurs, these students develop their FRLD competencies, while they help satisfy important social needs across a wide variety of organizations and communities (see Table 10.1 for a sample of organizations that have benefitted from these efforts). We have observed that student leaders frequently display inspirational motivation to keep everyone motivated. This was necessary even when everyone knew that they were working on something important and valuable to the community. People need to be continually energized and motivated, even at the peak of success. That's why FRLD is so critical.

As you examine Table 10.1, think about ways that you can work with entrepreneurs to address a pressing social need in your community and expand opportunities for happiness for those in need. For example, we were very much impressed by our colleague Sue Kershner's volunteer work through Calvery

Table 10.1 Sample of Social Entrepreneurial Ventures Aided With FRLD

Organization	Website	Overview of Project Mission
Camp Dreamcatcher, Inc.	www.campdreamcatcher.org/	Developing a business plan for buying land to establish an all-season facility that can be used by Camp Dreamcatcher, a nonprofit organization serving HIV/AIDS-infected/affected children for the past 20 years, and also be available for other nonprofit organizations serving all children with diverse and special needs.
PainBeGone™ Central	n/a	Develop a business plan for PainBeGone Central. PainBeGone Central offers products and services for individuals in chronic pain. Write a well-conceived business plan for PainBeGone Central that describes the proposed venture to an audience of investors. No longer a going concern.
George Fox Friends School	http://gffs.org	Investigate feasibility of proposed expanded programming—after school program, adult evening classes, "specials" for homeschooled and cyber-schooled children. The school closed in 2015 due to a lack of enrollment and funding.
Ray of Hope Children's Hospital of India	www.partnersindia.org/roh/	Strategy development to establish a state-of-the-art pediatric network to provide low/no-cost health care; prioritize core service lines, identify funding and partnership opportunities.
Selene Whole Foods Cooperative, Inc.	n/a	Build a publicity campaign to attract more members/customers, and a strong involved membership in the community of Media (the first fair trade town in the United States). Represent locally grown organic food, community orientation, environmental responsibility, contributing strongly to the town's sustainability, and support its members and citizenry with strong values. No longer a going concern.
West African American Trading Company	www.waatco.com/	Develop five-year strategic plan.
La Comunidad Hispania, Inc.	http://lacomunidadhispana.org/	Develop a marketing plan for an established endowment that was created through Chester County Community Foundation.
Pennsylvania Home of the Sparrow	www.homeofthesparrow.org/	Prepare a planned giving plan.
Friends Association for the Care and Protection of Children	www.friendsassoc.org/	Prepare a marketing plan to bring attention to the need for more foster families.
The ARC of Chester County	www.arcofchestercounty.org/	Develop a marketing plan and collect marketing research.

Fellowship Church in Downingtown, Pennsylvania. Sue's church partnered with Michelle Henry of Faith Bible Church in New Orleans immediately after Hurricane Katrina struck in August 2005. They were called into service to assist with the coordination of the teams of volunteers that were showing up at Faith Bible Church after Katrina hit. Sue's group made annual trips to New Orleans between 2005 and 2012 to help with recovery efforts. Her group also reached out to assist the needy of the U.S. Gulf region when Hurricanes Gustav and Ike struck in 2008 and Hurricane Isaac hit New Orleans in 2012. They responded to the devastation that Hurricane Sandy leveled on the New Jersey coast in the fall of 2012. They sent teams to help with the clean-up and rebuilding efforts for nearly two years, first on a weekly basis and then on a bi-monthly bias as long as they had volunteers.

Sue's work has inspired a group of our students to consider social entrepreneurial ventures in New Orleans and other regions affected by natural disasters. Even in 2017, many years after Hurricanes Katrina and Isaac, the New Orleans area is still reeling from effects of the devastating flooding. While the infrastructure for primary care has improved, many areas have not been redeveloped and over 100,000 former residents have not returned. Many business areas still lack access to basic food and shopping centers. The natural environment requires further restoring; there are needs for farm and gardening expertise, seeds, and tools. Each of these challenges provides opportunities for inspiring resilience, role modeling compassion, challenging the status quo, and coaching people to come back as a community reborn. Opportunities for social entrepreneurship are all around us. Look around, find one, and work hard to bring about positive change and help people realize their human potential.

Environmental, Health, and Safety Issues in the Workplace

There has been a sharp increase in attention being paid in organizations to environmental, health, and safety (EHS) issues in the workplace. Several of our manufacturing clients have requested training that utilizes aspects of FRLD to help reduce the number of injuries and fatalities on the job, promote safe work practices, and create a culture that promotes both safety and quality. We believe that these three goals are not mutually exclusive, and with FRLD, they can be sustained over a long-term period. In Box 10.2, we illustrate our belief with thoughts gleaned from the case of a global manufacturer of industrial access hardware and position control devices that has applied FRLD for this purpose.

While preparing for this application, we were reminded of the work of leadership scholar Julian Barling and his associates. They have conducted some interesting research that examines the intersection of transformational leadership and workplace safety outcomes. Their research indicates that executives who take a passive approach to workplace safety create a dangerous environment for their employees. Employees who work for such leaders take on the same lazy attitude toward safety, pay little attention to safety issues, and therefore raise the risk of serious injuries on the job. These results suggest that the passive approaches to FRLD (i.e., laissez-faire and passive management-by-exception) can actually make your workplace more dangerous.

Much more active forms of leadership are necessary to reduce such risk and raise levels of safety awareness. If action is taken after an incident occurs, active forms of management-by-exception may not be sufficient. The monitoring aspect of management-by-exception does have a place in EHS concerns, especially when leaders manage by walking around. It is amazing how the lazy and passive attitudes of some current leaders toward worker safety can be transmitted to the next generation of leaders. We can do much better by using the active behaviors in the FRLD model. More recent meta-analytic research conducted by Sharon Clarke supports our recommendation. Clarke found that when leaders display transformational leadership, followers perceive their workplaces to be safer and actively participate in safety initiatives, like the one Glenn Anderson led at Southco Inc. (see Box 10.2). She also found that when leaders display active transactional leadership behaviors (contingent reward and MBE-A), followers perceive even higher levels of workplace safety climate and comply with safety policies. According to the study, both participation in safety initiatives and safety compliance resulted in less occupational injuries.

Box 10.2 Environmental, Health, and Safety Application of FRLD

Southco Inc. is a global manufacturer of industrial access hardware and position control devices. It has been in business since 1899. With 17 manufacturing locations in ten countries and about 3,500 employees, Southco helps their customers solve and overcome engineering issues with its products. The manufacturing of products ranging from compression latches to locks, mounts, and screws to electronic access and locking systems requires a strong avocation of and support for safety initiatives. One of Southco's goals is to minimize the exposure of workers to environmental and physical hazards and ensure their wellbeing.

Southco has been the employer of engineer Glenn Andersen since he graduated from Louisiana Tech University back in the mid-1980s. Glen is currently responsible for custom product design reviews, position control product development, and strategic technical leadership. With keen interest, Glen decided to use his knowledge of FRLD to review the safety protocols and changes needed to implement safety procedures in a re-configured product engineering laboratory for prototype development. Glen met with his team of engineers to solicit constructive ideas, outline actions to be completed for safety procedures, and champion the results of the workplace safety meeting throughout their corporate campus.

Glenn and his team started the meeting with the use of constructive transaction behaviors, using goal setting for the expected outcomes. Then they identified current workplace hazards though brainstorming procedures and reviewed recent personal injuries of engineering staff. Most prior incidents were cuts, bumps, and pinched hands and fingers. Some incidents required medical attention for flying debris, imbedded debris in the skin, severe cuts,

---

and minor fractures. Glenn used idealized influence to address the importance of identifying safety hazards. He outlined the team's possible solutions to each of the items listed in the brainstorming output. He used intellectual stimulation to encourage the team to consider different perspectives on how to refine the safety procedures, and to develop monitoring and controls for the work area. He also required the team to develop a policy for corrective action if workers in the lab do not comply with the safety procedures.

The outcome of Glenn's meeting was a collective agreement to the safety procedures and equipment needed to ensure a safe work area. The work area would need to be kept clean and orderly using five actions tracked with a weekly scorecard. When the meeting ended, the team was happy they helped with this strategic safety initiative, and Glenn was proud of the outcome and enlightened by the positive effects of his FRLD application at his company.[29]

To become more actively involved in the safety arena, you should use a mix of transactional and transformational leadership. When safety conditions are high risk or involve life-and-death situations, MBE-A would be better to monitor circumstances that may be hazardous and nip the problem areas in the bud. For example, management-by-walking-around and complimenting those who practice or exceed EHS expectations are likely to work well because they put positive psychology into action. You should use contingent reward leadership to set four or five safety goals and work each day to make incremental progress toward each goal. You should provide feedback on progress made on the goals. And when the goals are reached, you should distribute appropriate rewards to those who helped achieve the goal to recognize their active contributions. Awarding those that exemplify the desired behavior will demonstrate management's commitment to EHS. These awards are forms of positive reinforcement so followers will continue to keep workplace safety in mind.

You should then build upon these contingent rewards by displaying the components of transformational leadership. As Glenn did, you can display *idealized influence* by talking about workplace safety as an important organizational goal, consider implications for safety in your decisions, and role model best safety practices. You can display *inspirational motivation* by setting high safety standards and clearly communicating them to associates in a way that is interesting and meaningful. You can display *intellectual stimulation* by urging associates to identify potential safety hazards and risks and thinking about causes of injuries as well as ways to eliminate them. And you can display *individualized consideration* by coaching and mentoring associates on safety issues, and listening to a wide variety of associates to get their perspectives on ways to improve safety. The good news is that training leaders at all organizational levels on these transformational leadership behaviors often results in future positive changes in their associates' attitudes toward safety and safety programs and fewer incidents and injuries.[30]

Environmental Leadership Initiatives

The environmentally conscious Beatle George Harrison once wryly sang, "We've got to save the world. Someone else may want to use it."[31] Soon after, scientists told us that there was a hole in the earth's ozone layer above Antarctica. Despite the advent of the ecology movement in the 1960s and more recent green initiatives, the number of problems facing our natural environment has been expanding rapidly. As mentioned in Chapter 1, the land has been excessively concreted over, and our human activities have produced a litany of environmental problems that need our immediate attention and proactive actions.

If business leaders are going to "save the world," they must view our many environmental problems not just as threats but as opportunities as well to create a better place for all of us while generating new sources of revenue. But often, environmental and societal interests are at odds with each other. Just like with workplace safety issues, you can use FRLD to develop a solution that balances these competing agendas and values. Today more than ever before, top executives need to partner with governmental agencies and the general public to empower people in their green initiatives and demand more socially responsible behavior from corporations. Intellectual stimulation is certainly critical in generating creative solutions that not only protect the environment but also create sustainable business opportunities. This process requires us to question old assumptions, consider alternative points of view, and rethink tried and true practices and policies. Once ideas are agreed upon, leaders should use inspirational motivation to achieve consensus and rally employees, volunteers, and others to put their ideas into action.

An interesting study of CEO transformational leadership offers some hope in finding ways to lead the process of making corporations more socially and environmentally responsible. Leadership scholar David Waldman and his colleagues studied the FRLD behaviors and corporate strategies of CEOs of 56 U.S. and Canadian companies. They found that those CEOs who displayed intellectual stimulation most frequently led companies that were more likely to engage in strategic corporate social responsibility initiatives.[32] Subsequent research has shown that transformational leadership behaviors, like intellectual stimulation, make followers think that business has a social responsibility beyond making a profit, and that these two goals are compatible.[33] These results suggest that the more top executives get their associates to "think green" and focus on the triple bottom line, the more environmentally responsible they will become. Ecomagination, a successful green initiative espoused by GE and its Chairman and CEO John L. Flannery, illustrates this point very nicely.[34]

Contingent reward leadership offers another avenue to lead such environmental initiatives. Since 1992, New York State's Agricultural Environmental Management annual awards program has recognized the outstanding efforts of farmers who preserve the environment through cutting-edge conservation and innovation. For example, one 2016 award winner was Tom Wickham of Wickham's Fruit Farm located near North Fork, New York. Wickham has been on the cutting edge of applying innovative ground and water protection practices that have boosted his farm's profits since 1999. He advocates and leads a cost-sharing program and fuel tank replacement program. These strategic actions not only reduced costs but also the risk of fuel contamination into the ground. He installed micro-irrigation systems to better manage water flow. He also introduced improved pest management and fertilizer reduction practices to reduce nitrogen contamination. Wickham and his farm are now role models for the protection and conservation of the soil and water in upstate New York.[35] This example shows that you don't have to be a corporate executive to use intellectually stimulating strategic initiatives. FRLD behaviors can be used by leaders in all walks of life to save our precious Planet Earth and its natural resources. When was the last time you challenged your followers to work toward such worthwhile goals?

Putting Full Range Leadership Development into Practice at the Strategic Level

While conducting research for the first edition of this book, John made a nostalgic pilgrimage back to the Center for Leadership Studies (CLS) at the State University of New York at Binghamton in July 2008. The CLS is where the great leadership scholar Bernie Bass was inspired to develop the notion of transformational leadership, and where we forged our passion for teaching and conducting FRLD research in our doctoral program. Although John has gone back to Binghamton many times since graduating in 1995, his return to the CLS after 13 years was still very much a refreshing homecoming.

As John perused the CLS library, he was filled with the same sense of wonder and excitement that he experienced as a student. The library contained many books from Bernie's personal collection, along with his publications and working papers. These items were moved into the CLS library after his death in October 2007. To peruse the personal effects of a leadership research legend and mentor was thrilling for his former student and admirer. One item that caught John's eye was an unpublished early working paper with implications for strategic leadership. In this paper, Bernie argued that transformational leadership should be fostered with appropriate organizational policies, practices, and strategies.[36] In honor of our esteemed mentor and "intellectual father," we draw upon this paper to provide you with six ways to apply transformational leadership to your own strategic initiatives.

Use Transformational Leadership Measures for Promotion and Transfer

To support the innovation and learning perspective of the balanced scorecard, consider using the Multifactor Leadership Questionnaire (MLQ) to select, screen, assess, and place leaders into higher-level or lateral positions for managing talent more effectively. This helps to ensure that your associates are in the most appropriate organizational roles or what the Gallup Organization refers to as an "appropriate fit" along the Gallup path.[37] Human resources staff can administer the MLQ on a yearly basis to build a healthy pipeline of transformational leaders for your company. By providing feedback from the MLQ report to these managers, the quality of mentoring and coaching typically increases, and you can accelerate your associates' leadership development. Remember that transformational leadership is all about creating a larger leadership capacity for the whole organization through active mentoring and developmental opportunities.

Recruit and Select the Best

Your search for new leadership talent should be constant. Today, the key to success is recruiting and retaining the best and the brightest. Social media and employment websites, such as Monster.com, LinkedIn, and careerbuilder.com, along with professional networks are great resources for identifying potential top talent to recruit. As a user of such resources, Google is a great example of building a highly successful company through the recruitment and careful selection of the best human talents available. When an intelligent prospective recruit is interviewed, she will pay attention to your organization's climate, culture, and reputation. When she sees that the climate is friendly, collaborative, energetic, and intellectually stimulating, she will be attracted to your organization. If the human resource managers conducting the interview treat her with individualized consideration, the candidate is likely to walk away from the interview with a positive attitude. Inspirational motivation also can go a long way to earn candidates' passion for your company if your associates share an exciting vision and purpose with them. We have witnessed these practices at successful organizations such as Apple, Southwest Airlines, Sanofi, and the Vanguard Group.

Use Transformational Leadership as a Career Development Tool

Your organization's training and development processes can benefit from FRLD. As we described in Chapter 5, the first supervisor of a new trainee can either make or break his potential to succeed. Research from the mentoring field indicates that the support and challenges provided to subordinates by superiors goes a long way in determining subordinates' career success. In order to move up the organizational ranks, subordinates often take on the behaviors and attitudes that their superiors display.[38] Therefore, it is important for supervisors to role model idealized leadership, show individualized consideration, and provide intellectually stimulating, challenging, and highly visible assignments. These behaviors can enhance the career development and psychosocial support you give your associates through mentoring and reduce their perception of job-related stress and be more effective while performing their jobs.[39] You might feel a lot of pressure to know that it is you who may either make or break the career of your new subordinate. But, you should also consider it to be a privilege to have such a big responsibility. After all, it is your job to develop your followers into leaders and advance their careers.

Reengineer Jobs and Processes

To support the internal business process perspective of the balanced scorecard, those responsible for operations management should consider introducing challenge, intrigue, and problem solving into jobs, processes, and systems. Our experience is that employees working in research and development, manufacturing, and engineering like to be constantly challenged. They enjoy taking on more responsibility in their jobs. People love being challenged so much that they are spending their personal time working on public projects on the internet, such as Wikipedia and Linux, or participating in virtual communities such as Second Life, Facebook, or Twitter. And they seem to love finding solutions to problems and expressing themselves even though they don't get paid a dime.

So, use intellectual stimulation to design or reengineer jobs with more challenge built into them. And get your associates excited with tasks that appeal to them and allow for self-expression. Use individualized consideration to review workflows and operational procedures from the production, engineering, and sales points of view. Be sure to design jobs with the talents, skills, and developmental needs of your associates in mind. Use inspirational motivation to show them the big picture of how their jobs contribute to organizational success from the perspectives of customers, their coworkers, logistics managers, and investors. These behaviors will keep them actively engaged in their work, generate interest in Six Sigma and continuous process improvement, and determine which activities add value to your products and services.

With the advent of advanced information technologies such as smartphones and tablet computers, leaders are being challenged to find time to think and perform creative tasks. There are simply too many interruptions these days with 24/7 operations and the electronic leashes that email, voicemail, and instant messaging place upon us. You can be an intellectually stimulating leader only if you are able to design your jobs to be relatively free of interruptions and constant demands. As we spend more time on communication than ever before, we need to make our communication process far more efficient and effective as well as less distracting. If you can, take the time to design your own job so that it gives you time to think. This will free you up to examine new strategic opportunities for your organization, learn from the past, solve problems that need fixing, come up with new ideas, and think ahead to envision a brighter future.

Build a Strong Brand and Corporate Image

To support the customer perspective of the balanced scorecard, consider developing strategies that project images of quality, excellence, and vision to your customers, like Steve Jobs and Tim Cook used at Apple (see Box 10.3). Your customers need to see value in what they buy, appreciate what is created and sustained over time by your organizational culture and top management. Create an image of your organization as having its eyes on the future, confidence in its strategic direction, collaboration, and teamwork, and valuing its intellectual capital, innovative processes, and development of its associates. A blend of inspirational motivation, idealized influence, intellectual stimulation, and individually considerate behaviors displayed by individuals and teams at all levels of the organization can help you attain this goal. Their passion can create strong emotional connections with your customers and a reputable brand for your product and services.[40]

Box 10.3 Apple CEOs: Consistently Applying FRLD for People, Profit, and Planet

As of January 2018, Apple was the world's biggest brand, well on its way to a stock market capitalization value of $1 trillion. When it comes to building a brand, Steve Jobs learned three things from Mike Markkula, Apple's CEO in the early 1980s. Jobs first learned to inspire his employees to work hard to build a long-term emotional connection with customers based on superior product quality and excellent customer service. This lesson reflects inspirational motivation and individualized consideration. After all, the business of business is (and always will be) people. Maintaining high-quality relationships with them through quality products and service is essential. This lesson sets up the second lesson of focusing on a few great products and avoiding unnecessary distractions and ventures into markets that are at odds with one's core competencies. This second lesson reflects a blend of inspiration motivation and constructive transactional leadership with their focus on goal setting.

The third lesson that Jobs learned was the importance of designing products in ways customers will "impute" or perceive as being the highest of quality in terms of ascetics, design, and function. When it comes to product design and marketing, style and substance are equally important. The goal is to present not just an effective and nice-looking product, but a work of art. This lesson requires a great deal of intellectual stimulation and MBE-A leadership. Taken together, these lessons illustrate charismatic leadership infused with intellectual stimulation. That's because Jobs always aimed to empower people not only to "think different" and use his products to change the world, but also to "make a dent in the universe."

Current CEO Tim Cook has continued Jobs' transformational strategic approach with Apple's product offerings, slick marketing, and captivating annual Worldwide Developers Conference. Although he is less visionary and charismatic than Jobs was, Cook has consistently been rated by *Fortune* and *Forbes* as a highly effective CEO and socially responsible leader. He has championed social initiatives such as LGBT rights, corporate diversity, philanthropy, and renewable energy. He has even taken on the U.S. Federal Bureau of Investigation (FBI) over privacy rights when the FBI demanded that Apple provide the code to unlock an iPhone used by a shooter in San Bernardino, California in 2015. He has instituted sustainability programs with detailed progress reports that track Apple's efforts to eliminate their carbon footprint, encourage their suppliers to switch to renewable energy, and power Apple's own facilities with it. Cook's notion of what it means for a company to be successful transcends beyond the traditional financial perspective to non-financial perspectives prized by socially responsible organizations. And with Apple's jaw-dropping stock market capitalization value, it seems to be paying off quite well.[41]

Periodically Examine and Redesign Your Organizational Structure

Conditions change, and your organizational strategies and the structures required to carry them out change as well. To adapt to market conditions, organizations conduct strategic planning sessions and design an appropriate organizational structure to support the execution of the plan. In most industries, business markets are fraught with turbulence, uncertainty, risk, competition, ill-structured problems, and unforeseen opportunities and ever-lurking threats. Organizations fight with competitors to secure limited financial, intellectual, technological, and material resources. Such vexing environmental conditions demand constant renewal and change. Many companies, such as Kodak, Sears, Motorola, and Xerox, have faced crises due to organizational inertia, which prevents these big companies from reinventing themselves as the market changes constantly.

To overcome these challenges, you should use transformational leadership to create an *organic organizational structure* with little hierarchy and specialization of functions and a fluid and flexible network of highly skilled associates. Transformational leadership allows your company to develop organic structures. Their flexibility and broad reach, in turn, allow you to detect new trends ahead of your competition and create appropriate strategies. Recognizing the implications of these trends for your organization requires you to also inspire your colleagues with a compelling vision that unifies them to execute the objectives laid out in the balanced scorecard. If this vision is communicated effectively, it can add clarity to the purpose and meaning underlying your objectives and goals.

Making progress toward these goals involves creating product/service value and a strong brand image, improving the activities that create value, and developing the knowledge, skills, and abilities of people who enable these processes. These are the leading indicators of organizational success that can result in your financial success down the road. We believe that promoting transformational leadership in your organization through high-quality recruiting, selection, training, job design, marketing, and organizational structuring will pay off in increased economic and market value over time.[42]

Leaving Your Own FRLD Legacy of Prosperity and Wellbeing

Bernie Bass would have been most pleased to see how people from all walks of life are embracing and benefitting from FRLD. Whether promoting the prosperity of colleagues, building companies and communities, or working to save our precious planet, these people have helped FRLD to become what sociologists call "part of the culture." We have highlighted many of these people throughout the pages of this book. Many of them are our clients, associates, and adult graduate students. They work in the education, military, government, for-profit, and non-profit sectors. They are not famous CEOs of global companies. They are people just like you—ordinary people capable of doing extraordinary things and making a truly remarkable difference in the world. They are able to accomplish great and exciting things because they have made FRLD part of who they are. May their fine examples guide you on your own fantastic journey of leadership development throughout your life. May they inspire you to help others to reach their full potential as both leaders and human beings.

If you have followed the pathways we have paved throughout this book to becoming a transformational leader, you can be an example for others in the future. We hope that your example will be about the changes you initiate at home, work, and in your community. You now have the potential to be a brand-new leader who embraces FRLD to create positive change in your life and the lives of others. Remember that *leadership is all about making positive change*. If you are not creating change in your life and others' lives, you are just managing and not leading people. So be a champion of change! But as the pioneering social entrepreneur Bill Drayton once said, "You can't be a change-maker by reading a book."[43] You have to emotionally connect with the people you want to help, empathize with them, and take action to initiate a positive social change that is a win for humanity. Whether your victories are big or small, for many people or just one person, you will have made your mark on humanity as a transformational leader. You have been empowered to succeed. So, the best time for you to initiate change in your life and work is now. Your journey as a leader who champions positive change in people, profit, and planet begins this very minute. Godspeed!

Summary Questions and Reflective Exercises

1. Interview a member of the senior leadership team at your organization or an organization that you admire. This person should be a C-level executive (e.g., CEO, CFO, CIO, COO). Inquire about the organization's vision, mission, core values, and major objectives. Summarize your ideas regarding how aspects of FRLD can be used to support these elements of organizational strategy. Present your findings to your learning partner, team, or class. Better yet, present your findings to the executive who you interview and reflect upon this person's response.

2. Building upon your response to Exercise 1, identify how specific aspects of FRLD can be used in the organization you selected to support or enhance each of the following strategic initiatives:

   a. Leveraging core capabilities
   b. Building a foundation for future growth
   c. Addressing an unmet need in the market
   d. Establishing a strong, differentiated position in the market
   e. Improving process efficiencies and effectiveness
   f. Developing new businesses
   g. Penetrating a large new market.[44]

3. Review the accounting and organizational literatures for information on the *balanced scorecard*. This strategic leadership concept describes

how an organization's mission drives the major strategic objectives in the customer, employee, operational, and financial functional areas of an organization. What are your organization's major strategic objectives in these four areas? What metrics or measures can be used to assess the progress made toward these major strategic objectives? How can specific FRLD behaviors be used to help achieve each of these objectives in your organization?

4. Conduct an external environment assessment for your organization. List the top three most relevant trends pertaining to the following areas for your organization:

   a. Economic
   b. Sociocultural
   c. Global
   d. Technological
   e. Political/legal
   f. Demographic
   g. Competitors
   h. Industry (e.g., threat of new entrants, power of suppliers and buyers, product substitutes, intensity of rivalry).

   For each of these factors, how can you use specific FRLD behaviors to help shape strategies or adapt to the trends you identified?

5. Lead a team advocating improved workplace safety in your organization. Remember that the key to success here is reducing the amount of exposure to hazards for your associates. What changes in systems, culture, and equipment are needed to reduce exposure risk and severity level? How can the 5Is of transformational leadership be used in this regard?

Notes

1   Anonymous. (2015, April 2). *Leadership Experiential Exercise Post* [LEAD 555]. Malvern, PA: The Pennsylvania State University, Great Valley School of Graduate Professional Studies.

2   Retrieved from https://experiencematters.blog/2017/03/30/lexus-and-kia-earn-top-customer-experience-ratings-for-auto-dealers/; and http://temkingroup.com/research-reports/2016-temkin-experience-ratings/.

3   www.gmsustainability.com/_pdf/landing/highlights.pdf; and www.usatoday.com/story/money/cars/2017/06/04/ceo-mary-barra-shakes-up-gm/102484738/.

4   For detailed information on how FRLD behaviors can support the functions of executives, see Sosik, J. J., Jung, D. I., Berson, Y., Dionne, S. D., & Jaussi, K. S. (2004). *The dream weavers: Strategy-focused leadership in technology-driven organizations.* Greenwich, CT: Information Age Publishing.

5   Laureani, A., & Antony, J. (2017). Leadership characteristics for Lean Six Sigma. *Total Quality Management & Business Excellence, 28*(3–4), 405–426; and Sosik, J. J., &

Dionne, S. D. (1997). Leadership styles and Deming's behavior factors. *Journal of Business and Psychology, 11*(4), 447–462.

6   Bass, B. M. (1997). Personnel selling and transactional/transformational leadership. *Journal of Personal Selling & Sales Management, 17*(3), 19–28; and https://public relationssydney.com.au/pr-marketing-whats-difference/.

7   Senge, P., Kliener, A., Roberts, C., Ross, R. B., & Smith, B. J. (2014). *The fifth discipline fieldbook: Strategies and tools for building a learning organization.* New York: Crown Publishing Group.

8   Schneider, B. (1987). The people make the place. *Personnel Psychology, 40*(3), 437–453.

9   Bernard, C. I. (1938). *The functions of the executive.* Cambridge, MA: Harvard University Press; Cameron, J. C., & Sosik, J. J. (2016). Corporate citizenship: Understanding the character strength of citizenship from corporate law and leadership perspectives. *Journal of Behavioral and Applied Management, 17*(1), 3–32; Schoemaker, P. J. H., Krupp, S., & Howland, S. (2013, January–February). Strategic leadership: The essential skills. *Harvard Business Review,* pp. 131–134, retrieved from https://hbr.org/2013/01/strategic-leadership-the-esssential-skills; and www.sterling-resources.com/docs/RolesAndRespCEO.pdf.

10   Sosik et al. (2004). As cited in Note 4.

11   Hoque, Z. (2014). 20 years of studies on the balanced scorecard. *The British Accounting Review, 46*(1), 33–59; and Kaplan, R. S., & Norton, D. P. (2004). *Strategy maps: Converting intangible assets into tangible outcomes.* Boston, MA: Harvard Business School Press.

12   Blazek, K. (2016, March 4). The transformational leadership style of Elon Musk. *The Booth Company.* Retrieved from www.boothco.com/360-feedback-resources/leadership-style-of-elon-musk/; Bonnell, S. (2016, August 10). Every entrepreneur can learn from these 5 leadership traits of Elon Musk. *Entrepreneur.* Retrieved from www.entrepreneur.com/article/279971; Solomon, F. (2017, May 5). Elon Musks says robots will help Tesla catch up to Apple in value. *Fortune.* Retrieved from http://fortune.com/2017/05/05/elon-musk-tesla-apple-robots/; and Vance, A. (2017). *Elon Musk: Tesla, SpaceX, and the quest for a fantastic future.* New York: HarperCollins.

13   Kaplan & Norton (2004). As cited in Note 11.

14   Fleming, J. H., & Asplund, J. (2007). *Human-sigma: Managing the employee-customer encounter.* New York: Simon & Schuster.

15   Fleming & Asplund (2007). As cited in Note 14.

16   Associated Press (2017, April 3). Companies start implanting microchips into workers' bodies. *Los Angeles Times.* Retrieved from www.latimes.com/business/technology/la-fi-tn-microchip-employees-20170403-story.html; and Enthoven, D. (2014, April 18). How to track your employees' productivity without becoming Big Brother. *Inc.* Retrieved from www.inc.com/daniel-enthoven/how-to-track-your-employees-productivity-without-becoming-big-brother.html.

17   For more information on EVA™, visit http://sternvaluemanagement.com/consulting-services-strategy-governance-financial-policy-operations/eva-training/.

18   Welch, D. (2004, May 13). Mutual of Omaha's healthy preoccupation with talent. *Gallup Business Journal.* Retrieved from www.gallup.com/businessjournal/11608/mutual-oma-has-healthy-preoccupation-talent.aspx.

19   Sosik et al. (2004). As cited in Note 4.

20   Drucker, P. (1954). *The practice of management.* New York: Harper & Row; and Kaplan, R. S., & Norton, D. P. (1996). *Balanced scorecard: Translating strategy into action.* Boston, MA: Harvard Business School Press.

21   O'Reilly III, C. A., & Pfeffer, J. (2000, p. 33). *Hidden value: How great companies achieve extraordinary results with ordinary people.* Boston, MA: Harvard Business School Press.

22 Bower, J. L, & Paine, (2017). The error at the heart of corporate leadership. *Harvard Business Review*, *95*(3), 50–60.

23 Elkington, J. (1994). Towards the sustainable corporation: Win-win-win business strategies for sustainable development. *California Management Review*, *36*(2), 90–100; Elkington, J. (1998). *Cannibals with forks: The triple bottom line of 21st century business*. New York: Capstone Publishing; and Hunt, S. D. (2017). Strategic marketing, sustainability, the triple bottom line, and resource-advantage (R-A) theory. *AMS Review*, *7*(1–2), 52–66.

24 For details on such legislation and emerging triple-bottom-line corporate organizational forms, see www.bcorporation.net/; and www.gov.uk/government/organisations/office-of-the-regulator-of-community-interest-companies.

25 Hendricks, D. (2017). Seven companies proving triple bottom line is possible. *Earth 911*. Retrieved from http://earth911.com/business-policy/triple-bottom-line-7-companies/; and Savitz, A. W., & Weber, K. (2006). *The triple bottom line: How today's best-run companies are achieving economic, social and environmental success—and how you can too*. San Francisco, CA: Jossey-Bass.

26 Burns, J. M. (2003). *Transforming leadership: A new pursuit of happiness* (p. 230). New York: Atlantic Monthly Press.

27 Kickul, J. R., & Lyons, T. S. (2012). *Understanding social entrepreneurship: The relentless pursuit of mission in an ever-changing world*. New York: Routledge; Litzky, B. E. (2017). *LEAD 582 entrepreneurship and community leadership syllabus*. Malvern, PA: Pennsylvania State University School of Graduate and Professional Studies; Mumford, M. D., & Moertl, P. (2003). Cases of social innovation: Lessons from two innovations in the 20th century. *Creativity Research Journal*, *15*(2–3), 261–266; and Schaper, M. (2016). *Making ecoprenuers: Developing sustainable entrepreneurship*. New York: Routledge.

28 Felício, J. A., Martins-Gonçalves, H., & da Conceição-Gonçalves, V. (2013). Social value and organizational performance in non-profit social organizations: Social entrepreneurship, leadership, and socioeconomic context effects. *Journal of Business Research*, *66*(10), 2139–2146.

29 Anderson, G. (2017, March 30). *Leadership Experiential Exercise Post* [LEAD 555]. Malvern, PA: Pennsylvania State University, Great Valley School of Graduate Professional Studies; Anderson, G. (2017, April 13). *Leadership development plan* [LEAD 555]. Malvern, PA: Pennsylvania State University, Great Valley School of Graduate Professional Studies; and www.southco.com/en-us/.

30 Barling, J., Loughlin, C., & Kelloway, E. K. (2002). Development and testing of a model linking safety-specific transformational leadership and occupational safety. *Journal of Applied Psychology*, *87*(3), 488–496; Clarke, S. (2013). Safety leadership: A meta-analytic review of transformational and transactional leadership styles as antecedents of safety behaviors. *Journal of Occupational and Organizational Psychology*, *86*(1), 22–49; and Innes, M., Turner, N., Barling, J., & Stride, C. B. (2010). Transformational leadership and employee safety performance: A within–person, between jobs design. *Journal of Occupational Health Psychology*, *15*(3), 279–290.

31 Harrison, G. (1981). Save the world. On *Somewhere in England* [CD]. Hollywood, CA: Dark Horse/Warner Brothers Records.

32 Waldman, D. A., Siegel, D. S., & Javidan, M. (2006). Components of CEO transformational leadership and corporate social responsibility. *Journal of Management Studies*, *43*(8), 1703–1725.

33 Groves, K. S., & LaRocco, M. A. (2011). An empirical study of leader ethical values, transformational and transactional leadership, and follower attitudes toward corporate social responsibility. *Journal of Business Ethics*, *103*(4), 511–528.

34   For details on GE's Ecomagination, see www.ge.com/about-us/ecomagination.

35   www.agriculture.ny.gov/SoilWater/esa/2016.html.

36   Bass, B. M. (1986). *The nurturing of transformational leadership*. Working Papers Series 86–99. Binghamton, NY: School of Management, State University of New York at Binghamton.

37   Coffman, C., & Gonzalez-Molina, G. (2002). *Follow this path: How the world's greatest organizations drive growth by unleashing human potential*. New York: Grand Central Publishing; and Sorenson, S. (2013). How employee engagement drives growth. *Gallup Business Journal*. Retrieved from www.gallup.com/businessjournal/163130/employee-engagement-drives-growth.aspx.

38   Wang, M., & Wanberg, C. R. (2017). 100 years of applied psychology research on individual careers: From career management to retirement. *Journal of Applied Psychology, 102*(3), 546–563.

39   LePine, M. A., Zhang, Y., Crawford, E. R., & Rich, B. L. (2016). Turning their pain to gain: Charismatic leadership influence on follower stress appraisal and job performance. *Academy of Management Journal, 59*(3), 1036–1059; and Sosik, J. J., & Godshalk, V. M. (2000). Leadership styles, mentoring functions received, and job-related stress: A conceptual model and preliminary study. *Journal of Organizational Behavior, 21*(4), 365–390.

40   Fleming & Asplund (2007). As cited in Note 14.

41   Fiegerman, S. (2016, August 24). Apple under Tim Cook: More socially responsible, less visionary. *CNNtech*. Retrieved from http://money.cnn.com/2016/08/24/technology/apple-tim-cook-five-years/index.html; Issacson, W. (2011). *Steve Jobs*. New York: Simon & Schuster; Kharpal, A. (2016, March 29). Apple vs FBI: All you need to know. *CNBC*. Retrieved from www.cnbc.com/2016/03/29/apple-vs-fbi-all-you-need-to-know.html; and https://images.apple.com/environment/pdf/Apple_Environmental_Responsibility_Report_2017.pdf.

42   Bass (1986). As cited in Note 36.

43   Thompson, L. A. (2014). *Be a changemaker: How to start something that matters*. New York: Simon & Schuster.

44   Adapted from Anonymous (2008, August). *LexisNexis corporate innovation strategies*.

Appendix

Master of Leadership Development Program

The FRLD model provides the foundation for Penn State's Master of Leadership Development (MLD) graduate degree program. The MLD degree program, which is a professional graduate program offered on a part-time basis by Penn State's School of Graduate Professional Studies, enrolled its first cohort of students in January 2005. By the end of the 2016 Fall Semester, slightly more than 11 years after it began, the program had enrolled more than 1,800 students and graduated approximately 250. Separate and distinct from the School's MBA program, the MLD program is included under the specialized accreditation received from the Association to Advance Collegiate Schools of Business International (AACSB). Faculty in the program and in the Management Division as a whole, as well as the administration, have been very pleased with the success of the MLD program. It has attracted a more senior level of professionals to the student body; the diversity of the student body is richer than in many of the other programs at the School in terms of gender and ethnicity; and the feedback from students, their employers, and various other constituents has been very positive according to results of teaching evaluations and exit survey comments from graduates. The program underwent revisions in 2010 and 2017. This appendix describes the MLD's philosophy, structure, and content as an example of how an individual's leadership can be developed more systematically.

MLD Versus MBA: A Difference in Focus and Philosophy

The MLD teaches students how to be exemplary leaders, while the MBA teaches students how to be exemplary managers. The MLD and MBA programs are quite different in their emphasis and content. For example, Penn State's MBA program prepares professionals to manage in an ever-changing, increasingly global economic environment. The curriculum includes both behavioral and more technical and functional courses on organizational operations. It provides students with the intellectual tools to integrate finance, accounting, marketing, information systems, operations management, human resource management, and organizational behavior, and articulate a vision, motivate colleagues and employees, and develop and execute business strategy. The MBA's primary focus is on constructing and maintaining organizational systems, emphasizing improvements in efficiency and bottom-line financial performance.

In contrast, the MLD program includes courses focusing on behavioral and ethical elements, such as adult human development, positive psychology, creativity, motivation, interpersonal and group influence tactics, role modeling, and moral development. This curriculum is primarily aimed at educating students regarding what constitutes authentic transformational leadership and enhancing the full positive potential of individuals, groups, organizations, and communities. It is directed toward challenging the status quo and initiating and managing change, formulating visions and meaning for others, innovating the entire organization, transforming cultures, inducing change in values, attitudes, and behavior using personal examples and expertise, and empowering associates with shared values. While the MBA program provides an overview of leadership, the MLD program provides an *in-depth* analysis of the theory, research, and practice of authentic transformational leadership. The MLD program provides an environment in which faculty and students can have a complete and open collaboration on what constitutes exemplary leadership. The MLD's primary focus is on promoting positive change in individuals, teams, organizations, and communities emphasizing improvements in effectiveness and triple-bottom-line performance.[1]

The MLD degree is designed to help students develop their leadership potential. The program considers leadership across the life span, from early career through retirement, including parenting and community service, as well as leadership in the corporate realm. The program employs a multidisciplinary approach stressing social responsibility, ethics, and the value of the individual. Instruction develops real-world skills to foster positive change in individuals, groups, organizations, and community.

The MLD provides the competencies and actionable behaviors that can be readily applied in students' professional and personal lives. Cutting-edge information on leadership development is shared in an interactive, collaborative learning environment. The program's life span perspective on authentic transformational leadership development is reinforced through strong bonds formed with leadership practitioners, faculty and students, and the university's leadership events and alumni association.[2]

MLD Program Structure

The MLD is a 36-credit interdisciplinary professional program that blends the social and behavioral sciences with ethical studies to develop outstanding organizational and community leaders. It is accredited by the AACSB. At the time of this writing, the faculty were considering a second program revision integrating pre-program requirements and an expanded offering of online courses. We will describe the proposed program revision here.

When we originally designed the MLD's course structure in 2004, we decided to use Fulton J. Sheen's notion of "correlation of courses"[3] to tightly integrate various aspects of FRLD, especially transformational leadership, throughout the courses. This approach serves to reinforce in the student's mind interrelationships between course concepts and the broad array of practical applications for transformational leadership. The conceptual overlap of several key topics illustrates the complex system of interdependencies often found in leadership activities in organizations. This approach is quite different from the "cafeteria style" of curricular design, where students select courses to check off a curricular requirement, without evaluating interdependencies of concepts within and between courses. This latter approach does little to develop strategic or systems thinking skills in students. Such thinking is required at the upper echelons of organizations for leaders to synthesize information from a variety of domains, identify similarities and differences between situations, and create entirely new solutions to novel problems. These requirements are similar to tasks we challenged you to perform in the beginning of this book (see Chapter 1).

This correlation of tightly integrated courses offers students a challenging and interesting overview of leadership development. To earn the MLD degree, students must complete five pre-program requirements, three Leadership Cornerstone courses (9 credits), four Leadership Competency courses (12 credits), four Leadership Context courses (12 credits), and a Leadership Capstone course (3 credits). The Leadership Cornerstone courses provide basic foundation material that introduces the program's philosophy and FRLD concepts and assessments, including the Multifactor Leadership Questionnaire (MLQ). The Leadership Competency courses elaborate upon the components of transformational leadership and other leadership models and research methods as well. The Leadership Context courses teach students about the environment that surrounds their personal leadership situation and how to lead strategically and in a socially responsible manner. In the Leadership Capstone course, students apply FRLD and strategic leadership tactics to an organizational field project and a competitive online leadership game. The revised MLD curriculum is depicted in Figure A.1.[4]

Pre-Program Requirements

Over the past ten years, the faculty has perceived variation in the level of developmental readiness of students enrolled in the MLD program, especially with Millennial Generation students. While the faculty is striving to work closely with these younger, less experienced students to help them succeed, it is imperative to increase their developmental readiness in the application and pre-program requirements processes, so as to attract and admit more capable students in the future. To this end, five pre-program requirements (measuring motivation to lead, perspective-taking capacity, growth mindset, statistical and writing acumen) have been proposed. The MLD program prescribes the writing style of the American Psychological Association (APA).

Upon program admission and before enrollment in LEAD 501 *Leadership Across the Lifespan* (the first course in the MLD program), students will complete online self-assessments of their Motivation to Lead[5], Perspective-Taking Capacity[6], and Growth vs. Fixed Mindset.[7] These assessments are administered via Qualtrics[8] and results and developmental feedback are provided to students during the first week of LEAD 501. At the same time, students will complete online training primers covering Basic Statistics and APA Writing for Graduate Students. These assessments will be administered via Lynda.com and results

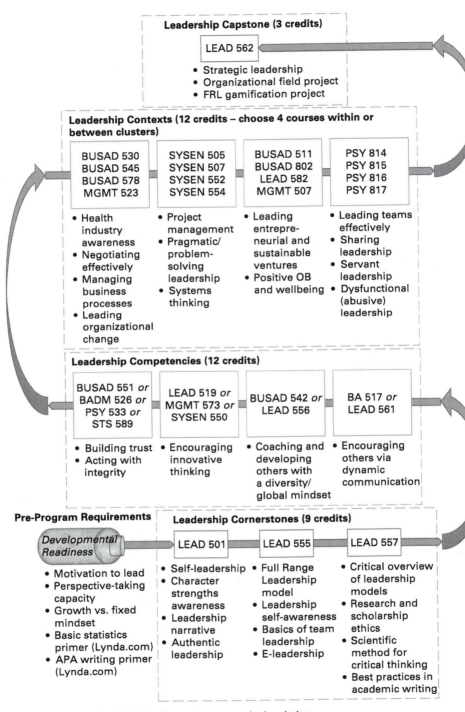

Figure A.1 **Master of Leadership Development program revised curriculum.**

and developmental feedback will be provided to students during the first week of LEAD 557 *Leadership Models and Methods* (the third course in the MLD program) and LEAD 501, respectively. Students also complete an online discussion module and test of topics pertaining to the responsible conduct of research once they begin their coursework.

Leadership Cornerstone Courses
Students complete the cornerstone courses lockstep as a cohort. We have found that the sequential completion of these first three courses by students creates cohesiveness, common identity, and pride in the cohorts as they enter and progress through the program. The cohort also serves as a learning community where students share best leadership practices, network with their colleagues in professional and social settings, and form friendships. The content of these courses is a challenging and comprehensive introduction to the elements of the FRLD leadership system that are elaborated upon in more detail later in the program.

LEAD 501—Leadership Across the Life Span
In the first course, we introduce students to the MLD program by framing leadership as a noble lifelong journey of personal development. We use a strengths-based approach to leadership development to transform students' innate talents into strengths, and build their hope, optimism, confidence, and resilience for success in the program itself, and in life in general. The course builds upon the concepts of self-leadership, positive psychology, positive organizational scholarship, and authentic transformational leadership to examine key developmental processes associated with leadership across the life span. Topics include an overview of leadership thought and theories, character strengths and virtues, individual differences, emotional intelligence, cross-cultural issues, self-construals, stages of moral and adult human development, personal meaning and vision, group dynamics, and self-leadership and its application in students' careers and lives. Through both written and oral presentation assignments, students analyze results of executive coaching experiences, moral development tests, leadership narratives, assessment centers, 360-degree feedback leadership development planning, and leadership and human development-related movies to enhance their self-leadership. This course also introduces students to the FRLD model.

LEAD 555—Full Range Leadership Development
The second Leadership Cornerstone course is the keystone of the MLD program. This course presents all components of the FRLD as measurable, trainable, and actionable behaviors as they relate to the student. Learning modules include values clarification, leadership purpose, goal setting, contingent rewards, idealized influence, inspirational motivation, intellectual stimulation, individualized consideration, perspective taking, team leadership, shared leadership, cross-cultural dimensions of FRLD, and e-leadership (i.e., leadership in virtual or distanced settings). The MLQ is administered to students as a baseline measure of their FRLD potential. Students analyze results of their personal applications of the FRLD model, MLQ

reports, current events, personal values clarification, mission statements, and personal leadership development plans to enhance their transformational leadership potential. This course introduces students to issues of ethical decision-making, role modeling, inspirational communication, innovation processes, team building, and diversity. These topics are elaborated upon later in the program.

LEAD 557—Leadership Models and Methods

The third and final cornerstone course expands students' understanding of the array of leadership theories and models other than FRLD and the research methodology used to conceptualize and test them empirically. Students learn to explain these leadership models, identify their strengths and weaknesses, and discover potential applications for them. Because science backs the material taught in the MLD program, students are trained how to construct and evaluate leadership theories, test them, and draw conclusions from their analysis. This course develops students' critical thinking, logical reasoning, and technical writing skills required for contemporary leaders. As a result of these academically rigorous components of the MLD program, a growing number of our students have applied to doctoral leadership programs after completing the MLD. Learning modules include leadership theory overview, philosophy of science, conceptualizing theory, study design, measurement issues, data analytic procedures, and interpretation of results. Through both written and oral presentation assignments and *Kahoot!* quizzes, students critique manuscripts and theories, conduct formal debates, and design and present an empirical study to become more informed consumers and producers of leadership research.

Leadership Competency Courses

Once students have completed the Leadership Cornerstone courses as a cohort, they branch out on their own to enroll in the Leadership Competency courses. They complete four courses in the areas of leadership communication (inspirational motivation), individualized consideration, intellectual stimulation, and idealized influence.

Leadership Communication Course Block

Students choose one of two courses that demonstrate inspirational motivation and communication effectiveness. These courses teach students skills that encourage others through dynamic communication:

- *LEAD 561—Dynamic Communication for Leadership Contexts* expands students' understanding of the concept of inspirational motivation through theory and techniques of persuasion and rhetoric for articulating and promoting a vision, and facilitating interaction and communicating within and between groups. Students learn to craft and deliver visionary and charismatic speeches that inspire collective confidence, trust, team synergy, intrinsic motivation, and engagement to create potent and cohesive teams and organizations with a common identity. Learning modules include meaning-centered communication and discursive leadership, intrapersonal and interpersonal communication, articulating a vision and promoting positive change, persuasion, social influence, and framing. Students present team talks on a leadership rhetoric topic, prepare a dynamic communication improvement plan, complete a series of essays, and make an emotive presentation to become more inspiring leaders.

- *BA 517—Leadership Communications* teaches students to reframe their view of themselves, and seek solutions to organizational issues through effective information collecting, analysis, and vision articulation. It focuses on four different themes: positioning leaders and followers as problem solvers, clarifying complex information, framing value to shareholders, and creating a common vision.

Individualized Consideration Course Block

Students choose one of two courses that provide a framework for coaching and developing others with a diversity or global mindset. These courses provide skills required to better understand psychological, cognitive, demographic, and cultural differences:

- *LEAD 556—Diversity Leadership* expands students' understanding of the concept of individualized consideration through the analysis and application of models, theories, and strategies for managing an increasingly diverse workforce and customer base. Through guided exercises in self-reflection, students learn to appreciate the individual differences people bring to the workplace and how to leverage these differences to create potent and cohesive teams with a common identity. Learning modules include implicit bias, majority–minority identity development, intercultural communication, team diversity, and group identity and life experiences' impact on leadership. Students lead class discussions on diversity leadership issues, analyze Diversityinc.com articles to identify best practices, and participate in an activity where they become a minority. The capstone assignment is the Diversity Leadership Improvement Plan. The student assesses his or her skillset against an evidence-based set of diversity leadership competencies and develops an action plan for self-improvement. Students review a representative sample of the published research in the following areas: career experience of diverse individuals, the effect of diversity on team performance, the influence of leadership on setting and achieving diversity goals, best practices in diversity leadership at the organizational level, and the impact of best practices on organizational outcomes. The course moves the student systematically through the consideration of diversity leadership at the individual, team, and organizational levels.
- *BUSAD 542—Global Intercultural Management* develops students' global cross-cultural competencies and cultural intelligence in order to enhance their ability to lead and manage in global contexts. This course also helps students to work across cultural boundaries with both internal and external stakeholders. Culture is broadly defined to include national, regional, organizational,

vocational, and other cultures and subcultures relevant to the global work environment. Upon course completion, students are able to demonstrate their understanding of the theoretical, empirical, and applied managerial efforts to define cultural dimensions and cultural intelligence. They can also identify and describe specific global, national, regional, organizational, and professional work cultures and cultural dimensions that are relevant to global managerial practice.

Intellectual Stimulation Course Block

Students choose one of three courses that promote creativity and innovation. These courses expand students' understanding of the concept of intellectual stimulation through theory and practices from business, science, and the arts to foster creativity within people and teams, and innovation throughout organizations. Students learn the antecedents, processes, and outcomes associated with creativity and innovation methodologies in individuals, teams, and organizations.

- *LEAD 519—Developing High-Performance Organizations* uses a liberal arts and natural science approach to create high-performing organizations. Learning modules include philosophy of aesthetics, meaning making, behaviors and traits of creative individuals, and the elements of creative products. Students' assignments include assessment of original works of practicing artists, musicians, actors, scientists, and writers, and creating executive briefs on creativity topics. These activities help students become more intellectually stimulating contributors to the overall performance of their organization.
- *MGMT 573—Corporate Innovative Strategies* surveys the issues involved in formulating and implementing innovation initiatives and large technology projects. Learning modules include the innovator's dilemma, stimulating new ideas through dialogue, identifying attributes of disruptive technologies and their threats and opportunities, discussing how existing business models constrain new ventures, and using storytelling and story listening to facilitate change and innovation. Through both written and oral presentation assignments, students learn through homework, presenting on issues of adaption, innovation, resilience, sustainability, globalization, and organizational learning. They examine these issues through storytelling and story listening to become more intellectually stimulating leaders.
- *SYSEN 550—Creativity and Problem Solving* explores the cognitive and behavioral approaches to fostering creativity in individuals, with an emphasis on pragmatic or problem-solving approaches to leadership and the paradox of structure. Learning modules include the brain's organization of problem solving, the catalytic nature of change, individual assessment of problem-solving style, and problem-solving leadership models. Through homework assignments, exams, and class participation that emphasize precision, students learn to use their own respective problem-solving abilities and cognitive styles to become more intellectually stimulating leaders.

Idealized Influence Course Block

Students also choose one of four courses that teach role modeling and ethical decision-making. These courses expand students' understanding of the concept of idealized influence through an ethical lens focusing on virtues, values, moral development, ethical reasoning models, philosophy, and application to their personal leadership context. Students learn philosophies and frameworks for conducting themselves and their businesses in an ethical, morally developed, and socially responsible manner:

- *BADM 526—Ethical Dimensions of Leadership* takes a historical approach to the philosophical study of Western and non-Western ethical frameworks, with implications for contemporary ethical leadership. Learning modules include how the economy influences our ethics, the interrelationships between the ethical issues we face, ethical issues facing the earth and its life-sustaining systems, doing business in an ethical way, and ethical issues raised by the larger context of our life as part of a developing universe. Students prepare and present a research paper on the life, work, and significance of leaders such as Paul Robeson, Susan Adams, Desmond Tutu, and Eleanor Roosevelt; prepare news briefs that connect class readings with ethical issues in the news; and analyze case studies to enhance their idealized leadership.
- *BUSAD 551—Business, Ethics, and Society* focuses on the exploration and analysis of the ethical, political, technological, social, legal, and regulatory environments of business. Learning modules include ethical problems in business and their importance, moral standards, famous cases in business stakeholders' relations, making moral decisions, corporate social responsibility, globalization, government regulation, consumer protectionism, "green" initiatives that protect the environment, economic regulation, and the political lobby. Through class discussion and debate, and report writing assignments, students learn to better understand the ethical obligations of today's transformational leaders.
- *PSY 533—Ethics and Leadership: Psychological and Social Processes* examines ethics through a behavioral science lens with an emphasis on ethical decision-making and ethical leadership. Roles of being both an ethical leader and ethical manager are examined and applied to personal and work applications so that students better understand the relationship between ethical leadership and idealized influence.
- *STS 589—Ethics and Values in Science and Technology* examines ethics through a problem-solving lens. An emphasis is placed on preventive ethics along with the professional responsibility to enact ethics within the technical community. Students learn about what it means to demonstrate idealized influence by framing and analyzing moral problems that occur within information technology, engineering, and research and development contexts.

Leadership Context Courses

Leadership does not occur in a vacuum. Transformational leaders are aware of the strategic opportunities and challenges that surround them. To gain such

---

Box A.1 Leadership Context Elective Courses

- BUSAD 530—Biotechnology and Health Industry Overview
- BUSAD 545—Negotiation Strategies
- BUSAD 578—Managing Business Processes
- MGMT 523—Organizational Change: Theory and Practice
- SYSEN 505—Technical Project Management
- SYSEN 507—Systems Thinking
- SYSEN 552—Creativity and Problem Solving II
- SYSEN 554—Problem-Solving Leadership
- BUSAD 511—New Ventures
- BUSAD 802—Cornerstones of Sustainability
- LEAD 582—Social Entrepreneurship and Community Leadership
- MGMT 507—Positive Organizational Behavior and Wellbeing
- PSY 814—Psychology of Leading Work Groups or Teams
- PSY 815—Psychology of Servant and Authentic Leadership
- PSY 816—Dysfunctional Leadership
- PSY 817—Psychology of Shared and Collective Leadership

---

awareness, aspiring leaders must learn systems thinking skills, how to lead change in organizations, and how to address special issues they face in their personal leadership situation, among other skills and knowledge bases. Students choose four courses among those listed in Box A.1. Context electives come from multiple academic departments within the university and are too numerous to describe here in detail.

Leadership Capstone

When we designed the MLD program, we wanted students to finish the program by applying what they learned about FRLD in local and global businesses and communities. As a result, we felt that they would make life better for others. We also wanted to teach them the importance of measuring their organization's success in terms of the balanced scorecard and triple-bottom-line philosophies described in Chapter 10.

To this end, students complete their capstone experience, LEAD 562 *Strategic Leadership*. This course focuses on executive-level leadership of larger systems and organizations. The course applies FRLD concepts to illustrate the impact of developing human, intellectual, social, structural, financial, and reputation capital that create wealth for shareholders. Students learn to think and lead strategically, guided by strategy tools such as the Gallup Path™ and Balanced Scorecard™. Learning modules include upper echelons theory, creating multiple forms of capital, environmental scanning and shaping, internal and external environmental analysis, the visioning process, shaping organizational culture and values, supporting innovation and learning, and measuring real profit and economic value-added. As part of an organizational field project, students interview top executives responsible for their firm's strategy, assess their leadership style and culture, and create an executive coaching plan for them. They also analyze their own company's performance using strategy and performance management tools to become more effective strategic leaders, as well as compete as teams using an online business game developed by Recurrence Inc.[9]

Notes

1 Indro, D. C., Sosik, J. J., & Holway, C. A. (2010). *Proposal for a change in the Master of Leadership Development Program.* Malvern, PA: Penn State University; and Master of Leadership Development Task Force. (2004). *Master of Leadership Development program proposal.* Malvern, PA: Penn State University.

2 Retrieved from http://greatvalley.psu.edu/academics/masters-degrees/leadership-development.

3 Sheen, F. J. (1999). *Life is worth living* (pp. 243–250). San Francisco: Ignatius Press.

4 Revised curriculum based on Avolio, B. J. (2016). *The leadership development footprint.* Foster Center for Leadership and Strategic Thinking Briefing 2016-1. Seattle, WA: University of Washington; and The Gallup Path © 1996–2002. The Gallup Organization, Princeton, NJ.

5 Chan, K.Y., & Drasgow, R. (2001). Toward a theory of individual differences and leadership: Understanding the motive-to-lead. *Journal of Applied Psychology, 86*(3), 481–498.

6 Escoffier, M. R., & Kroeck, K. G. (1990). *Test of business issues.* Miami: University of Miami.

7 Niemivirta, M. (1998). Individual differences in motivational and cognitive factors affecting self-regulated learning—A pattern-oriented approach. In P. Nenninger, R. S. Jäger, A. Frey, & M. Woznitza (Eds.), *Advances in motivation* (pp. 23–42). Landau, DE: Verlad Empirische Pädagogik.

8 For details, see www.qualtrics.com/.

9 For details, see http://recurrenceinc.com/.

Index of Leaders and Authors

General Index